Hiking the Blue Ridge Parkway

Hiking the Blue Ridge Parkway

Parkway

The Ultimate Travel Guide to America's Most
Popular Scenic Roadway

Second Edition

Randy Johnson

FALCONGUIDES

GUILFORD, CONNECTICUT
HELENA, MONTANA
AN IMPRINT OF GLOBE PEQUOT PRESS

FALCONGUIDES®

Copyright © 2003, 2010 by Morris Book Publishing LLC

FalconGuides is an imprint of Globe Pequot Press. Falcon, FalconGuides, and Outfit Your Mind are registered trademarks of Morris Book Publishing LLC.

All interior photos by Randy Johnson except where otherwise credited.
Maps by Topaz Maps Inc. and Daniel Lloyd © Morris Book Publishing LLC
Project editor: Julie Marsh
Layout artist: Kevin Mak

The Library of Congress has catalogued the earlier edition as follows:
Johnson, Randy, 1951–
   Hiking the Blue Ridge Parkway: the ultimate travel guide to America's most popular scenic roadway / Randy Johnson—1st ed
     p. cm. — (A Falcon Guide)
    ISBN 0-7627-1105-1
     1. Hiking—Blue Ridge Parkway (N.C. and Va.)—Guidebooks 2. Blue Ridge Parkay (N.C. and Va.)—Guidebooks. I. Title II. Series

GV199.42.B65J64 2003
917.55—dc21

                    2002041646

ISBN 978-0-7627-5531-8

Printed in the United States of America
10 9 8 7 6 5 4 3 2 1

To past and present Appalachian families—the people who know how much you have to love the mountains to live there.
And to the men and women of the Blue Ridge Parkway—who help the rest of us appreciate why it's worth the effort.

CONTENTS

The Hikes

The North-Central Blue Ridge

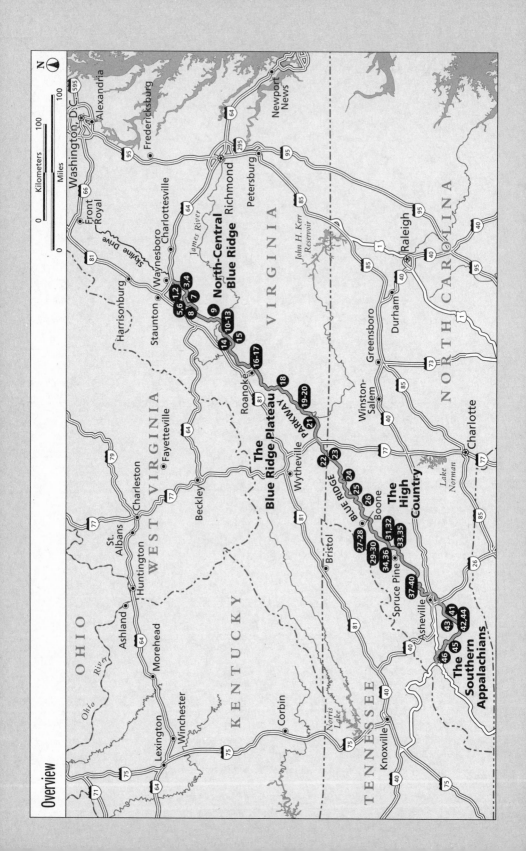
Overview

The Blue Ridge Plateau
Mileposts 121.4 (US 220, Roanoke, VA) to 276.4

The High Country

The Southern Appalachians

Parkway paths invite you into the lushness of one of the nation's most diverse natural environments. Boone Fork Trail, Price Park, North Carolina

How to Use This Guide

Hiking the Blue Ridge Parkway is designed for anyone who visits the Parkway—America's longest and most popular national park and the premier portal to the Southern Appalachian experience.

Serious hikers and casual motorists alike should refer often to the final section of this book for a mile-by-mile log to the overlooks, entrances and exits, interpretive sites, museums, visitor centers, and craft shops along the way. The log also highlights the easy "leg-stretcher" trails and more strenuous hikes that line the Parkway—all keyed to the numbered mileposts you'll see dotting the roadside. Besides keeping you on track with your trip, the Mileage Log (like the table of contents) directs you to the interior of the book, where you'll find detailed write-ups of the featured hikes. Another good reason to keep your eye on the Mileage Log: Some of the very tiniest trails appear only there.

But this book is more than just a guide to hikes and facilities on the Blue Ridge Parkway. By including the best trails in the national forests, state parks, and private preserves that lie just off the 469-mile scenic road, *Hiking the Blue Ridge Parkway* provides a single-volume resource for the serious explorer, whether on foot or in a car.

Included here are challenging day hikes to some of the East's highest peaks, overnight backpack trips, and multiday explorations of the most isolated wilderness enclaves. The Mileage Log also highlights these hikes, so you know where to read about them in the body of the book and how to find them while traveling.

With all these hikes come detailed descriptions that will boost even casual motorists' appreciation of the surrounding scenery—and might even entice them off the beaten path.

Author Randy Johnson has helped design Parkway trails and has explored the unique richness of Appalachian culture. This book meshes the best of the Parkway's outdoor experiences with a keen sense of the cultural heritage and travel opportunities that make the Parkway a national treasure—a motor trail through the heart of the United States' least homogenized region.

INTRODUCTION

Hiking the Blue Ridge Parkway

With the 2010 arrival of the Blue Ridge Parkway's seventy-fifth anniversary, there has never been a better time to explore what travel writers continually call "America's most scenic highway." Stretches of road elsewhere in the United States may indeed be spectacular, but nothing matches this manicured, uniquely uncommercialized half-a-thousand-mile thoroughfare through the lofty heart of America's first frontier. That's what makes the Parkway a globally recognized icon of the American road.

Scenery aside, the recent completion of the Parkway's main visitor center in Asheville and the ongoing finalization of the Blue Ridge Music Center near the Virginia–North Carolina state line are reminders that the experience just keeps getting richer for visitors.

A Parkway vacation—tackling the length of the roadway from the southern end of Shenandoah National Park in Virginia to Great Smoky Mountains National Park in North Carolina—is a singular experience, a dazzling juncture of earth and sky.

Most of the time spent in the Southern mountains—in a car or on foot—involves either going up or coming down. But the Parkway follows almost continually along the crest—truly a skyline traverse.

At the Parkway's 45 mph speed limit, the drive could be completed in eleven hours. But the point of this book is that it shouldn't. With vistas beckoning from dozens of overlooks, and trails everywhere, this is a motorized wander that could—and surely should—be given at least a week. The Parkway is a visual feast of vignettes every step or mile of the way.

It's a place of raw springtime, where deep winter gives way to a season of hoar-frosted trees and rich earth-toned forests full of snow-flattened leaves. You dip down from cloud-shrouded, winter-whitened trees to suddenly open views that stretch for miles into valleys unseen only moments before. The bite in the air takes your breath away.

As spring progresses, your car sails through a lime-green swale lit by a pale beam of sun. Overhead, a cold-shadowed summit towers through the trees. This is when everything bursts into shades of green and pink and one of the world's most diverse natural environments explodes into bloom. The Parkway becomes the perfect place to play Aaron Copland's *Appalachian Spring* symphony on the car audio system.

Summer is a delicious time on the Parkway—a season of golden high-altitude light and refreshing breezes. The sunniest days elicit rich forest aromas, from the fecund pungency of galax spread beneath a grove of lower-elevation oaks to the perfume of

◀ *Raven's Roost Overlook, near Humpback Rocks, shows off the pastoral beauty of the Shenandoah Valley.*

spruce and fir warming in a rare still day on the summits. During this short, poignant pause in an otherwise harsh climate, it's cool enough to induce a summer-colony subculture. Century-old inns attracted sweltering flatland Southerners long before the Parkway was built. New resort communities prosper in the same tradition.

Autumn brings brilliant clarity and color, with crystal-clear days alternating with misty highland rains. Winter brings moody fogs that randomly hide and expose eerie, ghostlike forests and sudden vistas. Winter can be stunningly beautiful—when Parkway travel is possible.

Whatever time of year you motor the Parkway, you'll marvel at ever-changing perspectives. A chasm suddenly yawns in a curve—and is gone. As you pass an overlook, a father and son stand silhouetted against the sunset.

The Parkway isn't literally a national park, but it is a unit of the National Park Service—and the nation's most visited one at that. More than half the population of the United States lives within a day's drive of the Parkway. Average annual visitation hovers just below 20 million. The record was set in 2003 at 23.5 million.

Best of all, this national treasure has trails along its entire length, making the Parkway a perfect destination for hikers. Indeed, a drive on this high road is a motorized metaphor for the trail experience itself. The Parkway is an Appalachian Trail for autos. But don't just settle for looking through the windshield—getting out of the car is a must. Nevertheless, the wonder of this motor trail is that what you see while driving is a lot like what you see in the woods. That includes wildlife.

Be on the road early or late and you'll likely have to stop and sit amazed behind the wheel as a herd of deer gambol across the road. Ravens soar with the air currents above evergreen-covered summits. Peregrine falcons, reintroduced at Parkway-adjacent sites since 1984, now nest and dive all along the road. Flocks of turkeys, also successfully reintroduced, prefer trailside Parkway meadows.

Groundhogs munch everywhere; the Parkway's handcrafted stone walls seem to be their favorite seats. Mountaineers ate groundhogs—or whistle pigs—and used their hide for shoelaces. Renowned mountain musician "Doc" Watson, a native of Watauga County, North Carolina, which lies astride the Parkway near Boone, once recorded the traditional song "Ground Hog." The lyrics reflect the importance of the animal to early Parkway residents:

I dug down but I didn't dig deep, I dug down but I didn't dig deep, there lay a whistle pig fast asleep. Oh Groundhog.

Pick up your gun and whistle up your dog, Pick up your gun and whistle up your dog, off to the woods for to catch a Groundhog. Oh Groundhog.

Eat up the meat and save the hide. Eat up the meat and save the hide. Make the best shoe strings ever was tied. Oh Groundhog.

There's culture as well. Since our nation's earliest westward migrations, the fertile valleys to the east and west of the Blue Ridge Mountains have filled up with farms, towns, and eventually cities. A relative few of those newcomers, Scots-Irish and Germans among them, settled into the very highest elevations of the Blue Ridge and adjacent ranges. Long traditions of music and crafts were thus preserved in these storied hollows. In some ways, Appalachian mountaineers were living a pioneering lifestyle long after the West was settled.

Luckily for today's hikers and motorists, early mountain farms, cabins—even a mill—have been preserved at key places along the Parkway, and they impart a sense of what life on the heights must have been like. These exhibits incorporate some of the Parkway's shorter, tamer trails, but they're deeply insightful and worth a wander. Note-

The meandering miles of the Blue Ridge Parkway are a direct route to a legendary "land of do without," rich in culture and raw in spectacular scenery.

worthy stops include the Mountain Farm Trail at Humpback Rocks (Milepost 5), Trail's Cabin at Smart View Picnic Area (Milepost 154.5), the Johnson Farm at Peaks of Otter (Milepost 85.9), and Mabry Mill (Milepost 176.2).

Handcrafts were essential for survival in this "land of do without." That rich tradition of crafts comes to life in a variety of places on and adjacent to the Parkway. Don't miss the Northwest Trading Post (Milepost 258.7), the Parkway Craft Center in Moses Cone Park (Milepost 294), and the Folk Art Center near Asheville, North Carolina (Milepost 382).

The Parkway's craft centers and mountain lifestyle exhibits are just the beginning. Skilled crafters often demonstrate their skills at the Parkway's various craft centers. Reenactors at the lifestyle exhibits depict the kinds of domestic and commercial activities it took to wrest a living from a harsh climate and primitive facilities. If you make time for these programs, an amazing part of America's past will come to life for you.

The National Park Service also tries to remind Parkway travelers of the past by leasing lands along the road for farming and other traditional activities. And while you surely will see vacation homes perched in plain sight of the road (Who wouldn't want a perpetual Parkway view?), organizations such as the Blue Ridge Parkway Foundation (336-721-0260; www.brpfoundation.org) and Friends of the Blue Ridge Parkway (704-687-8722; 800-228-7275; www.blueridgefriends.org) purchase land and scenic easements to preserve the Parkway's viewshed and update visitor centers and other facilities.

Life on the Parkway

With all these attractions, many visitors slow down and take weeks to tour the Parkway and meet the "who's who" of significant Appalachian summits that line the route. That means visitors need places to stay and eat, and the Parkway comes through.

Picnicking is a quintessential Parkway experience, at more than a dozen formal picnic areas with restrooms, at a wealth of overlooks with picnic tables, or just on the roadside. (You can park on the grass—just pick a spot that will support your car and be well away from traffic.)

Camping is another must-have experience, and the Parkway's nine campgrounds—an average of one every 43 miles—offer 712 tent sites and 332 RV slips. All the Parkway's campgrounds charge a daily rate for "first-come" campers. And you can reserve a campsite in advance for a slightly higher rate at Julian Price Park, Linville Falls, and Mount Pisgah Campgrounds (Web site www.recreation.gov or call toll-free: 877-444-6777).

At press time, Mount Pisgah is the only campground with showers, but when funding permits, more campgrounds will provide that amenity. Major campgrounds can have camp stores with firewood and basic supplies for sale (charcoal, starter fluid, snacks, flashlights, batteries, ice, canned goods, etc.), but don't expect a wide selection.

There are also commercial campgrounds just off the Parkway, as well as nearby campgrounds run by the USDA Forest Service. These are concentrated in the national forests at the northern and southern ends of the Parkway and include Sherando Lake and Cave Mountain Lake in Virginia and Black Mountain and Davidson River in North Carolina. And North Carolina's Mount Mitchell State Park offers the East's highest tent camping.

The Parkway has four lodges, including Peaks of Otter Lodge (the only year-round lodge) and Rocky Knob cabins (built during the Depression by the Civilian Conservation Corps) in Virginia. In North Carolina you can stay at Bluffs Lodge and Pisgah Inn.

Peaks of Otter Lodge and Pisgah Inn have the most sophisticated restaurants, but there are less-formal snack bar/restaurants at Otter Creek and Mabry Mill in Virginia and at Doughton Park and Crabtree Meadows (as well as at Mount Mitchell State Park) in North Carolina.

The facilities above are referenced in the introductions to each section of the Parkway and in the Mileage Log.

The Climate

A mix of serious seasons reigns on the ridgetops. Dramatically different microclimates emerge with each bend of the road.

Summer on the Parkway comprises June through September. June forests are fully leafed out—except on the very highest summits, where it remains spring till late in the season. Rhododendron crowns that last stage of spring with a high-altitude bloom of legendary appeal. Target the third week of June for the best bloom at the loftiest elevations.

July is when temperatures peak along the Parkway. That differs from the rest of the South, where August and even September bring the hottest days. By August, temperatures along much of the Parkway are heading down the road to fall.

The hottest summer days at the lowest elevations—principally in Virginia—can be hot, up to the low 90s. On the higher parts of the road, summer temps climb to the low to mid-70s; the hottest days will reach the low 80s. But those days are rare. On the very highest peaks, summer days can be downright chilly. Add misty conditions, and temperatures can stay in the 60s and even 50s. Summer nights often dip to the mid-50s and mid-60s. The coolest summer nights can drop to the upper 40s at higher elevations.

Expect rain through the summer months. The loftiest peaks are home to a kind of temperate rain forest. You will encounter sunny periods principally after cold fronts that yield refreshing mountain temps, but generally summer is a time for daily thunderstorms and, possibly, sustained periods of wet weather. September usually ushers in a change—by late in the month, the highest areas are drying out and showing the foliage of fall.

May and October, the months when Parkway facilities routinely open and close, can bring hoar-frosted trees and cold. Even light snowfall is possible, especially at the highest elevations. Normally May sees spring in full bloom, with warm days and chilly nights (consult appendix A for a Parkway bloom calendar). October brings peak foliage color—from the tenth to the fifteenth of the month at the heights and during the last two weeks of the month in most other places.

April and November—the months before Parkway facilities open and after they close—can be beautifully clear and cool. Expect April to be the rainiest month, but the volatility of late-winter weather often quickly replaces rain with shine. The year's best long-range views are November's reward—with low humidity, infrequent rain, and no leaves to block the vistas. A November "Indian summer" can be one of the best times on the Parkway. But April and November are, respectively, the latest and earliest months when snow is expected. Both months have received substantial accumulations at the heights and atmospheric dustings lower down.

March and December are fickle. The Parkway's heaviest snowfalls can occur in March, when the first of spring's substantial rains run into the last of winter's cold. Outside of that, March is often clear and cold—perfect hiking weather. December

The Parkway can be an exciting drive in winter for hikers and even cross-country skiers wanting to experience the high road's most austere season.

is drier, but snow becomes more likely as fall gives way to winter. The highest peaks have a fifty-fifty chance of seeing a white Christmas.

Winter is the Parkway's truly quiet time. The peaks are often snow covered for weeks at a time from January through mid-March—to the delight of cross-country skiers. Even when snowless, trails and waterfalls are often covered in ice. Temperatures can dip well below 15°F at night and stay below freezing during the day. High winds, arctic temperatures, and deep snow can make the Parkway impassible. Expect gates to block Parkway access points during those times (in late fall and spring as well).

Virginia's Peaks of Otter Lodge (Milepost 85.9) is open and may be one of the region's best winter holiday bets. The Parkway is plowed from Moses Cone Park at US 321 near Blowing Rock, North Carolina, past Price Park to US 221—a nearly 7-mile section with particularly enticing winter trails for Nordic skiing. Snow doesn't stay all winter; coverage fluctuates with the weather. Tune into the Weather Channel for the latest report on the Parkway microclimate, or log on to www.weather.com for updated forecasts according to Parkway-area zip codes.

Note: The weather described above is what you can expect on the Parkway itself.

Being Prepared

Practical Cautions on a Lofty Road

It's refreshing when a road can be a natural experience—but tackle this trip with particular caution. The Parkway is a driving challenge for many "flatlanders"—an unrelenting combination of curves and grades for every one of its 469 miles.

Stick to the 45 mph speed limit, and note that it is 35 mph in a handful of places.

Wildlife should be your first concern. Be especially alert at dusk, dawn, and after dark. Driving during daylight hours is best—for views and the safety of the many animals that live along the road.

Sheltered and exposed parts of the Parkway pose their own respective hazards. In warmer months dry pavement can suddenly become wet in a shady curve. That can mean a sudden change to snow or glare ice in colder months, hence the BEWARE OF SUDDEN ICING signs. Parkway fatalities often occur under just these conditions. Fog also necessitates slower speeds. You'll never see it denser than on the Parkway. Such weather hazards explain why signs urge motorists to avoid the Parkway in fog, snow, and ice. In the worst winter weather, motorists have been stranded and even died on the Blue Ridge Parkway.

Taking the above concerns seriously doesn't mean that you should delay the motorist who shows up on your rear bumper. Bear in mind that locals drive these roads every day and know every curve. The Parkway is often the best way for locals to get to work, so just pull over at the next overlook. The almost endless supply of these effortless on-and-off options give visitors no excuse for blocking traffic. Please be especially conscious of this if you're driving an RV. Also of interest to RV owners, the Mileage Log includes the minimum height of the Parkway's twenty-four tunnels.

Selecting a Trail

The uniqueness of the Parkway creates an unusual mission for this guide. A Parkway road trip between Shenandoah and Great Smoky Mountains National Parks can be a seamless experience of the Southern Appalachians, and this guide is designed to provide that opportunity.

How many times have you crossed a park boundary only to have your trail guide say, "See the guide to _____ National Forest for that hike"? The Parkway is bordered by state parks, national forests, and private wildlands throughout its length. There are countless trail options, and if you miss the best of those options, you haven't made the most of the Parkway. This guide covers the Parkway as well as the best off-Parkway hikes along the route—often lesser known and less crowded.

When deciding on a Parkway hike, first match the trail to your level of ability. Luckily, the Parkway's famous leg-stretcher trail philosophy means that many of its trails—dozens, in fact—are easy ambles to a great view or secluded spot. You can just pull off the road and go. Signs tell you which trails are very short; so does the Mileage Log in this guide.

Times haven't changed that much. National Park Service rangers still stand ready to help Parkway motorists. PHOTO BY LOU HARSHAW/COURTESY ASHEVILLE CHAMBER OF COMMERCE

Hikes in this guide are listed—and described—as easy, moderate, or strenuous.

Easy: Generally, regardless of length, an easy trail has a graded or benched treadway, meaning that the tread has been excavated, like a mini road grade, for predictable footing. An easy hike is relatively level, with a grade that's gradual and consistent.

Moderate: A moderate trail, besides often being a longer hike, may involve a rougher, rockier treadway and fluctuations in the rate of rise, though the climb is usually gradual.

Strenuous: Strenuous trails are longer and steeper overall or in places, require substantial exertion, and often have uneven footing or involve the use of ladders or climbing over rocks.

When a trail is said to "slab around a peak," it means that it avoids a summit, generally keeping to a gradual grade at one elevation. Add these basic terms to the descriptions in the trail entries. For instance, the Nuwati Trail on Grandfather Mountain (rated easy) is considered untaxing because of gradual grades. Nevertheless, the text mentions that the trail has rocky footing, a fact that hikers will need to consider.

Trail entries often use the term "loop" to describe a hike—a route that resembles a circle—but there are at least two different types of loops. A lollipop loop is a single trail that leaves a trailhead, splits some distance away, then returns to the split (forming that circle) and then to the trailhead—a frequent occurrence on the easiest Parkway paths. Others are actually a "circuit" hike—a route that originates on one trail but turns onto different trails on the way back to roughly the same starting point. Many longer hikes on the Parkway and adjacent to it are circuit hikes.

This book suggests lollipop loops and circuits wherever possible. On a high-elevation, linear park like the Blue Ridge Parkway, many possible hikes are out-and-back treks that descend off the ridge and require a slog back up. The most egregious of these are not included here to concentrate on the kinds of trails most people want to take.

Trail entries also specify the elevation gain in a given hike—that, after all, is where most people truly feel the effort. In many places trailheads are the trail's low point, often where a trail reaches a road. On the Parkway, the trail often descends first then climbs back to the trailhead.

Mileages are given for most hikes, often with "about" appended to them. This is done where seemingly reliable data conflicts with the author's own experience or other information, such as park brochures or official publications. All mileage information should be considered a best estimate. Certain kinds of terrain make it difficult to measure with certainty a trail's exact length. In addition, the varying levels of experience that hikers bring to a trail can make mileage information less meaningful. Trail descriptions and ratings are often more valuable than simple mileage figures.

I often suggest ways for inexperienced or less physically fit hikers to sample longer, more strenuous trails. Most entries, for instance, suggest places to turn around or alternative routes that avoid the most difficult terrain. Still, a person in very poor condition could find an easy-rated trail to be a challenging hike, so the trail descriptions in this book are subjective. If you are overweight, do no regular exercise, or are unsure of foot, expect an easy hike to be moderate and a moderate hike to be strenuous. The nice thing is that with consistent exercise, your personal rating system can match—or exceed—the ratings in this book.

Don't Forget the Net

Nature-loving hikers also tend to be people who are comfortable with the Internet. If you're online, definitely check out the exploding trove of hiking information to be found on the World Wide Web. The richness starts with individual home pages for national, state, and private parks; you'll find information, maps, directions, and even the latest campground rates.

Turn to appendix B for a listing of Internet sites of interest to Parkway travelers.

What to Carry

The shortest, easiest nature trails in this book require that the hiker carry nothing other than a camera or binoculars. But hikers who venture more than a mile into fields or forests will want to carry a few essential items. A small backpack or fanny pack is big enough for the essentials:

- a water bottle or hydration system
- a snack or extra food
- spare clothing and other protective items (raincoat, sunscreen, insect repellent, sunglasses, and a hat.)

- a small first-aid kit (bandages, antiseptic, extra-strength aspirin/acetaminophen, moleskin for blisters)
- this guide—or the relevant photocopied pages/map
- the recommended hiking maps
- any trail permits required by managing agencies

The ultimate item you'll want to carry isn't in your pack but in your head: knowledge. The information contained here is timely and extensive, but no single trail guide can do it all. Explore the variety of resources available to those who enjoy the outdoors, including FalconGuides and other books on survival, route finding, mountaineering, and backpacking. To be truly prepared, take courses in first aid and CPR.

Maps

A strip map for finding the trailhead, available from Parkway headquarters and visitor centers, provides the perfect main map for your trip. That map plus the highly detailed and accurate trail maps in this book should be all you need. The Parkway also publishes its own stylized and less detailed trail maps of many of the major developed recreation areas. These are often referred to in the text as the "handout maps" that are available at the local visitor center, campground, etc. If you want to be sure you can find these, download them before your trip from the Parkway Web site. Nevertheless, other maps, notably USGS topo quads and wilderness area trail maps, are recommended for many hikes. (See appendix B for additional resources.)

Clothing

Choose clothing that is comfortable and protective.

Any summer outdoor activity on the Parkway might seem to call for shorts and T-shirts, but when choosing hiking clothing, the best policy is to be prepared for the worst weather the season and place can deliver. This means being flexible and dressing in layers and being prepared for rain and wind. Luckily, the latest trail shirts and pants (the latter with zip-off legs) are virtually weightless, dry fast, have antimicrobial properties that eliminate odor, and are even sun protection formula (SPF)-rated.

The best choices for outer garments are waterproof and breathable jackets and pants made of synthetic fabrics. They're expensive but highly recommended. In spring, fall, and especially winter, your outer layer is the first line of defense. Under that, wear more layers—how many varies by season. Synthetic fabrics that are warm even when wet are the best choices. Look for polypropylene T-shirts, long underwear, pants, and zip-up or pullover pile jackets.

Major insulating garments are definitely necessary in severe winter weather. The choice for insulation is, again, synthetic materials that won't lose their insulating value when wet. Although waterproof fabrics are bringing down back into vogue.

Footwear

On the Parkway's easy trails you'll need only a sturdy pair of walking or running shoes. But on moderate or more difficult hikes—or even easy hikes with rocky footing—you'll want a good pair of hiking boots.

The newest-generation boots are lightweight and relatively inexpensive, boasting waterproof fabrics and various kinds of nonskid soles. They add comfort, safety, and enjoyment to any hike and are a worthwhile purchase for even a casual hiker.

Serious winter hikers will need more than a lightweight three-season boot. And those who walk wilderness or primitive trails may need to cross streams without the aid of bridges. Rather than avoid these trails, carry a pair of aqua shoes, which slip over bare feet, or sport sandals for wading. They also make great in-camp wear.

Weather Dangers

It is not enough to own the proper clothing. Be sure to put on your high-tech garments before you become thoroughly wet or chilled.

Hypothermia results when lack of food and/or exposure to severe weather conditions prevent the body from maintaining its core temperature. Hypothermia can occur at any time of year—at temperatures well above freezing—with the dramatic cooling effects of wind and rain. To prevent it, stay dry and protected with the right clothing—especially a hat, since up to 70 percent of heat loss can emanate from your head. Don extra layers when you stop for a rest, before you get chilled. And remove layers before you get sweaty, starting with that hat. Adequately fuel yourself with food and water; drink plenty of fluids (in winter, simply breathing robs you of moisture), and nibble energy foods (such as trail mix, sandwiches, and hot soups). Set up camp early to accommodate any inexperienced or less physically fit members of your party.

The best way to treat hypothermia is to stop it before it starts, but you may not be able to. Do not ignore such symptoms as uncontrollable shivering and, later, slow and slurred speech, stumbling gait or clumsiness, and disorientation. Take immediate action to shelter and refuel anyone with these symptoms—including yourself. If the victim is uncooperative or unconscious, sandwich the lightly dressed hiker in a sleeping bag between two similarly dressed helpers to share their body heat.

Frostbite. Frozen flesh can result from severe cold, and its first sign is reddened skin. Next, the frozen site—often toes, fingers, or portions of the face—will turn white or gray. The best prevention is to stay warm so that your extremities receive the blood flow they need. If you can avoid it, do not venture into extreme conditions or exposed areas where windchill factors are below minus 20°F. In severe conditions hikers should monitor one another's faces and suggest shelter when the need arises. Do not rub frozen skin or slap frozen extremities together. When an area with severe frostbite begins to thaw, expect severe pain; use aspirin or acetaminophen to ease the pain on the way to medical assistance.

Lightning. In summer a hiker's major danger is lightning, especially on exposed mountaintops—and the Parkway is full of them. At the first rumblings of thunder, move off ridgetops and seek shelter in a group of smaller trees rather than under one tall one. Rest in a low, dry area (but not a gully or near a pond, where water can conduct the current). Avoid overhangs or small caves where ground current might pass through you. In a lightning storm you're better off sitting in the open below surrounding high points and atop a low-lying rock that is detached and thus insulated from the ground. To further insulate yourself, crouch low or kneel on top of your pack or sleeping pad.

Heat stroke and heat exhaustion are warm-weather equivalents of hypothermia. The Parkway isn't known for hot hikes, but be sure to carry and drink plenty of fluids, especially if you're sweating heavily. Avoid hiking in the hottest part of the day, and cool off by slipping into one of the trailside pools often mentioned in this guide's hike descriptions. (*Note:* Swimming is prohibited in Parkway waters.) If you feel dizzy and drained, heat exhaustion may be the culprit. Relax, drink fluids, and let your body recover. Heat stroke is a more extreme—and dangerous—condition. Rather than being damp and drained, you'll be dry and feverish, signs that the body has given up the attempt to cool down by perspiring. Immediately cool the affected person with cold, wet compresses. Administer water, and seek medical attention.

Trailside Pests

Winter weather largely eradicates the Parkway's most bothersome bugs, reptiles, and plants. But spring, summer, and fall are different matters.

Bees. Do everything you can to avoid contact with concentrations of bees. Be cautious around fruit and flowers, and be on the lookout for nests hanging from limbs, in hollow trees and logs, or on the ground. And don't act like a flower. You can't avoid sweating, which attracts some types of bees, but don't entice them with perfume or scented body care products.

As long as you're not allergic, most stings are minor and easily treated. Simply scrape an imbedded stinger out with a knife blade. (Don't squeeze it out, which releases even more venom into your bloodstream.) A paste made of water and unseasoned meat tenderizer that contains papain (a papaya enzyme) can neutralize bee venom; baking soda paste does not.

Some stings are not so simple. A person who is allergic to bee stings or is stung many times can suffer anaphylactic shock—even death. Around a hundred people a year die from bee stings in the United States. An over-the-counter antihistamine that contains diphenhydramine (such as Benadryl) can help control mild allergic reactions. Serious toxic reactions and anaphylactic shock can either set in immediately or after some delay. If you know you are allergic to bee stings, always carry an epinephrine syringe bee sting kit—and be sure your companions know where it is and how to use it.

Ticks. The Piedmont and coastal forests of Virginia and North Carolina are favorite warm-weather habitats for ticks. Hikers on the Parkway's highest mountains are less likely to find ticks, especially where spruce and fir forests prevail. Ticks can carry Lyme disease and Rocky Mountain spotted fever—potentially deadly diseases.

North Carolina is infamous for the latter. Both diseases can take up to two weeks to gestate before symptoms develop. Among the signs are arthritis-like joint pain, high fever, and/or a circular rash.

The best defense against ticks is three-pronged: First, at the lowest Parkway elevations, use a tick and insect repellent that contains N, N-diethyl-3-methylbenzamide, more commonly known as DEET. Second, whether you use repellents or not, wear long-sleeved shirts and long pants and avoid walking through tall grass, brush, or dense woods. Third, frequently check yourself for ticks, especially at night and when you finish a hike. Focus on armpits, ears, scalp, groin, legs, and where clothes, such as socks, constrict the body. It takes awhile for ticks to attach and transmit disease, so you have a good shot at preventing infection if you find them early.

If a tick becomes embedded in your skin, use a bit of repellent, rubbing alcohol, or a hot, extinguished match to encourage the tick to back itself out. If you must use tweezers to remove a tick, grasp the head to avoid squeezing toxins into the wound. And don't hesitate to pull a little bit of your skin out with the tick so that mouthparts do not remain to cause infection.

Many Parkway paths are easy "leg-stretchers," but serious hikers will find challenging hikes and even overnight backpacking trips all along the high road.

Flies. In spring (mid-April to mid-June), hikers on the Parkway's higher elevations can be troubled by the same tiny black flies that pester North Country hikers in Minnesota and Maine. More often hikers here see common houseflies and horseflies; the latter are particularly vicious at the coast. The best defenses are to use insect repellent, keep food and garbage covered or stored elsewhere when picnicking and camping, and cover your body. The newest trick is to reduce the use of chemicals and buy and wear the new Buzz-Off treated clothing, the first bug-banning technology to get the EPA's nod.

Mosquitoes and gnats are prevalent, especially on cool mountain evenings. Again, the Buzz-Off garments are effective, or use repellent with DEET.

Poison ivy, poison oak, and poison sumac are all found everywhere on the Parkway except the highest peaks. All produce contact dermatitis—rash and watery blisters that appear twelve to forty-eight hours after skin rubs against the plant resin. The outbreak usually runs its course in ten days, but isolated cases can be severe or cause allergic reactions. Learn to identify these plants ("Leaves of three, let it be"), and be wary of wading through brush in shorts.

If you realize that you just touched one of these poisonous plants, remove and isolate contaminated clothing until it can be washed at home. Flush the affected skin with water but no soap—your skin's natural oils will protect you temporarily. Cover rash areas with calamine lotion. See a physician if face, genitals, or more than 25 percent of your body is affected. Preventive creams you can apply before exposure are also available.

Snakes rank high on the list of hiker fears, but these animals play their role in nature, and only two venomous types are found in the Blue Ridge: timber rattlesnakes and copperheads. Snakes are not a problem on the Parkway's higher peaks.

The best way to avoid being bitten is to be observant—and be able to recognize poisonous snakes *before* they can bite. Rattlesnakes and copperheads are generally heftier than nonvenomous snakes and have triangular or arrow-shaped heads and vertically slit pupils (versus tube-shaped heads and round pupils for nonvenomous snakes). Don't reach blindly behind logs and rocks, inspect wooded sites before you sit, and watch where you step. Luckily, of the 20,000 people bitten by venomous snakes annually in the United States, fewer than 15 die. The venom of these two species is also relatively slow acting, almost half of all bites don't transmit venom, and antivenin is widely available in local hospitals.

If bitten, be able to report what kind of snake bit you. Observe your wound: The bite of a pit viper includes two or more prominent fang marks, while a nonvenomous snakebite usually leaves two rows of indentations and no big holes. If possible, use a commercial snakebite kit within three minutes of the bite. Immediately remove all watches and rings that may cause constriction from swelling. Do not make incisions with a knife or try to suck out the venom. Do not use tourniquets, cold water, or ice packs, which increase the possibility of gangrene. Instead, loosely splint and immobilize the affected limb, and mark on the victim with a pen the time and spread of swelling. If you are within twenty minutes of the trailhead, carry the victim (or permit the person to walk slowly, with frequent rests) to a vehicle for immediate transfer to a hospital. If hiking alone—not necessarily a good idea—walk as calmly as possible back to your car for help. Hikers who are far from a trailhead should send a companion for help and wait for emergency personnel to return with antivenin.

Bears. Most other animals in North Carolina are harmless to hikers. The exception is the rarely seen black bear. Most of the time, a backcountry glimpse of one of these reclusive mammals includes its rear end sprinting away. If you have a sudden encounter with a nearby bear, especially a mother with cubs, steadily and calmly back away. Leave the area. Do not turn your back on the bear. Do not run or climb a tree, since this may provoke a chase—and you cannot outrun a bear. Stand your ground if charged; bears often bluff.

The most problematic locations for bear encounters are popular campsites, where marauding bears forage through garbage. There they can be aggressive, especially if you approach while they are enjoying food. Stay away. The best defense against such encounters with bears—and with skunks and other animals, even mice—is to keep your food away from camp. Safely hang bagged food by tossing a rope over a tree limb, tying on your food container, running the food into midair away from the trunk, and tying the other end where you can reach it. Generally bears are much more of a problem in Shenandoah and Great Smoky Mountains National Parks than along the Blue Ridge Parkway. But problems with bears seem to be on the rise at Parkway campgrounds and picnic areas, many of which now provide bear-proof trash receptacles.

Waterborne pests. The other animal threat is a microscopic one. Ingestion of waterborne pests can cause a variety of backcountry infections. Perhaps the best known is *giardia lamblia,* but an E. coli infection can be deadly. Hikers have even contracted Type A hepatitis from drinking untreated water in the "wilderness." Unfortunately, even pristine-looking streams may contain these and other disease-producing agents. All hikers should carry water from treated sources, carry commercially bottled drinks, or treat the water they use. Boiling water for at least five minutes (before adding food or flavoring) will kill the tiny protozoan that causes giardia, so campers can often prepare hot foods with water from streams and springs. Boiling can cause drinking water to taste flat, so pour boiled water back and forth between clean containers to restore its oxygen content, or add flavorings. Better still, carry a portable backpacker's water purifier. Do not attempt to disinfect water with halazone, chlorine, or iodine.

Zero Impact

Everyone's heard the dictum "Take only pictures, leave only footprints." Well, even footprints cause soil compaction and erosion in many of the popular wilderness areas that line the Parkway. However, damage to the environment can be minimized.

Zero-impact hiking and camping starts with an effort to minimize any evidence of your presence. That starts with staying on defined trails and restricting your outings to a small party of people. Intelligent strategies for protecting trails, such as not shortcutting switchbacks, also reduce the likelihood that you'll brush directly through poison ivy or step on that snoozing copperhead. Groups of four to six hikers can more easily find campsites and deal with emergencies and don't disturb other hikers' wilderness experience. Whatever your party's size, try to keep your noise level down, especially when camping in the vicinity of others. Noise travels far after dark; there's no excuse for loud conversation or rowdy behavior after 9:00 p.m.

Littering is the number-one trail pollution problem. The dictum "Pack it in, pack it out" has become the basic backcountry credo. Too many people lug food and drink into the woods in heavy containers, then leave the bottles and cans behind when they're empty. Pack properly, using lightweight plastic, and you won't be tempted to jettison the refuse. Bag trash immediately to avoid attracting bugs and animals, and consider picking up litter left by others.

Everyone generates waste in the woods, so proper disposal is another element of zero impact. Where restrooms are available, use them before hitting the trail. When hiking or camping, use proper methods of disposal to keep urine, feces, soap, and garbage out of water sources. To make a "cat hole" for body waste, use a small trowel to remove a cap of sod (keep it intact) and dig a hole at least 6 inches deep in organic soil (damp but not wet) at least 200 feet from surface water, trails, campsites, or other places where people congregate. This is your "toilet." Use natural wipes such as leaves, or pack out toilet paper in a plastic bag. After using your pit, mix soil into the waste to hasten decomposition, then cover with the sod cap. When urinating, avoid hitting plants; try to go on mineral soil or sand. Choose a sunny spot to hasten evaporation.

Camping impacts the environment in ways that hiking does not. Hikers who intend to camp should read up on clean camping: How to choose a campsite, the safety and environmental benefits of carrying a camp stove (where allowed), and many other topics are addressed in several fine publications. A touchy topic for campers is how to keep your body and equipment clean without polluting streams and lakes. Some camping purists choose not to bathe in the backcountry; others wouldn't camp if they couldn't get clean. The best way to wash and not pollute nearby drinking water is to carry a large pot or bucket of water at least 200 feet from the water source. Lather minimally with biodegradable soap, and rinse; dilute and disperse any suds on the ground with more water. To brush your teeth, go the same distance away and use the smallest amount of paste and water possible. Disperse by spitting, and rinse away residue with water.

Hiking with Pets

Woodsy forays with Fido are fun. There's nothing like sharing the exercise and camaraderie of the great outdoors with your favorite friend. But be aware that dogs can be a headache for other hikers and for park managers, so restrictions apply. The Blue Ridge Parkway requires that all dogs be leashed at all times, and pets are not allowed in campgrounds.

Sadly, not everyone out there loves dogs (or, at the very least, your dog). It can be frightening to see an unleashed animal charging down a trail at you, especially if you're a parent with children or another pet owner with your own dog on a leash. Many national parks actually prohibit dogs because their territorial instincts can complicate life for wildlife populations already trying to survive in shrinking natural areas. While out of sight of their owners, unleashed dogs can trample fragile plants, dig up animal dens, even kill wildlife, and leave their scent (not to mention piles of pooh, sometimes on the trail).

There are real virtues to using a leash. Many dogs get permanently lost in wild areas, severely injured in encounters with wildlife, or hurt in falls. For more guidelines visit the American Dog Owners Association Web site: www.adoa.org.

Hiking with Kids

Hiking is a wonderful way to instill a love of the outdoors, an enjoyment of physical fitness and exercise, and less-tangible values of environmental and personal responsibility in young people.

You don't have to wait until a child is ten years old to take him or her out into the woods. Many of the hikes in this guide are great for kids—the leg-stretcher trail philosophy makes the Blue Ridge Parkway particularly well suited to children. On the Parkway, even a short walk can lead to high adventure.

The Parkway can be a formative experience for kids. Paths like the Price Lake Trail (Milepost 297.2) even make great winter walks.

Trail descriptions highlight paths suitable for toddlers (on their first unaided woods walks), family hikes, beginner backpacking trips, and saunters with the elderly and physically challenged. Sample some of these, but don't expect to make the entire hike or reach that intended campsite. Be flexible with tiny hikers—let them set the pace.

Many parents purchase sophisticated child-carrier packs that include a pouch for kid items. These increase your mobility, but remember to duck below tree limbs and other obstacles. Also, children often fall asleep in these packs, and few have a way to stabilize a sleeping tyke's head. Be prepared to use a scarf, pillow, or other items to cushion a napping child's head, and be sure to work out the system in advance.

Cool-weather hiking with children poses more challenges. Since children in carriers aren't active, it is easy for them to become cold, especially in winter. Don't overdo winter hikes. Carry hot drinks or soup in a thermos. Be aware that just bundling a child in urban-style outerwear may not keep her or him warm. There is no substitute for effectively layered high-quality clothing. Foam-lined, heavily insulated boots with polypropylene or wool socks and substantial mittens should also be basic requirements. A word to the wise: Children who have a bad experience will not be enthusiastic about hiking in the future.

Focus on comfort and safety at any time of year. In warm weather, such items as sunscreen, hats, insect repellent, topical anesthetic for bug bites or sunburn, and snacks and drinks are the ingredients for a successful family hike.

Trail Etiquette

You can enhance your safety and limit human conflict in the outdoors just as you can limit impact on the environment. Conflict between recreationists occurs in many ways.

Camping can be a touchy topic—hence the rule that Parkway campers observe quiet time between 10:00 p.m. and 6:00 a.m. Serious campers cope with darkness by going to sleep; when nearby tenters build a giant bonfire and party until midnight, the result can be unpleasant.

Avoid such conflict in the backcountry by choosing your sites according to your preferences. Choose an isolated campsite if you are a wilderness purist. A car-accessible campground may be more appropriate if you're taking the neighborhood kids on their first camping trip. With a little forethought and consideration, you can minimize conflicts between you and other Parkway recreationists.

Trails have their own particular form of etiquette. Unless it's unsafe to do so, step aside when other hikers approach, even if you have the right-of-way. Be diplomatic at all times. If the chemistry in a given situation is negative, be the first to back down and move on.

Criminal violence is rare on trails, but instances of robbery and rape seem to be increasing. Be friendly but reasonably wary. Do not hike alone; if you do, dress conservatively, don't flaunt expensive equipment or jewelry, and don't hesitate to say you're with a group of friends. Backcountry users have much in common, and the camaraderie of the woods can cause some people to treat everyone they meet as though they were old friends. But it is far better to keep an urban sense of security about you—which means not leaving your pack and other gear unattended and not volunteering information about yourself or your belongings.

Don't leave valuables in your vehicle. The number-one crime associated with hiking is the trailhead auto break-in. When your trek begins at an isolated trailhead, consider parking at a nearby business and arranging to be shuttled. At the very least, lock valuables out of sight in the trunk.

Always let a responsible party know where you are going and when you'll return. Religiously comply with hiker registration and user permit systems, which exist at many places on the Parkway and at parks and preserves along the way. These function as a safety net and, where fees are collected, support the maintenance and management of the trails you've come to enjoy.

Enjoyment is, after all, what trails are all about. There's the exercise, the good times you share with those who accompany you and those you meet, and the scenic views, both vast and intimate. Sadly, today's nature lovers often find themselves spending a lot of time in cars. Fortunately, the American fascination with being "on the road" finds its ultimate expression on the Blue Ridge Parkway, where trail after trail makes it easy to turn a road trip into an unforgettable encounter with the outdoors.

Seventy-five years after the birth of the Parkway, hybrid vehicles may be cruising the road, but the goal is the same: Tempt motorists out of their cars and onto the trail. Near Cumberland Knob (Milepost 217.1).

Map Legend

Transportation

Blue Ridge Parkway	═══════
Interstate Highway	═(81)═
U.S. Highway	═(60)═
State Road	═(43)═
County/Forest Road	[CR 90][FR 90]
Unpaved Road	= = = = =
Railroad	+—+—+—+
Tunnel	[ ]
Featured Trail	━ ━ ━ ━ ━
Other Trail	- - - - - -
Track	....

Hydrology

Lake/Reservoir	
River/Creek	～
Intermittent Stream	—·—·—
Spring	o—
Waterfall	≋

Symbols

Bridge	≍
Campground	▲
Capital	⊛
City/Town	○
Cross-County Skiing	🎿
Dam	—
Entrance Kiosk	▮
Gate	•—•
Mine	⚒
Mountain/Peak	▲
Overlook	◓
Parking	🅿
Pass	≍
Picnic Area	🅰
Point of Interest	■
Restroom	🚻
Trailhead (Start)	❶
Visitor Center	❓

The North-Central Blue Ridge

Mileposts 0.0 (I-64 at Shenandoah National Park) to 121.4 (US 220 at Roanoke, Virginia)

The northernmost 120 miles of the Parkway is the perfect introduction to the Blue Ridge. Motorists starting on this section approach the mountains as people have for centuries. This is the Blue Ridge at its most definitive—the Appalachians, rearing sharply above the Piedmont to the east and the Shenandoah Valley to the west.

Indeed, the ridge seems sharper here than it does in Shenandoah National Park, just north of the Parkway. The 100 miles of Shenandoah's Skyline Drive is a nice prelude that turns the Parkway's 469 miles into a nearly 600-mile mountain experience.

From Rockfish Gap (Milepost 0) to US 220 in Roanoke, Virginia (Milepost 121.4), the dramatic spinelike ridge offers what some other sections of the high road don't—views from towering forested peaks into valleys checkerboarded with farms. These summits are largely unsettled; national forests wrap the Parkway corridor in multi-hundred thousand–acre woodlands. In the evening these dark shapes bulk mysteriously against the twinkling of valley towns far below.

The ridge is high and airy until Otter Creek (Mileposts 55–64), when the Parkway dips through intimate forests to its lowest point—the James River, at 650 feet. Then up it climbs again, past the James River Face Wilderness and the high road's northern high point—3,950 feet, near Apple Orchard Mountain. Next are the Peaks of Otter's famous summits. From there it's a long scenic slide into the Roanoke Valley.

The Parkway's homage to the culture and history of the Southern highlands includes wayside exhibits and visitor centers. That starts immediately at Humpback Rocks Visitor Center and on the Mountain Farm Trail (typical late-1800s mountaineer farm). Don't miss this cultural side of the Parkway—trails are integral to its interpretation. Major interpretive sites include the James River Water Gap canal exhibit and Peaks of Otter's early-twentieth-century mountain farm and mid-1800s inn, Polly Wood's Ordinary.

Parkway service sites include a restaurant at Otter Creek and Peaks of Otter Lodge. The latter is also a highly regarded, spectacularly scenic spot to spend the night (even

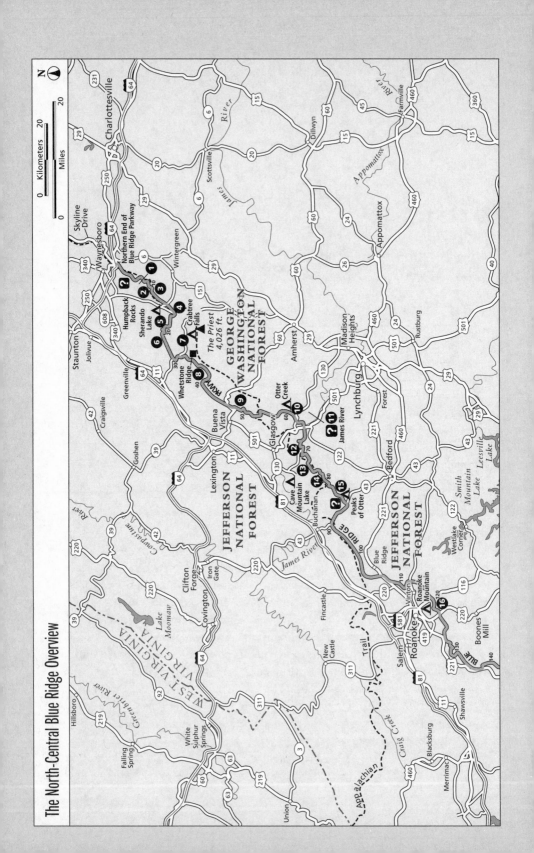

The North-Central Blue Ridge Overview

in winter, if you like to hike in the snow or cross-country ski). Campgrounds are available at Otter Creek, Peaks of Otter, and Roanoke Mountain.

The USDA Forest Service Sherando Lake Recreation Area is a premier base for campers near the start of the road. Just across the Parkway from there, Wintergreen Mountain Resort represents the upscale end of the recreation and lodging experience. It's one of the South's premier ski areas and usually rated among the country's top tennis and golf resorts (with its own extensive trail system).

Anchoring the north and south of this section of the Parkway are cities worth a pause. The shaded sophistication of Charlottesville is on the north end, with the University of Virginia and an up-and-coming wine-producing region named for Thomas Jefferson's nearby home, Monticello. Near Lynchburg, Jefferson's summer home, Poplar Forest, is also open. At this section's south end, Roanoke has typical urban amenities; but a historic farmers' market is noteworthy.

Take the time to sample other cities and towns along this part of the Parkway—great attractions are within easy reach. There's the Frontier Culture Museum in Staunton. Civil War history saturates the Shenandoah Valley, and Virginia Military Institute is just one of Lexington's attractions. Other sites honor George C. Marshall, "Stonewall" Jackson, and Robert E. Lee. There's historic downtown lodging at the Alexander-Withrow House and McCampbell Inn.

Natural Bridge, which Jefferson once owned and George Washington once surveyed, is near the town of the same name. The offbeat free attraction Foamhenge—yes, a life-size replica made of foam—is just to the west on US 11. Bedford, just east of Peaks of Otter, is the site of the National D-Day Memorial. The town lost more soldiers per capita during the invasion of France than any other place in the country.

The first section of the Parkway will leave you wanting more of these mountains. Luckily, there's 350 miles to go.

Check appendix B for a wealth of relevant Web sites and contact information.

Mill Mountain Park surrounds Roanoke's illuminated star and offers a stunning view of the city.

1 Humpback Rocks Recreation Area

Mileposts 5.8–6.0

Just 5 miles south of the Blue Ridge Parkway's first milepost, the Humpback Rocks Recreation Area provides a perfect introduction to the cultural and natural riches of this linear park. An interpretive trail through a hardscrabble farm explores the rustic life led by mountaineers up to the turn of the twentieth century. Don't miss the "1850–1950 Life along the Blue Ridge" exhibit at the small visitor center (where water and restrooms are available). The fascinating display emphasizes how the nearby Howardsville Turnpike and more distant canal on the James River (see that entry) created surprisingly diverse occupations and access to urban consumer goods for mountain residents in this area. Just across the road, a short, steep trail lifts hikers to Humpback Rocks and truly awe-inspiring vistas that stretch north and south along the Blue Ridge, east to the Piedmont, and west into the Shenandoah Valley. There's also a small picnic area.

Option 1: Mountain Farm Trail

An eye-opening glimpse into the rustic lives led by nineteenth-century Appalachian mountaineers who lived near what is now the Parkway.

Parkway mile: 5.8
Distance: 0.5 mile out and back
Difficulty: Easy (wheelchair accessible)

Elevation gain: Negligible
Maps: *USGS Sherando;* Parkway handout map, available at the visitor center

Finding the trailhead: Park at the Humpback Rocks Visitor Center and take the paved sidewalk south (left when facing the building).

The Hike

What a difference a century or so makes. The cabins and outbuildings of the re-created William J. Carter farm—plus interpretive plaques, seasonal programs, and costumed interpreters—give startling insight into the lives of Appalachian families. This pioneering lifestyle still existed in some places when the Blue Ridge Parkway was built in the mid-1930s. The 1890s farm found on the Mountain Farm Trail isn't the original; it was re-created in 1950 using period structures. Nevertheless, it is an authentic setting explored by a very easy trail.

Buy the trail's inexpensive booklet at the visitor center and take the paved side-walk that becomes a gravel lane. On the left, you first reach a cabin and chicken house and then a "gear loft," where the family stored their "plunder" (supplies and equipment). Past those structures and across the lane, a contorted barn is surrounded by a stone-walled pigpen. Farther on, a springhouse channels cold water through a sheltered food storage structure. Beyond that is "kissin' gate"; pass through and you're in

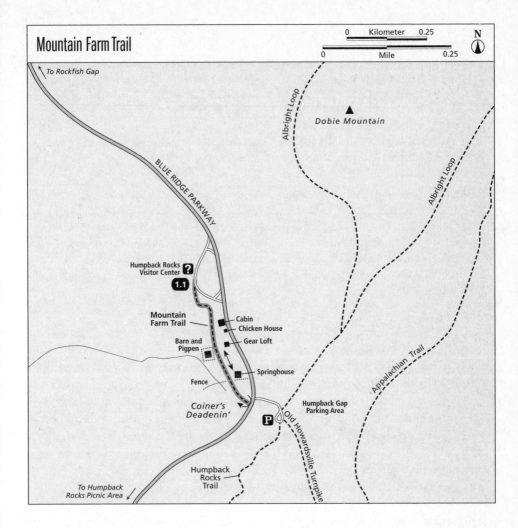

Mountain Farm Trail

0   Kilometer   0.25

0   Mile   0.25

N

To Rockfish Gap

BLUE RIDGE PARKWAY

Albright Loop

Dobie Mountain

Albright Loop

Humpback Rocks Visitor Center

1.1

Mountain Farm Trail

Cabin

Chicken House

Barn and Pigpen

Gear Loft

Springhouse

Fence

Coiner's Deadenin'

Appalachian Trail

Humpback Gap Parking Area

Old Howardsville Turnpike

Humpback Rocks Trail

To Humpback Rocks Picnic Area

"Coiner's deadenin'," grass-covered meadows under the towering crag of Humpback Rocks. Here mountaineers cleared fields the slow way—by girdling trees to kill them and planting crops between the leafless giants (which were later felled).

You can walk beyond the gate, gradually rising to Humpback Gap and trailhead parking for the Humpback Rocks Trail. Retrace your steps, or park at the gap and take both trails from one central spot.

Option 2: Humpback Rocks Area Trails

A short, steep hike and a longer circuit from Humpback Gap reach superb panoramic views at Humpback Rocks. Other circuit hikes in the area include the new Albright Loop and an overnighter to an Appalachian Trail shelter. From Humpback Rocks Picnic Area you can take the Catoctin Trail leg-stretcher and an AT hike to Humpback Mountain.

Parkway mile: 6.0 (Humpback Gap) and 8.5 (picnic area)

Distance: From Humpback Gap Parking Area, 2.0-mile out-and-back hike to Humpback Rocks and 4.3-mile circuit using the Appalachian Trail. Other circuits: 3.1-mile Albright Loop and 5.5-mile overnight backpack to Appalachian Trail shelter (10.0 miles from the Parkway near Milepost 0). From Humpback Rocks Picnic Area, the Catoctin Trail is 0.5 mile round-trip; using the AT, Humpback Mountain is 4.0 miles round-trip and Humpback Rocks is 6.0 miles round-trip.

Difficulty: Strenuous; easy for Catoctin Trail

Elevation gain: Approximately 720 feet to the rocks

Maps: *USGS Sherando;* Parkway handout map, available at the visitor center

Finding the trailhead: The Humpback Gap Parking Area has three entry points for these hikes. On the south end of the lot, by the big orientation sign, the blue-blazed trail leads directly to Humpback Rocks. From the north end of the parking area, the blue-blazed trail leads to the Albright Loop hike, the AT, and on to the Paul C. Wolfe Shelter. From the middle of the parking area, the Old Howardsville Turnpike connector also reaches the AT. The Catoctin Trail and AT hike to Humpback Mountain leave the middle of the back loop of the Humpback Rocks Picnic Area, at Milepost 8.5.

The Hikes

Humpback Rocks

The classic Blue Ridge Parkway hike to Humpback Rocks is no easy leg-stretcher. Nevertheless, the effort is rewarded with some of the best views in the northern Blue Ridge. The basic hike is a strenuous, 1.0-mile climb to Humpback Rocks, a massive greenstone outcrop at 3,080 feet. The rocks jut west but offer expansive views of the patchwork of farms on both sides of the Blue Ridge—the Shenandoah Valley to the west and Virginia's Piedmont to the east. Please follow these descriptions carefully—rangers say people often get confused in a few spots. I've personally met hikers here who have failed to find the rocks after even a few tries.

The blue-blazed trail to the rocks was once a punishing part of the white-blazed Appalachian Trail. Since then the AT has been substantially rerouted to bypass the rocks. The now nicely graded, gravel trail still ascends steeply, but there are benches along the way.

At 0.5 mile the steep, gravelly trail with wide steps crests and flattens out and continues straight beneath the towering crags of Humpback Rocks. At that leveling off spot, too many people turn left where the old trail used to go. That extremely steep ascent was closed in the early 1980s, but it still confuses some people; even hard-core hikers should avoid this old route. Bear right, actually straight, on the "new" trail with great uphill views. The trail soon ascends a set of wooden steps then switchbacks a half dozen times over increasingly rocky turns to a gap and a signed junction at 0.9 mile. Take a left and in 0.1 mile reach the cloven crags of Humpback Rocks. The best photos may be from the left crag of people on the right crag.

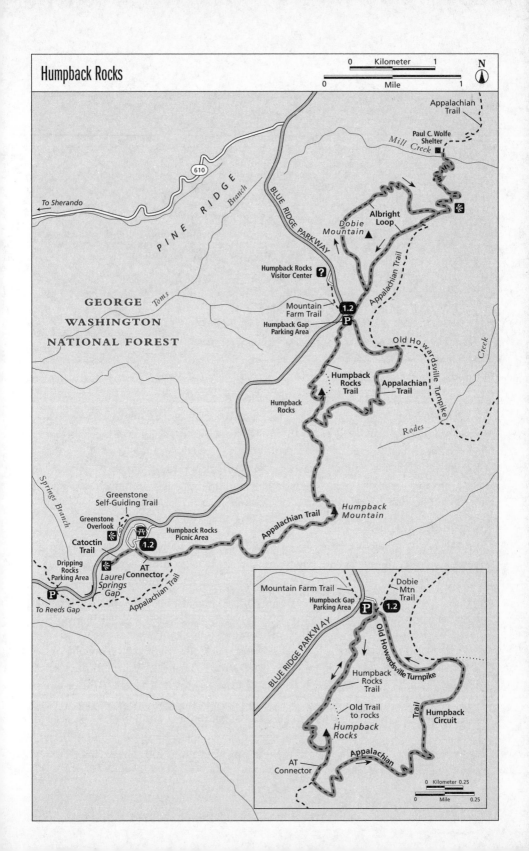

A father and son have a stellar view of the valley from Humpback Rocks.

Caution: When you leave the rocks and enter the woods, don't bear left or you'll get sucked down the old trail. Enter the woods from the rocks and bear kind of right to reach the signed junction—and be sure to turn right there to go back down the trail you came up for a round-trip of 2.0 miles. Parkway rangers report that some hikers miss this turn back down the mountain and unknowingly continue on toward the AT and beyond. Searches and unplanned overnight hikes have resulted.

Humpback Circuit

To make a counterclockwise circuit out of the hike to Humpback Rocks, don't turn right back down the mountain, but go straight at the signed junction to reach the AT in 0.2 mile. Turn left onto the AT at about 1.2 miles. Descend on the AT; there's a spring beside the trail on the left 0.8 mile below the junction, about 2.0 miles into your hike. Continue descending on the AT. At 3.6 miles the trail jogs left on an old road grade that is actually part of the Old Howardsville Turnpike.

This atmospheric avenue is fern fringed and quiet now. Built between 1846 and the mid-1850s, the road long linked the farms of the Shenandoah Valley on the west with the Rockfish Valley and the James River canal system on the east. (Check out where the canal breached the Blue Ridge on Parkway trails near Milepost 63.) The old road actually crosses the Parkway between Mileposts 4.0 and 5.0. Coming from that direction, wagon masters used to track their progress by sighting Humpback Rocks. If you hop off to the right of the trail on this section, you can see how artful rockwork underlies the grade.

When the AT bears right off the trace at 4.1 miles, go left at the sign, staying on the blue-blazed old turnpike (which has become a designated trail since the first edition of this guide). You'll reach Humpback Gap Parking Area in 0.2 mile, for a 4.3-mile hike.

If the 4.3-mile circuit to the rocks appeals to you, my suggestion is to reverse the above direction. That way, the climb to the rocks is far more gradual and you see far fewer people. But use caution. Leave the gap on the old trace and continue when it joins the AT, but keep a sharp eye out for when the AT turns right to climb toward the rocks (at about 0.7 mile). This is another place where novices are drawn left and can end up lost down in the drainage. Hike the circuit in this direction, and the spring is on the right at 2.3 miles. Then it's all right-hand turns at junctions back to your car. Turn right off the AT at 3.1 miles; go right at the next junction to the rocks. Leaving the rocks, again go right at that intersection to reach the parking lot at 4.3 miles.

Albright Loop Circuits

At busy times, you'll encounter fewer people by heading north out of Humpback Gap on the new 3.1-mile, moderate Albright Loop trail, named for an Old Dominion Appalachian Trail Club AT maintainer and field guide editor. The trail was created by adding a new trail west of Dobie Mountain to an AT access trail that already existed to the east of the peak.

The blue-blazed trail leaves the north end of the parking area and goes left at 0.3 mile on the new trail. It slabs the summit and follows old road grades as it switchbacks down to a junction with the AT at 2.0 miles. Go right on the AT for 0.1 mile then right again as the trail climbs over the flank of Dobie Mountain and back to the loop junction at 2.8 miles and the parking lot at 3.1 miles.

The Albright Loop also can be used to create a nice 5.5-mile overnight circuit to the Paul C. Wolfe Shelter, where there's a privy behind the shelter and a waterfall and swimming spot not too far downstream on Mill Creek. Camping isn't permitted on the Parkway except at designated sites, and this is one of those places. Take the Albright Loop left and then left again on the AT at 2.0 miles. There's a nice view east at 2.2 miles. Cross Mill Creek at 3.1 miles; the shelter is just beyond, at 3.2 miles. Return with a right off the AT at the second junction with the Albright Loop for a round-trip of 5.5 miles. (*Note:* The leg of the AT down to the Old Howardsville Turnpike and the turnpike trail connection back to the Gap also form a circuit with the east side of the Albright Loop that can be hiked by itself or added to other hikes.)

Another nice overnighter to the shelter uses the more northerly section of the AT. Just south from the developed area where I-64 passes under the Parkway near Shenandoah National Park, the AT goes left off the Parkway through a break in the guardrail. It's 5.0 miles to the Paul C. Wolfe Shelter for a 10.0-mile round-trip.

Picnic Area Options

For a few more great hiking options, drive south on the Parkway to Humpback Rocks Picnic Area (Milepost 8.5). Two trails start on the outside loop of the picnic area. To the right, the easy 0.5-mile Catoctin Trail leads to a nice stone wall–encircled view of the Shenandoah Valley. Humpback Mountain and Humpback Rocks can also be reached from here. Take the blue-blazed side trail to the left that reaches the AT in 0.2 mile. (Off to the left, notice the remnants of stone walls that you'll also see in the picnic area.) A left at the AT reaches Humpback Mountain in about 2.0 miles (4.0 miles round-trip). If you continue past Humpback Mountain to Humpback Rocks, it's a 6.0-mile round-trip, with a lot less elevation gain than the hike from Humpback Gap—and much more solitude.

This beautifully convoluted barn is a highlight of the Mountain Farm Trail.

2 Greenstone Self-Guiding Trail

Milepost 8.8

Take this twenty-minute self-guiding loop trail to learn about the geology of the northern Blue Ridge and see how mountaineers used their most abundant resource—rock—to wrest a living from harsh surroundings.

Parkway mile: 8.8
Distance: 0.2-mile loop
Difficulty: Easy

Elevation gain: Negligible
Maps: *USGS Sherando;* no Parkway map available

Finding the trailhead: Park at the end of the overlook near the woods.

The Hike

This engaging self-guiding interpretive trail explains the natural setting and alerts you to the telltale signs of human habitation that are a stirring subtext to the Parkway experience.

The Mountain Farm Trail's extensive living-history exhibits at Milepost 5.8 re-create the picturesque side of the rustic Appalachian lifestyle. The Greenstone Trail imparts an anthropologist's insight into how to detect the evidence of a former mountain farm.

The overlook's interpretive sign explains that "hog-walls" were scattered through-out many places in the mountains. Built in the early 1800s and maintained in winter by slaves from lower-elevation plantations (Jefferson's Monticello is only 40 miles away), the walls penned nearly wild hogs that otherwise were permitted to roam the mast-covered slopes, becoming "free-range" delicacies. Before you hit the trail, look over the front of the overlook. Whether by accident or sensitivity, the builders of the Parkway spared the hog-walls below, and the Park Service's vista maintenance crews periodically expose them to view.

Pass the trailhead sign and go right along the gravel path. A sign describes the ubiquitous green rock of the overlook and the general area—Catoctin greenstone—as an ancient lava flow, evidence that volcanoes once existed in the region. Were the lava to liquefy today, notes the sign, it would fill the Shenandoah Valley. Undulating along over occasional steps, the trail bears left around the end of the loop and across a dome of greenstone. Mountain laurel and Virginia pine cling to this steepening side of the ridge.

Pause at the sign that describes how tremendous earth forces 200 million years ago uplifted the lava, sandstone, limestone, and shale of the area, transforming it into ridges and peaks. Between Mileposts 20 and 60, the shale and limestone are particu-larly visible in road-cuts—a favorite haunt for geology students touring the Parkway. At that sign, look to your right and behind, just below where the trail crosses the crag,

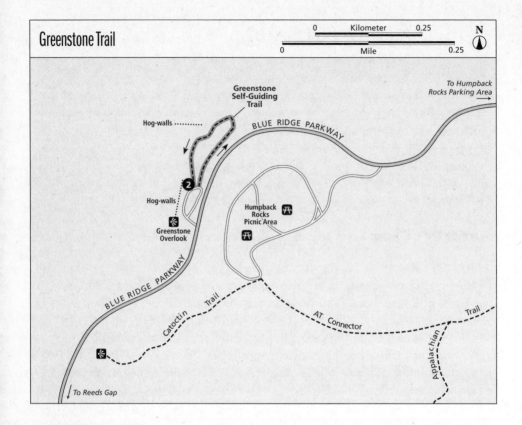

and you'll see another hog-wall—this one quite disheveled—arcing down through the rough woods. The sure of foot could go down and, being careful not to dislodge or alter the rocks, explore this high-mountain holding pen from centuries ago.

Swinging right, squeeze between a pine and a crag and emerge onto an open ledge with great views of the Shenandoah Valley. The vista here, on the nearby Catoctin Trail at Humpback Rocks Picnic Area at Milepost 8.5, and at the clifftop Raven's Roost Overlook at Milepost 10.7 showcase the outstanding pastoral scenery that recommends this first part of the Parkway. When the leaves are off the trees, look ahead to the opposing ridge and notice the huge greenstone outcrops—like the one you're on—off in the woods.

Descending a flight of stone steps, the trail then rises over more steps past a crag where kids might hop off left into a greenstone cleft. An interpretive sign notes that you'll see all three types of rock along the Parkway—igneous (greenstone and lava), metamorphic (quartzite and schist), and sedimentary (limestone and sandstone). The trail climbs through a crag, to the right, and back into the parking lot.

3 Wintergreen Mountain Resort Trails

Milepost 13.7

This environmentally sensitive resort near the Parkway takes preservation and good hospitality seriously.

Parkway mile: 13.7
Distance: 0.3 mile to 12.0 miles on a diverse system of trails
Difficulty: Easy to strenuous

Elevation gain: Negligible for Shamokin Springs Trail
Maps: The resort publishes its own trail map.

Finding the trailhead: Leave the Parkway at Reeds Gap (Milepost 13.7) and go east 1 mile on VA 664, then take the second left into the resort's main entrance. (The first left is actually the exit.)

The Hikes

Environmentalists weren't happy when private land beside the Parkway across Blackrock Mountain was purchased in the 1970s and became Wintergreen Mountain Resort. The Appalachian Trail was rerouted as a result.

Not that it will satisfy the most ardent environmentalist, but Wintergreen's lodge and condominium accommodations and its status as a ski, golf, and tennis resort may actually be exceeded by its renowned preservation program and 30-mile trail system. More than 6,000 of the resort's 11,000 acres will remain as wilderness or forested open space by restrictive covenant. Wintergreen actually gave 3,000 acres of land to the Blue Ridge Parkway—and the resort's best roadside views are Parkway-style overlooks, one above the ski area. Accommodations range from lodge-style

Steps start the drop to The Plunge overlook at Wintergreen, one of many great trails at the resort.

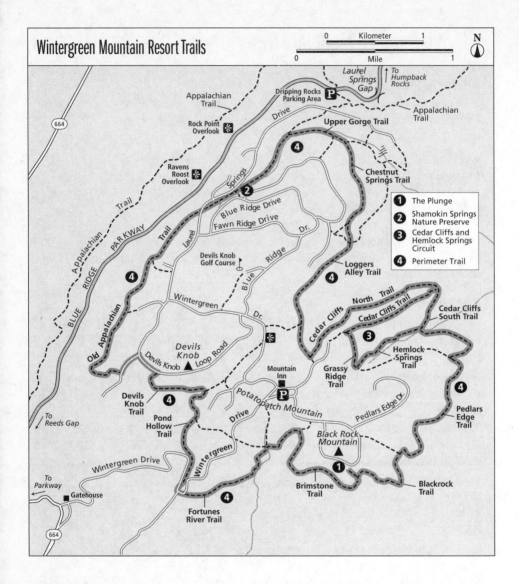

Wintergreen Mountain Resort Trails

Kilometer

Mile

N

664

Appalachian
Trail

Laurel
Springs
Gap

To
Humpback
Rocks

Dripping Rocks
Parking Area

P

Rock Point
Overlook

Upper Gorge Trail

Appalachian
Trail

Drive

Ravens
Roost
Overlook

Springs

Chestnut
Springs Trail

Blue Ridge Drive

Fawn Ridge Drive

Dr.

1 The Plunge
2 Shamokin Springs
   Nature Preserve
3 Cedar Cliffs and
   Hemlock Springs
   Circuit
4 Perimeter Trail

Trail

Appalachian

BLUE RIDGE PARKWAY

Trail

Laurel

Devils Knob
Golf Course

Blue Ridge

Dr.

Loggers
Alley Trail

Wintergreen

Dr.

Cedar Cliffs North Trail

Cedar Cliffs Trail

Cedar Cliffs
South Trail

Old Appalachian

Devils Knob Loop Road

Devils
Knob

Hemlock
Springs
Trail

Wintergreen

Mountain
Inn

P

Grassy
Ridge
Trail

To
Reeds Gap

Devils
Knob
Trail

Pond
Hollow
Trail

Potatopatch Mountain

Drive

Pedlars Edge Dr.

Pedlars
Edge
Trail

To
Parkway

Wintergreen Drive

Gatehouse

Wintergreen

Black Rock
Mountain

Brimstone
Trail

Blackrock
Trail

Fortunes
River Trail

664

studio rooms in the slope-side Mountain Inn to condominiums and single-family homes, all with access to resort dining spots, recreational facilities, and resort-wide shuttle bus service.

The respected Wintergreen Nature Foundation offers diverse interpretive programs—a highly regarded annual Wildflower Symposium in May and Virginia's Natural History Retreat Weekend in September—from its base in a stunning structure near the resort's Wintergarden Spa. Staff naturalist Doug Coleman was given a key role from the start in keeping the "green" in Wintergreen. Development is carefully sited, and sensitive plants are rescued beforehand.

In one case, Coleman went to bat for a thirteen-acre spot scheduled for home development, and the Shamokin Springs Nature Preserve was born. Today it's still home to its old residents—botanical rarities for Virginia, such as the spotted coral-root orchid and the northern starflower. Shamokin Springs is a popular trail in a rare Blue Ridge resort that other developers would do well to emulate. Here are just a few of many possible hikes for Parkway visitors who make Wintergreen a base of operations.

The Plunge is only about 0.4-mile round-trip, but it is a steep, rocky hike on the way down and even tougher coming out. Nevertheless, it's fine for anyone over the age of nine or ten and ends with a spectacular view of the Rockfish Valley. The deep clefts of Wintergreen's protected open space make up a good portion of the 160-degree view. Most people complete the hike in forty-five minutes to an hour.

Shamokin Springs Nature Preserve features a 0.3-mile loop trail through an amazingly diverse area. A braided stream is the focal point of this trail, and you meet it over and over as you cross and recross the many streamlets that eventually form Stoney Creek, the primary stream that flows through the resort's lower acreage. This flat area atop the mountain has a great diversity of plant life, and kids love to play on the bridges along the trail.

The circuit formed by Cedar Cliffs Main, Cedar Cliffs South, and Hemlock Springs Trails yields about 2.0 miles of ridgeline hiking that eventually follows a beautiful creek. The trail starts on Grassy Ridge Drive, and there are great views at the center of the loop. This is a moderate trail, suitable for most, with difficult and easy parts—all in all a great hike.

The Perimeter Trail is a 12.0-mile loop that goes around the entire mountaintop area of the resort. Designed to explore many different habitats and ecosystems, this trail is quite difficult in places and includes some truly rigorous hiking. Avid hikers are rewarded by forest and ridge walking, distant views, and intimate settings beside rushing mountain streams.

Though the Appalachian Trail has been rerouted away from Wintergreen, the former AT is now part of the Perimeter Trail and leads hikers through much the same environment as it once did.

THE APPALACHIAN TRAIL

Each spring, nearly 1,500 people hoist heavy packs and strain down a misty trail, intent on accomplishing the most difficult task of their life: trekking between Georgia and central Maine along the Appalachian Trail (AT). When regional planner Benton MacKaye first proposed an Appalachian Trail in 1921, he labeled the idea "an experiment in regional planning" aimed at preserving the East's wilderness.

Within two years of MacKaye's first article proposing the AT, the major trail organizations, including fledgling groups in the South, had endorsed the plan and built the first sections of the trail in New England. In 1925 a meeting held in Washington, D.C., formally created the Appalachian Trail Conference, Inc., forerunner of the organization that manages the trail today.

With railroad imagery fostered by MacKaye, the trail's "main line" from Georgia to Mount Washington in New Hampshire was intended to link various "branch lines" that would funnel

An icon of the outdoors—an AT blaze in the James River Face Wilderness.

jaded urban workers into the refreshing green corridor. "The path of the trailway should be as 'pathless' as possible," MacKaye maintained. In the late 1920s, that's exactly how it was.

In reality, the AT was built largely out of existing trails in the North and through unexpected devotion from trail clubs and the Forest Service in the South. Energetic Southerners helped build other sections, too: The Potomac Appalachian Trail Club completed the trail through Maine to Mount Katahdin.

Nearly 600 miles of the Skyline Drive and Blue Ridge Parkway were built during the early days of the AT. The roads claimed dozens of miles of the trail's early route and were ardently opposed by many trail clubs. Appalachian Trail Conference chairman Myron Avery called the scenic roads "a major catastrophe in Appalachian Trail history." The Civilian Conservation Corps (CCC) was enlisted to revise the route.

The trail in any form became a symbol. Long before wilderness preservation was achieved in the East, die-hard hikers built the trails by following ridgetops and linking dwindling remnants of a wild heritage. By 1937 the first version of the trail was complete. Thousands of catastrophes—from hurricanes to commercial development—have claimed portions of the trail. But each time, a new generation of trail enthusiasts has stepped in and carved the path anew. As Myron Avery observed, the AT was the trail of which it could never be said, "It is finished—this is the end!"

In 1968 the AT became the first National Scenic Trail under the landmark National Trails System Act. The act gave the Appalachian Trail Conference control over the AT and authorized acquisition of the 1,000 miles of trail in private hands. A late-1970s Appalachian Trail bill accelerated the process, and today most of the trail is in public ownership.

Maintenance of the AT never wanes, through the efforts of thirty affiliated organizations—now joined under the Appalachian Trail Conservancy—working on some 2,150 miles of trail. Though four million persons take to part of the trail annually, only 150 to 200 hikers a year complete the trail. Fewer than 10,000 have accomplished the feat since the trail's inception.

Almost a century later, MacKaye's proposal has had the philosophical impact he'd hoped for. More than perhaps any other recreational facility in the world, the Appalachian Trail symbolizes the power of nature to work wonders for those who take the time to wander in the woods.

4 Three Ridges Wilderness

Milepost 13.7

One of Virginia's newest wilderness areas, 4,600-acre Three Ridges was designated a wilderness in 2000. The great circuit hike it affords follows the Appalachian Trail as it swerves east of the Parkway and up and over Three Ridges, at 3,970 feet. The route descends from the peaks then skirts 1,000 feet higher than the AT's southerly trailhead on VA 56 to turn right on the Mau-Har Trail and loop back to the Parkway. The oddly named Mau-Har Trail uses the first syllable of the names of the two backpacking shelters you pass, Maupin Field and Harper Creek.

The shelters make nice out-and-back day or overnight hike destinations—Maupin Field is less than 2.0 miles from either of its trailheads, and Harper Creek is 2.6 miles. From the VA 56 trailhead there's a nice, secluded waterfall hike near the shelter on Campbell Creek. The route described below takes in the entire circuit, starting on the AT from the north. The shelters and their adjacent campsites are arranged best that way for either a one- or two-night camping trip. And, very important, the elevation gain is far less taxing than it is from the south.

Three Ridges Wilderness Circuit

One of the best backpacking loops on the northern portion of the Parkway, with a number of nice views, plentiful campsites, a waterfall, and two overnight backpacking shelters and adjacent campsites (each pretty accessible for easy out-and-back overnighters).

Parkway mile: 13.7
Distance: 13.5-mile circuit and a variety of shorter out-and-back day hikes
Difficulty: Strenuous

Elevation gain: 3,495 feet
Maps: *USGS Sherando;* Appalachian Trail Conference: Pedlar Ranger District, George Washington National Forest

---

Finding the trailhead: There are two Parkway trailheads for this circuit hike. Park in the gravel trail parking slip on VA 664 just east of Reeds Gap at Milepost 13.7 or beside the gated fire road at Milepost 15.4 in Love Gap. To get to VA 56, exit the Parkway at Milepost 27.2 and go east on VA 56; parking is on the right at 11.2 miles. The trail crosses the Tye River on an impressive suspension bridge.

The Hike

The white-blazed Appalachian Trail leaves the meadows of Reeds Gap at 0.2 mile and climbs gradually, then steeply to a ridgetop campsite on the left at 0.8 mile. There's a nice view just across the trail to the right. The AT dips off the ridgetop and switchbacks to a T junction with a fire road at 1.7 miles. The fire road from the right makes a great alternative route to this campsite for Parkway backpackers who want an easier path to a quick overnighter. The fire road goes west 1.5 miles to Love Gap

At nearly 4,000 feet, the loftiest peaks of the Three Ridges Wilderness bulk over Virginia's western Piedmont.

and is much more gradual than the AT from Reeds Gap.

At this junction the AT goes left along the fire road. Straight ahead, where a sign directs hikers to as many as twenty designated campsites in the vicinity, a trail leads 100 yards to Maupin Field Shelter and the headwaters spring of Campbell Creek behind it. The blue-blazed Mau-Har Trail, your return route, leaves just south of the shelter and crosses then follows Campbell Creek down to the AT on the other side of Three Ridges.

Going left on the road, the AT immediately passes another trail to Maupin Field Shelter on the right that also passes a privy. The AT quickly leaves the old road and continues over Bee Mountain (3,022 feet) at 2.0 miles. It dips off the summit and climbs to the right of the ridgeline to commanding clifftop views from Hanging Rock at 3.7 miles. The Priest dominates the vista to the southwest. The trail continues up across the forested double summit of Three Ridges at 4.2 miles then, at 4.4 miles, switchbacks steeply off the peak. It passes a number of views, then Chimney Rock at 5.9 miles. Descending the ridgeline to a nice view at 6.3 miles, the trail turns north and descends again on an old road. A side road leads off to the right at 7.9 miles to Harper Creek Shelter and a privy. The stream in front is the water source.

The AT crosses Harper Creek and climbs to a junction on the right with the

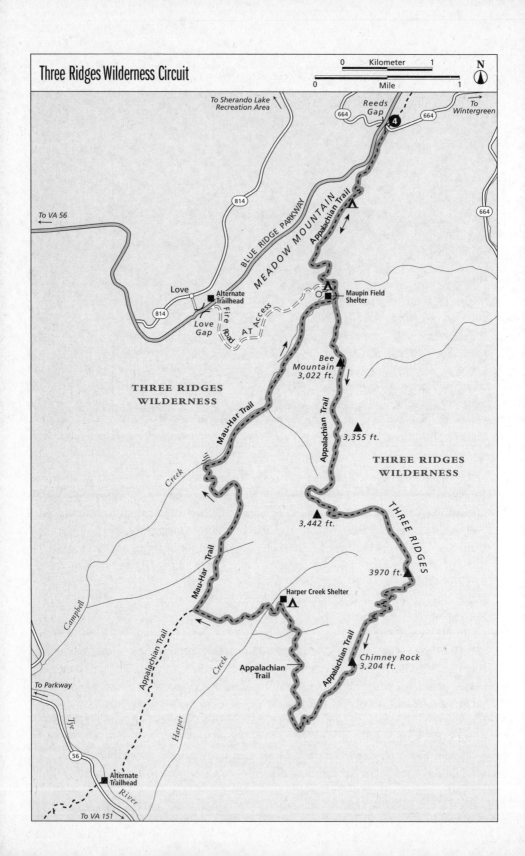

Three Ridges Wilderness Circuit

0 Kilometer 1
0 Mile 1

N

To Sherando Lake
Recreation Area →

Reeds Gap
664 · 4 · 664

→ To Wintergreen

BLUE RIDGE PARKWAY

MEADOW MOUNTAIN

Appalachian Trail

814

To VA 56 ←

664

Love

814

Alternate Trailhead

Love Gap

Fire Road

AT Access

Maupin Field Shelter

THREE RIDGES WILDERNESS

Bee Mountain 3,022 ft.

Mau-Har Trail

Appalachian Trail

3,355 ft.

THREE RIDGES WILDERNESS

Creek

3,442 ft.

THREE RIDGES

3970 ft.

Mau-Har Trail

Campbell

Harper Creek Shelter

Appalachian Trail

Appalachian Trail

Appalachian Trail

Chimney Rock 3,204 ft.

To Parkway ←

Tye

Creek

Harper

56

Alternate Trailhead

River

To VA 151 →

Mau-Har Trail at 8.8 miles (VA 56 is 1.7 miles to the left on the AT). Turn right and follow the blue-blazed trail along Campbell Creek. Mau-Har slabs the flank of Hanging Rock as it slides into the stream drainage. It rises and falls repeatedly until reaching Campbell Creek near a nice waterfall at 10.3 miles (3.2 miles from VA 56, for a 6.4-mile out-and-back day hike from there). A more gradual ascent along the upper trail brings you to Maupin Field Shelter at 11.8 miles. A left to your car at Love Gap creates a 13.1-mile circuit. Continuing another 1.7 miles on the AT to Reeds Gap—with a much more gradual uphill than on the way in—creates a circuit of 13.5 miles.

Key Points

1.7 Road grade right to Parkway and Love Gap; side trail to Maupin Field Shelter and Mau-Har Trail.

3.7 Viewpoint atop Hanging Rock.

4.2 High point of the hike at Three Ridges summit.

5.9 Chimney Rocks view.

7.9 Harper Creek Shelter.

8.8 Right turn onto Mau-Har Trail.

10.3 Waterfall on Campbell Creek.

11.8 Return to Maupin Field Shelter.

An assortment of backcountry campsites surround Maupin Field Shelter.

5 White Rock Falls Circuit and Sherando Lake Recreation Area Hikes

Milepost 19.9

This strenuous but worthwhile circuit adjacent to the Parkway can be expanded to start at Sherando Lake Recreation Area, a recommended National Forest campground convenient to the first section of the high road. The campground itself has a few nice, easy hikes.

Parkway mile: 19.9
Distance: Shorter hikes include a 2.6-mile out-and-back moderate hike to White Rock Falls and 1.0- and 1.2-mile easy loops around Sherando Lake. Longer, strenuous hikes include a 4.9-mile White Rock Falls circuit from Slacks Overlook and circuits from Sherando

Lake of 8.2 and 9.5 miles.
Difficulty: Easy to strenuous
Elevation gain: 860 feet for the entire circuit from Slacks Overlook
Maps: *USGS Big Levels;* USFS Saint Mary's Wilderness map (best)

Finding the trailheads: From Slacks Overlook enter the woods on the east end of the parking area past a picnic table to a signed junction (blue plastic diamonds) with the Slacks Trail.

To start the White Rock Falls Trail from Slacks Overlook, exit the overlook on foot. Cross the Parkway, turn left, and walk north along the road 200 feet to a right turn into the woods on the signed, yellow-blazed trail.

The lower end of the White Rock Falls Trail and access to the Slacks Trail is available from an informal dirt parking area (every time I've pulled in, it's been through a puddle or mud) on the north side of the Parkway in White Rock Gap (Milepost 18.5). From there the White Rock Falls Trail enters the woods across the Parkway at a yellow blaze and a trailhead sign. The orange-blazed White Rock Gap Trail (to the Slacks Trail and Sherando Lake Recreation Area) leaves the north side of the gap to the right on an old road grade.

To start at the lower end of the White Rock Gap Trail—or hike the lakeshore loops—make the quick trip to Sherando Lake by turning north off the Parkway on VA 664 from Reeds Gap (Milepost 13.7). Turn right at 2 miles past VA 814 to the left, and at 2.6 miles turn left onto FSR 91 to the campground. The first right on FSR 91B at 3.6 miles leads to the fishermen's parking trailhead for the lakeshore hikes. Sherando's main trailhead for the lakeshore and larger loops is located 0.9 mile past FSR 91B, past the bathhouse on the right, just across the bridge by the picnic area. To reach the trailhead beside Upper Sherando Lake, pass the main trailhead, various campsites, and a small parking area at the base of the dam to where the trail starts through a gate on the left at 0.7 mile. Park just uphill of the gate in the lot on the left.

Option 1: White Rock Falls Circuit

The best short waterfall walk and the best circuit hike start at the same spot—Slacks Overlook.

Cross the Parkway and descend into the woods past a sign honoring the Youth Conservation Corps crew that built the trail in 1979. Another sign prohibits camping, hunter access, and dogs without leashes. The trail meanders down and is soon within earshot of tumbling water. Bearing right across a small side stream at 0.3 mile, the path crosses a bridge at 0.5 mile over White Rock Creek and follows the stream until it plummets into a chasm then bears away right and reaches a crag with great views of the gorge below.

Following clifftops away from the crag, the trail switchbacks left along the base of the cliffs. When the trail reaches the bottom of the first crag encountered above, at 1.2 miles, it switchbacks sharply right—but don't be fooled. The best waterfall view on the entire White Rock Falls Trail continues straight ahead another 0.1 mile on an obviously used but unsigned and seemingly informal trail below the cliffs. The path dips down to a beautiful cataract and pool amid encircling stone walls. A return to the Slacks Overlook from here makes a moderate and rewarding 2.6-mile hike. *Caution:* If you miss this rather obscure side trail to the falls, you could hike the entire White Rock Falls Trail and not see a waterfall!

Back at the switchback, descend steeply on a rocky tread, passing a boulder beautifully striped with quartz intrusions (the falls and nearby gap are named for the prevalence of quartz). Steep, rocky switchbacks continue. The trail approaches the stream again at a deep pool but steeply switchbacks two final times before crossing White Rock Creek below a large pool. Crossing the stream, the trail climbs steeply then

A less-than-obvious side trail leads to the rocky grotto that hides White Rock Falls.

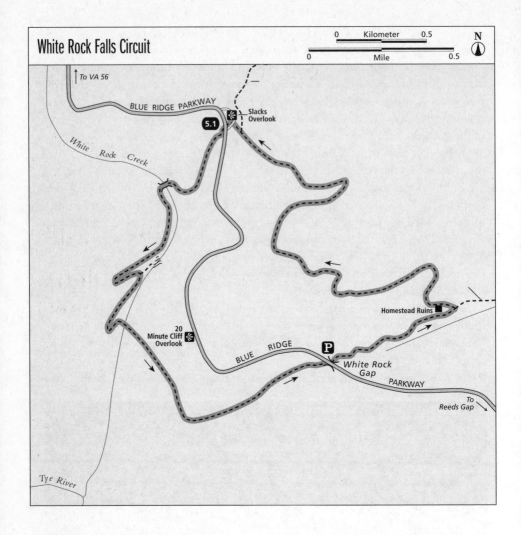

White Rock Falls Circuit

0   Kilometer   0.5

0   Mile   0.5

N

To VA 56

BLUE RIDGE PARKWAY

5.1

Slacks Overlook

White Rock Creek

20 Minute Cliff Overlook

BLUE RIDGE

P

White Rock Gap

Homestead Ruins

PARKWAY

To Reeds Gap

Tye River

rises into a startlingly scenic pine grove. Turn left onto an old wagon road that climbs steeply toward White Rock Gap at 2.2 miles. The old road levels off; a stream and then an old rock wall appear on the right—the latter no doubt part of the homestead you'll see across the gap on the White Rock Gap Trail. Three small bridges span seeps, and the Parkway appears high on the left. The trail climbs past roadside signs to the Parkway at 2.5 miles. If you can park a second car here, the hike is mostly downhill. Going from here up to the falls is a strenuous 2.8-mile hike.

Crossing the Parkway, the old grade reappears as the orange-blazed White Rock Gap Trail and descends to the site of an old homestead at 3.1 miles. By the late 1700s, the Blue Ridge was full of hardscrabble farms like this one. The Parkway showcases a number of such homesteads.

Just beyond the homesite, turn left on the blue-blazed Slacks Overlook Trail. (To

Sherando Lake Trails

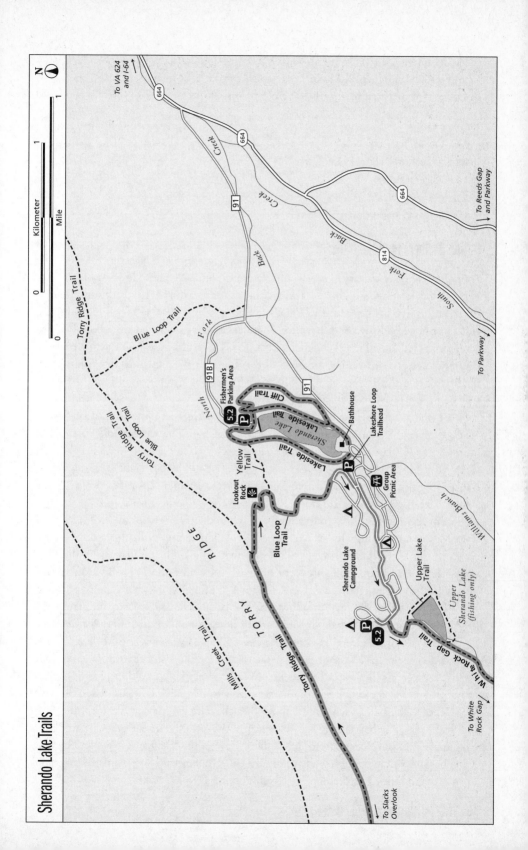

N

Kilometer
0   1

Mile
0   1

To VA 624
and I-64

664

664

Creek

91

Creek

Back

664

Back

814

South Fork

To Reeds Gap
and Parkway

To Parkway

Torry Ridge Trail

Blue Loop Trail

North Fork

91B

Fishermen's
Parking Area

5.2
P

Cliff Trail

Lakeside Trail

91

Sherando Lake

Batthouse

Lakeshore Loop
Trailhead

P

Group
Picnic Area

Williams Branch

Torry Ridge Trail

Blue Loop Trail

Torry Ridge Trail

Blue Loop

Yellow
Trail

Lookout
Rock

Lakeside Trail

Cliff Trail

Blue Loop
Trail

Sherando Lake
Campground

Upper Lake Trail

Upper
Sherando Lake
(fishing only)

White Rock Gap Trail

To White
Rock Gap

TORRY   RIDGE

Mills Creek Trail

Torry Ridge Trail

5.2
P

To Slacks
Overlook

the right, Sherando Lake Campground is 2.0 miles down the White Rock Gap Trail.) Climb steeply along another old grade, with evidence of quarrying off to the right. In open scrubby forest at 4.9 miles, turn left into Slacks Overlook.

Key Points

0.5 Cross White Rock Creek.

1.3 Arrive at White Rock Falls.

2.5 White Rock Gap.

3.1 Old homesite and left turn just beyond.

4.9 Return to Slacks Overlook.

Option 2: Sherando Lake Trails

Sherando Lake Recreation Area, where the lengthiest hike and a few very easy ones begin, is a great place to camp on this northernmost portion of the Parkway. The lake has been known as the "jewel of the Blue Ridge" since 1936, when the beautifully rustic facilities built by the Civilian Conservation Corps opened on a twenty-five-acre spring-fed lake. There's a beach; a classic CCC bathhouse (with a small visitor center/gift shop); swimming, boating, and fishing on the big lake; and fishing and boating only on seven-acre Upper Sherando Lake. The campground is open for full service from April 1 to October 31.

To make a long circuit from Sherando with a variety of options, start on White Rock Gap Trail at the Upper Sherando Lake trailhead. This gradual old road grade follows orange-plastic blazes southward along pretty Back Creek to a junction at 2.0 miles with the Slacks Trail near the old pioneer homesite. Go right, pass the access trail to Slacks Overlook at 3.7 miles, and turn right again at 4.4 miles on the Torry Ridge Trail. (Left, it's only 1.2 miles to the sparsely wooded summit of Bald Knob, a nice campsite. You can drive to this trailhead when the gate is open on FSR 162 from Bald Mountain parking area at Milepost 22.1.) Descending with the yellow-plastic blazes of the Torry Ridge Trail, at 6.4 miles turn right onto the first leg of the blue sign–blazed Blue Loop Trail. Just past Lookout Rock, take another right at the junction with the Yellow Trail and descend to site A-6 of the White Oak Campground at 7.3 miles. Go left to the main trailhead by the bathhouse and follow the main road through the campground back to the starting point for a loop hike of 8.2 miles.

For the easiest area hikes, park at the main trailhead by the bathhouse or take FSR 91B to Sherando Lake's fishermen's parking area by the dam. Starting at the main trailhead, the 1.0-mile loop of the Lakeside Trail is very easy in either direction.

There's also a nice circuit east of the lake that pairs one side of the Lakeside Trail with the steeper Cliff Trail, which climbs above the lake. The easy option starts to the right and then bears right beyond the bathhouse across the grass and up the gradual part of the Cliff Trail. Overlook Rock affords a peephole view of the lake halfway along. The trail switchbacks down its steepest grade to the Lakeside Trail by the fishermen's parking (and a privy) at 0.5 mile. Go left along the lakeshore for a 1.2-mile walk.

6 Saint Mary's Wilderness

Milepost 22.1

The 10,090-acre parcel is the largest of Virginia's federal wilderness areas. The tract lies west of the Blue Ridge Parkway between Milepost 22.1 (Bald Mountain Overlook) and Milepost 27.2 (Tye River Gap).

The Saint Mary's area was never logged. But although the forests may be virgin, rugged slopes and thin soil have not produced towering trees. Many trails in the area were once railroad grades; manganese and other mines operated from the early 1900s to the 1950s. The scenery is nevertheless impressive, and ruins from the mining era are part of the appeal. Oak and hickory forests predominate, and the summits are covered with pitch pine, table mountain pine, bear oak, and mountain laurel. Barren talus fields appear as gray jumbles of rock on otherwise lush, green slopes.

The Saint Mary's Trail starts west of the Parkway in the vicinity of Steele's Tavern and follows the Saint Mary's River. Large pools below waterfalls, some 10 feet deep, attract dippers in the heat of summer. The falls on the Saint Mary's aren't dramatic, but quartzite cliffs and large streambed boulders make the setting a scenic one.

This wilderness is very popular. Regulations prohibit camping around the trailhead parking area, and campfires are banned in the vicinity and within 150 feet of the trail from there to beyond the falls, about 2.0 miles. Groups are limited to ten persons. Weekdays are the best time to visit during the warmer months.

Luckily, that kind of popularity is absent in the upper part of the wilderness. Parkway hikers have easy access to the scenery below—and quick escape to the less-popular area above. The upper Saint Mary's Trail climbs gradually up the valley, where two trails connect to the Parkway.

Deer, turkey, grouse, and a respectable population of black bear call Saint Mary's home. Trout are prevalent in the Saint Mary's River, although increased acidity from acid rain and related phenomena is having a negative impact on at least one species of tiny native fish.

A circuit hike dips from the Blue Ridge Parkway into a lush watershed of the Saint Mary's Wilderness and returns via scenic Green Pond, a natural high-elevation tarn.

Parkway mile: 22.1 or 23.0
Distance: Circuits of 10.3 and 3.8 miles; out-and-back hike of 9.4 miles
Difficulty: Strenuous for the 10.3-mile circuit and 9.4-mile out-and-back; moderate for the 3.8-mile circuit
Elevation gain: 1,280 feet for the longer circuit; 1,400 feet for the out-and-back hike
Maps: USGS *Big Levels, VA*, USFS Saint Mary's Wilderness map

Finding the trailheads: The Mine Bank Trail enters the woods on the opposite side of the Parkway from Fork Mountain Overlook (Milepost 23.0) at a roadside parking area not indicated on the USFS map. The Bald Mountain Trail soon branches to the right.

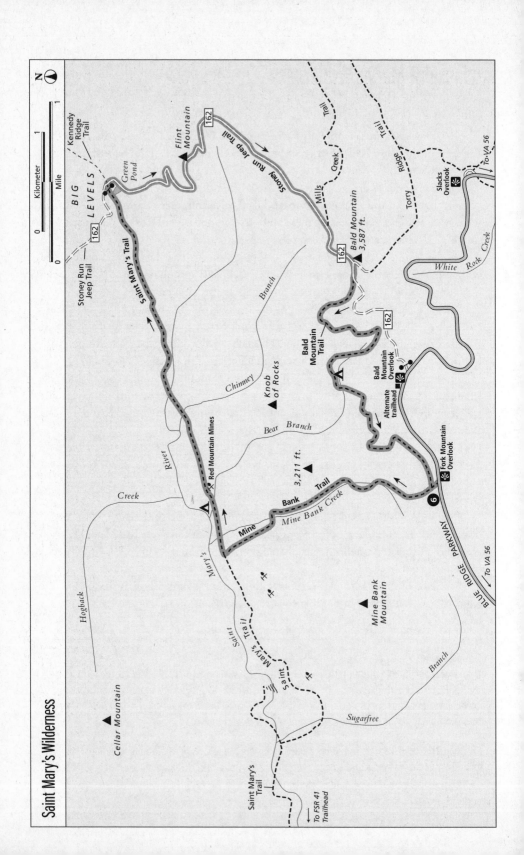

Saint Mary's Wilderness

N

BIG LEVELS

Kennedy Ridge Trail

Stoney Run Jeep Trail

162

Green Pond

Flint Mountain

162

Saint Mary's Trail

Stoney Run Jeep Trail

Mills Creek Trail

Branch

Chimney

Knob of Rocks

Bald Mountain 3,587 ft.

162

Torry Ridge Trail

Slacks Overlook

White Rock Creek

162

Bald Mountain Trail

Bald Mountain Overlook

River

Red Mountain Mines

Bear Branch

3,211 ft.

Alternate trailhead

Creek

Mine Bank Trail

Mine Bank Creek

Fork Mountain Overlook

6

Mary's Trail

Mine Bank Mountain

BLUE RIDGE PARKWAY

To VA 56

Hogback

Saint Mary's Trail

Sugarfree

Branch

To VA 56

Cellar Mountain

Saint Mary's Trail

To FSR 41 Trailhead

0   1   Kilometer
0   1   Mile

Another trailhead for the Bald Mountain Trail is located on a usually gated gravel road (FSR 162) that leaves the Parkway on the north end of the Bald Mountain parking area (Milepost 22.1). The trail branches left from FSR 162 at about 0.7 mile from the Parkway. At certain times of year, this road is ungated and accessible to four-wheel-drive vehicles. The hike uses part of that route. A branch of the road goes right at 0.2 mile beyond the Bald Mountain trailhead and climbs to a trailhead for the Torry Ridge Trail and a nice campsite clearing at the former site of a fire tower atop Bald Mountain (3,587 feet).

The Hikes

This Saint Mary's Wilderness circuit adjacent to the Blue Ridge Parkway offers a combination of streamside and mountaintop scenery and an absence of crowds. Two hike options range from under 5.0 miles to more than 10.0 miles. The longer circuit is a nice overnight trip, with camping on a stream or at Green Pond—a rare, natural pond located on an open ridgetop.

At the parking area across the road from Fork Mountain Overlook, the orange-blazed Mine Bank Trail enters the wilderness. One hundred yards from here, the yellow-blazed Bald Mountain Trail goes right to the other trailhead on FSR 162. Stay on the Mine Bank Trail. The trail quickly descends north to Mine Bank Creek and follows the stream 2.0 miles, dropping nearly 1,100 feet

A trail sign points the way in Saint Mary's Wilderness.

to a junction with the blue-blazed Saint Mary's Trail.

The Saint Mary's Trail runs up and down the stream. Turn right and follow the gradually ascending trail, a railroad grade that once served nearby mines. Cross two creeks to excellent campsites in the vicinity of Bear Branch. The mining that once took place in the area is visible here at Red Mountain Mines. Local mining focused on manganese, coal, and iron. There used to be more than twenty buildings, including residences, in this mining community; foundations are still visible.

The gradual grade of the Saint Mary's Trail continues and then steepens before leveling out on a ridgetop appropriately named Big Levels. The trail exits the wilderness and reaches Green Pond—a tarn surrounded by pines—at about 4.8 miles.

Sedges and a colony of cranberry grow in the boggy area. There are excellent campsites by the pond, but camp in a zero-impact manner. The trail continues 0.3 mile farther to reach FSR 162, called the Stoney Run Jeep Trail, at 5.1 miles.

Reaching the jeep trail, turn right and hike the primitive road along a gradually ascending ridge for 3.0 miles. At about 8.1 miles turn right onto the yellow-blazed Bald Mountain Trail. The trail dips into the beautiful headwaters of Bear Branch, where it passes fine campsites before turning out of the stream drainage to ascend and intersect the Mine Bank Trail at about 10.3 miles. A left on the Mine Bank Trail leads to the parking lot. This lengthy hike can be taken in either direction and started from either parking area.

Whether you start at the Parkway or take the lengthy drive down to start at the bottom of the Saint Mary's Trail, the Green Pond circuit described above isn't just a nice upper circuit in the wilderness—it may be the best in Saint Mary's. Problems with development of private land on the west side of the wilderness have made it less attractive to form circuits with the Cold Spring and Cellar Mountain Trails.

You can also shorten this hike to a less than 4.0-mile loop of the Bald Mountain Trail. Park at either trailhead, hike to the other trailhead on the 2.2-mile Bald Mountain Trail, then walk between the trailheads on the combination of the Blue Ridge Parkway (0.9 mile) and FSR 162 (0.7 mile) for a 3.8-mile total hike. The FSR 162 section is a pleasant walk in itself.

These trails offer other options. Campers wanting to reach a secluded Saint Mary's backpacking spot quickly can park at either trailhead and take the Bald Mountain Trail to nice campsites in the upper Bear Branch area.

From the Mine Bank Trail's intersection with the Saint Mary's Trail, you could go downhill to the waterfalls, either on a day hike or as a side trip during an overnighter. This is a railroad grade trail after all, and it's only 3.6 miles from the intersection down to the main trailhead. As a side trip from a campsite on a backpacking trip, it's 1.5 miles downstream to an old mining building that's still standing and 2.2 miles to where a side trail goes right 0.5 mile to a waterfall at the base of the Saint Mary's River Gorge. That's the heart of the wilderness area, and the key factor is that it's only about 300 feet lower in elevation than the Mine Bank junction.

A highly recommended day hike down from the Parkway to the falls (Mine Bank Trail to Saint Mary's Trail and back), the 9.4-mile round-trip involves only 1,400 feet of elevation gain back to your car.

Key Points for the Longer Circuit

0.05 Bald Mountain Trail goes right. Continue straight.

2.0 Turn right from Mine Bank Trail onto Saint Mary's Trail.

4.8 Green Pond.

5.1 Turn right onto FSR 162.

8.1 Turn right onto Bald Mountain Trail.

10.3 Go left on Mine Bank Trail to Parkway and your car.

7 Crabtree Falls

Milepost 27.2

One of the South's best waterfall walks also has barrier-free access.

Parkway mile: 27.2
Distance: 6.0 miles round-trip. The upper falls make a nice turnaround point for a 3.4-mile hike from the bottom trailhead or a 2.6-mile hike from the upper trailhead
Difficulty: Strenuous from the bottom of the falls; moderate from the top

Elevation gain: 1,500 feet for the entire falls trail from the bottom; 1,000 feet to falls from the bottom; 500 feet to falls from the top
Maps: *USGS Montebello* and *Massies Mill;* Appalachian Trail Conference: Pedlar Ranger District, George Washington National Forest

---

Finding the trailheads: Exit the Parkway at Milepost 27.2 and descend east on VA 56 for 6.6 miles to the lower trailhead on the right side of the road. The upper trailhead for the falls is on VA 826, an unpaved road suitable for use in good weather by higher clearance vehicles (an SUV is the best choice). To reach that trailhead, go east on VA 56 from the Blue Ridge Parkway; in about 3.8 miles turn right onto VA 826. The upper trailhead is on the left in just under 4 miles.

The Hike

This Crabtree Falls isn't the last cataract you'll encounter with that name while driving south on the Blue Ridge Parkway. This Virginia hike is in the George Washington National Forest. The second—actually a Blue Ridge Parkway trail—is in North Carolina at Milepost 339.5.

Various publications describe this falls as "the highest in Eastern America," the "highest in Virginia," and the "highest in the Virginia Blue Ridge." Which of those claims to believe probably depends on a long list of qualifiers and arguable assumptions. Chances are they at least qualify for "highest in the Virginia Blue Ridge" status—and that's being conservative.

Suffice to say that this path follows Crabtree Creek's 1,800 feet of descent to the Tye River. Along the way, five major waterfalls create a truly spectacular cascade.

Starting at VA 56, hikers are in for a climb, but this trail is highly developed and gradual over its entire length. The newest renovation, completed in late 2002, included the construction of a seventy-car parking area, new barrier-free restrooms, and an extensively reworked approach that provides barrier-free access to the first overlook on the falls. The trail's improvements are largely designed to keep hikers away from the cascades, which have claimed more than twenty lives. Stay on the trail, and watch children closely.

Developed observation areas overlook the falls at four places along the trail, the first just above the parking area on the new trail. There's a wood deck overlook at 0.7 mile, and at 0.8 mile you can use a small cave to rejoin the trail above. An overlook at 1.4 miles looks up at the upper falls. The last overlook, at about 1.7 miles, surveys

The sculpted ridges of The Priest are the scenic highlight of Virginia's Religious Range.

the Tye River Valley from above the upper falls. A return from that point makes a nice 3.4-mile hike.

Continuing, the trail follows a gradual old grade and at 3.0 miles reaches an upper trailhead on VA 826. Keep this trailhead in mind for summer and fall weekends, when the lower trailhead may be jammed. Indeed, the upper cascade is actually an easier hike starting from the top. With two cars, a descent of the trail is an easy walk.

VA 826, a bumpy dirt road with a few easy stream fords, is a worthwhile side trip in its own right. Camping is not permitted at the Crabtree Falls Trail trailhead or along the trail, but camping is allowed in Crabtree Meadows, an expanse of fields across the split rail fence from the trailhead and privies. The area looks exactly like what it was as recently as the early twentieth century—the rustic setting for a sawmill community.

Key Points from below the Falls

0.2 First waterfall overlook.

0.7 Wooden deck overlook on second cascade.

0.8 Cave route.

1.7 View of upper falls. This is the turnaround point for a 3.4-mile out-and-back hike.

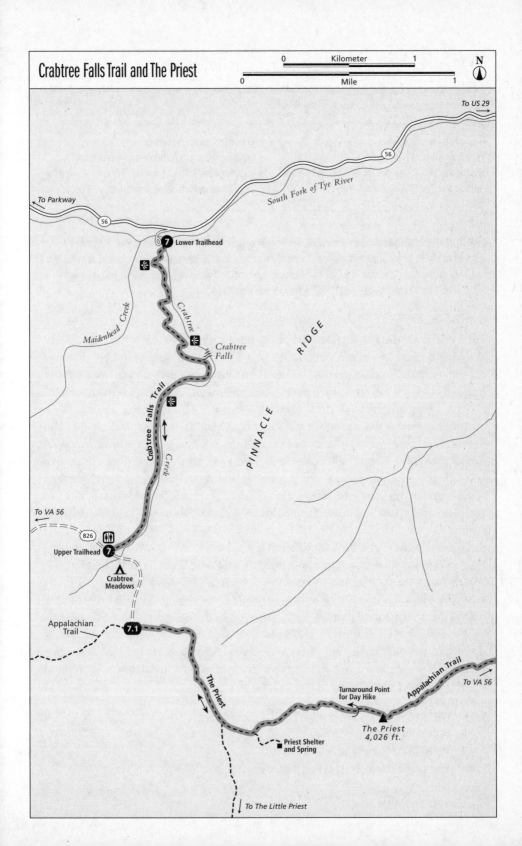

Crabtree Falls Trail and The Priest

N

| 0 | Kilometer | 1 |

| 0 | Mile | 1 |

To US 29

56

To Parkway

South Fork of Tye River

56

7 Lower Trailhead

Maidenhead Creek

Crabtree

Crabtree
Falls

P I N N A C L E   R I D G E

Crabtree Falls Trail

Creek

To VA 56

826

Upper Trailhead 7

Crabtree
Meadows

Appalachian
Trail

7.1

The Priest

Appalachian Trail

To VA 56

Turnaround Point
for Day Hike

The Priest
4,026 ft.

Priest Shelter
and Spring

To The Little Priest

Option 1: The Priest

This popular AT hike to a shelter and campsites reaches one of the most beautifully shaped summits in the central Blue Ridge.

See map on page 53.	**Elevation gain:** 975 feet
Parkway mile: 27.2	**Maps:** USGS *Montebello* and *Massies Mill*;
Distance: 2.6 miles out and back; 5.7 miles one-way to Tye River parking area	Appalachian Trail Conference: Pedlar Ranger District, George Washington National Forest
Difficulty: Strenuous	

Finding the trailhead: Go east on VA 56 from the Blue Ridge Parkway; in about 3.8 miles turn right onto VA 826, an unpaved road suitable for use in good weather by higher clearance vehicles (an SUV is the best choice). The upper trailhead for Crabtree Falls is on the left in just under 4 miles. The Priest hike starts just 0.5 mile beyond this trailhead.

The Hike

From the west, the massive, dramatically sculpted major summit of the 6,000-acre Priest Wilderness Area is easily accessible. It's a 1.4-mile hike and almost 1,000 feet of rise from an AT parking area just 0.5 mile past the upper parking area for Crabtree Falls. Of course if you truly want to "earn it," more than 3,000 feet and forty switchbacks of ascent are always available from VA 56 via the AT's Tye River trailhead.

Not only is this the way to see the summit of The Priest (4,026 feet), but it's also the direction in which to hike this portion of the AT. Leave the trailhead where VA 826 ends at Shoe Creek Hill (3,300 feet). Head left on the AT and pass through a fence, then ascend through a gap at 0.3 mile, going right. (Option: Go left here for a rewarding side trip across the spectacularly sculpted crest of Cone Mountain that's so visible from the Parkway.) After gaining the ridge, the trail to The Little Priest leads right at 0.7 mile. That summit is 1.5 miles away and requires 500 feet of descent and the same amount of rise back up to reach the peak.

At 0.9 mile a blue-blazed trail goes right to the Priest Shelter. The shelter, a spring, and tent sites are 0.1 mile off the main trail. Heading north, the trail reaches rocky viewpoints at 1.3 miles. The summit is 0.1 mile farther on, making the rocks at 1.3 miles a great turnaround point.

If you're continuing, the trail takes a plunge. A viewpoint at 3.0 miles looks directly down into the cleft of the Tye River where you're going. A bridge crosses Cripple Creek at 4.3 miles, and then a series of road grades carry the trail. The VA 56 trailhead is across the road from the Tye River at 5.7 miles.

Key Points across The Priest on the AT

0.0 Start at the trailhead off VA 826.

0.7 Trail to The Little Priest leaves AT to the right.

0.9 Blue-blazed side trail right to the Priest Shelter.

1.3 Views near summit; turnaround point for day hike.

3.0 View of Tye River Valley.

4.3 Bridge over Cripple Creek.

5.7 Tye River parking area on VA 56.

Option 2: Spy Rock

This spectacular view is the perfect introduction to the central Blue Ridge—the perfect place to take a map and compass to identify the major surrounding summits.

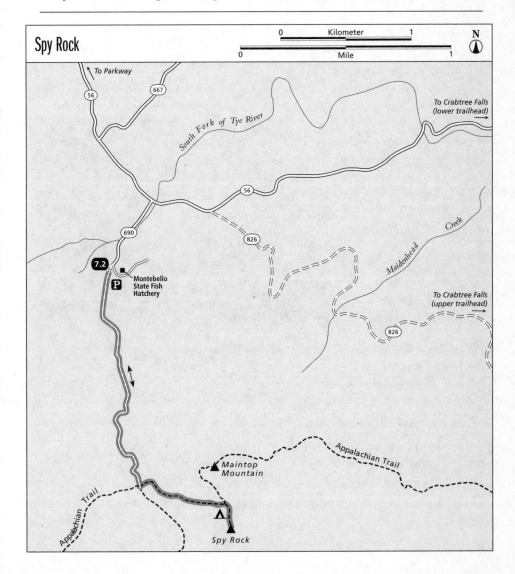

Parkway mile: 27.2
Distance: 3.2 miles out and back
Difficulty: Moderate
Elevation gain: 1,000 feet

Maps: *USGS Montebello* and *Massies Mill;* Appalachian Trail Conference: Pedlar Ranger District, George Washington National Forest

Finding the trailhead: Leave the Parkway to the east, descending on US 56, and in 3.4 miles turn right onto VA 690 at signs for the Montebello State Fish Hatchery. Pass the fish hatchery and turn right at 3.8 miles on an informally signed rough road to trailhead parking on the left at 3.9 miles.

The Hike

If you want a truly awesome view, hike to Spy Rock. This is one of the best views in the central Blue Ridge. Much of the hike is on a gradual road grade, and there's a campsite near the viewpoint.

Strike off across the small stream and up gated Spy Rock Road on the right from the trailhead on the way to the AT junction at 1.0 mile. Go left; the trail crosses a fence at 1.1 miles. At 1.5 miles the AT bears left at a campsite. Turn right onto the side trail to Spy Rock. The trail emerges on the rocky dome of Spy Rock (about 3,900 feet) in just under 0.1 mile.

The all-encompassing summit view includes an excellent vista of the Religious Range—The Priest, The Cardinal, The Little Priest, and The Friar. Retrace your steps from the summit for a 3.2-mile hike.

Azaleas are often seen blooming above Shenandoah Valley vistas along the first 30 miles of the Parkway, especially near Milepost 11.

Key Points

1.0   Turn left onto the AT.
1.5   Turn right onto the Spy Rock side trail.
1.6   Spy Rock summit.

8 Yankee Horse Overlook Trail

Milepost 34.4

This is a quintessential Parkway leg-stretcher trail. Great views of Wigwam Falls combine with an interesting exhibit about the logging railroads that carried off the region's virgin timber.

Parkway mile: 34.4
Distance: 0.1 to 0.2 mile
Difficulty: Easy

Elevation gain: Negligible
Maps: *USGS Montebello;* no Parkway map available

Finding the trailhead: Start on the right side of the overlook, by the interpretive sign.

The Hike

Blue Ridge Parkway interpretive trails impart an amazing sense of how people affected the mountain environment. If you open yourself to the insights, you'll start noticing the remains of old cabin sites and stone walls where you'd least expect them. This trail will change the way you look at trails wherever you hike in the eastern United States.

Remnants of the virgin forests encountered by the colonists are rare in the Appalachians today. The last of that timber was carried away in the early twentieth century on narrow-gauge railroads that climbed into the most impassable places on grades excavated by hand and lifted over precipitous gorges on log trestles. This trail explores a section of railroad reconstructed on the actual grade used by the Irish Creek Railway to transport more than 100 million board feet of lumber. The railway, built in 1919 and 1920, was 50 miles long.

As you climb stone steps, the trail rises and turns right onto railroad tracks across a log-supported bridge that spans gushing Wigwam Creek. The path goes left beyond the bridge, but don't turn yet. Follow the tracks as the rails end and the ties continue.

On the Yankee Horse Overlook Trail, you'll see how old railroad grades fade back into the forest.

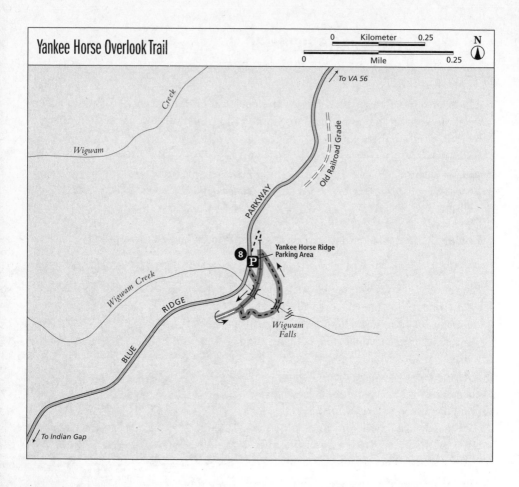

0   Kilometer   0.25

0   Mile   0.25

N

To VA 56

Wigwam Creek

Old Railroad Grade

PARKWAY

Yankee Horse Ridge Parking Area

8 P

Wigwam Creek

RIDGE

BLUE

Wigwam Falls

To Indian Gap

When the ties stop, keep going a short distance and see how the grade softens and the woods encroach.

Many trails use portions of grades like this, and most hikers assume they're old farm or auto roads. Some of the grades you encounter on the Parkway, especially near gaps, may be wagon roads from centuries past. But many are railroad grades, and now you may be better able to recognize them. When you finish the hike, drive north a short distance from the overlook. Where the hillside recedes from the road on the right, you can see the continuation of this railroad grade slicing through the woods.

Return to where you would have gone left, and turn right (uphill). Pass a tree growing over a huge boulder on the right and then go left across two bridges below Wigwam Falls, most impressive when the small stream has seen recent rain. The trail continues left, levels out above the stream, and then descends on a log-lined treadway to rejoin the tracks. Head left, back toward the bridge, and then take a right to return to your car. Or go right on the tracks toward a picnic table and then left down steps to the overlook.

9 Indian Gap Trail

Milepost 47.5

Parents with children will like the hands-on experience that Indian Rocks gives to young mountain climbers.

Parkway mile: 47.5
Distance: 0.3-mile loop
Difficulty: Easy

Elevation gain: Negligible
Maps: *USGS Buena Vista;* no Parkway map available

Finding the trailhead: The trail leaves the north end of the parking area.

The Hike

Take the stone-paved pathway toward the north and pass a picnic table. An old grade comes in from the right, and the trail follows it through a gully. The trail bears right off the grade to a ridgetop with a small peak off in the woods to the left. Amid stand-

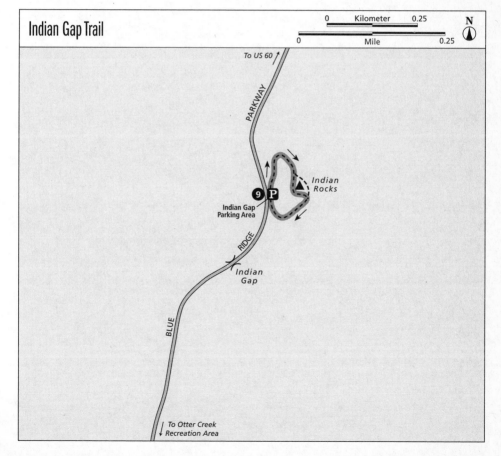

ing dead timber that's popular with woodpeckers, the trail turns right and wanders through mountain laurel to Indian Rocks.

Bootleg trails seem to go everywhere—you can turn left and go below the rocks. Stay to the right on the formal trail and you soon realize that a few of these impressive "rocks" are the size of small houses. Descend rocky steps and go left below a huge boulder that's been blackened by a campfire. The path weaves back and forth below the crags, but you can head left at many points and find yourself at dead ends in rocky fissures. There's even a small cave to crawl into. This is the perfect place for kids to scramble around with adult supervision and really get in touch with the environment.

The trail turns right, away from the rocks, and levels off through a corridor in the mountain laurel. The road appears ahead, and the gravel-covered path becomes paved before swinging into the south side of the parking lot.

10 Otter Creek Recreation Area

Mileposts 60.8–63.6

For almost 10 miles, Otter Creek memorably parallels the Parkway on a descent from 1,100 feet to the James River at 650 feet. Though this is not a lofty portion of the high road, the mixed forest of hardwoods (oaks, sycamores, and beeches) and evergreens (white pines and hemlocks) is reminiscent of higher elevations. All along the 8.5 miles of Otter Creek's dance with the Parkway, broad flats and inviting woods lie beside the meandering stream. Luckily, a wonderful series of overlooks—and the lengthy Otter Creek Trail—permit you to revel in the rich streamside forest. This entire area is one of the most recommended places to pause along the northern part of the Parkway.

This stroll sticks close to the Parkway for its entire 3.4-mile length, so if you hike it one-way you end up miles from your car. You could enjoyably backtrack for a 6.8-mile round-trip hike—the terrain is so gentle that even that distance would qualify as a moderate hike for honed Parkway hikers.

The best bet may be to start at one or the other end and make Otter Lake your destination. The 1.0-mile loop around this scenic lake is a high point of the trail and divides the Otter Creek Trail into two nice day hikes of different lengths. The longer, 5.8 miles, starts at the Otter Creek Campground trailhead. The shorter, which starts at the James River Visitor Center, is only 2.4 miles. The trail descriptions reflect that organization.

The Otter Creek Trail begins at this major Parkway campground, which has a small pine-paneled restaurant/snack bar and gift shop.

Option 1: Otter Creek Trail

Enjoy awesome streamside strolling in a memorable mixed forest of hardwoods and evergreens.

Parkway mile: Major starting points at Mileposts 60.8 and 63.6 (other overlook access included in the text and mileage log)
Distance: 5.8-mile lollipop from Otter Creek Campground and 2.4-mile lollipop from James River Visitor Center
Difficulty: Moderate

Elevation gain: 222 feet from the campground; 128 feet from visitor center (including lake loop)
Maps: USGS *Big Island;* Parkway handout map combining the Otter Creek Recreation Area and James River Water Gap, available in season at the visitor center and campground

Finding the trailhead: Starting at the campground, park at the restaurant (or nearby parking) and head south past the front of the building on the paved then gravel-surfaced trail that dips into the woods along the stream. Starting at the James River Visitor Center, park near the trail map sign. Descend below the front of the building on the paved path and turn left just beyond the visitor center to follow another paved path above the picnic tables and down into the woods.

Tumbling Otter Creek grows quiet and still where it meets the mighty James River.

The Hikes

From Otter Creek Campground

The Otter Creek Trail leaves the parking area and immediately passes circular concrete stepping-stones that cross the stream left into the campground (you'll see more of these 1950s-looking conveniences all along the trail). Passing campsites, the trail crosses to the east side of the creek at 0.1 mile then slips under Otter Creek Bridge #6 at 0.3 mile and wanders west to stone steps that lead left up to Terrapin Hill Overlook at 0.6 mile (Milepost 61.4).

The trail swings south with the stream and goes under two bridges at 0.7 mile, both through the leftmost water tunnels. The Parkway's stone Otter Creek Bridge #7 is followed by the concrete modernity of the VA 130 bridge. Just out of the tunnel, the trail turns right and crosses to the other side of the stream. Along the river rocks on the shore, the stream is deflected hard right by a towering green palisade; turn with it (a side trail across this bend could avoid the streambank in higher water). Paralleling VA 130, the trail again hops to the east side of the stream and rises steeply left to parallel above the Parkway (which has crossed above the other road). The path rises higher and higher along a log-lined treadway through an impressive forest of white oak, hemlock, and white pine to a bench at 1.0 mile. After a dip left into a dry

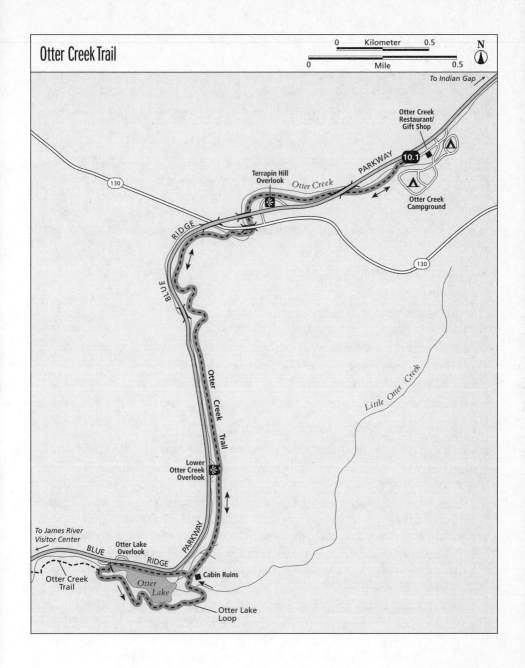

0   Kilometer   0.5

N

0   Mile   0.5

To Indian Gap

Otter Creek
Restaurant/
Gift Shop

PARKWAY

10.1

Otter Creek
Campground

Terrapin Hill
Overlook

Otter Creek

130

RIDGE

BLUE

Otter Creek Trail

Little Otter Creek

Lower
Otter Creek
Overlook

130

PARKWAY

To James River
Visitor Center

BLUE   RIDGE

Otter Lake
Overlook

Cabin Ruins

Otter Creek
Trail

Otter
Lake

Otter Lake
Loop

drainage, the trail swings out again and back in to a bridge at 1.3 miles. Swinging into another drainage, then out, the trail is again above Otter Creek, which has come back under the Parkway and is now below. Entering into another drainage, side steps lead to a huge crag with an overhanging shelter spot and a bench. Leaving that rock, the trail swings out and steeply down to Otter Creek at about 1.5 miles.

From here to Lower Otter Creek Overlook (Milepost 62.5) at 1.9 miles, the trail stays near the stream, barely undulating with nice views into clear, cold, and at times invitingly deep water. Mountain laurel crops up and you pass another bench. Entering the overlook's picnic table area, take a right across the steel bridge. Walk left along the parking area and immediately go left across the next bridge (the zigzag avoids a cliff face).

Back along the stream, this time on a sandier shore, the Otter Creek Trail enters a more open deciduous forest and at 2.4 miles intersects the Otter Lake Loop. Go right at this junction, crossing two steel bridges. Staying right, emerge from the woods to walk along the Otter Lake Overlook (Milepost 63.1). This is the best way to circle the lake and is the route described under the Otter Lake Loop Trail (see Option 2 of this hike). At the end of that loop (3.4 miles), retrace your steps along the Otter Creek Trail for a 5.8-mile day hike.

Key Points on the Longer Lollipop

0.3   Under first bridge.

0.6   Terrapin Hill Overlook.

0.7   Under second and third bridges.

1.9   Lower Otter Creek Overlook.

2.4   Junction with Otter Lake Loop; turn right onto loop.

3.4   Return to Otter Creek Trail.

5.8   Return to campground.

From James River Visitor Center

Heading down to the woods line above the visitor center picnic area, leave the paved path and join Otter Creek. Here it's a quiet stream, backed up into stillness by the lumbering flow of the nearby James River. Soon, though, the stream comes to life as its rise creates a rush of incoming water.

Following the creek beneath the visitor center parking, the path runs atop a stone reinforcement wall at 0.3 mile that protects the road from the curving waters of Otter Creek. Across the stream, hemlocks grapple to stay rooted among mossy-green crags. The trail swings right then left around a bend in the river (where you can see evidence of an old road off to the left) and then crosses more round stepping-stones.

The trail joins an old grade at 0.5 mile and leaves it at 0.6 mile to cross a small stream. This atmospheric evidence of early wagon roads and later logging railroads jibes with the chimneys and other ruins that the alert hiker will notice hereabouts. This was a region of rich soil and impressive forests, and the Kanawha Canal—on the James, just 0.5 mile down Otter Creek—was one of early America's thriving commercial thoroughfares.

Continuing through hemlocks, white pines, and a carpet of running cedar, the river straightens out and the trail dips down railroad-tie steps to cross stepping-stones at 0.7 mile. Just beyond is the stair-stepping cascade of water over the Otter Lake Dam.

You could cross the stream and walk up the steps beside the dam to the overlook. Instead go right before the stepping-stones and start the Otter Lake Loop. Hiking the 1.0-mile lake trail (described below) and retracing your steps along Otter Creek to the James River Visitor Center creates a 2.4-mile lollipop hike.

Option 2: Otter Lake Loop Trail

This intensely scenic loop around a man-made lake includes a ruined mountaineer cabin.

Parkway mile: 63.1
Distance: 1.0-mile loop
Difficulty: Moderate
Elevation gain: 108 feet

Maps: *USGS Big Island;* Parkway handout map combining the Otter Creek Recreation Area and James River Water Gap, available in season at the visitor center and campground

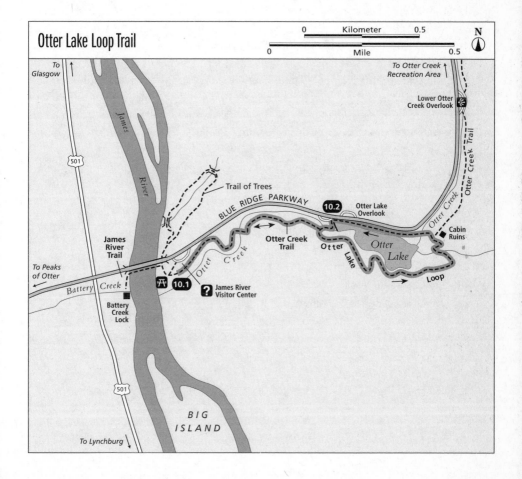

Finding the trailhead: Park at the Otter Lake Overlook. The trail starts at the end of the parking lot near the dam.

The Hike

Starting at the end of the parking lot near the dam, go down the steps and cross the stream on concrete stepping-stones. Go left and ascend stone steps past crags along the stream and above the dam at 0.1 mile. At lake level, the trail slides around a point and into a drainage to cross a small stream, then switchbacks around the ridge to a bench above the lake at 0.3 mile. A small side trail leads to another view of the lake.

The main trail rises gradually to its high point in the mixed deciduous and evergreen forest. At 0.4 mile another bench amid towering white pines announces the drop down a gully from the ridgetop. Bearing left across a small creek, the trail wanders through sycamores and blond grasses in the wetland where inlet brooks feed the lake. Cross a small bridge at 0.5 mile over Little Otter Creek, and then rise into a white pine grove on a knoll where an old cabin sits in ruins. The huge base of the chimney is nicely intact, but the upper rocks have fallen in much the way the rocks were stacked, directly across the interior of the cabin. A perimeter of rock foundation stones and the remnants of large logs are all that's left. A bench is across the trail.

Dipping down into the floodplain below the once artfully sited cabin, turn left at the signed junction and cross two steel bridges at 0.6 mile. At the edge of the Parkway, head left. Rounding a ridge above the wetland, walk into the parking area, past a wooden observation deck on the lakeshore, and back to your car for a 1.0-mile loop.

Note: The lake is plentifully signed with fishing regulations (swimming, boating, and ice skating are prohibited).

Key Points

0.1 Cross stream and go left to top of dam.
0.3 First bench at side trail to view.
0.4 Second bench.
0.6 Cross bridges to go left.
1.0 Arrive back at dam beside Parkway.

11 James River Water Gap

Milepost 63.6

For all the might of the mountains, the sight of Virginia's biggest river flowing plac-idly through the breach is sure to impress. Trails on the Blue Ridge Parkway and in the James River Face Wilderness provide an impressive experience of the titanic natural forces at work in this water gap.

The Parkway's two riverside paths are advertised as thirty-minute interpretive walks. Each, in turn, features interpretive signs about the human and natural history of the James River Water Gap. Both begin beside a visitor center that in season offers a variety of other exhibits about the canal and the river.

Be sure to consider the picnic area beside the visitor center. Twelve or so tables and grills dot a split-rail fence–flanked meadow beside the James. You can picnic in the open or just inside the edge of the woods. The Otter Creek Trail starts here near the visitor center, but a lower path also leads along the first part of the stream from a number of picnic sites. It's a wonderful chance to leave the placid silence where Otter Creek merges with the massive James and walk into the woods to see—and hear—the creek come noisily to life as a tumbling mountain stream.

Option 1: Trail of Trees

The geology of the water gap and the diversity of the floodplain forest are the focus for one of the Parkway's best interpretive trails. The path crosses crags with great views of the river.

Parkway mile: 63.6
Distance: 0.5-mile loop
Difficulty: Moderate
Elevation gain: 50 feet

Maps: *USGS Big Island;* Parkway handout map combining the James River Water Gap and Otter Creek Recreation Area, available in season at the visitor center and campground

Finding the trailhead: Park at the visitor center near the trail map sign and descend on the paved path to the right past the building. Continue under the Blue Ridge Parkway's river bridge and go right up the steps. (The pedestrian walkway left across the river leads to the James River Trail.)

The Hike

From the paved patio beneath the bridge, the trail steeply switchbacks right then left up stone steps to where the loop splits just below the level of the Parkway. Heading left, descend a bit to a stone wall–encircled patio and a sign that explains the water gap—a formation typical of the Appalachians (see photo). These gaps played a key role in westward expansion, and the James River Water Gap so dramatically displayed here was particularly important. An early turnpike, railroad, and canal were part of the gap's transportation network. The canal is gone, but a major highway and rail line still course above the river on the opposite bank.

Parkway interpretive signs offer a wealth of environmental insight.

The trail rises away from the view on a soil treadway, passes below some crags, and then climbs again directly above the river. All around are dramatic cliffs and crags that lost the battle with the James. The scenery conjures the romantic early lithographs of canal traffic you see on nearby interpretive signs.

Down more steps and under an overhang, the path dips into a drainage and descends to switchback left along the stream. A bridge spans the stream just before it slips into the James. Rising to a headland, there's another river view and then a second formal stone viewpoint at the top of more stone steps. The view is of plunging cliffs and nearby islands in the river.

The trail turns away from the river and slabs above the stream you crossed, eventually recrossing it on another bridge. There's a bench in this quiet spot, then more stone steps lift you out of the drainage.

Dozens of signs do a particularly fine job of identifying the trees and explaining the ecosystem of a typical lower-elevation Appalachian forest (at 650 feet, this is the lowest part of the Parkway). A sign here explains that eastern hemlocks "indicate the presence of a stream." Groves of these graceful evergreens (now being decimated by the hemlock woolly adelgid) usually grow in the moist soil along watercourses. But even when these trees climb a ridge, "beneath the seemingly dry rocks are pools of water that supply the hemlock's thirsting roots."

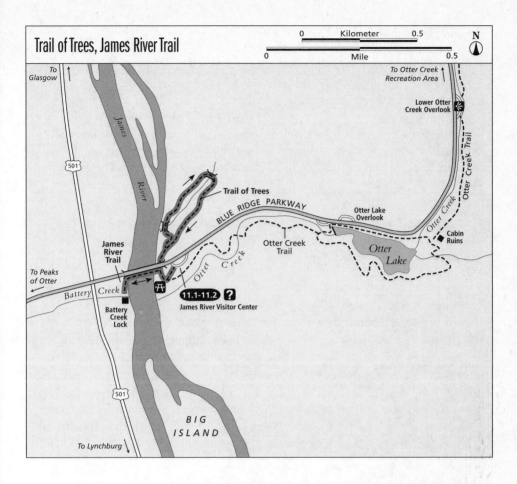

Trail of Trees, James River Trail

The trail continues a steep climb past another bench, then levels along the edge of the drainage below. You can see directly down on the first bridge you crossed near a sign for the tulip tree, or yellow poplar, the tallest broadleaf tree in North America. Topping out, the path swings right along the height of land past other interpretive signs and scrubby Virginia pine. As you skirt just above the trail you started on, a small fenced graveyard appears off to the left, with headstones—some just rocks—from the early and mid-1800s, when the water gap funneled settlers into the wilderness beyond. A set of steps closes the loop and takes you back down the steeper steps the way you came.

Key Points

0.1 First viewpoint.

0.2 Cross first bridge.

0.3 Cross second bridge at bench.

Option 2: James River Trail

A pleasant walk across a scenic river bridge leads to a self-guiding interpretive exhibit at a canal lock built in the mid-1800s.

See map on page 69.
Parkway mile: 63.6
Distance: 0.4 mile out and back
Difficulty: Easy
Elevation gain: Negligible

Maps: *USGS Big Island;* Parkway handout map combining the James River Water Gap and Otter Creek Recreation Area, available in season at the visitor center and campground

Finding the trailhead: Park at the visitor center and descend to the right on the paved path from the trail map sign. Continue under the Blue Ridge Parkway's river bridge and take the pedestrian walkway left across the river.

The Hike

The James River Trail crosses the impressive pedestrian span beneath the Blue Ridge Parkway bridge. Descend the steps on the south side of the river and go left across the grassy riverside meadow to Battery Creek Lock. Built in 1848 and used between

1851 and 1880 on the James River and Kanawha Canal, the lock lifted and lowered boats around part of the river's 13 feet of drop from nearby Buchanan, a Shenandoah Valley town and western terminus of the canal.

Signs interpret the lock and the system that used river water to feed the adjoining canal and operate its gates. To lengthen the walk, go beyond the lock to the river or walk along the creek before returning to the bridge on the way back.

Key Points

0.2 Battery Creek Lock.

The Battery Creek Lock is still in use to tame the James River.

12 James River Face Wilderness

Mileposts 63.9–71.0

The 9,000-acre James River Face Wilderness is a rugged and scenic area that clings to the cliffs where the mighty James River breaks through the Blue Ridge. Designated in 1975, Virginia's first wilderness area lies north of Petites Gap, a major trail access point at Milepost 71 on the Blue Ridge Parkway. Thunder Ridge, added in 1984, is a 2,450-acre wilderness just south of Petites Gap. That tract is essentially just the sloping western side of the Blue Ridge below the parkway, though that description doesn't do justice to the unique plants that grow there. Together, the James River Face and Thunder Ridge make up a wilderness tract that rises from the deceptive calm of the James River (about 650 feet) to the lofty altitude of Highcock Knob (3,073 feet) and the Blue Ridge Parkway.

Much of the area was logged early in the last century, and many of the trails follow old grades that were part of the process (these roadlike trails are one reason horses are permitted in the wilderness on the Balcony Falls, Sulphur Spring, and Piney Ridge Trails). Nevertheless, the rugged, precipitous faces that plummet toward the James River possess significant parcels of timber that escaped early loggers. But don't expect

Remnants of old Camp Powhatan mark the trailhead for the Devil's Marbleyard hike in James River Face Wilderness.

trees of major proportions. The thin, rocky soils support scrubby communities of Virginia pine, chestnut oak, and heath-type undergrowth, such as mountain laurel. The deeper coves are home to hemlocks and white pines, but few trails venture there. In general the area is steep and scrubby enough to discourage bushwhacking. But for the serious wilderness purist, the trail-less James River Face is a wealth of hard-to-reach places that offer pristine, primeval scenery and total solitude. As in other Virginia wilderness areas, group size is limited to ten persons.

This is an area of well-signed, radiating ridgetop trails with numerous out-and-back hiking options. Unfortunately, a desire to circuit hike through the James River Face will be largely frustrated. For that reason, this entry offers an overview of the trail network then recommends a few circuit hikes. (Check the accompanying maps while reading this description.)

South of Petites Gap, Milepost 71 on the Parkway, the Appalachian Trail is the single significant trail through the Thunder Ridge tract. From Petites Gap north, the AT runs into the James River Face, over the summit of Highcock Knob, then around the ridgetops, eventually dropping east past Matts Creek Shelter to wander along the James. The trail crosses the James on an impressive 625-foot trail bridge dedicated in 2000 to the late William T. Foot, a Natural Bridge Appalachian Trail Club member who worked to make the bridge a reality.

At the very crest of the wilderness, 2.3-mile sections of the Appalachian and Sulphur Spring Trails undulate along on opposite sides of the main ridge, creating a 5.6-mile circuit with junctions to the north and south. That's a key feature for hikers—a number of basically out-and-back day hikes/overnighters can become circuits by adding that summit loop.

Climbing from the east to meet the above trails are the Matts Creek Trail (part of the AT until the year 2000), which runs from US 501 to the shelter, and the Piney Ridge Trail, part of the original 1930s AT that rises to join the Sulphur Spring Trail on the crest of the wilderness. That trailhead is also very near US 501, on FSR 54. Both trails figure in circuits described here.

Four trails climb to the AT from the west. Northernmost is Balcony Falls, which rises from VA 782 to a junction with the Sulphur Spring Trail and, following that trail, reaches the AT in another 1.4 miles. Gunter Ridge Trail climbs from a trailhead in the vicinity of VA 759 to join the Belfast Trail 0.4 mile from the AT. The Belfast Trail leaves VA 781 and climbs to pass a junction with the Gunter Ridge Trail and then join the AT. Luckily for hikers, the lower ends of the above two trails are linked by the relatively new Glenwood Horse Trail, permitting one of the area's best circuits, also described here.

Option 1: Appalachian Trail Circuit to Matts Creek Shelter

A newer section of Appalachian Trail crosses the James River to a popular trail shelter. This is a perfect riverside hike for anyone who enjoyed the river-related Trail of Trees and canal exhibit at the Parkway's nearby James River Visitor Center.

Parkway mile: 63.9
Distance: 2.8 miles out and back to a camp-site turnaround on the bank of the James; 4.4 miles out and back to the shelter on the AT; 4.8 miles to the shelter on a circuit with Matts Creek Trail

Difficulty: Easy for the riverside walk; moderate for the Matts Creek hikes
Elevation gain: 650 feet
Maps: *USGS Snowden* and *Glasgow;* Appalachian Trail Conference: Glenwood-New Castle Ranger Districts, Jefferson National Forest

Finding the trailhead: Exit the Parkway at Milepost 63.9. From the stop sign on US 501, go west toward Glasgow, crossing the Snowden Bridge over the James. The trailhead for the Matts Creek Trail, the former AT, is just before the bridge on the left, at about 2.9 miles, beside an Amherst County historical marker. Across the bridge on US 501/VA 130, a major AT parking area is 4 miles from the Parkway. Leave the lot and go under a railroad bridge to cross the James River footbridge.

The Hikes

North to south, hikers face a nearly 2,500-foot climb from the James to the crest. But that climb doesn't kick in until you've passed Matts Creek Shelter. That makes this a rare north-to-south AT day hike that's recommended for its ease and a great turnaround point—a trail shelter that makes a nice lunch stop or campsite, especially during the week.

There are a few versions of a Matts Creek hike. The rerouted AT crosses the James on an impressive trail bridge and then follows the river, giving hikers views they never had before because the old AT (now the Matts Creek Trail) was in the woods all the way.

Either one of those routes leads to the shelter and, with two cars, makes a nice circuit hike—especially with the two parking areas so close together.

Head under the railroad bridge and cross the stunning trail span with awesome views of the wilderness area's namesake face dropping into the river. No camping is permitted for the first mile. Turn right and the white-blazed AT follows the riverbank above the watery grave of a nineteenth-century turnpike and the James River and Kanawha Canal.

At 1.4 miles the trail enters the James River Face and goes left at various camp-sites where Matts Creek tumbles into the James. A turnaround here makes a 2.8-mile day hike or camping trip. Leading away from this memorable meeting of a mountain stream and a major river, the trail ascends gradually into a rich forest. At 2.1 miles the old AT goes left, now called the Matts Creek Trail and marked with blue blazes.

It's another 0.1 mile to the shelter (and picnic table) where the Natural Bridge AT Club has built an impressive bridge across the gorgelike stream. Unlike the various shelters once located higher up at what is now an AT campsite called Marble Spring, the six-person Matts Creek Shelter is likely to stay, despite being located in a wilderness area. This is a popular camping spot, so a variety of alternative tent sites have been designated in the area. Midweek and off-season are your best bets for solitude.

A return to your car via the AT is a 4.4-mile hike. To descend Matts Creek Trail,

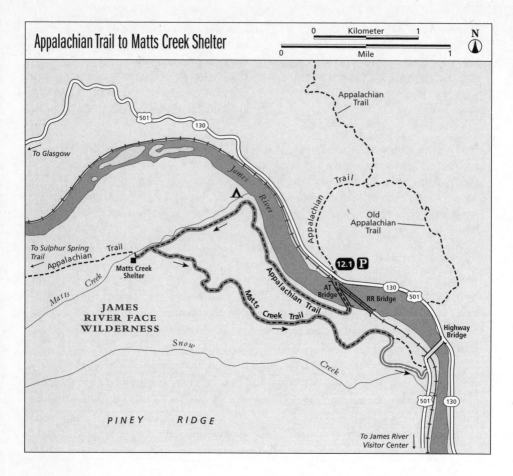

Appalachian Trail to Matts Creek Shelter

head back on the AT 0.1 mile and go right. That route involves some initial elevation gain before descending along an old road grade for the last mile or so to US 501 at 4.8 miles and a second car.

Key Points for Circuit

1.4 Campsites where Matts Creek meets the James.

2.1 Matts Creek Trail goes left.

2.2 Matts Creek Shelter.

2.3 Return to Matts Creek Trail and go right.

4.8 To US 501.

Option 2: Devil's Marbleyard Circuit

This circuit takes in one of the wilderness area's most interesting features—an open slope of bizarre boulders. It also permits a side trip to upper-elevation campsites and views along the Appalachian Trail.

Parkway mile: 71
Distance: 8.1-mile circuit
Difficulty: Strenuous
Elevation gain: 1,700 feet

Maps: USGS *Snowden* and *Glasgow;* Appalachian Trail Conference: Glenwood and New Castle Ranger Districts, Jefferson National Forest

Finding the trailhead: From the Blue Ridge Parkway at Milepost 71, go west on FSR 35 past the Petites Gap AT parking area. Park on the right in the lot at 4.2 miles. The trail has limited roadside parking, and the Forest Service asks that you not impede residents of the homes that border the trailhead.

The Hike

The Belfast Trail leads hikers to one of the wilderness area's most interesting natural features, the Devil's Marbleyard. This trail is also the start of the best circuit hike in the James River Face Wilderness.

The blue-blazed trail crosses the East Fork of Elk Creek on a footbridge and passes between the atmospheric entrance pillars to Camp Powhatan, an old Boy Scout camp. The trailhead sign is just beyond, surrounded by the interesting remnants of the camp. The orange plastic–blazed Glenwood Horse Trail comes in from the right (the horse trail does not cross the trail, as it may appear). The two trails climb together along an old road grade before the horse trail goes left (your return route). The Belfast Trail climbs the tightening drainage to the Devils Marbleyard at 1.4 miles, where an open boulder field provides great views of the Arnold Valley and Thunder Ridge Wilderness.

The Marbleyard's local legend is an odd tale. The site was supposedly the secret worship place of a peaceful Native American tribe who lived in the valley. It was lush and grassy and had a stone altar where the people would worship on full-moon nights. One day, two strangers appeared. The man and woman were welcomed, and because they were so strikingly different, the Native Americans wanted to worship these newcomers as spirits. But the man told the Indians that he worshipped a higher power. The Indians eventually were converted, but after a summer of horrendous drought, they blamed the newcomers and their new god. They dragged the missionaries to the altar and burned them alive. As the flames rose, a great storm exploded in the sky. Lighting bolts shattered the altar—scattering its remains all over this once-lush mountainside. Of divine origin or not, the screelike slope of Antietam quartzite is quite a sight. A return from here makes for a 2.8-mile round-trip hike.

After the steep stretch past the Marbleyard, the trail becomes more gradual and passes the Gunter Ridge Trail (about 2,500 feet) on the left at 2.4 miles and reaches the AT at 2.8 miles (with options in either direction for an overnighter). Head left down the blue-blazed Gunter Ridge Trail and run the ridge past a small summit at about 3.8 miles. The trail goes sharply off the ridge and drops down a strenuous series of switchbacks to intersect with the Glenwood Horse Trail at 6.0 miles. Turn left for

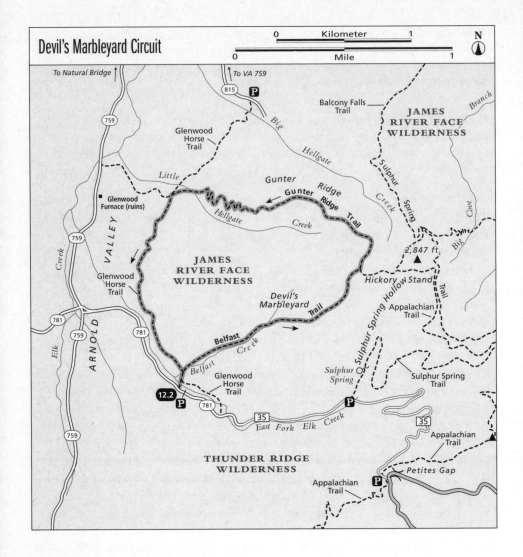

Devil's Marbleyard Circuit

0 _____ Kilometer _____ 1

0 _____ Mile _____ 1

N

To Natural Bridge

To VA 759

815 P

Balcony Falls Trail

JAMES RIVER FACE WILDERNESS

Branch

759

Glenwood Horse Trail

Big

Hellgate

Little

Gunter Ridge

Gunter Ridge Trail

Sulphur Creek

Spring

Cove

Glenwood Furnace (ruins)

Hellgate

Creek

2,847 ft.

Big

VALLEY

JAMES RIVER FACE WILDERNESS

Devil's Marbleyard Trail

Hickory Spring Hollow Stand

Glenwood Horse Trail

Appalachian Trail

Creek

ARNOLD

Belfast

Creek

Sulphur Spring Hollow Trail

781

759

781

Belfast

Sulphur Spring Trail

Sulphur Spring

759

12.2

P

Glenwood Horse Trail

781

P

35

East Fork Elk Creek

35

Appalachian Trail

759

THUNDER RIDGE WILDERNESS

Appalachian Trail

Petites Gap

P

Elk

1.9 miles on the horse trail and reach the Belfast Trail again at 7.9 miles. Turn right and follow the Belfast Trail back to the parking area for an 8.1-mile circuit.

Key Points

0.2 Bear right on Belfast Trail where horse trail goes left.

1.4 Devil's Marbleyard.

2.4 Go left onto Gunter Ridge.

6.0 Turn left onto Glenwood Horse Trail.

7.9 Go right onto Belfast Trail to parking.

Option 3: AT End-to-Ender and Summit Circuits in the James River Face

This rugged Appalachian Trail traverse of the James River Face Wilderness requires two cars or a ride and a few summit circuits with access from either the Piney Ridge or Sulphur Spring Trails.

Parkway mile: 71
Distance: 9.9 miles end to end; circuits of 11.4 miles via Sulphur Spring Trail and 12.6 miles via Piney Ridge Trail
Difficulty: Strenuous

Elevation gain: 1,647 feet
Maps: USGS Snowden and Glasgow; Appalachian Trail Conference: Glenwood and New Castle Ranger Districts, Jefferson National Forest

Finding the trailheads: The southern end of this section of the Appalachian Trail begins on FSR 35 just west of the Blue Ridge Parkway at Milepost 71 in Petites Gap. The Sulphur Spring Trail starts on the north side of FSR 35, 2.7 miles west of the Petites Gap AT parking area.

To reach the Appalachian Trail parking area to the north, exit the Parkway at Milepost 63.9. From the stop sign on US 501, go west about 4 miles; the parking area is on the left.

For the Piney Ridge Trail, exit the Parkway at Milepost 63.9. From the stop sign on US 501, go west toward Glasgow. In 2.0 miles make a left onto FSR 54, about 1 mile before the James River bridge. The small parking area is 0.6 mile on the right.

The Hikes

The white-blazed trail begins its 9.9-mile traverse of the James River Face (8.5 miles in the wilderness area) in Petites Gap. FSR 35 leaves the Parkway there and descends to the Devil's Marbleyard circuit. (See Option 2 of this hike.)

Hike the AT south to north to minimize the nearly 2,500-foot climb from the river. The trail heads north from Petites Gap, climbing the first 1.2 miles steeply to the wooded summit of Highcock Knob (3,073 feet). Plummeting very steeply off the peak, the trail levels off and arrives at the former site of Marble Spring Shelter, about 1.0 mile from the summit and just over 2.0 miles from the road. The shelter site is now a big, pebble-strewn camping area, with a spring 150 feet down the side trail to the left.

At about 2.7 miles the Sulphur Spring Trail, an old road grade, crosses the AT. Left, it descends to VA 781/FSR 35 and is part of another circuit hike. To the right, the trail soon passes the Piney Ridge Trail, also a circuit-hike option, on its way to meet and cross the AT a second time at the 5.0-mile mark—the 5.6-mile summit circuit mentioned above that figures in two hikes described below.

For the next few miles, the AT undulates southwest of the main ridge, skirting the summits of a crest called Hickory Stand on the way to a junction with the Belfast Trail at about 4.5 miles. This trail to the left and the Gunter Ridge Trail that branches from it make up a portion of the Devil's Marbleyard circuit.

From its route along the southwest side of the main ridge, the AT turns sharply right at the Belfast Trail junction and swings around the north end of the ridge about 5.0 miles from the parking area. The Sulphur Spring Trail crosses here. Left, it goes

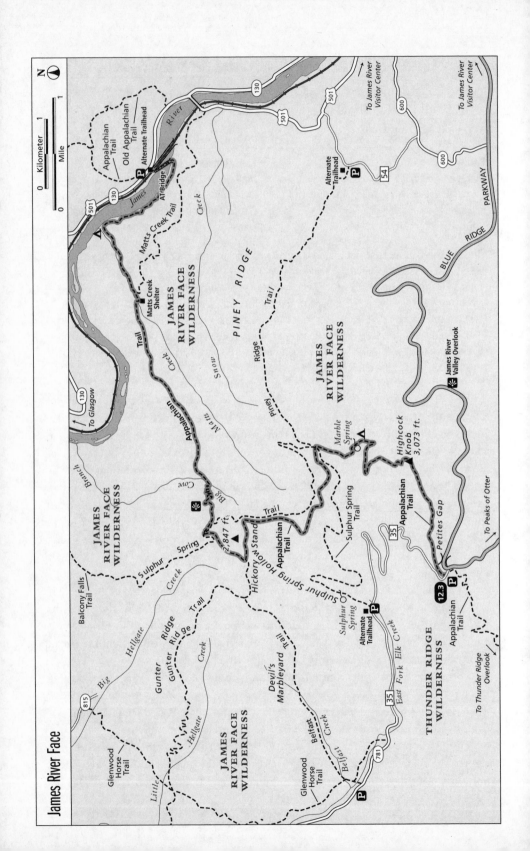

James River Face

1.4 miles to a junction with Balcony Falls Trail (that trail drops 4.4 miles to a valley trailhead). Right, the Sulphur Spring Trail runs back along the north side of the main ridge to rejoin the AT in 2.3 miles—again, part of the summit loop that figures in two inviting circuits covered below.

Swinging northeast, the AT slips across the main ridge of the James River Face and begins a descent of nearly 2,000 feet to the James River—the lowest point on the southern half of the Appalachian Trail. There's a view of the James just beyond the ridgecrest and another in 0.5 mile (winter is the best time for views in this wilderness area). At 5.8 miles, Big Cove Branch is a worthwhile water source. Following a narrowing ridge above Matts Creek, the trail turns right off the ridge and descends to cross a bridge at Matts Creek Shelter (picnic table and a privy) at 7.7 miles. This section of the AT between the ridgetop and Matts Creek Shelter offers great views of the James and glimpses of the area's wildest scenery. Day hikers or overnighters bound for Matts Creek Shelter (see Option 1 of this hike) could climb to these vantage points before turning around.

Just past the shelter, the blue-blazed Matts Creek Trail turns right. The AT continues northeast, following Matts Creek to campsites at 8.5 miles where the mountain stream empties into the James. Swinging along the river (beneath the impounded water lie the remains of a nineteenth-century canal and a turnpike), the path undulates for 1.0 mile before turning left to cross a 625-foot trail bridge to the AT parking area on US 501/VA 130 at 9.9 miles.

The summit minuet between the Appalachian and Sulphur Spring Trails turns a number of otherwise out-and-back routes into circuits.

Sulphur Spring is the southernmost of the westside trails and provides horse and hiker access to the heart of the wilderness area. The trail climbs via a road grade from FSR 35, past Sulphur Spring, to cross the Appalachian Trail at 2.9 miles. The trail then gradually slabs the side of the ridge opposite the AT, passing the Piney Ridge Trail on the way and offering nice views to the river. Out and back on the Sulphur Spring Trail, including the summit circuit with the AT, is 11.4 miles. The Piney Ridge Trail climbs a scenic ridge to the AT from the opposite side of the wilderness and joins the AT at 3.5 miles. Taking the summit circuit from there, the total hike is 12.6 miles. Because they're not the steepest routes to the peaks, both of these side trails see some horse traffic.

Key Points for End-to-Ender

1.2 Summit of Highcock Knob.

2.2 Marble Spring campsite.

2.7 Sulphur Spring Trail crosses AT.

4.5 Belfast Trail goes left.

5.0 Sulphur Spring Trail crosses AT (left to Balcony Falls Trail).

7.7 Matts Creek Shelter, just 0.1 mile before Matts Creek Trail.

8.5 Campsites where Matts Creek empties into James River.

9.9 US 501/VA 130 trailhead.

13 Thunder Ridge Trail and Wilderness

Milepost 74.7

One of the most impressive rock wall–encircled vista spots on the Parkway, this is the perfect place to consider the impact of air pollution on the Southern Appalachians.

Parkway mile: 74.7
Distance: 0.2-mile loop
Difficulty: Easy

Elevation gain: Negligible
Maps: *USGS Snowden;* no Parkway map available

Finding the trailhead: Start on the northeast side of the Thunder Ridge Overlook parking area.

The Hike

This short loop overlooks the dramatic Arnold Valley and the upper slopes of the 2,450-acre Thunder Ridge Wilderness. It's an even shorter and easier hike to the

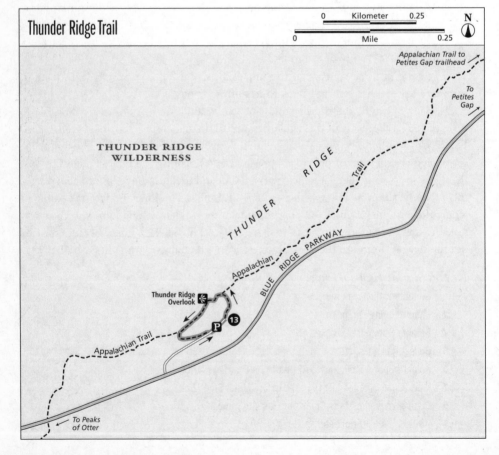

Thunder Ridge Overlook offers a great view and an easy stroll. James River Face and the Devil's Marbleyard are visible to the north.

viewpoint if you return the way you came. The Appalachian Trail through the wilderness provides a longer route.

After a few stone steps, the gravel trail leaves the parking area at the farthest corner from the Parkway. The path bears left past a picnic table. The Appalachian Trail comes in on the right to join the Thunder Ridge Trail from an alternative trailhead in Petites Gap. Just beyond the junction, the stone wall–encircled viewpoint offers a commanding vista of Virginia's Great Valley.

An interpretive easel appropriately titled "Seeing is Believing" shows three photos taken from this overlook that alarmingly illustrate how air pollution in the Southern Appalachians has diminished the area's famous views. Farther south on the Parkway, at the Nature Museum on Grandfather Mountain and in Mount Mitchell State Park, similar exhibits illustrate how air pollution has devastated the region's high-elevation spruce/fir forest—not just the view.

The combined Thunder Ridge and Appalachian Trails leave the viewpoint and thread through large boulders along the crest. Eventually the Thunder Ridge Trail turns left where the AT goes straight at a tree with a white blaze. The trail switchbacks left around smaller boulders and parallels the overlook spur road back to the opposite end of the parking area from where the hike started.

For a longer hike that follows an original section of the Appalachian Trail, start to the north at the AT trailhead just west of the Parkway at Petites Gap (Milepost 71). The trail climbs past a wet-weather spring on the left at 0.9 mile, traverses the peak of Thunder Ridge at 2.1 miles, and then descends to the overlook viewpoint at 3.3 miles. Retracing your steps creates a 6.6-mile out-and-back hike that passes through Thunder Ridge Wilderness to reach the Parkway viewpoint.

14 Apple Orchard Falls Trail and Cornelius Creek Circuits

Milepost 78.4

The Forest Service is justly proud of this waterfall circuit that features two scenic, well-maintained National Recreation Trails and spectacular Apple Orchard Falls.

Parkway mile: 78.4
Distance: 1.5- or 2.8-mile round-trip day hikes; circuits of 6.1 and 7.6 miles
Difficulty: Moderately strenuous for the easiest falls hikes from the Parkway and FSR 3034;

strenuous for the others
Elevation gain: 600 feet for the easiest waterfall hike; 2,000 feet for the lengthier circuit
Maps: *USGS Arnold Valley;* no Parkway map available

Finding the trailhead: From the Parkway, start at the Sunset Field Overlook at Milepost 78.4. For the shortest hike, start on Apple Tree Road (FSR 3034), an easy 4.9-mile drive from the Parkway. Leave north end of Sunset Field Overlook and descend on FSR 812. Turn left in 2.8 miles onto FSR 3034; the trailhead is another 2.1 miles.

To hike the circuits from the FSR 59 trailhead, start at the lower trailhead. Take the route to Apple Tree Road, but pass that turnoff and stay on FSR 812. Pass FSR 765, which goes right. At a T junction go left onto FSR 768. At the next junction turn left again onto FSR 59, which ends at the trailhead.

The Hikes

This figure-eight trail system explores a noteworthy north-facing watershed of old-growth forest below the highest peak in this part of the Blue Ridge. It's a best-kept secret for backpackers and birders. Neotropical songbirds such as the ovenbird, red-eyed vireo, and scarlet tanager can be seen and heard here. (The rare Peaks of Otter salamander is also a resident.) In the early 1990s the Forest Service designated 1,825 acres as a Special Management Area; the trails were upgraded and the focus shifted away from potential timber harvesting to enhancing recreation and wildlife.

Apple Orchard Falls is a short hike from the Parkway in the national forest just below the road.

From Apple Tree Road

The most direct route to the falls departs from the trailhead sign on Apple Tree Road. Take the 400-foot Apple Orchard Spur across two bridges and go left (southeast) onto the Apple Orchard Falls Trail. The forest here is alive with birdsong and the sound of water. It's a stiff but relatively short climb of 0.75 mile (1.5 miles round-trip) and 600 vertical feet to the falls. The stone steps get really steep as you near a wooden bridge that spans the base of the impressive falls, highest in the Glenwood Ranger District. The USDA Forest Service logo artfully adorns a bench on the bridge.

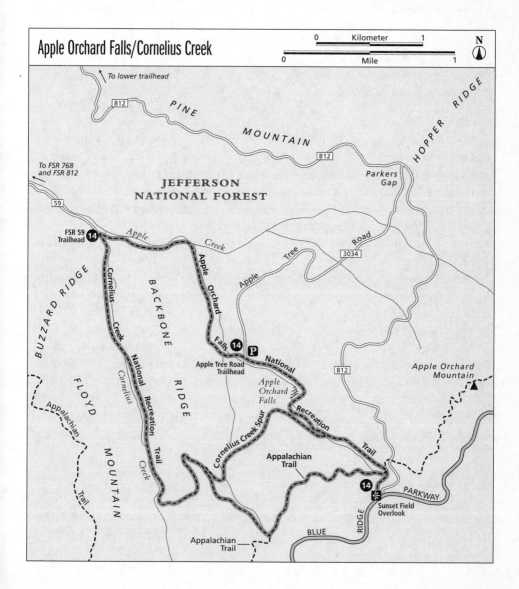

Apple Orchard Falls/Cornelius Creek

From the Parkway

Pass the APPLE ORCHARD FALLS TRAIL sign on the paved path and follow the blue-blazed route.

Cross the Appalachian Trail at 0.2 mile as you head northwest. At 0.8 mile a grassy woods road to the left leads to the Cornelius Creek National Recreation Trail and is part of a few loop hikes. Keep right; there's a sheltering overhang just before the drop to the falls starts at 1.2 miles. Turn around at 1.4 miles, the observation bridge below the falls. Return to the Parkway for a 2.8-mile round-trip with 1,000 feet of rise on the way back.

Key Points from the Parkway

0.2 Cross the Appalachian Trail.

0.8 Grassy woods road of Cornelius Creek Spur leads left to Cornelius Creek Trail.

1.4 Reach views at base of falls.

From FSR 59

A few day-hike or backpack circuits are possible. Starting at the FSR 59 trailhead and going southward, the Cornelius Creek Trail makes a gradual climb. Trails in this area follow old logging roads established before 1917, when the land was owned by the Virginia Lumber and Extract Company. The best day hike is a 6.1-mile waterfall circuit that goes up (south) Cornelius Creek, turns left (easterly) onto the Cornelius Creek Spur (a grassy fire road), then makes another left (northwest) onto the Apple Orchard Falls Trail to pass the falls on the way back to the parking area. This hike gains 1,400 feet.

A longer loop stays right at the grassy Cornelius Creek Spur, climbs to the AT, and goes left (northeasterly). Turn left (northwest) again onto the Apple Orchard Falls Trail. After passing the falls, arrive back at FSR 59 for a 7.6-mile hike (with 2,000 feet of elevation gain).

Campsites are particularly plentiful along this hike. Hikers could start at the Park-way—where it would similarly be best to walk the loop in a counterclockwise direction by descending past the falls northward and going up (south) Cornelius Creek.

15 Peaks of Otter

Mileposts 83.1–85.9

The Parkway's 4,200-acre Peaks of Otter Recreation Area is one of the most highly recommended places to spend a day or stop for the night. This lofty valley, formed by the stunningly pointed summit of Sharp Top and the bulk of Flat Top, is unique along the Parkway. Its facilities and colorful history are part of the appeal. Its name probably derives from the proximity of the Otter River.

Peaks of Otter Lodge, one of four concessionaire-operated accommodations on the Parkway, is open year-round for lodging and dining, with special buffets on Friday night and Sunday. Facilities operated May through October by the Park Service include a campground, picnic area, country store (where Sharp Top bus tickets are available), visitor center, nature center, and restored mountain farm.

Winter access is good because VA 43 is the best route between I-81, west of the Blue Ridge near Buchanan, and Bedford, east of the mountains. That link requires the highway not only to cross the Parkway but actually follow it for 5 miles in a "staggered crossing." Thus the Peaks of Otter stretch of the Parkway is plowed even when the rest of the road is "closed" due to snowfall.

Archaeological work has established that Native Americans hunted elk thousands of years ago on the fringe of a boggy meadow that is now the site of twenty-four-acre Abbott Lake, the Peaks of Otter's scenic centerpiece and the primary focus for guests at the lodge.

The land was first cleared by European settlers in 1766; by the 1830s an "ordinary" was established that offered lodging and dining to travelers crossing the Blue Ridge. You can still see Polly Woods Ordinary between the Peaks of Otter Picnic Area and Abbott Lake. Early tourist hotels, ancestors of the current Peaks of Otter Lodge, opened as early as 1857.

In 1820 a group of rowdies spent a few days trying to roll one of Sharp Top's summit boulders into the valley. They eventually succeeded with a little dynamite. When the Washington Monument was going up, local officials took a chunk of that boulder in 1852 and embedded it into the obelisk, where its inscription can still be read—"From Otter's summit, Virginia's Loftiest peak, To crown a monument, To Virginia's noblest son." Of course Sharp Top is not the state's highest peak—that's Mount Rogers (5,729 feet) in southwest Virginia—but such is the impressive appeal of pyramidal mountains. Nor does the rock actually crown the Washington Monument. It rests in the west wall at the twelfth stairway landing.

By the 1930s a community of more than twenty self-reliant families populated the high valley, including the last of the Johnson family, for whom the Johnson Farm Trail is named. A school and a church stood near the current site of Peaks of Otter Lodge. The families were mostly subsistence farmers, but the tourist traffic up the road to the Sharp Top summit and to the Hotel Mons (the site is visible on the Farm Trail) supplied cash for the locals who had jobs.

The Great Depression ended all that. The Johnson farm, which got its start in 1852, was sold in 1941, changed hands again, and was then purchased by the National Park Service. It deteriorated until the 1950s, when it was stabilized; it was restored in 1968. The interpretive loop of the Johnson Farm Trail is one of the best places on the Parkway to learn about the lives of the people who wrested subsistence from the rocky Appalachian soil. Warm weather living-history programs here are among the Parkway's most engaging and extensive. Summer programs also take place at Polly Woods Ordinary. (See the Abbott Lake Trail option for this hike.)

Early settlers generated some income from the primitive tourism economy created by the area's long history of mountain hostelries. Some mountaineers worked in the lodging establishments, and Peaks of Otter farmers grew the produce served in the dining rooms. Built in 1964, Peaks of Otter Lodge continues that long tradition.

When the lodge was built, the boggy mountain meadow was turned into Abbott Lake. This scenic jewel is appropriately named for Stanley W. Abbott, the Parkway's first landscape architect and the man largely responsible for designing what is today considered to be the quintessential scenic road. Ironically, today no one would even propose flooding a high-mountain bog.

A hiker peers into Polly Woods Ordinary, a Peaks of Otter hostelry that long predated the Hotel Mons and today's Peaks of Otter Lodge.

Option 1: Fallingwater Cascades Trail

A waterfall loop descends off the Parkway in a region known more for its peaks.

Parkway mile: 83.1
Distance: 1.6-mile loop
Difficulty: Moderate.
Elevation gain: 382 feet

Maps: *USGS Peaks of Otter;* Parkway handout map, available at the visitor center, lodge, and other Parkway facilities

Finding the trailhead: Park in either the Falling Cascades Parking Area (Milepost 83.1) or the Flat Top Parking Area (Milepost 83.5).

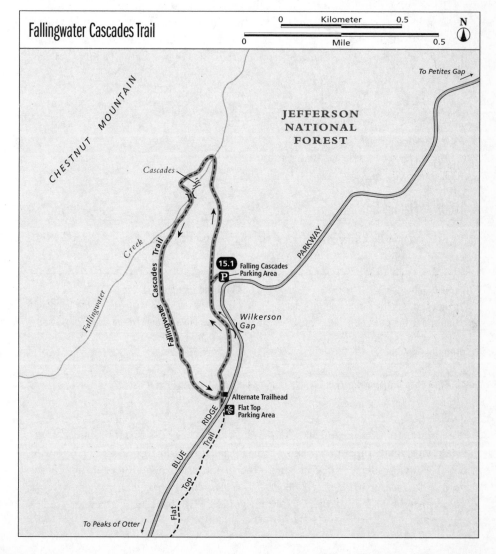

The Hike

This National Recreation Trail takes an unusual route for a Parkway path—it dips pretty immediately into the Jefferson National Forest. The attraction is a tumbling waterfall in a gorge that slips just past the Parkway boundary.

From Falling Cascades Parking Area, turn right down the rhododendron-bordered trail. After a steeper stretch and steps, Fallingwater Creek appears, tumbling downward to the cascades. Cross a bridge over the creek at 0.3 mile and go left, descending along the lush streamside through hemlocks, with hardwoods on higher slopes. A few benches offer rest spots on this steeply dropping part of the path, with numerous nice views back uphill to the falls. Pass the base of the cascade and go left back across the creek on another bridge at 0.6 mile. A backtrack return to the car from this point nets a 1.2-mile hike, about 0.4 mile shorter than taking the full loop.

Continuing on the loop, climb above the cleft of the falls past a bench, gradually entering the higher hardwood forest. At 1.0 mile you can go right on a side trail to the Flat Top Parking Area. Continue straight the last 0.6 mile to the Falling Cascades Parking Area.

Key Points

0.3 Cross bridge spanning Fallingwater Creek.

0.6 Recross the creek below the falls.

1.0 Pass side trail to Flat Top Parking Area.

1.6 Arrive back at Falling Cascades Parking Area.

Option 2: Flat Top Trail

A quiet, uncrowded hike takes you to the highest point at the Peaks of Otter—4,001 feet.

Parkway mile: 83.5
Distance: 4.4 miles end to end; 5.8 miles round-trip to the peak from the north, 3.2 miles from the south
Difficulty: Strenuous

Elevation gain: 1,391 feet
Maps: *USGS Peaks of Otter;* Parkway handout map, available at the visitor center, lodge, and other Parkway facilities

Finding the trailhead: Park in the Flat Top Parking Area at Milepost 83.5.

The Hike

Flat Top (4,001 feet) is the "other" summit of the Peaks of Otter. It's rounded compared with Sharp Top and was once actually called Round Top. Sharp Top's pointed popularity with hikers is due in part to the striking conical countenance it exhibits from a distance. It is stunning views of that pyramidal peak that make Flat Top a highly recommended hike (especially in winter). Flat Top Trail is a quieter, far less

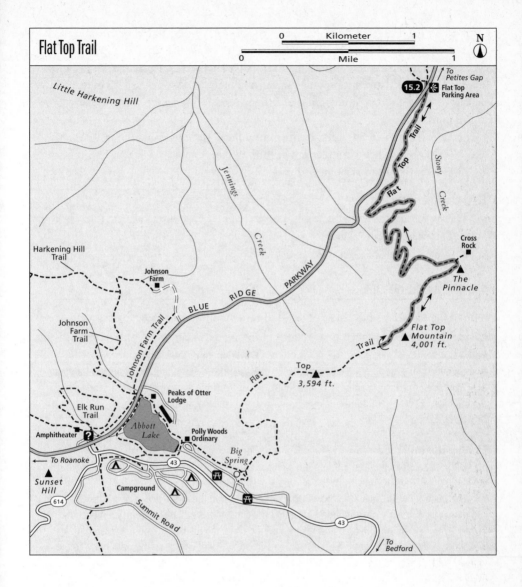

Kilometer

Mile

N

To Petites Gap

15.2 Flat Top Parking Area

Little Harkening Hill

Flat Top Trail

Stony Creek

Jennings

Creek

Cross Rock

Harkening Hill Trail

Johnson Farm

BLUE RIDGE PARKWAY

The Pinnacle

Johnson Farm Trail

Johnson Farm Trail

Flat Top Mountain 4,001 ft.

Trail

Top 3,594 ft.

Flat Top Trail

Peaks of Otter Lodge

Elk Run Trail

Amphitheater

Abbott Lake

Polly Woods Ordinary

Big Spring

To Roanoke

43

Sunset Hill

614

Campground

Summit Road

43

To Bedford

frequented path than the one to the summit of Sharp Top. Like the Fallingwater Cascades Trail, the Flat Top hike is a National Recreation Trail.

The crest of the mountain is littered with many crags and outcrops. A few, including the Pinnacle and Cross Rock, are named and accessible on the trail. The Pinnacle and the mountain summit boast the best views.

The easiest hike to the peak rises from the Flat Top Parking Area north of the visitor center/concession area. The Parkway itself is higher in that area—and therefore closer to the summit—although the trail is longer. You could also start at the parking area in the Peaks of Otter Picnic Area (see the Abbott Lake option for how to find the trailhead) if you want a greater elevation gain in a shorter distance.

Leaving the Flat Top Parking Area, the trail skirts along the Parkway boundary before beginning a 2.0-mile switchbacking ascent of the mountain's north side. At about 2.2 miles a side trail goes left to Cross Rock, then you pass the Pinnacle. At 2.9 miles the rocky summit provides panoramic views in all directions. Retrace your steps from here, or keep going another 0.1 mile for another nice view of Sharp Top to the southeast.

From that last view, 3.0 miles from your trailhead starting point, the trail descends steeply in spots another 1.5 miles down to the picnic area at 4.5 miles. This traverse is a nice hike if you can arrange two cars.

Key Points

2.2 Side trail to Cross Rock.

2.9 Summit views from Flat Top.

3.0 Another nice view of Sharp Top.

Option 3: Abbott Lake Trail

One of the Parkway's best lakeside strolls or cross-country ski tours.

Parkway mile: 85.6
Distance: 1.6-mile loop from picnic area; 1.7-mile loop from visitor center; 1.0-mile loop around lake
Difficulty: Easy

Elevation gain: Negligible
Maps: USGS *Peaks of Otter;* Parkway handout map available at the visitor center, lodge, and other Parkway facilities

Finding the trailheads: To start at the Peaks of Otter Picnic Area, turn east on VA 43 opposite the visitor center. Take the next left into the picnic area. At the T junction, park across the road at the Flat Top Trail Parking Area, or go left and park beside Polly Woods Ordinary.

For a shorter walk, park at Peaks of Otter Lodge; turn into the lodge and take the next right into the small lakeshore parking area by the first building. At busier times of year, you may have to park elsewhere in the lodge lot and take a paved path to the lakeshore. You may also park at the Peaks of Otter Visitor Center on the Parkway. Leave the visitor center on the path north to the Johnson Farm and take the right under the Parkway to Peaks of Otter Lodge.

The Hike

Abbott Lake was once a high-elevation mountain bog and a favored Native American hunting area—elk, bison, and other game were attracted to the watery site. Today the lake still attracts plentiful wildlife. This is a great place for bird watching—if you can divert your eyes from the knock-your-socks-off view of Sharp Top.

Sharp Top is so close and conical that the view is truly dramatic—especially with autumn color or hoarfrost in winter. It's great for very young, elderly, and even mobility-challenged hikers—not to mention cross-country skiers—because this trail is partially paved and extremely easy (hence suggested starting points that add to the distance).

From Sharp Top's rocky summit, it's easy to trace the entire Harkening Hill hike as it climbs the peak to the left of the lake.

The best starting point is the picnic area. The Flat Top Trail takes off from the parking area, so walk up the picnic area road 25 yards and take the trail into the woods by Big Spring, a reliable water source used for centuries by travelers traversing the Blue Ridge. The path passes Polly Woods Ordinary, a modest cabin used as a rustic inn by owner Mary "Polly" Wood between 1830 and 1855. Appropriately, given your destination, the building was originally located up near the lake and served travelers on the Buchanan to Liberty (early name of Bedford, Virginia) Turnpike. Wood's daughter ran the inn for five more years after Polly's death in 1855.

In 0.3 mile you'll turn right onto the paved Abbott Lake Trail and head northwest along the lakeshore. Cross an arched bridge at 0.4 mile and veer out into the lake on a promontory with benches and great views. Past the lodge and the small parking area by the last building, the pavement ends and a trail branches right at 0.7 mile to pass under the Parkway and then left on its way in about 0.4 mile to the visitor center (another good starting point). Continuing, the now unpaved path wanders south-westerly at the water's edge along the Parkway through open meadows dotted with dogwoods, cedars, and cattails. You'll cross the inlet brook on a bridge at 0.9 mile and pass a trail to Peaks of Otter Campground at 1.1 miles (campers can come in from this direction; campground trails link the campsites to Abbott Lake, the start of the Sharp Top Trail, and the visitor center). Cross the dam and at 1.3 miles turn right past Polly Woods Ordinary along the picnic area that you came in on. Back at your car, the round-trip is about 1.6 miles.

From the visitor center, hike 0.3 mile toward Johnson Farm to a trail junction. The Johnson Farm Trail loops left, but take the right toward the lodge and go beneath the road via an underpass. Turn right at the Abbott Lake Trail. This route is about 1.7 miles.

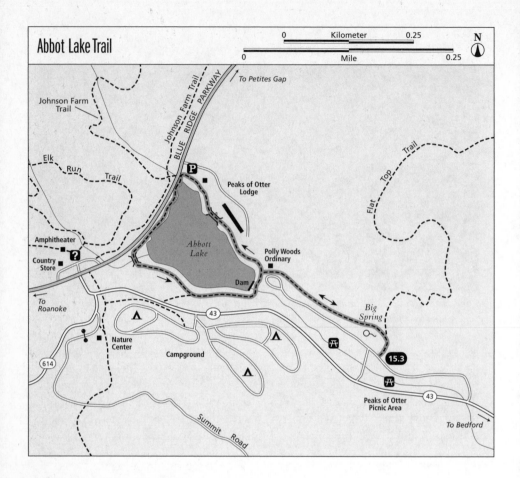

Abbot Lake Trail

Key Points from Picnic Area

- **0.3** Turn right onto Abbott Lake Trail.
- **0.7** Trail to Johnson Farm Trail and visitor center branches to the right.
- **0.9** Cross bridge over inlet brook.
- **1.3** Turn right to trailhead past Polly Woods Ordinary.

Option 4: Sharp Top Trail

This steep trail leads to great views from the rocky, conical summit of 3,875-foot Sharp Top.

Parkway mile: 85.9

Distance: 1.5 miles one-way with bus shuttle; 3.0 miles out and back

Difficulty: Moderate if you ride the bus up and hike down; strenuous from the bottom

Elevation gain: 1,340 feet

Maps: *USGS Peaks of Otter;* Parkway handout map, available at the visitor center, lodge, and other Parkway facilities

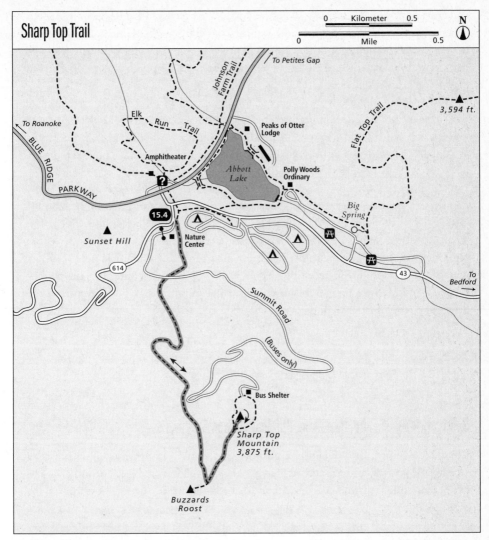

Sharp Top Trail

0 Kilometer 0.5
0 Mile 0.5

N

To Petites Gap

Johnson Farm Trail

Elk Run Trail

To Roanoke

BLUE RIDGE PARKWAY

Amphitheater

Peaks of Otter Lodge

Abbott Lake

Polly Woods Ordinary

Flat Top Trail

3,594 ft.

Big Spring

15.4

Sunset Hill

Nature Center

614

Summit Road

(Buses only)

43

To Bedford

Bus Shelter

Sharp Top Mountain
3,875 ft.

Buzzards Roost

Finding the trailhead: The trail begins near Milepost 86, opposite the Peaks of Otter Visitor Center and beside the Nature Center.

The Hike

Sharp Top is one of Virginia's sentinel summits and a major landmark of the Blue Ridge range. Its prominent conical peak, capped by rounded boulders, is visible for miles—from foothills far to the east and the Great Valley on the western side of the mountains. The views from the peak survey that same striking domain, making it possible to look down on springtime from a still frosty peak or see summer in the valley while immersed in colorful fall foliage.

This popular trail can be crowded on summer and fall weekends. Even though this hike is steep, it is often made by families and older persons intent on an adventure. Part of its popularity stems from the fact that a National Park Service shuttle bus ferries riders to the summit of Sharp Top for a small fee, making it easy for people to hike down who might not otherwise make the climb up. Ask about current rates and departure times at the Country Store where bus tickets are purchased. (*FYI:* The bus driver also sells tickets.)

The trail leaves the Nature Center, crosses the summit road used by the bus, and switchbacks through a deciduous forest before reaching a junction at 1.2 miles. This side trail is a half-hour round-trip to Buzzards Roost—a rocky crag that alternates between looking like a large foot or a dragon's head, depending on your vantage point. Here's the place to picnic if the surplus of humanity at the summit isn't for you.

Just above the junction, the trail to the top reaches its steepest section and actually climbs steps cut into solid rock. All of that is just preparation for the summit, a jumble of house-size boulders. Another side path descends to the mountaintop shuttle bus stop, and other highly developed trails lead to viewpoints that take in the entire 360-degree view. A large summit shelter is on hand in case of inclement weather, which can include direct lightning strikes. No camping is permitted in the shelter. Hikers should retrace their steps downhill on the trail or buy a bus ticket from the driver and ride down—walking is not allowed on the road.

Key Points

0.2 Cross summit road.

1.2 Junction; trail on right to Buzzards Roost.

1.5 Summit

Option 5: Johnson Farm, Harkening Hill, and Elk Run Loop Trails

These scenic, short to moderate-length interpretive trails impart a real sense of how Southern Appalachian mountaineers lived. The outer loop of the Johnson Farm and Harkening Hill Trails roll the human and natural history of the area into one wonderful walk.

Parkway mile: 85.9

Distance: Johnson Farm Trail, 2.0 miles; Harkening Hill Trail, 3.0 to 3.9 miles; Elk Run Trail, about 1.0-mile circuit hike

Difficulty: Easy to moderate for Johnson Farm; strenuous for Harkening Hill; easy for Elk Run

Loop Trail

Elevation gain: 814 feet for Harkening Hill

Maps: *USGS Peaks of Otter;* Parkway handout map, available at the visitor center, lodge, and other Parkway facilities

Finding the trailhead: All three of these interconnected loops start at the Peaks of Otter Visitor Center.

The Hike

The Harkening Hill and Johnson Farm Trails are interconnected, which creates an interesting situation: You can be on a section of two different hikes at once. Only the

Elk Run Interpretive Loop is a trail unto itself. All hikes are best started from the Peaks of Otter Visitor Center. Together or separately, they offer real insight into the lifestyle of Southern Appalachian mountaineers.

The easy-to-moderate Johnson Farm hike starts at the northern end of the visitor center parking lot. Take the scenic roadside path toward Peaks of Otter Lodge and reach a trail junction in about 0.3 mile. The first trail heading uphill to the left is best as the return part of the Johnson Farm Loop. Take a left at the second sign—the trail to the farm is flatter that way—and head out into the grassy meadow. (The trail that goes right leads under the Parkway to the lodge and Abbott Lake.)

Bear right in the meadow along the trees past a sign about the Hotel Mons, the post–Polly Woods Ordinary/pre–Peaks of Otter Lodge summer resort that operated here from 1857 to the late 1930s. Pass a trail sign farther down the meadow and enter

A couple glimpses an otter on the Abbott Lake Trail below Sharp Top.

the woods at a small bridge. The trail rises and goes left on a road grade into the farm at just under 1.0 mile from the parking area. If the farmhouse is closed, a sign outside has pictures, an interior layout of the building, and a map of the grounds. If the farmhouse is open—this is how the Waltons would have lived in the 1920s.

Leave the old Johnson place one of two ways. The easiest walk is to retrace your steps for the more gradual route. Or leave the house past the front porch and crop plantings and head uphill and left into the meadow beyond to the Johnson Farm return trail. At 1.3 miles the return trail goes straight at a junction where the Harkening Hill Trail turns right. (Go right for the 3.9-mile perimeter circuit formed by the Johnson Farm and Harkening Hill Trails.)

Stay on the Johnson Farm Trail and descend to the first junction you passed at the start of the hike. A right at the junction returns to the visitor center in about the same distance as the other route—around 2.0 miles.

The longest walk is the Harkening Hill Trail—you may choose to walk 3.4 miles (going left at the first sign from the visitor center on the Johnson Farm Trail) or about 3.9 miles (via the longer outer loop of Johnson Farm). This trail explores the now-wooded, wildflower-filled forest that in the 1930s was cultivated fields and road grades between the Johnson Farm and the peak directly above it—Harkening Hill (3,353 feet). The hike is rated strenuous, but it's only moderately so—800 feet of elevation gain from either direction.

The Johnson Farm Loop affords the best start for this hike by adding human context to a setting returning to nature. Whichever side of the farm loop you start on, branch off onto the Harkening Hill Trail. You'll pass through two small meadows at 0.5 mile. A side trail to Balance Rock—a boulder perched on a natural pedestal—heads left at about 0.7 mile. At 0.8 mile above your turnoff from Johnson Farm, you've slipped onto national forest land to the limited rocky viewpoint of Harkening Hill (2.1 miles via the eastern side of the Johnson Farm loop, 1.6 miles on the west).

The trail undulates down the broad, boulder-strewn summit ridge through scenic open woods with a number of descents, some of them steep. There's a sharp ridgeline and grass-fringed uphill a mile below the peak (3.1 miles from the visitor center via the east leg of the farm trail, 2.6 miles via the west). The trail descends by switchbacks then turns right between the rows of amphitheater seats through the visitor center breezeway at 3.9 miles (3.4 miles using the west leg).

The shortest hike in the three-trail network near the Peaks of Otter Visitor Center is the easy 0.8-mile Elk Run Loop Trail, which starts in the breezeway at the end of the Harkening Hill Loop. The interpretive signs of this educational nature trail tell of the ecological interaction between plants and animals. Follow the signs through the gap in the visitor center and bear right, coming to the first of many benches in 0.1 mile. An old grade becomes the path on its rise to a cemetery, at 0.7 mile, before dipping back to the visitor center.

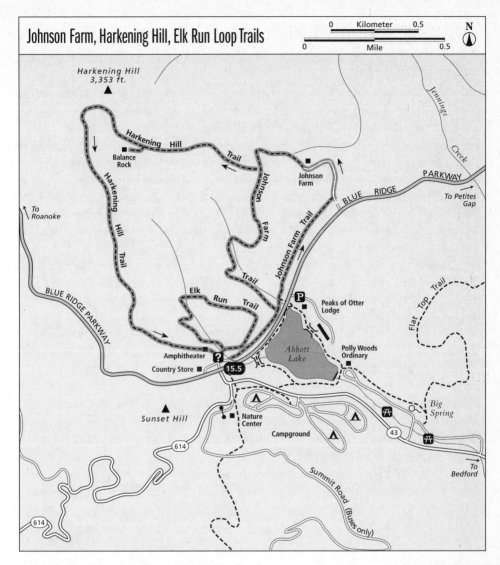

Johnson Farm, Harkening Hill, Elk Run Loop Trails

Kilometer 0.5

0 Mile 0.5

N

Harkening Hill
3,353 ft.

Harkening Hill Trail

Balance Rock

Harkening Hill Trail

Johnson Farm Trail

Johnson Farm

To Roanoke

BLUE RIDGE PARKWAY

PARKWAY

To Petites Gap

Jennings Creek

Elk Run Trail

Trail

P

Peaks of Otter Lodge

Flat Top Trail

Amphitheater

Country Store

15.5

Abbott Lake

Polly Woods Ordinary

Sunset Hill

Nature Center

Campground

Big Spring

43

614

Summit Road (Buses only)

To Bedford

614

Key Points for Harkening Hill Circuit Hike

0.3 Take the second left on the Johnson Farm Trail.

1.0 Johnson Farm.

1.3 Turn right on the Harkening Hill Trail.

2.0 Trail to Balance Rock.

2.1 Summit of Harkening Hill.

3.1 Sharp ridgeline before switchbacks.

3.9 Peaks of Otter Visitor Center.

16　Roanoke Area Trails

Mileposts 110.6–120.4

There are two truly urban areas on the Parkway—Roanoke, Virginia, and Asheville, North Carolina. Purists may be tempted to see them as interruptions in the natural experience of the Parkway, but these are worthwhile Appalachian cities.

Heading south, Roanoke is the first and larger of the two. Unlike the more southerly Asheville, where the Parkway plummets 3,000 feet down to pass the city then gains it all back on the climb beyond, Roanoke embraces the Parkway's glide through town, albeit with increasing suburban development. And in a situation very unlike Asheville, where Parkway facilities are located at high elevation well outside the city, Roanoke has a bona fide in-town Parkway campground and trails. Parkway maps do, after all, call these "Roanoke Valley Trails."

Asheville is a pause along the Parkway, but in Roanoke you can camp at a Parkway facility that's almost in the city. The spur road to the Parkway's Roanoke Mountain Campground leads quickly and directly into downtown and also passes Mill Mountain Park—a Roanoke city park with a nature center, a great summit view of the city from two overlooks, and a small zoo. There's even a trail that makes the overlooks a nice stroll. This is the best view of the city, not to mention the famous illuminated star that shines from the mountaintop. (The road is open to the star each night till 11:00 p.m.)

The best part: Head down the hill and you can be eating sushi ten minutes from your tent at Roanoke Mountain Campground. Go downhill 2.0 miles to a right on Jefferson Street—10 blocks later, turn right onto Campbell Avenue and you're in the Historic Farmers' Market District.

There's a long list of nearby attractions, and the international food court on Market Square is just one attraction of a compact, accessible city center. There's great diversity of dining, all kinds of interesting shops, and Center in the Square—a concentrated culture fix that combines the Art Museum of Western Virginia, the History Museum of Western Virginia, and the Mill Mountain Theatre. The outstanding Roanoke Transportation Museum is nearby, as is an urban interpretive walk along the railroad tracks that have made the city a hub.

That status may be why Virginia's earliest continuously operating farmers' market (1886)—and still one of the state's best (closed Sunday)—is a lively street scene in the heart of downtown. You will have no better meal in a Parkway campground than one based on produce fresh from Roanoke's Farmers' Market. Crafts and mountain music are often part of special events.

If you're not staying at the Parkway campground or backpacking, Roanoke has plentiful motels and B&Bs, and the city's resurgent landmark hotel is a special experience. The Hotel Roanoke, built in 1882, like Asheville's Grove Park Inn, is the quintessential mountain city hotel. It almost died in the late 1980s, but a public/

private partnership between Roanoke civic leaders and Virginia Polytechnic Institute (VPI) has kept this grande dame of the Blue Ridge alive. It's been reborn as a historic hotel/convention center that regularly earns accolades for Roanoke's finest dining and trains students in VPI's hospitality track to four-star standards. A pedestrian bridge takes you from the hotel across the tracks to the heart of downtown in a five-minute stroll.

Option 1: Stewarts Knob Trail

A stroll away from the parking lot leads to a broadened horizon over Roanoke.

Parkway mile: 110.6
Distance: 0.1 mile out and back
Difficulty: Easy
Elevation gain: Negligible

Maps: USGS *Stewartsville*; Parkway's Roanoke Valley Trails overview map, available in season at the campground

Finding the trailhead: The trail leaves the Stewarts Knob Overlook parking area in the turn between the upper and lower lots.

The Hike

This leg-stretcher heads slightly uphill into the woods and through a lush forest understory. Stay to the right where the prominent Roanoke Horse Trail goes left (1.5 miles to the Parkway's nearby Roanoke maintenance base). Where a small side trail goes left, the trail switchbacks right then left to a bench at a split-rail fence overlook perched above the spur road that leads to the overlook. Roanoke lies in the distance. The buildings are more impressive in morning light before you set off into the Parkway's green corridor. (For a more imposing city view, see the Mill Mountain Park option.)

Option 2: Roanoke River Self-Guiding Trail

This trail is actually two—a steep fishing trail to the riverside and a loop that offers a view of the river and a hemlock-dotted forest.

Parkway mile: 114.9
Distance: 0.4 mile out and back for the fishing trail; 0.6 mile out and back for a view trail; 0.9-mile loop that includes the view
Difficulty: Moderate

Elevation gain: About 100 feet from the river
Maps: USGS *Stewartsville* and *Hardy*; Parkway's Roanoke Valley Trails overview map, available in season at the campground

Finding the trailhead: Park at the Roanoke River Parking Area and take the paved path from the middle of the lot.

The Hike

Leave the lot on the gradual paved descent. A sign warns hikers that the river's boulders are treacherously slick and that strong currents can batter a person to death against the rocks. The now-earthen trail becomes nicely benched through scenic pines to a junction. Left, the blue-blazed fishing trail descends to the riverside. The white-blazed loop goes right.

Consider a short detour left on the nicely maintained upper portion of the fishing trail to an easel that shows early photos of the Niagara Power Plant, visible across the river. The dam and plant were built in 1906, and today, the sign says, it's the smallest hydroelectric plant in the country's electric power system. The plant brought the first electricity to Roanoke. Below the easel, the steeper, rockier trail terminates at the river.

Going right on the loop trail, pass under the Parkway bridge to a trail junction where steps descend left to a fern-flanked observation point overlooking a quiet, rocky spot in the river.

Back on the main trail, continue into a mixed evergreen and deciduous forest where you'll find black locust, white pine, tulip tree, eastern hemlock, and others. The wide, nicely graded and scenic trail bends to the right high above the river to pass a bench then cross a small bridge and go left, past another bench within earshot of the rapids below.

The trail crosses another little bridge and switchbacks right on the return route to cross a third bridge (on the same stream you crossed on the last bridge, just higher up). A plaque calls humus—decayed trees and other vegetation—the most valuable ingredient of soil. Ferns line the green forest trail; a bench appears and you're back at the junction. Take a left and return to the parking area.

A walk to the river on the fishing trail is about 0.4 mile; it's about 0.6 mile to the viewpoint at the start of the loop. The entire loop is about 0.9 mile.

Key Points

0.1 Junction—fishing trail to the left; loop to the right.

0.2 Side trail to view above river on loop.

0.4 Rejoin loop and go left.

Option 3: Roanoke Mountain Summit Trail

A short loop hike traverses a craggy summit.

Parkway mile: 120.3
Distance: 0.3-mile loop
Difficulty: Moderate
Elevation gain: 60 feet

Maps: *USGS Garden City;* Parkway's Roanoke Valley Trails overview map, available in season at the campground

Finding the trailhead: Take the Roanoke Mountain Loop Road to the top and start at either of the summit parking lots.

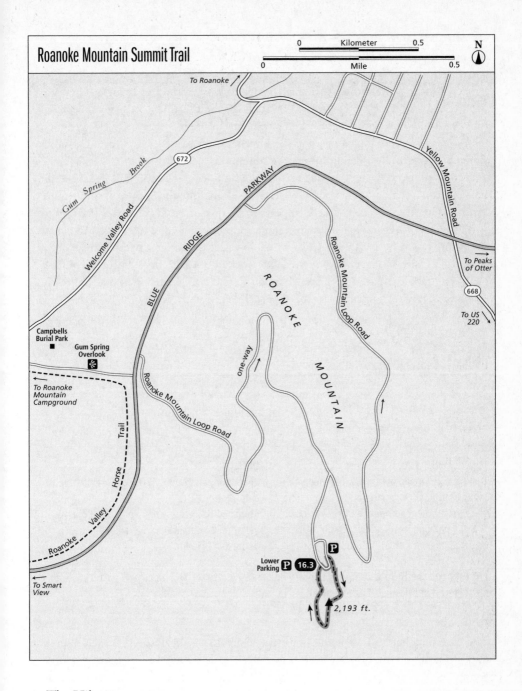

The Hike

Take one of only two mountain-climbing motor roads on the Parkway to reach this trail. At the other, Sharp Top at Peaks of Otter, only Parkway buses are permitted to drive to the summit.

At Roanoke Mountain, a 4.0-mile, mostly one-way loop road leads to a rewarding path across the summit at 2,193 feet. On the way up, a variety of overlooks are worth a look.

For a more adventurous hike, enter the woods from the upper lot by the sign to walk the loop clockwise. Descend through a boulder garden on a switchbacking flight of stone steps with a handrail. The trail dips through a dramatic little gap, goes left of crags up more flights of stone steps, and then weaves back and forth on more stone stairs to artfully ascend through the summit crags.

Descending across the rounded crest of the mountain, the loop trail returns back into the gap on an easy, pine needle–covered tread opposite the rocks you climbed up earlier. From here, the gap actually appears to be one of those craterlike quarry pits you'll also see at Roanoke Mountain Campground on the Chestnut Ridge Trail and the nature trail. Your path rises gently to the lower of the summit parking areas.

For an easier walk, start from the lower parking lot (the first you enter, on the right) and take the paved trail into the woods. The rise is gentler in that direction (counterclockwise), and most of the flights of stone steps—all with handrails—are downhill. Only one flight leads back up to the upper lot. Or just go out and back on this right side of the loop and avoid the stone steps for an easy walk.

Option 4: Chestnut Ridge Trail

A variety of different loops travel on generally gradual grades through oak and pine forests. A few hikes reveal bizarre topography, now nicely reforested, that was created by early mining operations.

Parkway mile: 120.4
Distance: 5.4-mile loop, which can become loops of 2.5 and 3.4 miles. A 1.7-mile nature trail circuit explores evidence of early mining. The campground has a small paved ridgetop trail that offers a barrier-free stroll of 0.2 mile.

Difficulty: Moderate
Elevation gain: About 320 feet for the entire loop
Maps: USGS *Garden City;* Parkway's Roanoke Valley Trails overview map, available in season at the campground

Finding the trailhead: Leave the Parkway on the Mill Mountain Spur Road and go 1.1 miles to the trailhead at Chestnut Ridge Overlook.

The Hikes

The Chestnut Ridge Trail is the one part of the 12.0-mile Roanoke Valley Horse Trail that will interest hikers. This red-blazed 5.4-mile trail makes an elongated loop around the Roanoke Mountain Campground. Its most interesting feature is evidence of quarrying. This campground trail system is complex—and both the Parkway's trail map and the sign map at the overlook leave much to the imagination. Keep your eye on the map in this guide.

These young hikers are about to set out on the Chestnut Ridge Trail.

Starting at the Chestnut Ridge Overlook, a trail goes left and right just off the left side of the parking area at a trail map sign. Right (southeast), it connects down to the loop trail; left (northwest), it crosses the Mill Mountain Spur Road to the campground and connects to the loop as well as the campground's network of paved "transportation trails." That connection permits you to turn the large loop into at least two smaller ones.

Go right (south) from the overlook, then turn immediately left (east) at a signed junction. The nicely benched trail rises gradually with brief steeper sections and rocky treadway that reflects use by horses.

The trail swings out southeast around a long ridge above a reservoir and then turns northwest around the ridge, following contours. It turns northeast along the Mill Mountain Spur Road before switchbacking lower at about 0.7 mile. The trail rounds a knob before swinging left into the gap where Yellow Mountain Road (VA 668) crosses the ridge. As the trail approaches the road at 1.6 miles, there's a junction. Avoid the right down to Yellow Mountain Road. Go up and left to cross the spur road at small posts with hiker symbols. You'll reenter the woods and go left again on the main trail. Here again a trail comes in from the roadside. Don't be confused. The paths permit riders to walk under the bridge and avoid crossing the spur.

Swinging in and out of the drainages below the spur road, the trail pulls away and rises under the campground's tent loop. Again side trails crop up—left to campsites;

right to residences largely out of sight. Bearing left (west) to miss the Parkway boundary, the trail crosses the ridge at a trail sign at 2.3 miles. A left here goes to the tent loop through pleasant piney woods. Across that road it becomes the campground's paved "transportation trail" and passes a comfort station (and can connect back to the Chestnut Ridge Overlook—see the map).

Pass the sign; other trails go left and right as the path swings in and out along the contours below the south side of the campground. Atop the long ridge above, a paved path passes campsites to a tiny end loop that would be suitable as a barrier-free stroll. (Park by the comfort station on the right—see the map.)

The trail swings deeply into drainages. At the second one, a sign points left to the campground's campfire circle amphitheater at 2.9 miles.

Passing the amphitheater, the trail swings out around another ridge to a trail sign in another turn at 3.1 miles. To return to the overlook, go left here on the obvious road-grade trail. At the next trail sign, the paved path from the amphitheater area crosses the trail (left to the amphitheater, right to the RV loop). Go straight on the old grade trail—it crosses the campground road, then the spur road, to the overlook for a 3.4-mile loop hike. (Coming that way from the overlook and going left on the route described below gives you a 2.5-mile loop.)

Continuing on the loop trail, the path rises past the RV loop. The trail parallels the loop before turning away from the campground among azaleas along an old railroad grade.

By now you've noticed the bizarrely disrupted topography of craters and hummocks—remnants of extensive quarrying that occurred in many places in the area. Roanoke is rich with quarries. A particularly odd jumble of these pits—which almost seem like wartime earthworks or the result of heavy shelling—is visible on the paved path through the RV loop (more below).

Not far from the campground, at 3.6 miles, a nature trail sign marks an interesting path to the left that leads back to the campground (see below for a short circuit there).

Continuing on the Chestnut Ridge Trail, round Chestnut Ridge, with views of Rockydale Quarry at 3.8 miles. Slabbing below Mill Mountain Spur Road along power lines, reach the grassy roadside of VA 672 at 4.5 miles. Across the road, the horse trail leads to a stable facility. Your trail goes left along the shoulder under the bridge, then left into the woods. The trail rises steeply then gradually along the spur road, arriving below Chestnut Ridge Overlook at the junction for a 5.4-mile loop.

Either side of this loop makes a good day hike.

Key Points

1.6 Pass VA 668.

2.3 Trail sign at apex of tent camping loop.

3.1 Easy left to trailhead overlook for half-loop hike of 3.4 miles.

3.6 Nature trail goes left to RV campground.

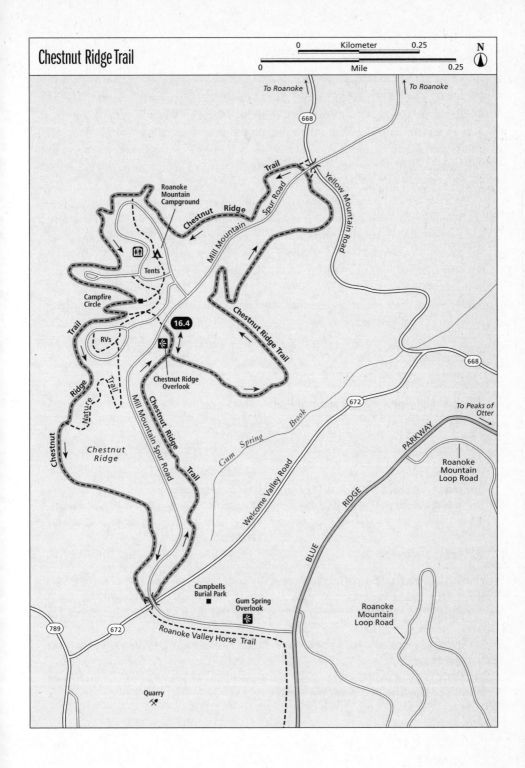

Chestnut Ridge Trail

N

0   Kilometer   0.25

0   Mile   0.25

To Roanoke

To Roanoke

668

Trail

Chestnut   Ridge

Mill Mountain Spur Road

Yellow Mountain Road

Roanoke Mountain Campground

Tents

Campfire Circle

Trail

Ridge

RVs

16.4

Chestnut Ridge Trail

668

Chestnut Ridge Overlook

Ridge

Nature

Trail

Chestnut

Chestnut Ridge

Mill Mountain Spur Road

Chestnut Ridge Trail

Gum Spring Brook

672

Welcome Valley Road

BLUE

RIDGE

PARKWAY

To Peaks of Otter

Roanoke Mountain Loop Road

789

672

Campbells Burial Park

Gum Spring Overlook

Roanoke Mountain Loop Road

Roanoke Valley Horse Trail

Quarry

4.5   Pass VA 672.

5.4   Return to trailhead.

You could also make a 1.7-mile hike out of the interesting quarry terrain to be seen on the nature trail. Go left (northwest) from the Chestnut Ridge Overlook, cross the Mill Mountain Spur Road and the campground road that leads to the RV loop, and bear left. At the first major trail sign, cross the paved path that goes left and right, and head straight to the next trail sign. Bear left there at 0.3 mile onto the Chestnut Ridge Trail and go left around the RV loop.

Make a left on the nature trail at 0.8 mile. It rises more steeply than the Chestnut Ridge Trail and follows the rim of an extensively crater-pocked area disrupted by mining but now nicely reforested. The trail descends from the crest of the crater. When the campground becomes visible below, the trail turns right (away from developed area), switchbacks left, and arrives back at the RV loop literally beside the trailer dumping station—about 1.2 miles from the Chestnut Ridge Overlook. A small roadside sign reads TRAIL. Cross the campground road, beside the comfort station, and turn right onto the paved path that bisects the loop. It undulates wildly up and down and all around more quarry pits. Cross the loop again and follow the paved path down to the trail sign at 1.4 miles where you first crossed the paved trail. Turn right and cross the roads to your car at about 1.7 miles.

Option 5: Mill Mountain Park and Star Trail

This is the best Parkway-adjacent view of Roanoke—bar none.

Parkway mile: 120.4
Distance: 0.4 mile out and back to Discovery Center from summit parking area; 3.0 miles out and back to summit and star from spur road
Difficulty: Easy to moderate

Elevation gain: Negligible for shorter hike; 670 feet for longer hike
Maps: USGS *Garden City;* Parkway's Roanoke Valley Trails overview map, available in season at the campground

Finding the trailhead: From Roanoke Mountain Campground, drive toward Roanoke on the Mill Mountain Spur Road. Turn left into Mill Mountain Park, 1.2 miles beyond the Roanoke Mountain Campground (2.5 miles from the Parkway). Start at either the Discovery Center (first left) or mountaintop trailheads.

To start at a lower trailhead below the park, go past the entrance to Mill Mountain Park 1 mile to a parking slip for a few cars on the right where the trail crosses the road. Above the road, the trail climbs to the peak. Below the road, the yellow-blazed trail runs about a half-mile to the lowest trailhead on Riverland Road beside the Roanoke River.

The Hike

The Star Trail provides a great view of the city—and that huge star. The historical marker above the view claims that the massive star is the world's biggest—but Texas

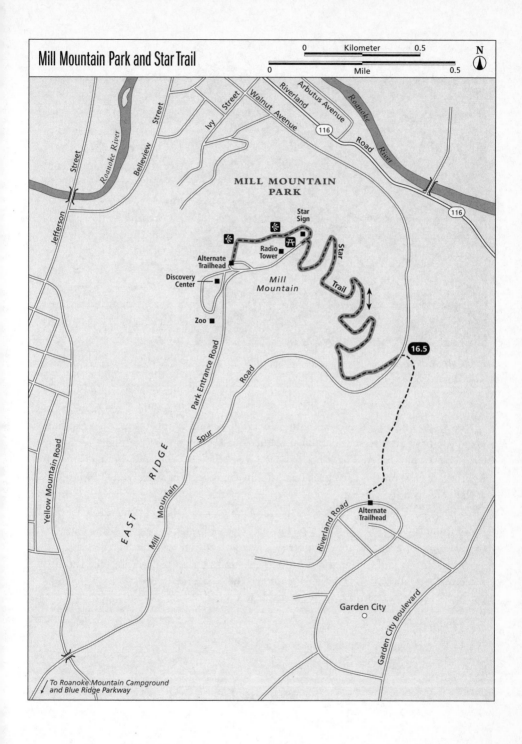

Mill Mountain Park and Star Trail

Kilometer
0   0.5

Mile
0   0.5

N

MILL MOUNTAIN
PARK

Star
Sign

Star Trail

Radio
Tower

Alternate
Trailhead

Discovery
Center

Mill
Mountain

Zoo

16.5

Park Entrance Road

Spur Road

EAST RIDGE

Mill Mountain Road

Yellow Mountain Road

Jefferson Street

Belleview Street

Ivy Street

Walnut Avenue

Riverland

Arbutus Avenue

Roanoke River

116

Road

116

Riverland Road

Alternate
Trailhead

Garden City

Garden City Boulevard

To Roanoke Mountain Campground
and Blue Ridge Parkway

From the Mill Mountain Spur Road, the Star Trail reaches a great summit view of Roanoke.

has since grabbed the honor. Perched at 1,847 feet—1,045 feet above the city—the star is 88 feet tall and can be seen for 60 miles. It was devised in 1949 by civic leaders as a Christmas decoration and has since taken on a life of its own.

Starting at the parking slip on the spur road, walk across the street, climb the steps, and bear left into the woods to begin half a dozen long and gradual switchbacks. The forest is mostly pines, oaks, redbuds, locusts, and maples. At the summit, about 1.5 miles, the trail comes to a T junction at a gravel road where a sign containing the trail's interpretive brochure points back down the trail. Head left; the gravel road goes 30 feet to the paved mountaintop parking area, where a right turn onto a paved path reaches the formal viewpoint below the star. Or turn right at the sign on the gravel road and follow it around the peak to the paved path at the viewpoint.

On the paved view path from the parking area, an asphalt trail descends left (west) off the summit, passing right of a picnic shelter to a lower viewpoint on the way to the main parking area at the Discovery Center and zoo in 0.2 mile.

The shortest and easiest way to reach the summit viewpoints is to take the first left into the Discovery Center. Park and take the trail across from the building; hike past the lower viewpoint to the higher one and return.

Key Points

1.5 Reach summit junction near star.

The Blue Ridge Plateau

Mileposts 121.4 (US 220 at Roanoke, Virginia) to 276.4 (US 421 at Deep Gap, North Carolina)

T he 155-mile portion of the Parkway from US 220 in Roanoke (Milepost 121.4) to Deep Gap at US 421 (Milepost 276.4) could be considered two sections if you split it at the Virginia–North Carolina state line—which some people do. I-77 is a nice central access point near the middle.

Both of these subsections share a common flavor. This is where the Appalachian Front undulates south from Roanoke at generally lower elevations to the Virginia line, then rises again in North Carolina. To the east, the Piedmont still lies below— just not as far below—and western views don't generally plummet to deep valleys. This is the Blue Ridge Plateau of rolling uplands, farms, and rural communities—a bucolic side of the Southern Appalachians.

Unlike other parts of the Parkway, here public lands don't lie beyond the National Park boundary. Residential and, increasingly, resort developments are more visible.

Groups such as the Blue Ridge Parkway Foundation and Friends of the Blue Ridge Parkway (see appendix B) are working closely with the Park Service to mini-mize the impact of what hikers would call "development" but residents of Appalachia often call "economic opportunity." For many of them, that opportunity has been a long time coming.

Fittingly, this part of the road is where human habitation of the mountains—and the culture of the mountain people—truly seems to stand out. This part of the road may come closest to fusing the Parkway's interpretation of the past with a sense of the present and future.

You'll see the Parkway's pioneer cabins and structures everywhere (most often on the trails in this book) and even "meet" some of the people who lived in them. Mabry Mill; Cool Spring Baptist Church; and Mathews, Trails, Puckett, Brinegar, Caudill, and Jesse Brown Cabins stand like silent portals to the past. Not all are exhibits. As you motor by, you may not even glimpse Sheets Cabin standing alone below the road at Milepost 252.3—with no nearby parking lot. You'll see fences, too, especially at the Groundhog Mountain exhibit. During the official season, living-history interpreters movingly personify this "land of do without" lifestyle.

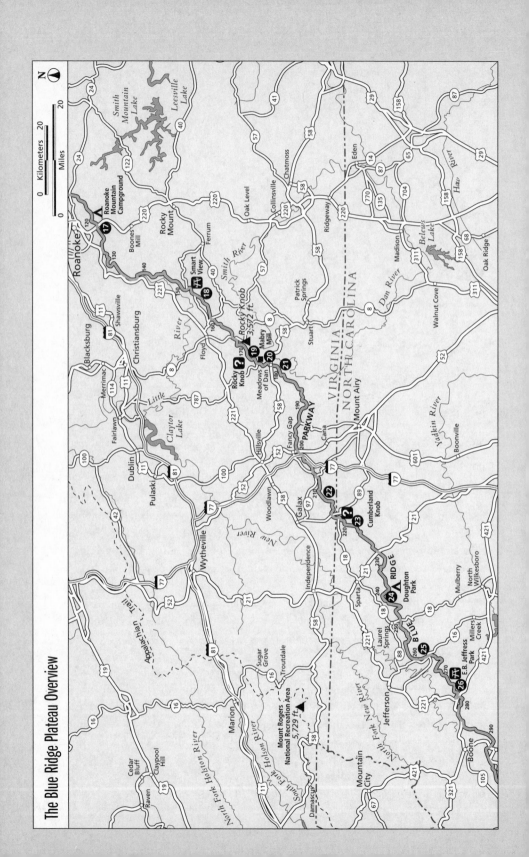

The Blue Ridge Plateau Overview

Even serious hikers will find something of interest at Parkway craft shops.

You'll see historic structures when you hike into Rock Castle Gorge (Milepost 167) or the backcountry of Doughton Park (Milepost 239), but there's more. You'll see where fields are becoming forests again. You'll see nature reclaiming a hardscrabble landscape where people struggled for generations attempting to make a living. Rock walls and stone chimneys are their monuments.

The people who once lived here are gone, but their progeny work or own businesses in the tourism and other industries, including Christmas tree farms, that you'll see all around you. They display their crafts at the Northwest Trading Post (Milepost 258.7), and the traditional mountain music so recently resurgent as a part of the country music scene is featured stunningly in one of the Parkway's newest facilities, the Blue Ridge Music Center (Milepost 213). Extensive exhibits complement the music center's in-season schedule of popular outdoor concerts. Not far off the road, from Galax (the Old Time Fiddler's Convention, second weekend in August) to Wilkesboro (MerleFest, last weekend of April), real music events still do what they've always done—tempt people, including Parkway tourists, out of the hollows.

The long list of major Parkway service sites on this 155-mile stretch include Smart View Picnic Area (Milepost 154.5), Rocky Knob Campground (Milepost 167.1) and Picnic Area (Milepost 169), Mabry Mill (Milepost 176.2), and Groundhog Mountain Picnic Area (Milepost 188.8)—and those are just to the Virginia–North Carolina state line at Milepost 216.9.

In North Carolina, Cumberland Knob Picnic Area (Milepost 217.5) is where Parkway construction started in 1935—75 years ago in 2010. Doughton Park is next, with a campground (Milepost 239.2), accommodations at Bluffs Lodge, a restaurant, and a picnic area (Milepost 241.1).

With so much private land along the road, this section has a wealth of smaller roads that come and go. Take a chance and explore a few of the public ones. There are surprises. The mountain town of Floyd, Virginia (Mileposts 158.9 and 159.3), is a destination on "The Crooked Road, Virginia Music Heritage Trail"—a 250-mile drive that crosses the Parkway and includes the Blue Ridge Music Center. There's great atmosphere and live music at Floyd Country Store. Nearby Chateau Morrissette's tours and tastings (Milepost 171.5) give a nod to the growing Blue Ridge region wine industry—with a reliably gourmet restaurant and vintages produced on premises.

The Mayberry Trading Post (Milepost 180.5) and the cluster of services at Fancy Gap (Milepost 199.4) are enjoyably oriented to tourism.

Check appendix B for a wealth of relevant Web sites and contact information.

17 Buck Mountain Trail

Milepost 123.2

A scenic trail made all the more fascinating by the fact that you can still see evidence of a 2001 forest fire.

Parkway mile: 123.2
Distance: 1.0 mile lollipop
Difficulty: Moderate to strenuous
Elevation gain: 300 feet

Maps: *USGS Garden City;* Parkway's Roanoke Valley Trails overview map, available in season at Roanoke Mountain Campground

Finding the trailhead: Park at Buck Mountain Overlook.

The Hike

In late 2001 a substantial fire burned this part of the Parkway and adjoining lands. The damage was severe enough that some hot spots no doubt destroyed major trees. Many standing burned trees were cut, perhaps as part of the firefighting effort. Fire

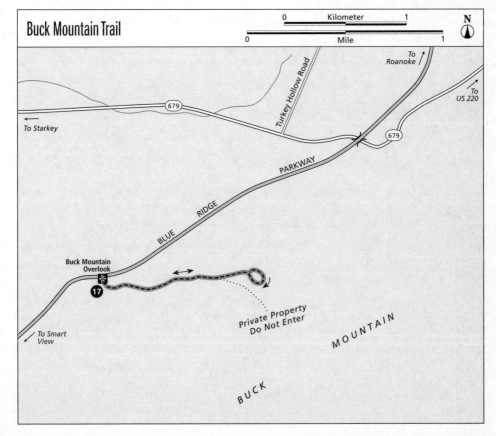

lines are still visible at various places along the trail. It will be years before all evidence of the fire is gone.

The paved trail rises out of the parking area and arcs up and left (eastward) over concrete water bars. The bluish-gray–blazed path stays to the left of the ridgeline, and the telltale red-tree blazes of a Forest Service property line appear just to the right of the trail.

At 0.3 mile there's a bench on the left with a partial view. Higher, the trail slides off to the right of the ridge. There's a major split in the trail at 0.4 mile where a well-used path goes right and may look like the start of a loop. It's not. This side trail dips off to the nearby gap then steeply climbs past NO TRESPASSING signs to the summit of Buck Mountain.

Go left on the Parkway trail with the faint bluish-gray blazes. Just above the junction, an obvious concrete National Park Service boundary post sits to the right of the trail. Bearing left, then right, the path again splits, this time into a tiny summit loop that encircles the rounded little mountaintop. Though there's no real view, it's a pleasant spot. There's a bench on the left branch of the loop.

Key Points

0.3 Bench to left of trail.

0.4 Stay left at major trail split—trail to right trespasses to summit of ridgeline.

0.5 Circle the tiny summit loop.

18 Smart View Loop Trail

Milepost 154.5

A picnic area loop that offers more, this trail mixes meadows with a deep stream drainage, a visit to a century-old cabin, and a wander through scenic forests.

Parkway mile: 154.5
Distance: Loops of 3.0, 2.1, and 1.6 miles
Difficulty: Moderate

Elevation gain: About 160 feet
Maps: *USGS Endicott;* no Parkway map
available

Finding the trailhead: Park immediately off the Parkway in the lot at the gate that closes the picnic area in winter. You can also park at the Smart View Overlook for a longer hike and the Trails Cabin Parking Area for a shorter walk.

The Hike

Start the hike through a fat-man squeeze in the fence to the left of the trail map sign. Strike off across the meadow to the northeast and pass a trail post and a bench at the woods line. The trail rises into the woods along a fence to a signed trail junction on the right at 0.2 mile. A right leads over a stile to the picnic area and a restroom visible

A wet, late-winter day lends a special atmosphere to the Parkway's historic cabins.

in the distance. Continue along a split-rail fence, then barbed wire. The trail continues away from the Parkway, dipping along a now-grassy path to a trail junction and a bench on the right at 0.4 mile. Straight ahead, the trail passes more trail posts and dips below then swings left into the Smart View Overlook. (Starting there adds 0.2 mile to the longest and shortest hikes described.)

Don't go to the overlook. Instead turn right at the trail junction and pass through a fat-man squeeze in the split-rail fence. The path dips down and bears right below the picnic area above a stream drainage that plummets left. The trail veers right into a side tributary, goes under a power line, then switchbacks left to cross a split-log bridge at 0.6 mile. Descending past the junction of two streams at a large rhododendron, the trail steepens its rise and emerges from the stream valley to switchback twice and turn right along the front of the Blue Ridge. The trail then levels off and rises again along the left side of the picnic area. Grills and distinctive rock-pedestal picnic tables appear on the right, and a large quartz rock announces the crest.

At 1.0 mile the trail swings past a paved and signed access to the easternmost bulge of the picnic loop beside a roofed picnic shelter and across from a restroom. Veering left, the trail swings above what in leafless times is a dramatic drop. Turning back toward the picnic area past old fence posts and a meadow, a side trail goes right to the picnic loop; just beyond, the main path reaches Trails Cabin at 1.2 miles. The unchinked cabin, built in the 1890s by the appropriately named Trail family, perches atop a wonderful view—"a right smart view" in the namesake vernacular of the region. From the cabin, a trail rises a short way along a split-rail fence to a parking area that permits easy access.

Continue the trail past a bench in front of the cabin. The trail dips down and around the ridge to a stream spanned by a nice stone bridge at 1.3 miles. The trail continues right toward a little meadow beside the picnic loop road and then switchbacks left back into the woods. At the switchback near the roadside, a sign points out to a small pond across the road. Walk the road a short distance in that direction back to your car to shorten the hike.

Go left on the switchback away from the stream crossing and around the ridge on a rock-underlain treadway. The trail crests above the pond and its noisy residents. Your parking area can be seen off to the right. Past a bench, the trail flattens in a tall pine forest. At 1.4 miles a signed trail goes right. This trail bisects the last part of the loop through the pines to your parking area (see the end of the entry for this option).

The pinewoods decrease in size as the loop descends away from the picnic area down a broadening ridge. The path rises around a few promontories left of the trail and continues level for some distance through a scenic area of big hardwoods, a fringed understory of pine, and a substantial carpet of running cedar. The trail goes left, back toward the edge of the Blue Ridge, then swings broadly right at 2.2 miles around and above Cannaday Gap, heading back to the picnic area. The dirt road through the gap appears below.

The Parkway comes in on the left, and the trail slides below a scenic, moss-

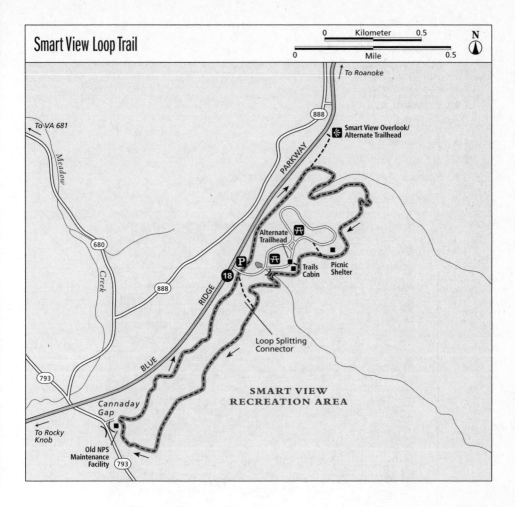

0   Kilometer   0.5

0   Mile   0.5

N

To Roanoke

888

Smart View Overlook/
Alternate Trailhead

To VA 681

PARKWAY

Meadow

680

Alternate
Trailhead

Trails
Cabin

Picnic
Shelter

18

888

Creek

RIDGE

Loop Splitting
Connector

BLUE

793

SMART VIEW
RECREATION AREA

Cannaday
Gap

To Rocky
Knob

Old NPS
Maintenance
Facility   793

covered outcrop through a forest dotted with hemlocks and quartz boulders. Past a bench, the path climbs through towering shagbark hickory and white pine. A signed junction on the right at 2.9 miles is the trail you passed earlier that bisected the loop. Go left through a fat-man squeeze and cross the picnic access road to your car.

To shorten this hike to an easier 2.1-mile loop that avoids the drainage and pairs the cabin with the best forest walking, start at the Trails Cabin parking area. Check out the cabin and then go right on the loop in the direction described above. Pass the trail that bisects the loop; when you encounter the trail again, at its second junction, turn right and bisect the loop back to the trail you just hiked. Go left at that junction back to the cabin and your car.

The stream-drainage (north) side of the loop can be a 1.6-mile hike from the original parking area. Take that hike in the above direction, but again use the trail that bisects the loop and return to the parking area beside the Parkway.

Key Points

0.2 Pass stile and side trail to restroom.

0.4 Turn right over stile.

0.6 Split-log bridge.

1.0 Access to picnic area.

1.2 Trails Cabin.

1.3 Stone bridge.

1.4 Trail bisects loop back to parking.

2.2 Trail turns back toward picnic area above Cannaday Gap.

2.9 Left to parking or right back to loop and cabin.

You'll see groundhogs all along the Parkway, often casually snacking atop roadside stone walls.

19 Rocky Knob Recreation Area

Mileposts 165.3–169.0

Like Doughton Park in North Carolina (Mileposts 238–245), Virginia's 3,589-acre Rocky Knob Recreation Area is a backcountry bulge from the Parkway that contains a trail system extensive enough to permit backpack camping. But unlike Doughton, with its various circuit hiking options, the 10.6-mile Rock Castle Gorge Trail is simply one big loop.

That makes it a strenuous day hike (except in sections). At first glance, backpacking trips seem similarly difficult, largely because the logical place to start, in the valley, is the location of the backcountry campsite where you should be ending up after a day on the trail. On second glance, some backpackers might like this arrangement. Start at the top and arrive at the campsite after a largely downhill hike. That means a significant climb back up the next morning—but your pack should be lighter. Best of all, if a long backpacking trip is not what you want, the backcountry site is so close to the trailhead that it makes a wonderfully accessible place for a quick overnighter.

Rocky Knob boasts a wonderful mix of high-elevation meadows, craggy-summit views, deep coves, scenic streams, and startling reminders that this and many a now-wild Appalachian wilderness were once places where mountain families lived out their lives. You will be startled into head-shaking wonderment at where people chose to establish farms.

Besides a Park Service campground and picnic area, you'll also find seven rustic cabins for rent. These classic Civilian Conservation Corps (CCC) structures are a rich part of the corps' heritage that you find nationwide in state parks, forests, and wherever the corps worked to wrest a legacy of service from the Great Depression. The corps labored to build the Parkway, too, and Rocky Knob's backcountry campsite is their former camp on Rock Castle Creek.

Though most people are likely to tackle the Rock Castle Gorge Trail in sections, a few other trails—the Black Ridge Trail for instance—coincide with parts of the Rock Castle Gorge Trail, further obviating the need to stick with the path for its full 10.6 miles. The options below treat the Rock Castle Gorge Trail first as a series of shorter day hikes.

Best bets include an out-and-back from the valley up Rock Castle Creek or Little Rock Castle Creek—perhaps as day hikes while spending a few nights at the backcountry campsite. Another good option would be a hike to the summit of Rocky Knob from a nearby overlook or from the vicinity of the backcountry campsite. And if you do hike the entire loop, up Little Rock Castle Creek from the backcountry campsite is the way to do it. It's pretty much all downhill from Rocky Knob.

If you choose to backpack, two overlooks make nice starting points for the backcountry campsite and do not require an overly long hike out the next day. Twelve O'Clock Knob permits a 5.1-mile hike to the campsite and an uphill return of 5.5

miles. From Rock Castle Gorge Overlook, it's 4.6 miles to the campsite and 6.0 miles back.

Option 1: Rock Castle Gorge Day Hikes

A streamside exploration of a scenic valley imparts a startling sense of what life was like for early-twentieth-century mountaineers.

Parkway mile: 165.3
Distance: 5.4 miles out and back to chimney; 10.6-mile loop
Difficulty: Moderate to strenuous

Elevation gain: 1,050 feet
Maps: *USGS Woolwine;* Parkway handout map, available in season at the visitor center and other facilities

Finding the trailhead: To start the Rock Castle Gorge Trail near the backcountry campsite, go east on VA 8 from Tuggle Gap (Milepost 165.3) and turn right at the bottom of the hill onto VA 605. Park at the end of this dirt road.

The Hikes

A day hike along Rock Castle Creek is one of the area's best. Leaving the parking area on VA 605, cross the gated bridge; the rugged, green-blazed Rock Castle Gorge Trail wanders for nearly 3.0 miles ever higher up the valley. Almost immediately,

The Austin House vividly recalls the isolated lifestyle of long ago in Appalachian hollows.

the higher-elevation side of the loop trail goes right and follows Little Rock Castle Creek. This is the best route if the entire loop hike is your goal (see Option 1a). Staying left in the valley, after a few short climbs you reach a long streamside stretch that leads into the broad flat of the old CCC camp at 0.3 mile. There's a privy and a variety of campsites—all with grills, many with benches.

The road climbs in steps, with Twelve O'Clock Knob on the high left (2,842 feet). Sycamores and copious quartz outcrops are everywhere. The prevalent six-sided quartz crystals reminded residents of castle towers; hence the name of the gorge. A half mile above the campsite, the road appears less traveled. The first stream crossing (1.2 miles) passes over one of four impressive metal bridges along the trail. The trail climbs steeply then levels with downstream valley views.

At 1.5 miles you enter a private inholding and come upon a barn and an early-twentieth-century white clapboard house with a privy and outbuildings. This is the Austin House, the only home in the gorge today. Built in 1916, it was the finest house in a community of thirty-plus families. The population dwindled when wage-paying industries came to surrounding communities and undermined a lifestyle of subsistence farming focused on growing oats, corn, buckwheat, apples, and the cash crop, chestnuts. The farm is a reminder of human transience—especially with jonquils announcing another spring in a long-untended garden.

Opposite the house, rough fields lie across the river. In the higher meadow to the left across the bridge, a stone wall enclosure makes a nice focal point for a picnic (but camping is not permitted). A return to your car from here is a moderate 3.0-mile day hike.

Back into the now rhododendron-filled forest, the road narrows with the valley and crosses another bridge back to the right of the stream at 1.7 miles. Soon another bridge crosses back to the left and the old road rises steeply and repeatedly, with great views straight down on the creek. A gorge forms to the right, and the road continues steeply, rising above it with views out the end of the valley.

Just beyond a bench at 2.4 miles, Rock Castle Cascades splash off the cliffs and shower down to the left of the roadside. The trail continues to gain and then crests at a junction and another bench. Left, the grade of the road continues much more gradually along Rock Castle Creek to a gate at the Rocky Knob cabins. Right, the Rock Castle Gorge Trail turns on its way to the Parkway and the high part of the loop. It first descends to another bench and the fourth metal bridge at 2.6 miles.

This makes another nice turnaround point, for a strenuous 5.2-mile day hike. But go just a bit farther. The upcoming 0.8-mile portion of the Rock Castle Gorge Trail used to be called the Hardwood Cove Nature Trail. A brochure, now out of print, used to interpret the uses for the trees along the trail. Just bring your tree book and head up the trail a short way, around at least a few more ridges, where a stout chimney stands alone in the woods. Imagine making a living here. This turnaround spot makes a 5.4-mile day hike. Or stick with it for another 0.1 mile or so to Bare Rocks—a major rib of boulders. From here it's only 1.8 miles farther to the junction with Black Ridge Trail and the crest portion of the Rock Castle Gorge Trail.

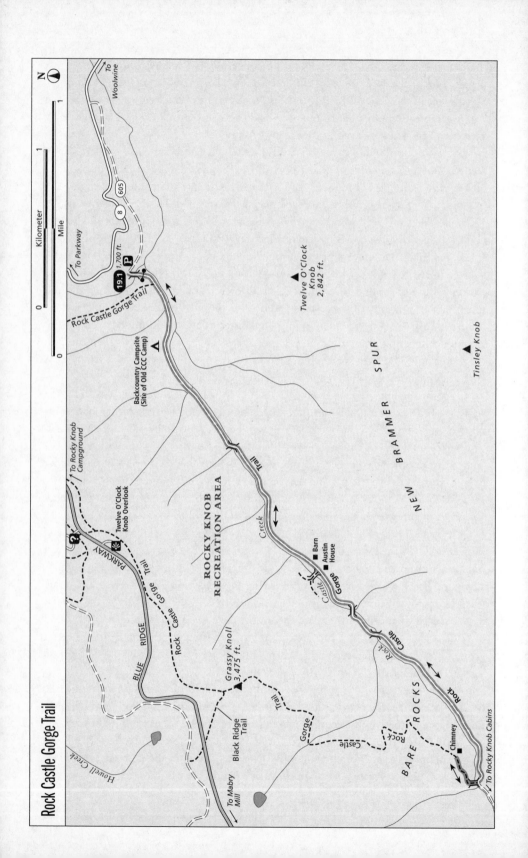

Rock Castle Gorge Trail

N

Kilometer

Mile

To Woolwine

To
Woolwine

605

8

To Parkway

19.1 1,700 ft.

P

Rock Castle Gorge Trail

Twelve O'Clock
Knob
2,842 ft.

Tinsley Knob

NEW   BRAMMER   SPUR

Backcountry Campsite
(Site of Old CCC Camp)

To Rocky Knob
Campground

Twelve O'Clock
Knob Overlook

PARKWAY

ROCKY KNOB
RECREATION AREA

Rock Castle Gorge Trail

BLUE RIDGE

Creek

Trail

Castle

Castle

Gorge

Barn

Austin
House

Rock

Castle

Rock

BARE ROCKS

Grassy Knoll
3,475 ft.

Black Ridge Trail

Gorge

Trail

Castle

Rock

Chimney

To Rocky Knob Cabins

Howell Creek

To Mabry
Mill

Key Points

0.3 CCC backcountry campsite.

1.2 Cross first bridge.

1.5 Arrive at the Austin House.

1.7 Cross second bridge and third bridge, 0.1 beyond.

2.4 Rock Castle Cascades shower left side of the trail.

2.6 Final bridge at bench; start of the former Hardwood Cove Nature Trail.

2.7 Chimney at old homesite.

Option 1a

An option from the same trailhead as the above hike is a walk up (north on) Little Rock Castle Creek (the opposite direction of the hike above, were you to make the entire loop). This is one of the least-used portions of the Rock Castle Gorge Trail and makes a nice uphill streamside hike to the meadows opposite the campground and even to the top of Rocky Knob. (See Option 2: Rocky Knob Day Hikes for more.) This is the direction to go to hike the entire loop. To the campground meadows, a hike up Little Rock Castle Creek is a 6.0-mile round-trip. On the way, you pass many benches for resting and more evidence of farming activity. Add the loop of Rocky Knob described below, and at 8.3 miles this hike becomes one of the area's most diverse longer walks—summit views and streamside hiking that's lacking on the hike up Rock Castle Creek. To the meadows the rise is 1,390 feet. To the summit of Rocky Knob, it's a stiff and strenuous 1,869 feet.

Option 2: Rocky Knob Day Hikes

A few day hikes climb to Rocky Knob's signature summit, one across scenic grassy meadows.

Parkway mile: 168
Distance: 1.1-mile loop from Saddle Overlook; 2.3-mile loop from campground
Difficulty: Easy to moderate

Elevation gain: 190 feet and 480 feet
Maps: *USGS Woolwine*; Parkway handout map, available in season at the visitor center and other facilities

---

Finding the trailhead: The trail leaves the south end of the Saddle Overlook. To park at the campground, leave your car near the entrance and walk directly across the Parkway—the fat-man squeeze provides a route through the fence. Turn right; signs direct hikers through the meadows.

To start at the picnic area, park at the visitor center. Pull past the building on the right and turn left into the lot before entering the picnic area. Walk across the road you took into the lot behind the visitor center and follow the yellow-blazed Picnic Loop Trail east.

The Hikes

Rocky Knob's namesake summit is known for some of the area's best views, especially of Rock Castle Gorge. Indeed, the entire crest of the Parkway across the Rocky Knob

The Appalachian Trail has relocated far to the west, but one of its earliest shelters still sits atop Rocky Knob.

area is a succession of meadow vistas. And there is also a historical oddity—the shelter on the summit of Rocky Knob was an Appalachian Trail shelter before Parkway construction forced the path far to the west. Ironically, when that relocation occurred, even the Blue Ridge Parkway was considered just another road destroying a trail.

Saddle Overlook is the best starting point for the easiest hike over Rocky Knob. Head south out of the overlook; when the green-blazed Rock Castle Gorge Trail goes left to climb the peak, bear right onto the easy, red-blazed side trail that avoids the summit. Another red-blazed side trail links left toward the summit trail—stay right. In 0.5 mile turn left; the trail climbs steeply to the crest of the ridge. Dipping through a swale on the crest, the path runs to the summit (3,572 feet) and the shelter at 0.9 mile. Descending steeply off the peak toward the Saddle Overlook, pass an intersection with the red-blazed linking trail. Rejoin the side trail that bypassed the peak, returning to the Saddle Overlook at 1.1 miles. This hike gains only 190 feet of elevation.

Extend the Saddle Overlook walk by starting farther north at the Rocky Knob Campground. That option adds another 1.2 miles for a 2.3-mile hike that includes summit views but begins and ends with wonderful meadow scenery. The elevation gain is still moderate at 480 feet. Start from the campground entrance, cross the road, and pass through the split-rail fence at a fat-man squeeze to a signed junction. Posts with arrows direct the route in either direction over the grassy areas. Left, the trail descends Little Rock Castle Creek 3.0 miles to the vicinity of the backcountry campsite. (See the end of the Rock Castle Gorge option. Starting there creates one of the best day hikes, at 8.3 miles.)

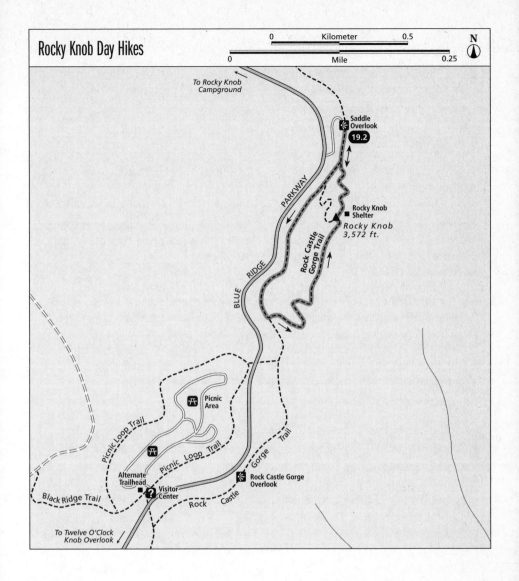

Turn right; the trail climbs the meadows with expanding views along the way. Cross a fence at the edge of the meadow at 0.3 mile and gain a small knob in another 0.1 mile. From there the trail descends to the north end of the Saddle Overlook at 0.6 mile. Do the loop described above for a 2.3-mile hike.

If you just stay left on the Rock Castle Gorge Trail, hit the shelter and summit and return, the trek is only 0.8 mile to the top, for a 1.6-mile hike.

You can start farther south; see the Rocky Knob Picnic Loop (Option 4) for that option.

Key Points from Saddle Overlook

0.05 Bear right on trail bypassing summit.

0.5 Turn left onto Rock Castle Gorge Trail to peak.

0.9 Reach summit of Rocky Knob.

1.1 Return to parking lot.

Option 3: Black Ridge Trail

This loop has a little bit of everything—dense forest, an old homestead, forest roads, and outstanding meadow views.

Parkway mile: 169
Distance: 3.1-mile loop
Difficulty: Moderate
Elevation gain: 486 feet

Maps: USGS Woolwine; Parkway handout map, available in season at the visitor center and other facilities

---

Finding the trailhead: Drive past the right side of the visitor center and turn left into the parking lot before entering the picnic area. To reach the Black Ridge Trail, walk across the grass from the lot toward the Parkway and to the right of the visitor center. Turn right at the trail signpost with a yellow arrow beside the building (technically the yellow-blazed Picnic Loop) and head into the woods. A blue-blazed trail heads left to and then across the Parkway (your return route for the Black Ridge Trail). Stay right; the trail is now a blue- and yellow-blazed combination trail.

The Hike

It's a bit hard to locate the trailhead for this hike (hence the detailed directions above). Heading away from the visitor center on the now blue- and yellow-blazed combination trail, the path weaves along a power line then descends through open woods. At 0.2 mile veer left on the blue-blazed trail where the yellow-blazed trail goes right into a meadow on its way around the picnic area.

The trail gets rockier on the descent through areas of running cedar then swings into and along a power line right-of-way that's full of beautiful ferns and mossy logs. A quiet brook appears off to the left. On the right, a towering chimney marks a cabin site at 0.4 mile. Here's as good a place as any to wonder about the people who lived here before the Parkway. With warm fertile valleys not so far away, someone chose this high, inhospitable place to scratch out a living. Cold fog, dreary mist, and winter snow all frequent this north-facing slope. Families waited up here for the three or four warmer months in a centuries-long experiment that eventually ended on the highest peaks and focused on valleys where agriculture was more practical.

Just past the chimney, the trail reaches a T junction with an old road grade that shows evidence of occasional use. Turning left, the trail hops the stream and follows the steep, at times eroded road through a not-so-scenic area. Note the huge burl at the base of a tree on the way up the first rise.

Eventually the road levels, becomes grass and moss covered, and parallels a fence-line beside expansive meadows with a high-elevation feel and extensive views to the right. The adjoining meadow has outcrops close to the trail that would make wonderful picnic viewpoints. (Be respectful—portions of this road lie on private property.)

The road continues to rise into hemlocks and rhododendron and turns right to closely parallel the Parkway. Passing a shed and a gate, the road swings right, away from the Parkway, and appears to be more frequently used by vehicles. Just past the start of a white wooden fence on the right at 1.5 miles, the path exits the road at a trail marker post that points left. Following trail posts across the crest of the meadow, the Parkway appears at 1.6 miles. Cross the road, climb the stile over the split-rail fence, and set off up Grassy Knoll.

This is high, scenic country. It can also be very foggy. If you cross the stile in zero visibility, set off straight into the meadow in the direction the steps are pointing (but bear just slightly right). In 100 feet you'll cross an odd depression. Walk between the two rocks that lie within it; not far beyond in the fog, you'll see the first blue-arrow trail post.

The posts cross the meadow and rise slowly to join an old grade along a fenceline on the right. Near the crest of the meadow, signs announce that the green-blazed Rock Castle Gorge Trail comes in from the right at 1.8 miles. Together the two paths turn left along the fenceline following posts with blue and green arrows. Protruding rocks, a bench—and cow pies—dot the meadow. Following the fenceline near the woods, the trail crosses a stile at 2.2 miles, dips into the forest around a ridge, bears left, and follows a lower meadow. Soon you're just to the right of the Parkway.

After veering away and climbing around a ridgeline, the trail passes a confusing connection to Twelve O'Clock Knob Overlook. At a sign that directs you ahead and behind on the trail you're hiking, an unmarked side trail goes left to the overlook. (See the map to get your bearings and see how another path from the overlook leads to an upcoming junction with the Black Ridge Trail.)

Staying on the main trail past the Twelve O'Clock Knob Overlook side trail, the path dips below the lot to a junction at 2.9 miles. The Rock Castle Gorge Trail heads off to the right for Rocky Knob. Go left; the blue-blazed Black Ridge Trail rises into the meadow. The formal trail from Twelve O'Clock Knob Overlook joins from the left as you continue up the grass to the Parkway roadside.

Here you could ascend the obvious trail steps, but instead cross the road into the visitor center driveway and walk across the grass to the left of the building to your car at 3.1 miles.

Key Points

0.2 Bear left when Picnic Loop goes right.

0.4 Old cabin site; left onto dirt road just beyond.

1.5 Turn left from road into meadow.

1.6 Cross Parkway.

Black Ridge and Picnic Loop Trails

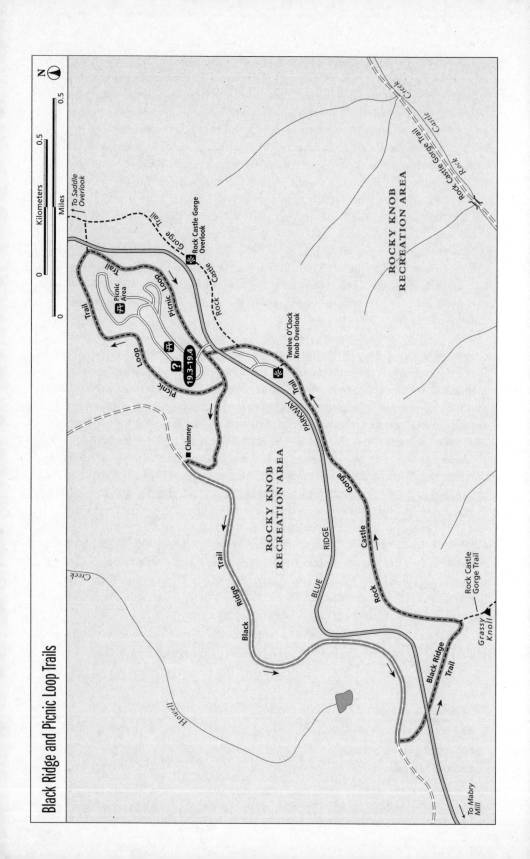

1.8 Turn left with Rock Castle Gorge Trail at signed junction near meadow summit.

2.2 Cross fence.

2.9 Turn left to Parkway and parking area when Rock Castle Gorge Trail goes right.

Option 4: Rocky Knob Picnic Loop

This easy loop around the picnic area makes a nice start to a hike up Rocky Knob.

See map on page 128.
Parkway mile: 169
Distance: 1.3-mile loop; 2.7- and 3.2-mile hikes that include the circuit over the summit of Rocky Knob

Difficulty: Easy
Elevation gain: 120 feet
Maps: *USGS Woolwine;* Parkway handout map, available in season at the visitor center and other facilities

Finding the trailhead: Drive past the right side of the visitor center and turn left into the parking lot before entering the picnic area. Two access points are possible.

To go to the west, walk toward the Parkway, across the grass from the lot to the right of the visitor center. Turn right at the trail signpost with a yellow arrow beside the building. Head into the woods and pass the blue-blazed Black Ridge Trail that goes left, staying right on the now blue- and yellow-blazed combination trail. The Picnic Loop soon turns right off that trail.

To take the Picnic Loop east, which is a nice way to start a hike to Rocky Knob, walk across the road you took into the lot behind the visitor center and follow the yellow-blazed trail.

The Hike

This is your basic picnic area loop through a scenic higher–elevation forest. Heading west, the yellow–blazed trail veers right, away from the Black Ridge Trail at 0.2 mile. (For a nice side trip, an old cabin site is just 0.2 mile left on the Black Ridge Trail.) Going right, the Picnic Loop wanders below and around the picnic area through hemlock and hardwood forest. Cross a small stream and the trail turns right toward the Parkway. After a bit of a climb at 0.9 mile, the red–blazed connector to Rocky Knob goes left, reaching the summit loop in 0.3 mile. Continue right and back to the lot for a 1.3-mile hike. Hiking the loop this way and adding a circuit over the summit of Rocky Knob is a neat option for a 3.2-mile hike.

Going the opposite direction, east from the visitor center, the connector to Rocky Knob peels off at 0.4 mile from the start. That permits a 2.7-mile hike over the summit—one of the best ways to tackle Rocky Knob.

Key Points Going West

0.2 Bear right where blue-blazed trail goes left.

0.9 Red-blazed trail goes left to Rocky Knob.

20 Mountain Industry Trail at Mabry Mill

Milepost 176.2

This highly developed and popular paved path (wheelchair accessible) explores a virtual mountain community. Mabry Mill, probably the Parkway's most photographed site, is surrounded by historic structures and informative exhibits about the early Appalachian economy.

Parkway mile: 176.2
Distance: 0.5-mile loop
Difficulty: Easy
Elevation gain: Negligible

Maps: *USGS Meadows of Dan;* Parkway trail map, available in season at the Mabry Mill restaurant/gift shop

Finding the trailhead: Parking is available at the restaurant/gift shop. Access to overflow parking lots is signed on the Parkway from both directions. See the accompanying map.

The Hike

How popular is this trail? One indication is that two Parkway trail maps are printed—one oriented from the restaurant/gift shop, the other from the overflow parking lot. Signs at those sites mirror the maps.

But don't let tour buses deter you. This trail features what is perhaps the Parkway's most photographed site, Mabry Mill—a scene notoriously claimed by postcards from states other than Virginia. A stop here also impresses with what is surely one of the more

The quintessential Parkway interpretive path surrounds postcard-scenic Mabry Mill.

complex systems of water flumes ever devised to feed an otherwise primitive water-powered facility. Indeed, Mabry Mill and the blacksmith shop are no relocated historic structures, as some are along the Parkway. This is their original, if landscaped, location. Surrounding structures—including an 1869 cabin—as well as a variety of implements were collected here in the 1940s and 1950s. Together they tell a compelling tale.

Before taking the trail, check out the shop and restaurant. (A few dining alternatives are close by on US 58 at Meadows of Dan, a recommended stop.)

Mabry Mill is among the most active interpretive sites on the Parkway. Signs throughout the area explain the exhibits, and during the warmer months, this is one of the Parkway's principal living-history sites. The gristmill often operates Friday through Sunday, and interpreters offer talks about the process. Blacksmithing demonstrations occur Wednesday through Sunday, and weaving and spinning take place at various times. Mountain music and dancing bring out the locals from 2:00 to 5:00 p.m. on Sunday.

Edwin Mabry, a miner, blacksmith, and chair maker, built the mill in 1910. He and his wife, Mintoria Lizzie Mabry, lived here until 1936, grinding corn for the Meadows of Dan community. In 1945 the National Park Service restored and landscaped the mill. Significant restoration of the structure took place over winter 2002 through the user fees that Congress allowed the Park Service to charge.

Starting at the mill side of the restaurant/gift shop, pass the NO PICNICKING sign and pause on the left at the paved patio. This is the quintessential view of Mabry Mill.

Head left at the first junction—the prescribed way to go. A short side trail veers left 100 feet beyond and showcases the action of the overshot wheel. Going uphill, take the boardwalk left along one of the many wooden aqueducts that permit this water-hungry mill to work so well. This is one of the auxiliary water sources that feed the main millrace—a necessity because this mill does not gain sufficient waterpower from its main stream. You'll see the origin of this side source of water, and perhaps gain a better understanding of Mabry's ingenious system, on the way back.

Off the boardwalk, turn left and go through the blacksmith shop and down to the mill. On the way you'll learn that the Mabrys eventually employed an engine to turn the wheel, just before the wide availability of flour from roller mills around the country made gristmills obsolete. Beyond the mill is a display of millstones.

Turn right along the Parkway and you'll next encounter a log cart used to haul timber. Not far beyond is one of the Parkway's neatest cabins—the Matthews Cabin. Built near Galax in 1869, the rustic structure was donated to the Parkway and moved here in 1956 after its metal roofing and outer weatherboarding were removed. In season you can go inside to see cloth being woven on an old loom. The Mabrys built a frame house on this site in 1914—not uncommon at the time due to the prevalence of small sawmills in rural areas. Hikers in the nearby Rocky Knob Recreation Area can see a home from that same era, the Austin House, just 1.5 miles from the lower trailhead on the Rock Castle Gorge Trail.

Past the cabin is a bark mill, a horse-powered machine that would grind oak and hemlock bark for tannin used to make bark liquor (a tanning treatment for hides).

Not far beyond, look over the edge of the bluff and down on the creekside makings of a different kind of liquor—a moonshine still. An illustration depicts how corn was efficiently turned into a portable, and potable, commodity—corn whiskey.

Corn meal, malt, and sugar were mixed with water and fermented in barrels like the ones you see to the right when you look down. When the fermented mash, called beer, was ready (the process can take two weeks), it was heated in the copper still atop the stone-lined furnace. The vapors would condense in a coil immersed in constantly circling cold water. The liquid then collected in a bucket and was usually run through the still twice to enhance its potency. Up to twenty gallons of corn whiskey could be produced in a night. Water was a key to the process in these well-watered mountains. If you look beyond the still, you'll see the dam that feeds the second of the mill's two flumes.

Continuing, the trail crosses the stream and then makes a right turn. A left leads to the overflow parking area and comfort station opposite the Parkway side of the mill. Just beyond is a sorghum press, another horse-powered squeezing device used to make the sweet substitute for maple syrup that became popular during the Civil War. Continue right; the evaporator where juice from the squeezing process is cooked sits on the left side of the path (one gallon of syrup is made from ten gallons of extract).

Bearing right, pass a horse-drawn wagon and go left back through the blacksmith's shop. The boardwalk you came in on goes right (the fastest way back to your car). Continue past a variety of plows and farm implements, over the not-so-rushing stream that should be the mill's main water source, and into a forest of white pines to the last leg of the loop. A paved left soon leads in a short distance to VA 603, access to overflow parking on the left by the comfort station, and a more remote employee lot to the right.

Just beyond the turnoff is a great view to the left of the impressive wooden aqueduct that feeds the upper end of the flume at the start of the hike. Off to the left, the neighboring stream that would otherwise rush into the millpond is raised up by a wooden aqueduct and carried to where it flows through the flume beneath you and into the mill's main race. An overflow on the wooden aqueduct permits excess water to spill out. To see how this stream is diverted into the aqueduct, take the paved trail behind you to VA 603 and walk right on the road to where the aqueduct starts behind the visitor center.

Returning, the path dips past the leftward view of the aqueduct. As you descend, remnants of the diverted stream flow to the left of the trail and into the pond at the spot where you started your hike. If you walk away with nothing else, an appreciation of Mabry's system aptly illustrates why the Appalachians have long been called the "land of make-do."

Key Points

0.1 Reach Mabry Mill.

0.25 Turn left to walk road to start of flume.

0.35 Return to trail and go left on last leg to lot.

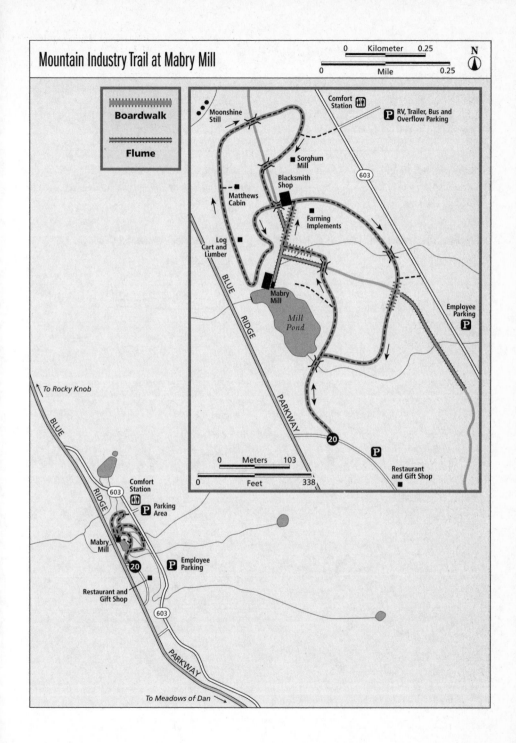

Mountain Industry Trail at Mabry Mill

Boardwalk

Flume

0   Kilometer   0.25

0   Mile   0.25

N

Moonshine Still

Comfort Station

RV, Trailer, Bus and Overflow Parking

603

Sorghum Mill

Blacksmith Shop

Matthews Cabin

Farming Implements

Log Cart and Lumber

Mabry Mill

Mill Pond

Employee Parking

0   Meters   103

0   Feet   338

20

Restaurant and Gift Shop

To Rocky Knob

BLUE RIDGE

603

Comfort Station

Parking Area

Mabry Mill

20

Employee Parking

Restaurant and Gift Shop

603

PARKWAY

BLUE RIDGE PARKWAY

To Meadows of Dan

21 Round Meadow Creek Trail

Milepost 179.2

This short loop hike along a rushing mountain stream is a twenty-minute leg-stretcher that might tempt you to tarry.

Parkway mile: 179.2
Distance: 0.5-mile loop
Difficulty: Easy

Elevation gain: 100 feet
Maps: *USGS Meadows of Dan;* no Parkway map available

Finding the trailhead: Take the right fork of the paved path at Round Meadow Overlook.

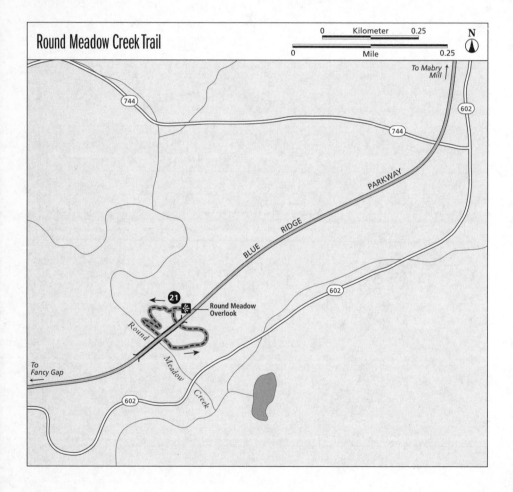

The Hike

The paved treadway soon becomes gravel as it meanders right and down over water bars and log steps. The forest is immediately interesting. A mix of deciduous hardwood trees and evergreen hemlocks, rhododendron, and mountain laurel, it's the quintessential Parkway woodland. Even if the weather hasn't been particularly wet, you'll probably hear the stream rushing below.

Past running cedar, the trail switchbacks to the streambank. At a trail post with arrows, head left on an old road grade along the river. The Parkway span is high above, and the opposite bank is covered in towering hemlocks and dense rhododendron.

Passing far below the bridge, follow a left-pointing arrow off the road grade. The pine needle–covered path strikes off into a white pine and hemlock forest. A state highway is visible off to the right when the leaves are down. The trail arcs up and left, eventually reversing direction back to the Parkway. The bridge you walked far beneath appears ahead. Go under it on a now-paved path; a right turn puts you back in the driver's seat.

Key Points

0.15 Turn left along the river on a road grade.

0.3 Turn left off the road grade.

Even if you're not a traditional music fan, check out the Blue Ridge Music Center's exhibits before hitting the trail.

22 Blue Ridge Music Center

Milepost 213.0

One of the Parkway's newest facilities, the Blue Ridge Music Center is dedicated to the stirring fusion of Irish, English, Scots-Irish, and African music and instruments that came together early in U.S. history to create the nation's traditional music. Exhibits trace Appalachia's early ballad-based music from the 1700s through the early twentieth century emergence of "hillbilly music," then bluegrass, and on to commercial country music and the growing popularity of traditional mountain music.

Musicians appear daily in summer, and there's a weekend concert series from June into autumn in an impressive outdoor amphitheater (dedicated in October 2001 by Ralph Stanley and the Clinch Mountain Boys). The National Council for the Traditional Arts organizes the series; visit www.ncta.net for more information. Two new red-blazed trails explore the surrounding fields and forests of the 1,700-acre park. One offers an out-and-back walk through meadows and wetlands, the other a longer loop hike up to forested Fisher Peak.

Parkway mile: 213

Distance: 2.0-mile out and back; loops of 2.5 and 2.7 miles

Difficulty: Easy to moderate

Elevation gain: 290 feet maximum

Maps: *USGS Lambsurg;* Parkway trail map available at the Music Center

Finding the trailhead: Enter the Music Center at Milepost 213. Continue straight at the intersection with VA 612 to the museum and park in the lot beyond; the trail branches near the left side of the building.

A second trailhead, located on VA 612, can be reached two ways. Leave the museum and go left on VA 612 at the junction you passed on the way in; park at 0.5 mile in the curve at the other trailhead. From the Parkway, turn onto VA 612 at Milepost 213.3 and park at the trailhead in the curve at 0.2 mile. *Note:* The gate to the Music Center trailhead is locked at 5:00 p.m., so it's recommended to start the hike on VA 612.

The Hike

From trailhead to trailhead, the High Meadow Trail runs 1.3 miles under Fisher Peak through fields near the forest edge. The elevation gain is only 100 feet if you want to hike a mile or so out from either trailhead for a round-trip of about 2 miles. Starting at the VA 612 trailhead, you'll skirt meadows and cross a bridge and boardwalk, slab under a rock outcrop in the woods, and cross a wetland bog boardwalk.

Two more bridges cross Chestnut Creek as you near the Music Center. The 1.6-mile Fisher Peak Loop branches from and returns to this lower trail not far from either trailhead. Starting from and returning to the Music Center trailhead, the total loop is 2.5 miles. From the VA 612 trailhead, the total loop is 2.7 miles.

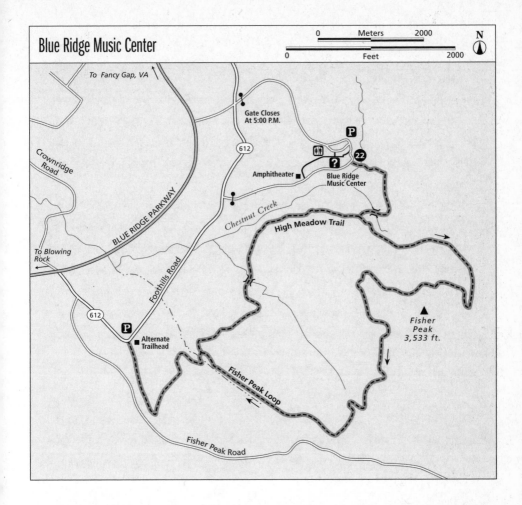

Blue Ridge Music Center

To Fancy Gap, VA

Gate Closes At 5:00 P.M.

Crownridge Road

612

BLUE RIDGE PARKWAY

Amphitheater

Blue Ridge Music Center

22

Chestnut Creek

High Meadow Trail

To Blowing Rock

Foothills Road

612

Alternate Trailhead

Fisher Peak Loop

Fisher Peak Road

Fisher Peak 3,533 ft.

Meters 2000

Feet 2000

N

The trail misses the top of Fisher Peak but explores the richly forested coves at the headwaters of the streams that feed Chestnut Creek. Depending on when you hike, you could hear mountain music echoing up from the hollow below.

THE BIRTH OF THE BLUE RIDGE PARKWAY—
HIGH ROAD TO THE PAST

The earliest parkways—among them New York's Westchester Parkway and the George Washington Memorial Parkway from Washington, D.C., to Mount Vernon, Virginia—were built to merge scenery with speed in an early ideal of motoring as both travel and recreation. That ideal got its start not long after the creation of great urban parks by Frederick Law Olmstead, himself an early Parkway proponent.

The original idea for a Blue Ridge Parkway–style road seems to have originated as far back as 1909 with Joseph Hyde Pratt, director of North Carolina's Geological and Economic Survey. He dreamed up a privately funded ridgetop Appalachian toll road, surveyed portions of a proposed route, and by 1912 had even constructed a section near Linville, North Carolina, that would later become part of the Parkway. The turmoil of World War I put an end to this dream.

By 1930 the possibility of actually building a Blue Ridge Parkway had been furthered by a number of developments. Building scenic roads between national parks had become a topic of discussion, and the Great Depression had prompted legislation permitting the Public Works Administration to build and maintain roads to counter unemployment.

But the Parkway can trace what may be its most immediate precedent to the creation of the Skyline Drive atop the Blue Ridge in Shenandoah National Park. Construction had begun on that 100-mile road in 1931 as a Depression-era relief project, and it wasn't long before the idea surfaced to extend the road into a park-to-park highway between Shenandoah and Great Smoky Mountains National Parks.

That's when the battle over where to locate that Parkway started—a struggle intriguingly detailed in Harley Jolley's highly recommended book, *The Blue Ridge Parkway*. The years-long controversy centered on the Parkway's strong suit—scenery. Virginia got the nod because the road had to start at Shenandoah National Park. But Tennessee and North Carolina were left to duke it out for the Smoky Mountain connection, each claiming the superior scenery.

Interior Secretary Harold Ickes wanted more objective information, so in summer 1934 he sent Forestry Director Robert Marshall to weigh the two routes. Marshall had early on challenged the idea of the Parkway on the grounds that it would further chop up what little wilderness remained. (Montana's Bob Marshall Wilderness today honors the man who ultimately devoted much of his life to wilderness preservation, both in the USDA Forest Service and as a founder of the Wilderness Society.) Marshall reported back to Ickes that he could defend either choice but favored the North Carolina route.

The political maneuvering of the route-selection process climaxed at a September 18, 1934, hearing in Washington, D.C. The Asheville Chamber of Commerce, motivated by a desire to sustain the city's century-long tourist economy, hired a train to pack the hearing. The group appeared to be winning until Tennesseans revealed the supposed secret that Ickes's selection committee had recommended the Tennessee route. But on November 10, 1934, Ickes overruled his own selection committee and gave North Carolina the Parkway (largely due to his opinion that the route was scenically superior). But controversy continued.

Indeed, the entire project—finessed into existence as a relief project by Roosevelt's Public Works Administration—was still in doubt because Congress had never approved it. Then North Carolina Congressman Robert Doughton introduced a bill to formally name the road the Blue Ridge Parkway and transfer control to the National Park Service when completed. On June 20, 1936, by a vote of 145 to 131—with 147 abstaining—the bill barely passed the House.

Parkway construction had already started in North Carolina, heading south from the Virginia state line in September 1935. The first construction in Virginia started south of Roanoke on February 29, 1936. Right-of-way problems and a desire to employ people first in the most economically depressed areas (most workers were unemployed locals) meant that for decades large uncompleted sections of road interrupted the route.

By 1970 the road was complete save for a short section at Grandfather Mountain. This "missing link" wasn't closed—and the Parkway completed—until 1987, two years after the Parkway's fiftieth anniversary. As the Parkway turns seventy-five in 2010, today's Parkway motorists and hikers enjoy a seamlessly scenic journey.

The building of the Parkway was in part intended to stimulate the Southern Appalachian economy. PHOTO BY HUGH MORTON

23 Cumberland Knob Recreation Area

Mileposts 217.5–218.6

Not far south of the Virginia–North Carolina line, an appropriately placed historic marker calls the Parkway "the first rural national parkway." Less than a mile south is Cumberland Knob, the Parkway's first recreation area and the spot where construction of the high road started on September 11, 1935. Cumberland Knob's information building (the Parkway's first "concession stand") and an atmospheric picnic shelter atop the Knob are among the Parkway's earliest structures.

At just about 2,860 feet, the area's namesake summit, Cumberland Knob, isn't a spectacular peak. But the 1,000-acre enclave embraces a wonderfully convoluted watershed that makes a great day hike. Cumberland Knob's primary facilities are a large picnic area and an information/comfort station.

A monument on the plaza in front of the information station honors the Parkway's fiftieth anniversary on September 11, 1985, and memorializes the contributions of the landscape architects who've shaped the park experience. Just a few feet away, a small cemetery reminds visitors how hard life was less than a century ago in these isolated mountains. The earliest of the nineteen graves is 1908. A sign tells of a sixteen-year-old mother-to-be who asked the landowner for permission to be buried under an apple tree on this spot. He assented, thinking that her death was far off. Nevertheless, Rebecca Smith Moxley's grave is here. She died soon after her baby was born.

Option 1: Gully Creek Trail

One of the most worthwhile trails that dip from the Parkway's heights, the Gully Creek Trail explores a topographically intriguing watershed.

Parkway mile: 217.5
Distance: 2.5-mile loop
Difficulty: Strenuous

Elevation gain: 820 feet
Maps: USGS *Cumberland Knob, Virginia/North Carolina;* Parkway handout map available

Finding the trailhead: Park near the information station in the Cumberland Knob Picnic Area.

The Hike

To start the Gully Creek Trail, leave the parking lot and cross the plaza in front of the information station (there's a nice view of Pilot Mountain). A trail sign directs hikers left and right on a two-hour hike it calls WOODLAND TRAIL. Go left of the building and downhill into the woods past trail signs.

One or the other of the two trails to the right will serve as your return from the Gully Creek Trail.

Head left from the WOODLAND TRAIL sign; as you near the Picnic Loop, take the paved trail that turns right and heads downhill.

The trail dips off the ridge and becomes gravelly and gullied. The descent levels out on a ridge at 2,650 feet. That's low for the Parkway, which explains why you soon leave the rhododendron as you turn hard right for the first of many switchbacks down the dry ridge to Gully Creek. Off to the east, two pine-forested ridges pinch in to squeeze the creek's exit from the valley. Beyond lie the green fields of farms, 1,000 feet below.

The trail switchbacks repeatedly on the sunny southeast side of the ridge. In the cleft of an abruptly projecting, rhododendron-covered ridge, the trail makes repeated lefts away from a small stream cascading down mossy slabs of rock. The growing stream continually blocks the trail's route, so the trail winds back and forth until you can hear a larger stream, Gully Creek, tumbling in from the left.

The trail crosses Gully Creek at 0.5 mile on rocks for the first of many times and passes a fern-covered ledge. It skirts under the ridge that blocked the trail higher up. The path crosses to the right of the stream then goes back to the left side on a wooden bridge. At a series of falls at 0.9 mile, stone steps descend then cross the stream to the right. Below and left of the crossing, the water flows back and forth over a series of ledges.

The trail rises above the stream, almost as though you're leaving the drainage, then descends again past flakes of rock that could serve as rain shelters. Down a flight of stone steps to creek level, the path straddles the stream for a few feet, crosses on big rocks, then traverses a steep and saturated seep on a rocky ledge (watch your footing here). Cross the stream again, and the trail levels out deceptively only to again cross to the left at another waterfall. More steps lead down to a pool and another crossing to the right, where you finally rise away from the stream at 1.2 miles. Off to the left, pines cap the portal where Gully Creek escapes into the Piedmont.

The trail rises now through open forest, switchbacking right and left. Dense rhododendron and a steep side slope signal the impending turn around Cumberland Knob's leading ridge. The trail steepens as it crosses the apex of the ridge at 1.4 miles. Here's a lesson in the importance of "aspect" to forest composition. As you round the ridge, bam! The ecosystem changes dramatically—from the lush and mossy rhododendron and hardwood forest of the wetter, colder, more northerly slopes to the dry and sunny southeastern-side forest of mountain laurel and pine, where a carpet of needles scents the air.

The trail switchbacks again to a view back into Gully Creek before arcing left on a steepening climb along the edge. The rocky, pine needle–covered trail levels out briefly across a saddle with sharp drops to the left and right, then rises again over stone steps. A left emerges onto a rocky viewpoint to the south. The second ridgetop on the high right is High Piney Spur, reached by a short paved path just south on the Parkway (see Option 3). Leaving the view, the path slides off the ridgetop to the right, back into rhododendron along the top of a drainage that's so steep the lower side of the treadway had to be elaborately reinforced.

After rejoining the crest of the ridge, the trail levels off along a mossy treadway as it swings right under the bulk of Cumberland Knob. At 2.2 miles a signed junction

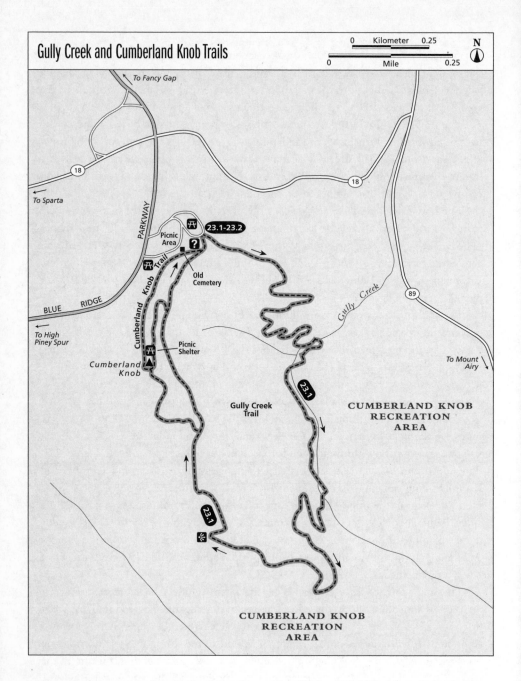

Gully Creek and Cumberland Knob Trails

To Fancy Gap

To Sparta

PARKWAY

18

18

Picnic Area

23.1-23.2

Cumberland Knob Trail

Old Cemetery

BLUE RIDGE

To High Piney Spur

Cumberland Knob

Picnic Shelter

89

Gully Creek

To Mount Airy

Gully Creek Trail

23.1

CUMBERLAND KNOB RECREATION AREA

23.1

CUMBERLAND KNOB RECREATION AREA

0   Kilometer   0.25

0   Mile   0.25

N

points left to a path that climbs 0.2 mile up Cumberland Knob to the picnic shelter. Go right; soon a second, unsigned path branches left to Cumberland Knob. Again go right; the trail becomes paved as you cross the meadow to the information station and the parking area.

Key Points

0.5 Cross Gully Creek.

0.9 Small falls at creek crossing.

1.2 Leave Gully Creek.

1.4 Dramatic change in vegetation.

2.2 Left goes to Cumberland Knob; keep right.

2.4 Another left to Cumberland Knob; keep right.

Option 2: Cumberland Knob Trail

An easy amble takes you to a classic stone picnic shelter atop Cumberland Knob.

See map on page 142.
Parkway mile: 217.5
Distance: 0.4 and 0.7 mile loops
Difficulty: Easy

Elevation gain: 100 feet
Maps: USGS *Cumberland Knob, Virginia/North Carolina;* Parkway handout map available.

Finding the trailhead: Park near the information/comfort station in the Cumberland Knob Picnic Area. Walk to the right of the building and through the porch to the sign that reads WOODLAND TRAIL.

The Hike

Two paved trails go right from the WOODLAND TRAIL sign. The shortest, easiest loop hike to Cumberland Knob goes hard right past the cemetery and up the paved path along the picnic tables near the parking lot. (The paved path on the left through the meadow is your return route.) As the path leaves the meadow beyond the picnic tables, the paving ends and the trail rises over a rougher treadway. The trail emerges at the summit to the right of an old stone-and-log shelter with a shake roof and a fireplace.

Turn left across the front of the shelter—there's not much of a view—and take the trail back into the woods. This gradual descent swings right to intersect Gully Creek Trail at an unsigned junction. (On the Gully Creek hike, this is the second path that branches left near the end of the walk.) Go left; the path is paved as it crosses the meadow to the information station for a loop of 0.4 mile. (The easiest hike to Cumberland Knob is an out-and-back walk on this return side of this loop.)

A longer walk starts the same way. But just past the shelter, turn right at a signed junction where a trail scoots through the rhododendron. The path descends rather steeply to a signed junction with Gully Creek Trail (the first trail to the left you encounter near the end of the Gully Creek Trail). A left at the sign soon passes the unsigned trail junction mentioned above and arrives at the information station for a 0.7-mile loop.

Note: You can reverse either of these routes or omit the trail that rises along the picnic tables and just use the two leftward paths.

Key points

0.2 Summit shelter.

Option 3: High Piney Spur

A level paved path leads to a striking viewpoint.

Parkway mile: 218.6
Distance: 100 yards
Difficulty: Easy

Elevation gain: Negligible
Maps: *USGS Cumberland Knob, Virginia/North Carolina;* no Parkway map available

Finding the trailhead: Take the spur road from Fox Hunter's Paradise Overlook to a lot at High Piney Spur.

The Hike

This flat, paved trail is so short that the sign just says PEDESTRIAN WALKWAY. The path departs from a shady bluff that projects away from the Parkway at 2,830 feet. It terminates at a stone observation deck on the very prow of the ridge. This is High Piney Spur, a dramatically airy perch with a great view into the Piedmont.

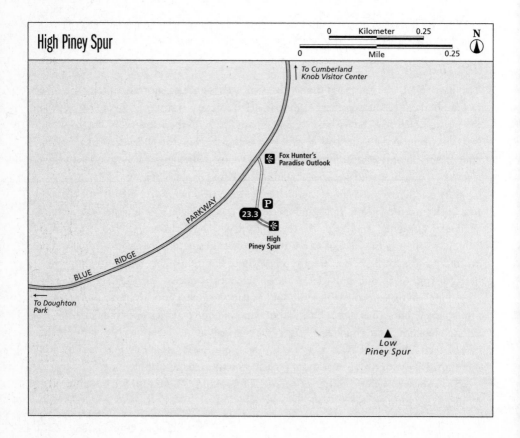

MOUNTAINS-TO-SEA TRAIL

The Mountains-to-Sea Trail (MST), which leaves the Blue Ridge Parkway south of High Piney Spur at Devil's Garden Overlook (Milepost 235.7) on its way to the coast, got its start in the 1970s with the dream of a statewide trail from the Great Smokies to the Outer Banks.

The trail through the mountains of North Carolina is quickly nearing completion, with much of that route skirting its way along the Blue Ridge Parkway. From Devil's Garden Overlook, the trail turns east and drops precipitously down the Blue Ridge to Stone Mountain State Park. South, many parts of the trail are still being built toward Deep Gap (Milepost 276.4), but south of there, much of the trail is in place, including stretches that flank the Parkway and should be considered by hikers.

The great plus for Parkway motorists is that at any crossing of the MST, and there are many, you can stride off into the woods for a leg-stretcher. (Check the Mileage Log in the back of this guide for the latest crossings.) The less-ideal side of the situation is that relatively few circuit opportunities exist. Especially on the Parkway, most walks on the MST will be out-and-back hikes (unless you use two cars). In addition, camping is prohibited on the Parkway except at formal sites. That complicates the end-to-end trek, but camping is easy along the MST in national forests.

MST hikes are suggested throughout this book. You'll find scenic out-and-back hikes as well as circuits. And some MST walks include camping, both on and off Parkway property.

A great burst of enthusiasm launched the MST effort in the 1980s, followed by a lull in the early 1990s. Enthusiasm was reignited when the route gained state park status and more funding. Growing participation in the Friends of the Mountains-to-Sea Trail organization's regional task forces has since sparked faster trail construction and consolidated funding. The trail is rapidly finding its way across the state, with an expected completion date of 2020. Where a path isn't practical, bikeable sections of road and paddleable sections of river are the choice.

Here's a brief list of awesome Mountains-to-Sea Trail hikes. Besides referring to the hikes in the body of this book, check the Mileage Log at the stated Mileposts below for additional access points.

MP 235.7: Devil's Garden Overlook

From Devil's Garden Overlook, it's a 3.3-mile descent to a scenic waterfall and streamside camping on the Widow's Creek Trail at Stone Mountain State Park's backcountry campsites. Backcountry permits are required and need to be picked up at the registration sign on the Widow's Creek Trail in the state park. If you hike down, you'll need to register while dropping a car. Your best bet is to start at the state park and hike up Widow's Creek Trail. (See Mileage Log, Milepost 229.7. Take US 21 east to a well-signed right turn onto NC 1100 for Stone Mountain State Park and access to Widow's Creek Trail.)

MP 242.4: Doughton Park

Doughton Park's Bluff Mountain Trail is a stunning meadow-covered section of the MST. See Hike 24, Options 2 and 3.

MP 272.5: E. B. Jeffress Park

Two separate paths at two overlooks are portions of the MST. Link them to create a great easy waterfall walk (Hike 26).

MP 291.8–294.6: Moses H. Cone Memorial Park

The MST snakes through Cone Park on an intricate assortment of moderate "carriage roads" that permit long loop hikes. For MST circuits, check out Hike 27, Options 6, 7, and 8.

MP 295.9–297.2: Julian Price Memorial Park

The Tanawha Trail starts/ends in Price Park, and the meadow-focused hikes include a nice circuit toward Grandfather Mountain that connects to Moses Cone Park (Hike 28).

MP 299.1–305.1: Grandfather Mountain

This trail offers some of the most scenic sections of the MST. By starting south of Grandfather Mountain (see Beacon Heights) and ending up at Julian Price Park, you could camp on national forest land just before the Tanawha, camp midway on Grandfather Mountain, and end up at Price Park Campground for a third overnighter hiking this section of trail. A more northerly campsite could extend that (Hikes 29 and 30).

MP 344.1: Mount Mitchell

The MST climbs from Black Mountain Campground to the top of the East's highest peak for those who want to take the full measure of the mountain (Hike 38, Option 1).

MP 359.8–355.3: Balsam Gap to NC 128

One of the most scenic sections of the MST runs for 5.0 miles from Balsam Gap to NC 128 along the junction between the Great Craggy and Black Mountains in an area that some say resembles the Pacific Northwest. Hike north or south to spectacular viewpoints on Blackstock Knob and return for ideal day hikes. (See the Mileage Log, MP 359.8).

MP 363.4: Craggy Mountains

Leave Graybeard Mountain Overlook and hike south for out-and-back hikes of 7.2 and 6.2 miles that reach Douglas Falls. Or wander the dramatic summit scenery of the Great Craggies through stunted high-altitude vegetation, where spring comes late and fall flames early (Hikes 39 and 40).

MP 396.4–407.6: Shut-In Trail

The Shut-In Trail section of the Mountains-to-Sea Trail follows the route that takes George Vanderbilt's access trail to his Buck Spring Hunting Lodge (Hike 41, Option 3, and Mileage Log).

MP 418.8: Graveyard Fields and Shining Rock Wilderness

The Graveyard Fields Overlook accesses the Mountains-to-Sea Trail for a few nice loops. One explores the waterfalls of Yellowstone Prong. Another crosses meadow-covered Black Balsam Knob (Hikes 42 and 43, Option 2).

Milepost 422.4: Devil's Courthouse

Take in Devil's Courthouse, then cross over a Parkway tunnel to the MST for a great view of the Shining Rock Wilderness (Hike 44).

24 Doughton Park

Mileposts 241.1–248.1

After the Parkway's journey south over pastoral rolling scenery to the Virginia state line, North Carolina's Doughton Park signals the road's return to loftier country.

Doughton Park rears to an abrupt escarpment of rocky cliffs and plunging coves. Across this crest—where the Parkway winds along the edge of prominent headlands—dramatic bluffs afford great views. This area was, after all, originally called the Bluffs.

Doughton—roughly Mileposts 238.0 to 246.0—contains classic scenery made famous in memorable photos of the Parkway. Bulging meadows hump left and right, cut by cliffs, edged by fences, and dotted with clumps of rhododendron that bloom dramatically in June. Fine photos of the road result from even a short walk through almost any roadside meadow.

Parkway overlooks in this area provide views of the rocky summits along the route, but the focal point for many vistas is the prominent and dramatic drop into Basin Cove, a watershed more than 2,000 feet deep that plummets southeast from the roadside. This 6,000-acre area is one of those bulges in the Parkway where hikers can get away from the sound of the road. The ridge that carries the Parkway encircles an isolated backcountry that's one of only two places on the Parkway where overnight backpacking is permitted.

Doughton Park is a great place to glimpse the pioneering tradition of these mountains. At Parkway Milepost 238.5, rustic Brinegar Cabin is the only Parkway log cabin listed on the National Register of Historic Sites. This and adjoining structures are the real thing: an original cabin built circa 1880 by Martin Brinegar at a lofty 3,500 feet. In summer there's a small garden behind the structure. Carolyn Brinegar's original loom is inside, and there are summer demonstrations. At the easy-to-reach viewpoint of Wildcat Rocks, a glimpse over the edge reveals Caudill Cabin, built in 1894. It sits far below at the very base of the cliffs, as far back in a hollow as Martin Caudill could get without climbing up the mountainside. Here he raised fourteen children—six fewer than his father, James Harrison Caudill, the area's first settler.

Despite the seeming wildness of the chasm, the isolated valley was once a thriving community with a school, store, church, and post office. The first residents moved in after the Civil War, and the last moved out after the flood of 1916. The tract was purchased in 1930 by Doughton Park's namesake, Robert Doughton, a member of the U.S. House of Representatives who played a key role in the creation of the Blue Ridge Parkway.

Most Parkway motorists just peer off the road at the cabin and drive on. Luckily for us, the bulk of Doughton's 30-mile trail system explores the old Basin Cove community. The cabin may be the best-preserved relic (it was last restored in summer 2001), but hikers will also encounter old chimneys, foundations, fences, fields being reclaimed by forest, and other remnants. Backpackers require a free camping permit to use the designated backcountry campsite. The best place to acquire permits is the Doughton Park Campground Ranger Kiosk, Milepost 239.2. If you have a few weeks before your trip, call (336) 372-8877 and request a permit by mail.

Doughton Park has a restaurant, camp store, and gift shop; a large picnic area and campground; and twenty-four-room Bluffs Lodge (one of the four rustic concessionaire-run accommodations that provide lodging on the Parkway).

Option 1: Wildcat Rocks and Fodder Stack

An easy paved trail to a view of Caudill Cabin and a rugged but short scramble to a spectacular crag—both head out from the same trailhead.

Parkway mile: 241.1
Distance: 0.3 mile out and back for Wildcat Rocks; 2.0 miles out and back for Fodder Stack
Difficulty: Easy for Wildcat Rocks; moderate for Fodder Stack

Elevation gain: Negligible
Maps: *USGS Whitehead;* Parkway handout map, available at the ranger station (Milepost 245.5) and other park facilities

Finding the trailhead: Turn east off the Parkway to the lodge and picnic area and bear left at the turn to the lodge. Park on the right in front of the second lodge unit for the Wildcat Rocks Trail, or continue left into the more distant parking lot for Fodder Stack (and a shorter trail to Wildcat Rocks).

The Hike

If you don't have much time for a hike here, this single location serves as a nice introduction to the scenic grandeur of Doughton Park. Both walks start near the lodge on the broad bluff that juts out into the void over Basin Cove.

Wildcat Rocks is the pinnacle beyond the lodge where a rocky outcrop and stone wall survey the entire watershed. Peer over to the southeast, past the summer wildflowers that cling to the rock, and Caudill Cabin sits far below. Start in front of the lodge and take the paved, gently rising path to the rocks and back. (For a shorter

Flowers cling to a ledge on Wildcat Rocks high above Caudill Cabin and Basin Cove.

Wildcat Rocks and Fodder Stack, Bluff Mountain

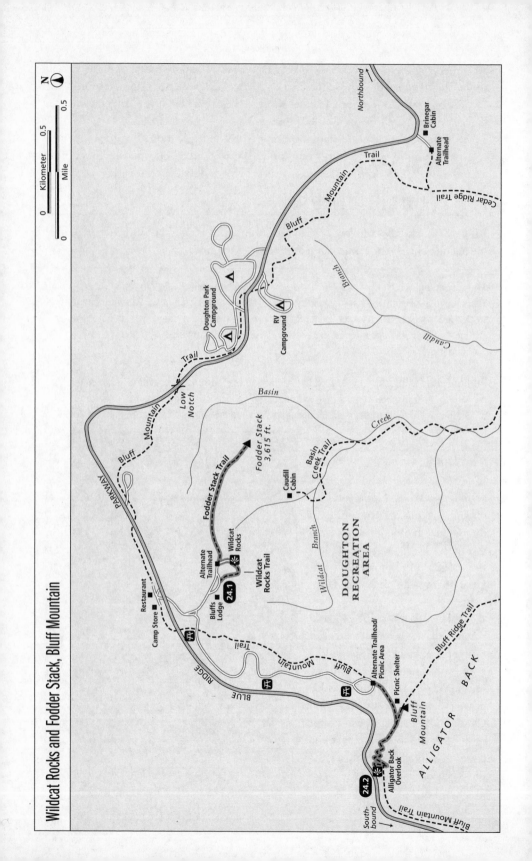

stroll, head to the second parking lot near the start of the Fodder Stack Trail, where a bas-relief bust honors Robert Doughton.) Take the ascending paved path up to the right. Some people picnic on the sunny rocks.

Nearby Fodder Stack is aptly named—it's a bumpy lump that juts out from the main ridge and stands on its own above steeply dropping terrain. It combines great views with moderate walking, and the Park Service recommends the hike to families. The trail veers left off the back of the parking lot and descends steeply down switchbacks to a bench amid great views down to Caudill Cabin. The trail passes a few more benches and a rocky viewpoint on the right as it reaches and follows the ridgeline then ends at a final bench on the summit. In the leafless seasons, the surrounding expanse creates a stunning feeling of being out in the middle of it all.

Key Points for Fodder Stack
- **0.1** Bench with a view of Caudill Cabin.
- **0.5** Rocky crag on right with nice view.
- **1.0** Bench at summit view.

Option 2: Bluff Mountain Trail to Bluff Mountain

Any stretch of this yellow-blazed 7.5-mile roadside path (part of the Mountains-to-Sea Trail) through meadows and forests is worth a wander. The two hikes of varying difficulty here feature a view from the trail shelter atop the crest of Bluff Mountain at 3,796 feet.

See map on page 150.
Parkway mile: 242.4
Distance: 1.6 miles out and back from Alligator Back Overlook; 0.6 mile out and back from the Doughton Park Picnic Area
Difficulty: Moderate to Bluff Mountain from Alligator Back Overlook; easy from the picnic area; other stretches easy to moderate
Elevation gain: 320 feet from Alligator Back Overlook; 50 feet from picnic area
Maps: USGS Whitehead; Parkway handout map, available at the Ranger Station (Milepost 245.5) and other park facilities

Finding the trailhead: Alligator Back Overlook is at Milepost 242.4; Doughton Park Picnic Area is at Milepost 241.1.

The Hike

The arching "alligator back" of the Parkway in this area is one of Doughton Park's most inspiring roadside sights. The summit of Bluff Mountain is one of its most impressive features—a point easily appreciated from Alligator Back Overlook. The cliffs and crags promise great views, and reaching the peak is worth the walk.

From Alligator Back Overlook descend the stone steps and turn left onto Bluff Mountain Trail. The path rises consistently then breaks into switchbacks that climb more steeply for a few tenths of a mile. As the switchbacks end, a deciduous forest yields to evergreens and the trail emerges onto clifftops. Dramatic views stretch south along the Parkway and directly down into the rugged defiles of the Cove Creek basin. Squeeze through a fence stile and soon turn right onto the red-blazed Bluff Ridge Trail. (Left, the Bluff Mountain Trail goes to the picnic area.) Pass through another fence and reach the three-sided trail shelter atop Bluff Mountain. This shake-roofed log-and-stone shelter is a perfect viewpoint destination—even when a summer thunderstorm seems likely.

The shelter is an easy hike from the end loop of the picnic area. Take the path through the expansive meadow. In about 0.2 mile turn left onto the Bluff Ridge Trail to the shelter. This is one of the Parkway's best easy hikes.

Key Points from Alligator Back Overlook

0.2   Trail starts to switchback.
0.5   Clifftop views.
0.6   Turn right onto Bluff Ridge Trail. (From picnic area, turn left at 0.2 mile.)
0.7   Reach trail shelter (0.3 mile from picnic area).

The rest of the Bluff Mountain Trail is best strolled out and back from your choice of starting points—it's one of those "transportation" paths that link roadside facilities but don't form loops. Nevertheless, its ridgeline location makes for nice views. Just see the map and pick a section. Here are two worthwhile starting points:

Brinegar Cabin. Enjoy the cabin and then walk to the end of the parking area; take the trail up the hill past the sign. Turn right onto Bluff Mountain Trail in about 0.2 mile. (The Cedar Ridge Trail goes left 4.4 miles into Basin Cove.) From here to the RV campground, about 1.1 miles, the path is a pleasant walk (2.2 miles roundtrip). There are nice meadow views at about 0.4 mile that might make a nice turnaround (0.8 mile out and back). The Doughton Park Campground isn't far beyond the RV camping area, so campers might also start there and hike this same stretch to Brinegar Cabin and back (1.4 miles one-way, 2.8 miles round-trip).

Campground. If you're camping at Doughton Park Campground, the Bluff Mountain Trail is a convenient way to grab a bite at the restaurant. The trail leaves the campground and reaches the restaurant, camp store, and gift shop in about 1.0 mile (2.0 miles out and back). Along the way, the trail crosses the Parkway twice, passes an overlook, and in many places offers truly inspiring meadow views.

Option 3: Basin Cove Circuit Hikes

The Flat Rock Ridge Trail–Grassy Gap Fire Road circuit is the easiest Basin Cove loop hike (though harder ones are covered). This is a moderate backpacking trip, one of the best on the Blue Ridge Parkway. It can easily include a side trip to Caudill Cabin.

Parkway mile: 244.7
Distance: Flat Rock Ridge Trail-Grassy Gap Fire Road circuit, 11.1 miles; Bluff Ridge Trail-Grassy Gap Fire Road route, 8.7 miles; Bluff Ridge Trail-Flat Rock Ridge Trail circuit, 13.0 miles

Difficulty: Strenuous, largely due to distance
Elevation gain: 1,800 to 1,900 feet
Maps: USGS *Whitehead;* Parkway handout map, available at the ranger station (Milepost 245.5) and other facilities in the park

Finding the trailhead: Park at Basin Cove Overlook (less than 1 mile from the ranger office at Milepost 245.5. Pick up camping permits at the Doughton Park Campground Ranger Kiosk (Milepost 239.2), or call a few weeks ahead of your trip at (336) 372-887 to request a permit by mail.

The Hikes

Basin Cove is nicely configured for a lengthy circuit hike or a backpacking trip. The Bluff Mountain Trail gradually parallels the Parkway along the upper rim of the cove, and four trails plunge into the drainage at various places to join at the base near the backcountry campsite. A fifth trail in the bottom of the cove, the Basin Creek Trail, provides the added appeal of a day-hike side trip to Caudill Cabin.

A circuit is doable in a day, but the 10- to 12-mile distance makes it a challenge. So unless you're a hiking animal, the cabin won't be accessible from the Parkway. (Start at the bottom for the cabin; see Option 1.) Luckily for day hikers who don't expect to reach the cabin, the route back up to your car on the Parkway is a bona fide easy grade—the Grassy Gap Fire Road.

Many hikes are possible; just look at the map. Unfortunately, the circuit made by the Cedar Ridge and Bluff Ridge Trails requires 4.0 miles of walking along the most developed part of the Bluff Mountain Trail—an arduous outing if you use the required backcountry campsite.

Having to camp in the required site is the rub with the northern route. (The dedicated could make it work with a second night in the park's main roadside campground.) Luckily, more doable overnighters lie on the southern end.

The best circuit for backpackers starts at the Basin Cove Overlook and drops 5.0 miles down the sky blue–blazed Flat Rock Ridge Trail to the Grassy Gap Fire Road. Leave the overlook and in 0.1 mile go right on the Flat Rock Ridge Trail at the junction where the Bluff Mountain Trail goes left. The Flat Rock Ridge is rugged, with frequent ups and downs, but it's well maintained and has the best scenery and most frequent views of the more rugged routes into the valley. Take the time to pause around the 2.0-mile mark at a great viewpoint.

Exit onto Longbottom Road at 5.0 miles. Go left across the bridge and left again back into the woods past the DOUGHTON PARK backcountry sign on the easy streamside stroll of Grassy Gap Fire Road. Soon pass the Cedar Ridge Trail on the right to Brinegar Cabin, then cross a lashed-log bridge on Basin Creek where the designated campsite appears on the left at 6.7 miles. This makes a premier base for a three-day camping trip with a hike to Caudill Cabin on day two and an easy fire road walk back to the Parkway on day three. (For more on the two-acre camping area, see the entry for Caudill Cabin via Grassy Gap Fire Road and Basin Creek Trail.)

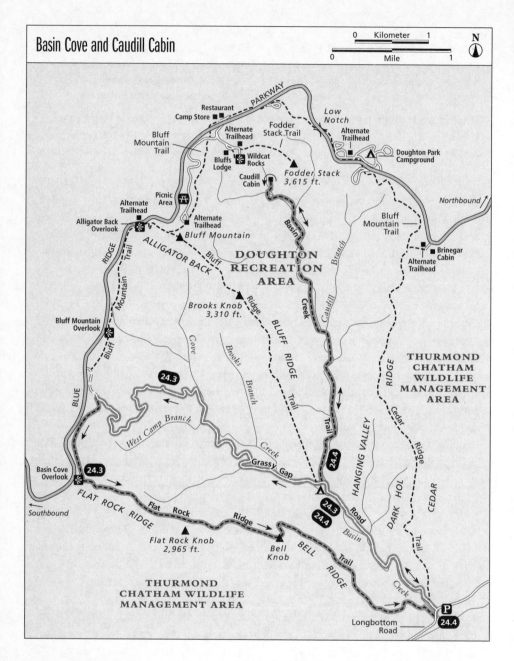

Basin Cove and Caudill Cabin

0   Kilometer   1

0   Mile   1

N

PARKWAY

Restaurant
Camp Store

Low
Notch

Bluff
Mountain
Trail

Alternate
Trailhead

Fodder
Stack Trail

Alternate
Trailhead

Doughton Park
Campground

Bluffs
Lodge

Wildcat
Rocks

Caudill
Cabin

Fodder Stack
3,615 ft.

Northbound

Picnic
Area

Bluff
Mountain
Trail

Alternate
Trailhead

Alligator Back
Overlook

Alternate
Trailhead

Brinegar
Cabin

Bluff Mountain

Alternate
Trailhead

ALLIGATOR BACK

DOUGHTON
RECREATION
AREA

Basin

Creek

Caudill

Branch

RIDGE

Mountain

Trail

Bluff

THURMOND
CHATHAM
WILDLIFE
MANAGEMENT
AREA

Bluff Mountain
Overlook

Bluff

Brooks Knob
3,310 ft.

Ridge

BLUFF RIDGE

Trail

RIDGE

Cedar

Ridge

CEDAR

BLUE

Cove

Brooks

Branch

24.3

West Camp Branch

Creek

Trail

24.4

HANGING VALLEY

DARK HOL

Trail

Basin Cove
Overlook

24.3

Grassy Gap

24.3
24.4

Road

Basin

Southbound

FLAT ROCK RIDGE

Flat

Rock

Ridge

Flat Rock Knob
2,965 ft.

Bell
Knob

BELL

RIDGE

Trail

Creek

THURMOND
CHATHAM WILDLIFE
MANAGEMENT AREA

P
24.4

Longbottom
Road

Day hikers just blow on by the campsite (or have lunch there). After a long gradual rise, go left on one of the easiest portions of the gradual Bluff Mountain Trail at
10.1 miles to Basin Cove Overlook at 11.1 miles.

There are two other possible circuits here. The shortest in the area (and perhaps
the best day hike without camping gear) also includes the Grassy Gap Fire Road but

starts at the Bluff Mountain Overlook (Milepost 243.4). Take the Bluff Mountain Trail left for a 1.0-mile warm-up before the climb to the Bluff Mountain Shelter and a rest at 1.9 miles. (See Option 2 for more suggestions) Backpackers with heavy packs could defuse the uphill to the shelter by parking on the end loop of the picnic area (saving the climb back up for a later day with a lighter pack). From the shelter descend the steep and forested Bluff Ridge Trail 2.8 miles to the campsite—4.7 miles from the start. That leaves an easy return leg of 3.4 miles on the fire road and 0.6 mile on the Bluff Mountain Trail back to the Bluff Mountain Overlook—only 8.7 miles if done in a day.

The most rugged loop—done the easiest way—deletes the gradual fire road and starts at the Basin Cove Overlook. Head left on the Bluff Mountain Trail and descend to the campsite on the Bluff Ridge Trail for a 6.3-mile first leg. Descend the fire road to Longbottom Road for a right turn, then make another right across the bridge onto Flat Rock Ridge Trail. Flat Rock Ridge is the best of the difficult uphill hikes because it's longer, sections of it switchback, and there are more views to admire during rest stops. Return to your car for a 13.0-mile round-trip.

For backpackers on any of these circuits, Caudill Cabin becomes a day hike from the designated campsite beside Cove Creek.

Key Points for Basin Cove Overlook Circuit

0.1 Go right on Flat Rock Ridge Trail where the Bluff Mountain Trail goes left.

2.0 Ridgetop view.

5.0 Left at road to another left on Grassy Gap Fire Road.

6.7 Pass campsite—or set up a tent.

10.1 Left on Bluff Mountain Trail.

11.1 Arrive back at trailhead.

Option 4: Caudill Cabin via Grassy Gap Fire Road and Basin Creek Trail

This is the easiest way to get to Doughton Park's most isolated and evocative spot—Martin Caudill's late-nineteenth-century cabin. It's a great but lengthy day hike and an easy backpacking trip.

See map on page 154.
Parkway mile: Milepost 248.1
Distance: 10.0 miles out and back
Difficulty: Strenuous due to distance and stream crossings

Elevation gain: 1,400 feet
Maps: *USGS Whitehead;* Parkway handout map, available at the ranger station (Milepost 245.5) and other park facilities

---

Finding the trailhead: Exit the Parkway at Milepost 248.1 and go east downhill on NC 18. About 6 miles from the Parkway, turn left onto NC 1728. At 4 miles turn left again onto NC 1730, Longbottom Road. Three miles from that turn, park on the right just past a bridge across Basin Creek. The Grassy Gap Fire Road begins on the left.

The Hike

The heart of Basin Cove, including Caudill Cabin, is most easily reached from below the Parkway, especially for day hiking. Easy access to the lower trailhead makes it well worth the effort.

Start on the green-blazed Grassy Gap Fire Road—a flat, wide trail over its entire length to a roadside junction with the Bluff Mountain Trail beside the Parkway. Follow the fire road along Basin Creek, past the junction of Cedar Ridge Trail on the right (at 0.1 mile). The fire road crosses Basin Creek on a bridge of lashed logs, passes campsites on the left, and reaches a pair of trail junctions on the right at 1.6 miles. The two-acre primitive camping area borders Cove Creek and contains eight widely spaced sites with fire grills. Maximum group size is twenty persons; maximum site capacity is forty. The Blue Ridge Parkway Foundation expects to build a campsite toilet here soon.

Turn right from the Grassy Gap Fire Road onto the blue-blazed Basin Creek Trail and consider that this was an old wagon road into an isolated community. Over the 3.3 miles from this junction to the cabin, the grade crosses Basin Creek or tributaries two dozen times—many likely to require wading in wet weather. (No big deal—bring water shoes!)

You'll pass a millstone in the creek after the first steep section and an old chimney and remnants of fence in the first mile (about 2.6 miles from your car). Rhododendron and hemlocks line the stream. The old grade deteriorates, and there's a waterfall with a swirling coldwater pool to soak in at 2.5 miles (4.1 miles from your start). Pass the second easily seen chimney not too far below the cabin as the trail wanders the streamside, rising and falling more frequently. The cabin sits in a clearing 3.4 miles from the campsite, 5.0 miles from Longbottom Road. Towering 800 feet above are Wildcat Rocks, Fodder Stack, and surrounding ridges. Have a picnic, plan which pool you'll chill out in on the way back, and try to imagine the hardships and rewards of a life lived in such a secluded, hardscrabble place.

Backpackers who use the designated campsite have the easiest day hike. Until the privy is installed, regulations require that campers keep toilet sites well away from camp and not closer than 200 feet from water. Campfires must be confined to existing fire sites, and no living or standing wood can be cut; use dead-and-down wood only. Water should be treated or boiled and all trash packed out. Quiet hours at the site are from 10:00 p.m. to 6:00 a.m.

A free camping permit is required so that the Park Service can limit use of the site. Pick up permits at the Doughton Park Campground Ranger Kiosk (Milepost 239.2), or call (336) 372-8877 a few weeks before your trip to request a permit by mail.

Key Points

1.6 Turn right at campsite onto Basin Cove Trail from Grassy Gap Fire Road.

2.5 Pass first old chimney.

4.0 Pass another chimney.

5.0 Reach Caudill Cabin.

THE CAUDILLS' CABIN

When Parkway visitors gaze down at Caudill Cabin from Wildcat Rocks, they see Appalachian isolation. Lenny and Larry Caudill look down and see where their great-grandfather Martin Caudill raised fourteen children.

The Winston-Salem and Wilkesboro residents—fifty-something years old—came to their family history at different times. Larry helped build the trail to the cabin in the 1980s with a local trail club after attending family reunions as a kid and "promising myself one day I'd visit that cabin far below." Lenny has delved deeply into genealogy—and he maintains the family history booklet he placed at the cabin for hikers.

Both men visit the rough-hewn 20- by 20-foot log structure a few times a year. On a 2009 hike they took along Lenny's then fourteen-year-old son, Alex, who was "born exactly one hundred years and one day after his grandfather Famon Caudill, the first child born in the cabin in 1895," says Lenny. Famon was one of the last residents of the Cove. He and most of the seventy-five residents left after the 1916 flood, which was caused by repeated hurricanes. His wife, Alice, her mother, and his brother were killed in the flood. Alice's grave is located at the backcountry campsite between the Basin Creek and Bluff Ridge Trails, not far from the foundation ruins of Basin Creek Baptist Church just beyond Grassy Gap Fire Road.

One chimney you see on the hike to Caudill Cabin, and many you don't, marks the cabins of other Caudills, and Lenny and Larry call each a relative's name. At the drop of a hat they exit the trail to other ruins—including pristine "Perfect Chimney." They're actively GPS-ing their discoveries.

Sadly, the Caudill family cemetery still eludes them. "We'll find it. I promise," Lenny says. "To have a place where your family history is preserved is a rare opportunity," he continues. "We're particularly grateful to the Park Service for preserving our heritage."

As the Parkway turns seventy-five, every citizen can say that the Park Service is doing that for all of us.

25 Jumpinoff Rocks Trail

Milepost 260.3

A classic leg-stretcher with a little up and down leads to a secluded stone observation platform atop rocks you should definitely not be "jumpinoff."

Parkway mile: 260.3
Distance: 1.0 mile out and back
Difficulty: Easy

Elevation gain: 196 feet
Maps: *USGS Horse Gap;* no Parkway map available

Finding the trailhead: Climb the flight of steps beside a picnic table on the right side of the Jumpinoff Rocks Parking Area.

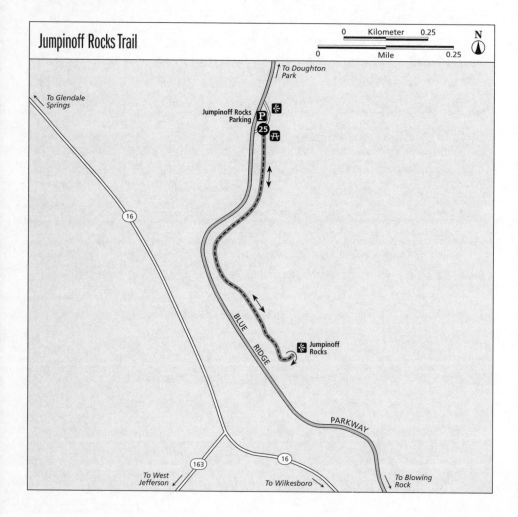

The Hike

The trail starts off in a rhododendron forest, slabbing to the right of a rising ridge. A gully on the left is no doubt the original trail, replaced by this more gradual and graded reroute. Reaching a small gap through a section of gullied trail, the path levels then turns right, ascending out of the gap and around the high point that rises off to the left. The path is a bit rooty on its rise. It eventually bears left around the receding bulge of the ridge and gradually dips to join an old road grade that comes in on the right. There's a bench at 0.3 mile, where a few short spurs go left to limited views.

The trail bears right off the graded path and dips gradually through pines and a carpet of galax into a quiet glade of white pines. Turning left, the route again reaches the edge of the drop-off beyond and steps down into a rock observation deck at 0.5 mile.

The view is expansive—and illustrative. Summer foliage softens the evidence of logging just below the view. This and other places in Virginia and northern North Carolina—where private land surrounds the Parkway—evidence increasing timber harvesting, development, and second-home construction. Who would have known back in the 1930s that this 0.5-mile-wide corridor would need to be even wider to provide isolation from the future. Ironically, the Parkway itself was designed to accommodate the primary instigator of all that change—the automobile. The Park Service and private organizations such as the Blue Ridge Parkway Foundation and Friends of the Blue Ridge Parkway are attempting to influence the future of surrounding lands.

Like other trails along this section of the Parkway, Jumpinoff Rocks Trail is to be linked north and south in the future by North Carolina's Mountains-to-Sea Trail.

Key Points

0.3 Bench.
0.5 Viewpoint.

Flame azalea blooms brighten the Parkway.

26 E. B. Jeffress Park

Mileposts 271.9–272.5

One of the Parkway's best self-guiding interpretive trails and evocative artifacts of human habitation make Jeffress Park a truly wonderful stop for hikers.

In 1933 E. B. Jeffress, chairman of the North Carolina State Highway and Public Works Commission, was one of the North Carolinians working to exclude Tennessee from the route of a mountaintop motorway between Shenandoah and Great Smoky Mountains National Parks. He also left no doubt that he and then Governor J. C. B. Ehringhaus were set against permitting the Parkway to be a toll road—as was Skyline Drive, the scenic road that had just opened through Virginia's Shenandoah National Park at the northern terminus of the future Parkway.

The Skyline Drive still charges a user fee, and the Parkway is still free. Jeffress Park, one of the Parkway's smallest roadside recreation areas (600 acres) memorializes the man who helped make that "No fee" message clear to Parkway planners.

It's appropriate that the newly four-lane US 421 can be seen from many overlooks on this stretch of Parkway as it courses up the mountainside into Deep Gap, a major Parkway access point 10 miles east of Boone, North Carolina.

Option 1: The Cascades Trail

One of the Parkway's best interpretive nature trails leads to a wonderful waterfall.

Parkway mile: 271.9
Distance: 1.0-mile loop
Difficulty: Moderate

Elevation gain: 170 feet
Maps: *USGS Maple Springs;* no Parkway map available

Finding the trailhead: Park in the Cascades Parking Area where the trail goes left at the restroom building. A picnic area surrounds the opposite end of the parking lot, where the Tompkins Knob Trail connects.

The Hike

This trail offers a great sense of the ecological community that teeters on the escarpment of the Blue Ridge. The path wanders the crest of cliffs overlooking the Piedmont and brings hikers to Falls Creek just as a waterfall leaps over the edge. The trail then swings back from the brink along the stream as it tumbles through a quiet valley toward the falls.

Trees are the subject of the trail's twenty interpretive plaques. Between the drier location at cliffside and the well-watered stream drainage, hikers will encounter many of the tree species that populate Blue Ridge forests.

Leave the parking lot on a paved trail that becomes gravel; go right at the start of the loop to undulate along the crest of the cliff. Winter views of an idyllic pastoral

Falls Creek tumbles along the crest of the Blue Ridge then leaps off the edge.

scene are particularly good. You'll marvel at the meadow-covered farming community suspended just below the Blue Ridge and surrounded by the forested slopes of lower mountains. There's a bench on which you can ponder what you're about to learn about dogwood, tulip tree, pignut, black locust, serviceberry, mountain laurel, white oak, flame azalea, minnie bush, highbush blueberry, and chestnut oak.

The trail dips left into the rhododendron and arcs down to a rustic log bridge across Falls Creek. Across the creek, the return loop trail goes left. Turn right past a dog hobble–describing plaque and quickly descend stone steps to an upper rock wall–encircled observation platform, where the stream jumps over the edge and down a steeply sloping slab of rock. The lower platform affords an even better view.

Please stay behind the guardrail. People have fallen to their death at these falls. The falls are best in spring, after a rain, or in winter, when ice holds water in place.

Go right at the return loop junction, with the stream on your left. A treadway nicely underpinned with rock leads to a bridge across the stream. With the stream now on your right, and the Parkway above it obscured by summer vegetation, pause at one of the two upcoming benches. Birches, rhododendron, sweet birch, witch hazel, eastern hemlock, black gum, and red maple are all species that favor these shady streambanks. The trail turns left and rises to the junction you passed earlier atop the ridge. Head right, back to the parking area.

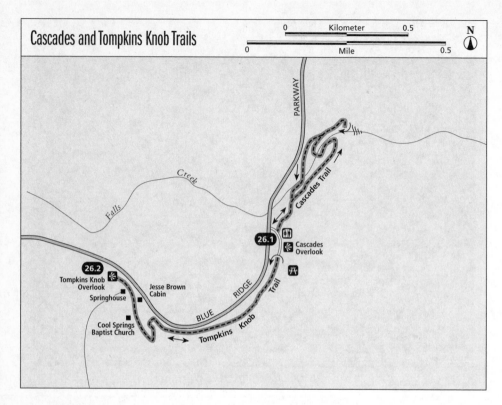

Cascades and Tompkins Knob Trails

There's evidence here of increasing off-trail wandering: Please heed the Park Service sign asking that hikers stay on designated trails.

Key Points

0.05 Go right where loop splits.

0.3 Cross log bridge over stream and go right at junction.

0.4 Upper falls view with lower platform 150 feet below.

0.5 Bear right at junction.

0.9 Bear right at final junction to parking lot.

Option 2: Tompkins Knob Trail

This trail through a white pine forest inspires appreciation for early mountain structures.

See map above.
Parkway mile: 272.5
Distance: 1.2 miles out and back
Difficulty: Easy

Elevation gain: Negligible
Maps: USGS Maple Springs; no Parkway map available

Finding the trailhead: Park at the Tompkins Knob Parking Area and take an immediate left from your car along the Parkway. The less-than-obvious path dips across the grassy decline into the woods, where it becomes more distinct.

The Hike

This pleasant path offers a stroll to three interesting historic structures and a longer walk to the picnic area at the nearby parking for the Cascades Trail. You could include the Cascades for an even longer option.

The stroll is highlighted by intriguing structures from the last century—a cabin, an adjacent springhouse, and a shelter that served as a rustic church (don't expect a steeple). No elaborate living-history displays take place here, and there's no popular Parkway concession area nearby—just quiet aplenty to imagine life a hundred years ago.

Head through the woods along the Parkway and emerge below Jesse Brown's cabin—a late-nineteenth-century residence moved here to be closer to Cool Spring, the lofty seepage trickling out of the ground in two places to your right beside a tiny decaying springhouse. Head down the short distance to examine this vanishing structure. Water gurgles out of the mossy rocks above the little building with some force. Below that sits a smaller seep that is artfully funneled through the springhouse. The water trickles from the ground along one channeled-out log and into a larger log that directs the flow through the structure. The water's summertime temperature of 40-some degrees no doubt nicely chilled food stored inside the shady, once-weatherized enclave.

The cabin and its impressive fireplace are worth a look, too. Farther up the gradual hill is the "Baptist church" named for Cool Spring—more a shelter used when the weather didn't cooperate while circuit-riding preachers were on hand to minister to high-hollow residents.

Head left at the sign describing the church and descend gently through shady hardwoods past a bench—the greatest elevation change on the whole walk. From here all the way to the Cascades Trail parking and picnic area, it's a largely level saunter under inspiring white pines, where the whisper of the trees mingles with the whoosh of the occasional passing car.

That last piney section of trail could be a nice out-and-back stroll from the Cascades Parking Area. The cabins are a nice walk from there, too. From either direction, the entire trail is 0.6 mile, with the round-trip a very easy 1.2 miles.

Better yet, ambitious hikers can start from the Tompkins Knob Parking Area and hike to the Cascades, turning the 1.0-mile waterfall walk into a really pleasant 2.4-mile trek.

Key Points

0.15 Pass between Jesse Brown's cabin and springhouse.

0.2 Enter the woods beyond Cool Spring Baptist Church.

0.25 Pass first bench.

0.5 Second bench.

0.6 Jeffress Park Picnic Area and Cascades Trail parking.

The High Country Overview

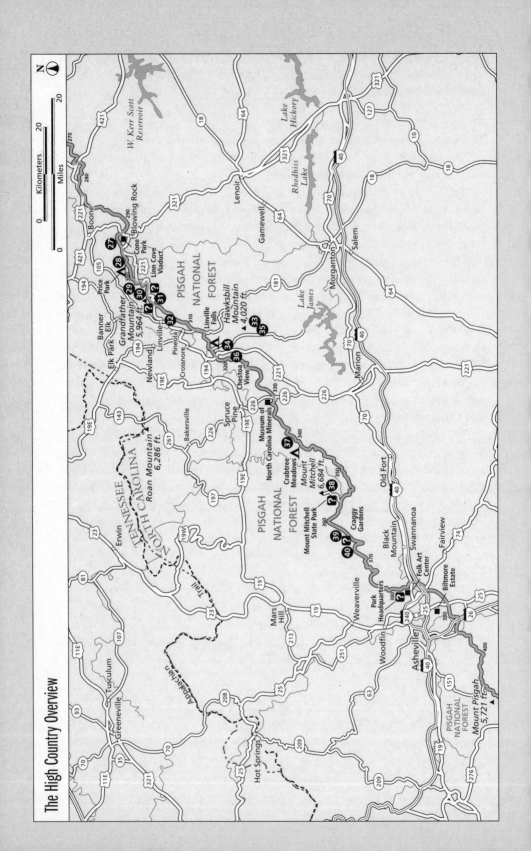

The High Country

Mileposts 276.4 (US 421 at Deep Gap, North Carolina) to 384.7 (US 74 at Asheville, North Carolina)

From Deep Gap at US 421 (Milepost 276.4) to Asheville, North Carolina, at US 74 (Milepost 384.7), the Parkway traverses what can only be called the High Country corner of North Carolina. Ironically, the highest spot on the Parkway is not here—it's south of Asheville.

But everything else about this area says lofty, indeed, almost alpine. At Grandfather Mountain, the Blue Ridge escarpment rises to its greatest relief—nearly a vertical mile above the surrounding Piedmont. The computer-designed span of the Linn Cove Viaduct—the Parkway's newest section, completed in 1987—puts you right in the middle of it. Easily accessible just 5 miles off the Parkway is Mount Mitchell (6,684 feet), the East's highest summit. Trails at both locations deserve your attention.

But there are two sides to the High Country. The first half of this Parkway section is bordered by private lands, some of it developed and popular as a resort area. The second half is again wrapped in national forest. In the High Country you get the Parkway at both ends of a spectrum.

The resort experience is on the northern end—where it's been since the 1880s, when the lowland rich first fled the summer heat to spark tourism in the mountains. They came for the South's coolest summer temperatures and, later, golf at classic, still popular hostelries like Blowing Rock's Green Park Inn and the chestnut bark–covered luxury of Linville's historic Eseeola Lodge.

The inns and shops of Main Street in the quaint town of Blowing Rock epitomize the appeal of the High Country tourist towns. The town's namesake destination, the Blowing Rock, is a crag with a great view and an Indian legend. It bills itself as "North Carolina's first travel attraction." Early history is the focus at Boone's summer outdoor drama *Horn in the West,* the inspiring, little-known story of how High Country mountaineers marched over their mountains and down to defeat the British in one of the American Revolution's pivotal battles, King's Mountain.

Other area burgs include Linville, at the base of Grandfather Mountain, one of the

Mast General Store is a High Country landmark.

United States' first planned resort communities. Banner Elk's special license plates call it the ski capital of the south for Beech and Sugar Mountains, the region's southernmost major ski areas. And Boone, the "Hub of the High Country," is a granola-inclined college town that's home to Appalachian State University. The village of Valle Crucis claims the Mast General Store (circa 1880), which the late Charles Kuralt called "America's premier country store."

It goes without saying that there are copious craft shops and country clubs here, and the area's diverse dining is as good as or better than that in most of the surrounding cities of the Piedmont.

Parkway facilities in the High Country include Julian Price Memorial Park (Milepost 296.9), a major picnic area and campground memorably sited beside Price Lake. Linville Falls (Milepost 316.4) also has a campground and a large picnic area. Crabtree Meadows (Milepost 339.5) has a campground and snack bar. The summit state park at Mount Mitchell (Milepost 355) also has a restaurant and small tent camp area (highest in the East).

Don't forget camping in the Pisgah National Forest. Nearer to Mount Mitchell are classic campgrounds such as Black Mountain, nestled in the virgin forest at the base of the mountain. There are a few additional campgrounds far below Grandfather Mountain in a huge dirt road–laced region called Wilson Creek.

Environmental awareness is easy to cultivate on this stretch of the Parkway. The Museum of North Carolina Minerals (Milepost 330.9) is newly renovated and one of the best such exhibits anywhere. Just off the Parkway, Grandfather Mountain's Nature Museum and environmental wildlife habitats are first rate. Mount Mitchell also has a new nature museum and a new wheelchair-accessible summit tower with horizon-identifying plaques. Just a few miles east of the town of Linville Falls on US 221 is Linville Caverns—North Carolina's only commercial cavern.

Museum-quality crafts are also in evidence. Between the Parkway Craft Center in Moses Cone's Manor House (Milepost 294) and the stunning original works of art for sale in the Folk Art Center (Milepost 382), you'll be astonished at the vibrancy of Appalachian handcrafts. The artisans who create these works get their training not far off the Parkway at the world-renowned Penland School of Crafts.

All in all, the High Country may be the high point of the Parkway experience.

Check Appendix B for relevant Web sites and contact information.

27 Moses Cone Memorial Park

Mileposts 291.8–294.6

Moses Cone Memorial Park's 3,500 acres are quite simply one of the Parkway's best places to pause—in part because Cone Park so well exemplifies the tourism tradition of the mountains and in particular the surrounding region. This is the heart of the North Carolina High Country resort area, and the village of Blowing Rock is its crown.

Moses Cone (1857–1908) helped launch that resort tradition. His Parkway contribution started in Greensboro, North Carolina. Together with brother Cesar, Cone amassed a fortune in North Carolina's post–Civil War textile industry with his Proximity Textile Mills. He built an empire popularizing blue denim cloth and became known as "The Denim King." Cone moved to the mountains at the turn of the twentieth century. With the heart of a preservationist and the mind of a forester, he created lakes in his mountain estate and offered jobs in the new apple orchards and fields to original landowners still living on the property.

He crowned his holdings with a Victorian mansion on the crest of the Blue Ridge. His Flat Top Manor is still a memorable structure, which celebrated its fiftieth anniversary as the Parkway Craft Center in 2001. The rich estate that sprawls from the mansion—down across wonderful white-pine forests to Bass Lake, up to the peaks of Rich and Flat Top Mountains, and below into hardwood and hemlock–filled drainages toward Grandfather Mountain—is quite simply one of the most beautiful and unique places on the Blue Ridge Parkway.

Cone also exemplified the role of wealthy benefactors in the very existence of this high road. John D. Rockefeller Jr.'s purchase of Linville Falls, Julian Price's donation of land just south of Cone Park, and Hugh Morton's granting of a free route across Grandfather Mountain and the pre-state park conservation easements granted across the mountain's crest also come to mind as pivotal contributions.

Cone's lifestyle also symbolizes the situation of so many today who are attracted to life in the hills while their livelihoods lie in the flatlands. Cone died in 1908, less than a decade after acquiring his estate; his wife followed forty years later. By then the land had been donated to the new Parkway. Today he and his wife lie in graves on the Flat Top Trail, surrounded by views and a sheltering grove of evergreens.

One of Cone's "hobbies" was road building, and he certainly indulged it here. More than 25 miles of road-width carriage paths were lightly laid on the land. They wander—indeed, they at times corkscrew (one section is called "The Maze") at very gradual grades with flat footing to create wonderful, easy avenues for carefree strolls. That's why even hikes of 5.0 miles or more can be rated moderate. These paths are perfect for families and are Nordic nirvana to cross-country skiers. Hard-core hikers should gladly trade steepness for distance and just take long walks that gobble up the miles. It's a good barter—a 10.0-mile hike here can go from hemlocks along a mountain lake to meadow-covered mountaintops. Cone Park is a superb place to reach an energetic easy stride and just enjoy the woods.

Today portions of this massive white-pine forest appear virgin in size and grandeur. Under the cathedral-like canopy, hikers experience a silent and beautiful setting, one of the scenic high points of the Parkway. And cross-country skiers are dazzled in winter. The Moses Cone and adjacent Julian Price Park parts of the Parkway are plowed between US 321 in the north (Milepost 291.8) and US 221/Holloway Mountain Road in the south (Milepost 298.6). Of course caution must still be exercised. When snow is on the ground, walkers should take care to help preserve smooth skiing conditions for skiers by not walking in ski tracks. Please create a hiker's path on one side of the trail.

Unlike Roanoke Mountain's horse trail on the Parkway in Virginia—more a favorite with riders than hikers—Cone attracts both horseback riders and walkers, so you'll surely find yourself stepping around reminders of equine passage. These are, after all, carriage paths, and the National Park Service chooses to reflect that historic use pattern by encouraging horseback riding (over the perhaps more widely popular sport of mountain biking). Nevertheless, one of the park's ongoing environmental problems is created by equestrians who wear deep troughs between trails by cutting switchbacks. Bicycles of any kind, however, are prohibited on the trails.

The leafy carriage paths of Moses Cone Memorial Park are the perfect place to soak up the autumn beauty of the North Carolina Mountains.

With so many junctions, Cone Park's system of carriage roads can be confusing, despite vastly improved signing in recent years. The following descriptions recommend circuits with carefully described junctions and turns, so you'll be sure to discover routes that many hikers and skiers only encounter by chance.

Cone Park's rolling uplands are an outstanding tribute to Moses H. Cone. Between the lakes of Cone and neighboring Price Park, this is the Parkway's best place for a "golden pond" experience of hissing breezes through lakeshore leaves, golden high-altitude summer light, and sunshine reflecting off the scintillating surface of a mountain lake. You can hike or camp by the water's edge; don't miss the A loop of Price Lake Campground for the quintessential lakeshore camping experience. Bass and Trout Lakes are among the most popular fishing sites in the High Country area.

Today Cone's Flat Top Manor is an impressive crafts center, visitor center, and gift shop, with frequent demonstrations by crafters and interpretive programs by park rangers (including weekend tours of the mansion's upstairs). The seasonal visitor center phone number is (828) 295–3782.

Option 1: Figure Eight Trail

This intriguingly designed trail explores a Northern–type forest. On one of the Parkway's most successful interpretive trails, hikers walk away with a sense of the local woods and Moses Cone, the industrialist whose estate became part of the Parkway.

Parkway mile: 294
Distance: 0.7-mile loop with figure eight
Difficulty: Easy
Elevation gain: Negligible

Maps: USGS Blowing Rock; Parkway handout map, available at the Cone Manor House/Parkway Craft Center

Finding the trailhead: Park at the Cone Manor House/Parkway Craft Center and descend to the Manor House. Cross the front porch and descend the front steps; turn right across the lawn to the sign by the woods.

The Hike

This very easy hike should be your first walk in Moses Cone Park. Even if you're not the artsy type, at least briefly explore the craft center in the Manor House (or save it for later), then take in Mr. and Mrs. Cone's favorite path, the one they shared with guests. It gives a real sense of their world—often in the evocative wording of plaques that introduce you to the forest and the culture of the mountaineers who were the couple's neighbors. The plaques "endeavor to interpret for you" the mountaineers' uses for the trees.

The gravel path barely climbs along the edge of the rhododendron and splits. Take the left turn at 0.1 mile through impressive rhododendron reaching for the sky. The trail parallels the road below the house, becomes underpinned on the left by stonework, then turns right and heads back the way it came.

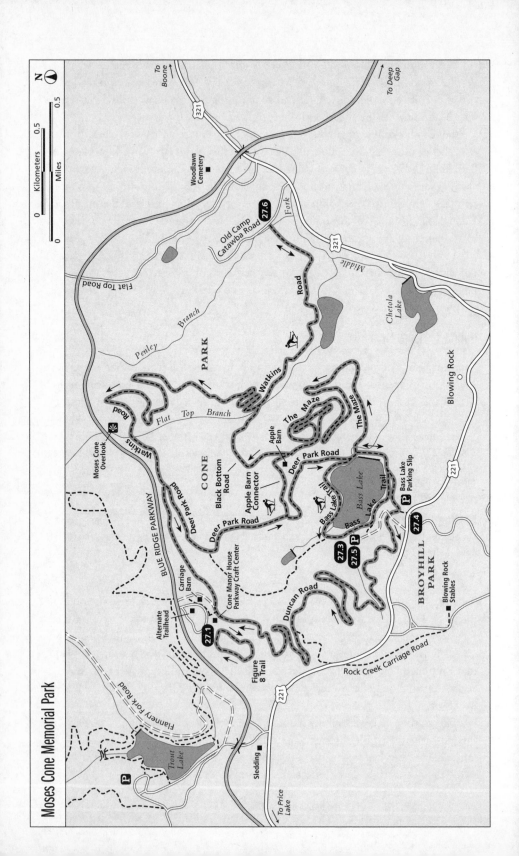

Moses Cone Memorial Park

N

Kilometers
0   0.5
Miles
0   0.5

To Boone

To Deep Gap

321

Woodlawn Cemetery

Old Camp Catawba Road   27.6

Flat Top Road

Fork

Penley

Branch

321

Middle

PARK

Chetola Lake

Watkins

Blowing Rock

Flat Top Branch

Road

CONE

The Maze

Moses Cone Overlook

Watkins Road

Apple Barn

The Maze

Black Bottom Road

Deer Park Road

Apple Barn Connector

Deer Park Road

Bass Lake Parking Slip

221

Deer Park Road

Bass Lake Trail

P

Deer Park Road

Bass Lake Trail

27.4

BLUE RIDGE PARKWAY

Carriage Barn

Cone Manor House
Parkway Craft Center

27.3

Bass Lake

P

27.5

Alternate Trailhead

27.1

Duncan Road

BROYHILL PARK

Blowing Rock Stables

Figure 8 Trail

Flannery Fork Road

Rock Creek Carriage Road

P

Trout Lake

Sledding

221

To Price Lake

Halfway back, a right turn at 0.3 mile leads into the namesake figure eight that's hidden within the loop. Like the much larger "Maze" section of carriage road above Bass Lake, this little detour through dense rhododendron is instantly disorienting— and no doubt reflective of what the Cones loved about their densely wooded Blue Ridge estate. Just follow the arrows around, taking a right back on the main path at 0.4 mile.

Impressive hardwoods such as oak, red maple, hickory, and black cherry cluster inside the trail loop. Toward the trail's end, spruce and fir mix in to lend a Northern feel. That and the flat terrain make this a good cross-country ski trail.

Signs tell how the mountaineers used the trees (tea made from black cherry bark was good for coughs, and the wood "warps not at all") or how a tree was named (serviceberry, "sarvis," bloomed when the circuit rider's church "sarvices" resumed in the spring).

By the time you leave the woods behind the massive Manor House at about 0.7 mile, you're in the perfect frame of mind to pause at one of the final plaques and "visualize the feudal elegance of this elite estate set down in the midst of mountaineer country."

At trail's end you're more than ready to nod at the man who "made his mark the classic American way, by hard work, dedication, and a dream" and left the fruits of his labors "for all Americans to enjoy."

Key Points

0.1 Turn left onto loop.

0.3 Turn right into figure eight.

0.4 Turn right out of figure eight.

0.7 Return to Manor House.

Option 2: Flat Top Road

This is the best hike to summit views of the Moses Cone Park area.

Parkway mile: 294
Distance: 5.6 miles out and back
Difficulty: Moderate
Elevation gain: 580 feet

Maps: *USGS Blowing Rock;* Parkway handout map, available at the Cone Manor House/Parkway Craft Center

Finding the trailhead: Park at the far end of the Manor House parking area, away from the house and above the Carriage Barn. A wheelchair-accessible route leads down toward the barn (and right to the house—the preferred way for skiers to avoid the steps near the house in winter). Take the gravel path left below the Carriage Barn.

The Hike

Flat Top Road, like the nearby Rich Mountain Road, is located north of the Parkway and is basically an out-and-back hike. Unlike the lower trails of Cone Park, both of

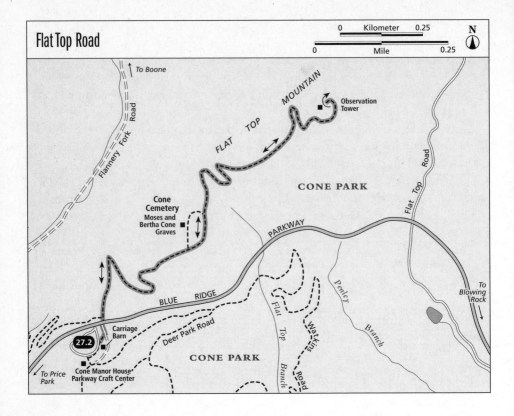

0   Kilometer   0.25

0   Mile   0.25

N

To Boone

Flannery Fork Road

FLAT TOP MOUNTAIN

Observation Tower

CONE PARK

Flat Top Road

Cone Cemetery
Moses and Bertha Cone Graves

PARKWAY

To Blowing Rock

BLUE   RIDGE

Carriage Barn

27.2

Deer Park Road

CONE PARK

Flat Top Branch

Watkins Road

Penley Branch

To Price Park

Cone Manor House
Parkway Craft Center

these hikes climb through open meadows. The Flat Top Road reaches spectacular views from occasional meadows and a tower on the summit of Flat Top (4,558 feet). Views encompass the entire North Carolina High Country.

From the Manor House parking lot, turn left below the Carriage Barn on Flat Top Road. Go under the Parkway via a tunnel to emerge at a junction amid beautiful meadows. The Rich Mountain Road goes left; bear right and go uphill and around the first turn. Leaving the meadow and entering the woods, the trail emerges again into meadows at 0.9 mile, where a spur to the left leads to the Cone family graves. Evergreens shelter the site. Mrs. Cone had four decades after her husband's death to appreciate her eventual place in this peaceful hilltop setting.

The road crosses the meadow, switchbacks right, and enters the woods. At one point the route swings just above cliffs that drop off into the forest. The trail makes very tight turns at 2.0 miles and then curves around the summit to reach the tower at 2.8 miles (5.6 miles out and back).

The tower was nicely restored in 2001. Nevertheless, expect to experience a touch of acrophobia on the breezy climb to the top. Views reach in all directions, including back to the meadow resting place of Moses and Bertha Cone.

0.1 Keep right at junction to climb along edge of meadow.

0.9 Cone family gravesite.

2.8 Summit tower.

Option 3: Bass Lake Loop Hike

This hike is a circumambulation of Cone Park's prettiest lake.

See map on page 170.
Parkway mile: 294.6
Distance: 0.8-mile loop from the lakeshore parking lot; 1.2-mile loop from US 221 trailhead

Difficulty: Easy
Elevation gain: Negligible
Maps: *USGS Blowing Rock;* Parkway handout map, available at the Cone Manor House/Parkway Craft Center

Finding the trailheads: Exit the Parkway at Milepost 294.6 to US 221. Turn left and descend in about 1 mile to the Bass Lake entrance and its two trailheads. The first is a left turn into a paved road that drops to a parking area on the banks of Bass Lake. Just beyond that turn, also on the left, the roadside Bass Lake parking slip is usable when snow complicates access to the lakeshore parking area.

The Hike

This is an easy, extremely scenic loop that, although unpaved, might be suitable for wheelchairs in dry weather. The Bass Lake loop is easiest from the lakeshore parking area below US 221. There is a new Blue Ridge Parkway Foundation–funded restroom at this parking area.

Take a right out of the lot. (You can just as easily go left as there is no preferred direction.) The grade weaves in and out along the grassy lakeshore amid maples and reaches a junction right at 0.2 mile—the 0.4-mile side trail to the parking slip on US 221.

Head left across the dam, with the Cone Manor House visible well above the lake. Across the dam, keep left as The Maze trail bears right. Cross a span over the lake's outlet and then a second road goes right (the return leg of the Cone Manor House circuit hike). In the area where the second carriage road veers right, you may notice the stone base of a boathouse down on the lakeshore at about 0.3 mile.

Continue left around the lake; your parking area is visible beyond an island on the opposite shore. The trail turns right and then left around the upper end of the lake where a bridge crosses the inlet brook at 0.6 mile. There's another bridge soon after, where hikers with dogs step off the trail to give their pets a drink. It's a few hundred feet back to the parking area for an 0.8-mile loop.

For the longer loop, start at the parking area on US 221. Pass an iron gate and gradually descend about 0.1 mile to a T junction with Duncan Road. The access road to the lakeshore parking area is just to the left, and a sign indicates that the Manor

House is 2.6 miles in that direction across the access road. Bearing right, reach the lake 0.2 mile from your car. Turn right to cross the dam. The added access distance makes this a 1.2-mile loop.

Key Points for 0.8-Mile Loop

0.2 Bear left where road goes right to US 221.

0.3 Keep left across dam; avoid two roads to the right.

0.6 Major inlet brook feeds Bass Lake.

0.8 Return to lakeshore parking area.

Option 4: Moses Cone Manor House Circuit Hike

The quintessential Cone Park day hike takes you to the Manor House and back from Bass Lake.

See map on page 170.
Parkway mile: 294.6
Distance: 4.7-mile circuit
Difficulty: Moderate

Elevation gain: 420 feet
Maps: *USGS Blowing Rock;* Parkway handout map, available at the Cone Manor House/Parkway Craft Center

Finding the trailheads: Exit the Parkway at Milepost 294.6 to US 221. Turn left and descend in about 1 mile to the Bass Lake entrance and its two trailheads. Avoid the first left turn into a paved road that drops to a parking area on the banks of Bass Lake. Just beyond that turn, also on the left, park at the roadside Bass Lake parking slip.

The Hike

The Cone Manor House is a fine destination for a day hike. Visitors gather here on the porch to relax in rocking chairs with the panoramic view of Bass Lake below. The Manor House circuit hike is on easy terrain but a moderate hike because of its length.

Park at the US 221 parking slip and pass through the iron gate. After a short descent to the T junction with Duncan Road, where a sign points left to the Manor House, go left across the road that drops to the lakeshore parking area.

At 1.1 miles the road swings out to meadows below the Manor House then switchbacks left. At 1.7 miles the Rock Creek Carriage Road goes left to circle an outlying summit on the way to Blowing Rock Stables (no horse rentals available). This popular horse trail doesn't hold much interest for hikers. After a meandering stretch through huge hemlocks and rhododendron, the road again swings back to and along the meadow, with views of the Manor House at 2.0 miles. Turn right at 2.3 miles onto the paved road that runs beneath the steps to the Manor House (craft center, restrooms, and water fountain) at about 2.6 miles.

To return to your car, bear right below the house, along the edge of the meadow on the paved Watkins Road (the pavement soon stops). At 3.2 miles turn sharp right onto the Deer Park Carriage Road where the Watkins Road goes left. The road descends (avoid one obscure old path that branches right) and emerges along the edge of the same area of meadows that you passed across the valley on the way up to the house. Just past this meadow, at 3.9 miles, the Apple Barn Connector goes left to The Maze and Watkins Road loops. A nice point of interest, the historic Apple Barn is only 0.2 mile (0.4-mile round-trip).

Continue to the right for 0.5 mile from this junction downhill through tall, stately white pines to join the Bass Lake loop at 4.4 miles. Go left and cross the span over the outlet brook. Pass the entrance to The Maze on the left and bear right. Cross the dam and at 4.5 miles bear left at a junction away from the lake and up to the T junction, where you first turned left on your way down from the parking area. A left here returns to the edge of US 221 for a 4.7-mile out-and-back hike, the last 2.0 miles of it downhill from the house. Adding the Apple Barn side trip makes this a 5.1-mile hike.

Key Points

0.1 Turn left onto Duncan Road.

1.7 Go right at junction; Rock Creek Carriage Road goes left.

2.3 Turn right onto paved road.

2.6 Reach Manor House.

3.2 Turn sharp right onto the Deer Park Carriage Road.

3.9 Go right at junction with Apple Barn Connector.

4.4 Bear right along the shore of Bass Lake and across dam.

4.5 Go left at junction to leave lake.

4.7 Make last left up to parking lot.

Option 5: The Maze Loop

A nice walk, with lakeshore views and deep forest, is made all the more interesting by the confusing route The Maze takes to get you where you've already been.

See map on page 170.
Parkway mile: 294.6
Distance: 3.6-mile loop from the lakeshore lot and from US 221
Difficulty: Moderate

Elevation gain: 220 feet
Maps: USGS Blowing Rock; Parkway handout map, available at the Cone Manor House/Parkway Craft Center

Finding the trailhead: Exit the Parkway at Milepost 294.6 to US 221. Turn left and descend in about 1 mile to the Bass Lake entrance and its two trailheads. The first is a left turn onto a paved road that drops to a parking area on the banks of Bass Lake. Just beyond that turn, also on the left, the roadside Bass Lake parking slip is usable when snow complicates access to the lakeshore parking area.

The Hike

The Maze twists and turns mysteriously through a mixed forest of mature hardwoods and towering white pines. Most hikers on this trail, especially during summer, are rarely sure where they are—be sure not to take shortcuts.

The best access is at the Bass Lake Carriage Road from the lakeshore lot. The hike is the same distance if you start at the parking lot on US 221.

Take a right out of the lot. The grade weaves in and out along the southern lakeshore and reaches a junction on the right at 0.2 mile—the side trail to the parking slip on US 221.

Take the first left across the dam, about 0.3 mile from the start or from US 221. Cross the dam and turn right at the sign into The Maze. From this entrance the carriage path corkscrews around for 2.3 miles before reaching the Apple Barn at 2.6 miles. The carriage path that drops off to the right at the Apple Barn, Black Bottom Road, leads to Watkins Road. That is the key to Cone's loneliest circuit hikes, including another version of The Maze. (See Option 6 of this hike.)

Go left past that junction. Pass the Apple Barn, and in another 0.2 mile, reach a T junction. To the right, Deer Park Road leads up to the Manor House. Make a left here at 2.8 miles and follow this last section of the Moses Cone Manor House circuit to Bass Lake at 3.3 miles. Bear left over the span that crosses the lake's outlet; pass The Maze entrance on the left, and bear right across the dam. Bear right again along the shore where the road goes left to US 221 and reach the lakeshore lot at 3.6 miles. If you parked at the US 221 parking slip, bear left just across the dam to end there for a hike that is also 3.6 miles long.

Key Points

0.3 Turn into The Maze.

2.6 The Maze ends at the Apple Barn.

2.8 Turn left at T junction.

3.3 Bear left along shore of Bass Lake.

3.6 Arrive at lakeshore lot.

Option 6: Watkins Road Circuit Hikes

A remote trailhead permits three lonely circuit hikes in a normally busy Blue Ridge Parkway hiking area.

See map on page 170.
Parkway mile: 291.8
Distance: 7.3-mile lollipop; The Maze, 6.0-mile loop; the Watkins Road–Deer Park Road circuit, 5.7 miles
Difficulty: Easy terrain, but long

Elevation gain: Greatest elevation gain 360 feet on Watkins Road circuit
Maps: USGS Blowing Rock; Parkway handout map, available at the Cone Manor House/Parkway Craft Center

Finding the trailhead: Exit the Parkway at Milepost 291.8 onto US 321 to Blowing Rock (the exit on the east side of the Parkway and on the south side of US 321). At the stop sign turn right toward Blowing Rock, and in 0.1 mile turn right again onto Old Camp Catawba Road. At 0.2 mile there's a tiny, single-car parking slip on the left before the gated carriage road goes left.

The Hikes

From its trailhead near US 321, Watkins Road is the centerpiece of three down-right quiet circuit hikes. This start is the choice for Nordic skiers wanting to avoid the chopped-up snow conditions of busier trails, but parking is almost nonexistent. (Please do not block private property.)

The longest hike—a 7.3-mile lollipop—comprises two smaller loops, formed by The Maze (6.0 miles) on the south side and the Watkins Road–Deer Park Road loop on the north side (5.7 miles). Both smaller loops join at the Apple Barn.

The Watkins Road branches from the Old Camp Catawba Road at a stream crossing with adequate stepping-stones. On its 1.0-mile jaunt to the first junction, dense rhododendron clusters under towering hemlocks. A meadow and small pond appear on the left at 0.7 mile.

To do The Maze loop, bear left onto Black Bottom Road at 1.0 mile where the Watkins Road goes right. At 1.5 miles go left again, this time into The Maze, at the Apple Barn. You'll emerge at Bass Lake at 3.8 miles. Turn right across the outlet brook bridge and make the next right. You'll ascend gradually through wonderful white pines to another right at 4.3 miles on the Apple Barn Connector. Just 0.2 mile farther, at 4.5 miles, turn left at the Apple Barn. It's another 1.5 miles retracing your steps back to Old Camp Catawba Road for a 6.0-mile loop hike.

To take the Watkins Road–Deer Park Road circuit, turn right at the first junction and stay on Watkins Road. The trail switchbacks four times then straightens as it climbs. Just below the Parkway's Moses Cone Overlook parking, the road again switchbacks before bearing left below the overlook and toward the Manor House. Turn left at 3.3 miles on the Deer Park Road. At 4.0 miles, just past meadows on the right, turn left onto the Apple Barn Connector for 0.2 mile. Make the next left, at 4.2 miles, onto the Black Bottom Road and bear right at 4.7 miles onto the Watkins Road again. Retrace your steps 1.0 mile for a 5.7-mile circuit.

The outer perimeter hike of both loops is 7.3 miles. Check the map for options. You could hike the smaller loops—or the outer perimeter—from either the Manor House or the Bass Lake trailheads to avoid the Catawba Camp parking.

Key Points on Watkins Road–Deer Park Circuit

1.0   Turn right to stay on Watkins Road.

3.3   Turn left to descend on Deer Park Road.

4.0   Turn left onto Apple Barn Connector.

4.2   Turn left onto Black Bottom Road.

4.7   Turn right onto Watkins Road and retrace route to car.

5.7   Old Camp Catawba Road.

Option 7: Rich Mountain Summit

This is the best hike to Cone Park's upland meadows.

See map on page 180.
Parkway mile: 294.6
Distance: 5.2 miles out and back from Rich Mountain trailhead; 3.6 miles from Mountains-to-Sea Trail

Difficulty: Moderate
Elevation gain: 510 feet from first trailhead
Maps: *USGS Blowing Rock;* Parkway handout map, available at the Cone Manor House/Parkway Craft Center

Finding the trailhead: Both trailheads are on Shull's Mill Road, best reached from the US 221–Parkway junction 0.5 mile south of Cone Manor. Exit the Parkway at Milepost 294.6 and turn right onto Shull's Mill Road (trip your tripometer at the junction). Descend under the Parkway tunnel and bear left. From this low point, the road climbs through curves to a crest where a fence and a pull-off on the right at 0.5 mile mark the first start of a connector trail that joins the Rich Mountain Trail. The paved road downhill is the Trout Lake Parking Area exit. (Be sure not to block the gate across the trail or the parking area exit.)

The second trailhead, for Mountains-to-Sea Trail access to the Rich Mountain Trail, is 1.3 miles past the first trailhead. Park on the left along a scenic line of mature maples and cross the road. Or park in the next curve, where the Mountains-to-Sea Trail also leaves the road south to slab around Martin Knob to a junction with the Boone Fork Trail.

The Hike

Called "Nowhere Mountain" by baby-boomer locals of the Boone area, Rich Mountain is a great hike or ski tour. The corkscrew ascent to its summit is an ongoing scenic experience as you preview the peak's summit view on the way around and around the peak. The hike described here is from either of two trailheads on Shull's Mill Road, but an even lengthier ascent can start at the Trout Lake Trail. (See Option 8.)

From the first trailhead on Shull's Mill Road, the carriage path connector climbs pretty steeply at first then becomes manageably gradual. At about 0.6 mile go left and arc across the meadow on the upper part of the Rich Mountain Carriage Road. (Don't bear right. A lower section of the Rich Mountain Carriage Road also descends to Trout Lake and is part of a longer hike from there.)

The trail leaves the meadow and wanders through a wonderful rhododendron tunnel. At 1.2 miles the Mountains-to-Sea Trail intersects on the left over a fence stile (it descends 0.4 mile to the second Shull's Mill Road trailhead). Continuing, the road turns right (an unmapped carriage road goes left at a gate) and right again at 1.7 miles as you leave the forest and slab across an open meadow. The peak is up to your right amid wind and ice–damaged trees.

The trail corkscrews twice before reaching the summit at 2.6 miles. At 4,370 feet, the peak has particularly good views across Blowing Rock and east off the Blue Ridge. Retracing your steps creates a 5.2-mile hike.

On the way down, or up, advanced hikers can alter the hike by wandering the meadows—just be sure to completely avoid the obvious routes that hikers, horses, and cattle (you could encounter some) are turning into eroded paths. Some of those trail-less options involve descents to the lower section of the Rich Mountain Road on its way to Trout Lake.

From the second trailhead ascend the Mountains-to-Sea Trail up the bank on a log with notched steps, and switchback into a white-pine forest. The trail straightens to climb directly up the slope. Turning right, it switchbacks a half dozen times to a stile over a barbed-wire fence at 0.4 mile to the carriage road. Turn left—the peak is 1.4 miles, 1.8 miles from your car—for a 3.6-mile round-trip. That route cuts 0.8 mile (1.6 miles round-trip) off the hike from the first trailhead.

The carriage road that goes left at the gate on the way to Rich Mountain is a nice quiet side trip (it's not shown on Parkway maps). A branch goes left not far from the gate that circles to the top of a tiny summit. The main road runs out a ridge to a few nice meadow views, the last down on one of Moses Cone's apple orchards. Turn around there for a 0.6-mile round-trip diversion.

Key Points

0.6 Take a left at the meadow onto Rich Mountain Carriage Road.

1.2 Mountains-to-Sea Trail goes left over stile.

1.7 Enter summit meadow.

2.6 Reach the peak.

Option 8: Trout Lake Loop and Rich Mountain Carriage Road

Unlike popular Bass Lake, with its grassy banks and deciduous trees, Trout Lake—its shores covered in a forest of towering hemlocks—is far less visited. This is also a great starting point for a long and quiet hike higher on Rich Mountain.

Parkway mile: 294.6
Distance: 1.0-mile lakeshore hike; 2.6-mile circuit of lower Rich Mountain Carriage Road; 6.6-mile circuit to Rich Mountain summit
Difficulty: Easy for lakeshore; moderate to strenuous for the longer walks

Elevation gain: Negligible around lake; 610 feet to Rich Mountain
Maps: USGS Blowing Rock; a Parkway handout map is available at the Cone Manor House/ Parkway Craft Center

---

Finding the trailhead: Access the trailhead from Shull's Mill Road, best reached from the US 221–Parkway junction 0.5 mile south of Cone Manor. Exit the Parkway at Milepost 294.6 and turn right onto Shull's Mill Road. Descend under the Parkway tunnel, avoiding the first, abrupt right to the unpaved Flannery Fork Road. Take the second, oblique right immediately past that. The scenic one-way road leads level above the lake to the Trout Lake Parking Area. The exit road returns to Shull's Mill Road at the first trailhead for the Rich Mountain hike (go left 0.5 mile back to the Parkway).

The Hike

Trout Lake makes for a memorable lakeshore walk or ski trip.

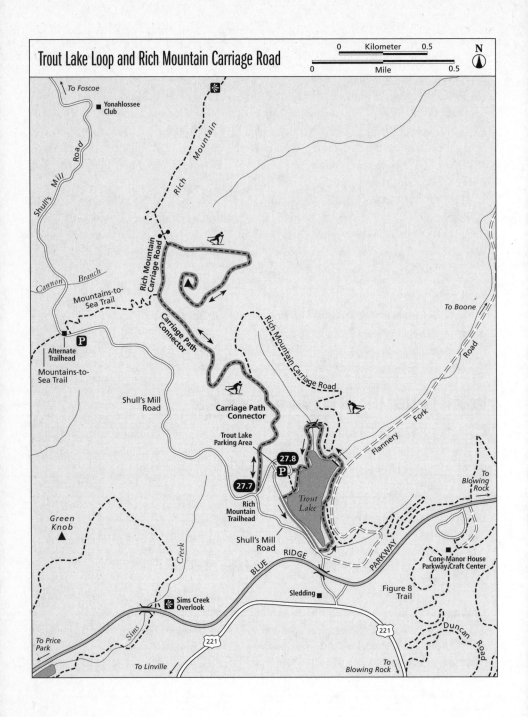

Trout Lake Loop and Rich Mountain Carriage Road

To Foscoe

Yonahlossee Club

Shull's Mill Road

Rich Mountain

Rich Mountain Carriage Road

Cannon Branch

Mountains-to-Sea Trail

P
Alternate Trailhead

Mountains-to-Sea Trail

Shull's Mill Road

Carriage Path Connector

Carriage Path Connector

Rich Mountain Carriage Road

To Boone

Flannery Fork Road

Trout Lake Parking Area

27.8
P

27.7

Rich Mountain Trailhead

Shull's Mill Road

Green Knob

Creek

Trout Lake

To Blowing Rock

Cone Manor House
Parkway Craft Center

BLUE RIDGE PARKWAY

Sledding

Figure 8 Trail

Sims Creek Overlook

Sims

To Price Park

221

To Linville

221

To Blowing Rock

Duncan Road

Kilometer   0.5

Mile   0.5

N

From the edge of the Trout Lake Parking Area, take one of the two access trails that dip to the carriage road below and go right. In a short distance turn left onto the road you just drove in on. As you near Shull's Mill Road, turn left and dip down into the woods again. You'll pass a junction at 0.4 mile where the Rich Mountain Carriage Road comes in on the right (the Cone Manor House is 1.0 mile to the right). At 0.5 mile reach Flannery Fork Road and turn left to cross the dam. Some Trout Lake hikers park here on the Flannery Fork Road (a secluded unpaved byway to Boone that's worth the detour).

Across the dam, the trail enters a towering, centuries-old hemlock forest that Cone found in the moist coves that became this lake. (Sadly, the hemlock woolly adelgid is killing these centuries-old trees.) There's a junction at 0.7 mile where the Rich Mountain Carriage Road goes right (more below). Stay left, across the bridge, to continue through tall trees and glimpses of a northern lakeshore scene. Take either of the two side trails right and uphill to the parking area for a 1.0-mile hike. The proximity of the trailhead for the Rich Mountain Carriage Road hikes—only a 100-yard walk up the exit road—makes this a nice start for more ambitious hikes.

To make a loop of the lake and lower Rich Mountain Carriage Road, take a left from the parking area and enjoy the lakeshore forest for 0.3 mile on the way to a left at the first junction with the Rich Mountain Carriage Road. The trail makes a switchback past a scenic water impoundment with a splashing spillway, then passes through a gate at 1.6 miles. The trail soon exits the woods and at 1.9 miles enters the meadow and reaches a junction just above the main Rich Mountain trailhead on Shull's Mill Road. To the right, the Rich Mountain Carriage Road goes across the meadow to the summit. Turn left and descend the carriage road access trail to Shull's Mill Road at 2.5 miles. From there, go left down the parking area exit road for a 2.6-mile hike.

You could also go right at the meadow above the Shull's Mill Road trailhead and reach the summit of Rich Mountain at 3.9 miles. Retrace your steps from there to the top of the carriage road access trail at 5.9 miles, then turn right down to Shull's Mill Road. A left there down the Trout Lake Parking Area exit road makes a 6.6-mile circuit.

Advanced hikers could shorten this hike. Leaving the summit of Rich Mountain, bear right as meadows open up to your right and drop down through the meadows and beautiful glades to join the lower Rich Mountain Carriage Road on its way to the lake. (See the map.)

Key Points on Trout Lake Loop

0.4 Rich Mountain Carriage Road comes in on right.
0.7 Rich Mountain Carriage Road goes right.
1.0 Parking area.

28 Julian Price Memorial Park

Mileposts 295.9–297.2

With the Parkway's largest campground, its second largest picnic area, and a forty-seven-acre lake that is one of the scenic high points of the entire Parkway, Price Park is justifiably popular. A trail circles the lake, and another path delves into the waterfall-filled Boone Fork drainage. The Greensboro-based Jefferson Standard Insurance Company donated the land to memorialize its founder and president, Julian Price, after his death in an automobile accident—an ironic tribute in a park dedicated to experiencing nature by car. Together, Julian Price and adjacent Moses Cone Parks exemplify the impact of wealthy donors on the Parkway—and the distinctive role played by the city of Greensboro, North Carolina (both men were residents).

Whether you camp at Price Campground, hike the lakeshore loop trail, or just glance across the placid waters from the Parkway as you cross the dam, the lake is the scenic centerpiece of Price Park. Grandfather Mountain towers in the distance—still snowy in the spring when lime-green trees line the lake or ablaze in autumn color while green branches still wave on the shore.

The lake is formed by Boone Fork, a stream named for Jesse Boone, a nephew of Daniel Boone who lived here in the early 1800s. Below the lake, the Boone Fork Trail forms a nice loop along the stream. Above the lake—and actually visible from Price Lake Overlook—you can see the stream's source in the high bowl-shaped valley scooped out under the peak of distant Grandfather Mountain.

Access is easy even in winter, when snow covers the ground and the entire surface of the lake can be frozen—often into jagged, jumbled sheets that groan and crack. Price and Moses Cone Parks lie virtually side by side, so the Park Service usually plows the Parkway past both parks between US 321 at Milepost 291.8, near Blowing Rock, and the US 221 exit at Holloway Mountain Road at Milepost 298.6 (but hazardous conditions can exist). That makes the parks' trails a nice target for winter hikers and cross-country skiers.

In summer, canoes and rowboats dot the surface of the lake—even sea kayaks have become popular of late. If you don't have your own boat, Price Park's boathouse, at Milepost 297, charges only a modest hourly fee to rent its dozen canoes and handful of rowboats. Boaters pay when they bring their boats back, so they're free to stay out longer when they realize how much fun they're having. In fall the rental schedule usually shifts to weekends only until the concession closes on November 1. Only paddle-propelled boats are permitted on the lake—no sails or motors of any kind.

Option 1: Green Knob Trail

This loop hike is a microcosm of one of the most scenic sections of the Parkway. It follows a stream from a lakeshore through towering trees to meadow-capped hilltops and panoramic views.

Parkway mile: 295.9
Distance: 2.1-mile loop
Difficulty: Moderate

Elevation gain: 460 feet
Maps: *USGS Boone;* Parkway handout map, available at Price Campground contact kiosk

Finding the trailhead: Park at Sims Pond Overlook, 1.3 miles south of the US 221 exit near the town of Blowing Rock. You could also use the Sims Creek Viaduct Overlook at Milepost 295.3.

The Hike

This hike takes the scenic gamut of the Julian Price and Moses Cone Parks and brings it together in one walk.

Leave the trailhead and cross the spillway bridge and the dam of tiny, scenic Sims Pond. You'll immediately turn left along the rhododendron-lined shoreline, passing fishing trails to the water's edge. As you leave the pond with the inlet stream, a new section of trail avoids the once wet and rooty route by climbing away from the stream then dipping more steeply back to cross it.

Then the trail rises gradually through the start of a long grove of towering hemlocks. There's a bench beside a pool at 0.4 mile. As stream sounds give way to the ka-thump of cars passing 85 feet above on the Sims Creek Viaduct, the trail rises above the stream and the gorge narrows. Inspiring views open up of hemlock wooly adelgid–challenged trees rising above a dense understory of rhododendron. You're high enough above the stream to really appreciate the carpet of rhododendron you've been under.

The trail undulates up and down and makes a handful of stream crossings, one over a rustic split-log bridge. Expect A+ scenery as the fern-lined path passes under the Parkway bridge amid massive hemlocks. At the next trail bridge, near a bench at about 0.6 of a mile, a side path climbs steeply right a short distance to Sims Creek Viaduct Overlook. Standing here in the open, sunlit forest, with the hemlock grove so close—not to mention the sound of people passing overhead with no clue of what lies below—you sense this is a secret spot. It's the perfect place to pull off the road and drop into the woods for a picnic or a rest, even if you don't hike.

The trail follows the stream from the bench, veers left, and steepens over the next 0.3 mile as it crosses three side streams and rises out of the Sims Creek drainage. Then the grade slackens, and ahead the sky beckons. Passing through a fat-man squeeze at the 1.0-mile mark, you rise into a broad meadow. Just ahead, a bench at a lone tree marks a perfect spot to admire profuse September wildflowers.

Beyond, the trail arcs leftward across the first of many meadows big and small. (Thirteen concrete posts with blue directional arrows appear at intervals to guide you across the grass.) In a short stretch of woods, the next meadow appears through the trees. As you prepare to leave that meadow through a fat-man squeeze near the woods, glance right—flocks of the recently reintroduced and increasingly profuse wild turkeys have been spotted in the distant corner of the fields.

Dipping into the hardwood forest past a weathered old bench, the trail levels off and enters a south-facing meadow (Price Lake is visible below Grandfather Moun-

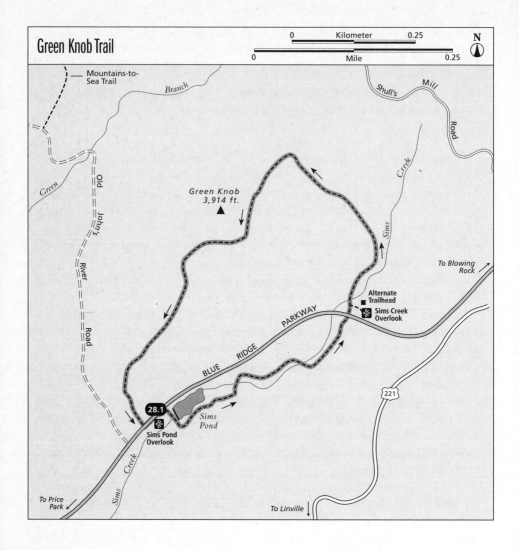

Green Knob Trail

0   Kilometer   0.25

0   Mile   0.25

N

Mountains-to-Sea Trail

Branch

Shull's

Mill

Road

Green

Old John's

River

Road

Creek

Green Knob
3,914 ft.

Sims

Alternate
Trailhead

To Blowing
Rock

Sims Creek
Overlook

PARKWAY

BLUE   RIDGE

221

28.1

Sims Pond
Overlook

Sims
Pond

To Price
Park

Sims   Creek

To Linville

tain). Descending more steeply now at times, you'll alternate between scenic woods and smaller meadows. The ridgeline route dips in and out of intimate swales, where the fringed green carpet of ferns runs off into open woods. You're near the bottom when a flight of log steps reaches a bench and spectacular view into the gaping bowl of Grandfather Mountain. To the mountain's right, the prominent (to be kind) Sugar Top condominium tops a peak of the Sugar Mountain ski area.

Heading down and left, you pass through a fat-man squeeze into another meadow and then exit into the woods at the sound of cars. A brief rhododendron-tunnel section of trail brings you to the Parkway. Your car is 150 feet to the left at the Sims Pond Overlook.

Option 2: Boone Fork Trail

One of the Parkway's longer trails wanders a significant distance away from the road and for much of its length follows a scenic mountain stream with rocky plunges and deep pools.

Parkway mile: 296.4
Distance: 4.9-mile loop
Difficulty: Strenuous

Elevation gain: 440 feet
Maps: *USGS Boone;* Parkway handout map, available at Price Campground contact kiosk

Finding the trailhead: Turn into the Price Park Picnic Area and go left into the first lot. Park beside the restroom building.

The Hike

The Boone Fork Trail is a standout for many reasons. Don't expect the Parkway's typical distant views. This is an "in the trees" trail that substitutes a stunning stream full of cascades and pools for vistas. And it's long by Parkway standards, so give this hike some time. It's perfect as a major midday walk that includes a picnic lunch. And there is insight aplenty—into the logging railroads that tamed unbelievable terrain to carry off the virgin timber a century ago and the beavers that build jaw-dropping dams visible along the trail.

Walk past the restrooms and take the bridge left across Boone Fork Creek. A map/sign marks the junction where this big loop branches. Head right, paralleling Boone Fork and the picnic area through what the signs say was once a lake. The path enters the woods, and boggy areas crop up. The trail tunnels along under rhododendron, the first of many times it will do so. Keep your eyes open on the right at about the 0.5-mile mark: Beavers are very active here. It's hard to believe they had been eradicated in the area by 1897.

In the next rhododendron tunnel, notice the obvious railroad ties in the tread-way—the grade you're on was an old logging railroad. At about 1.0 mile, where boulders cross the stream, the Mountains-to-Sea Trail goes right to Moses Cone Park. (The next trailhead, on Shull's Mill Road, is a starting point for the Rich Mountain hike.) Ahead, you're now on the combined Boone Fork–Mountains-to-Sea Trail, which immediately climbs a rock outcrop—subtle evidence of blasting on the rock and the upcoming road-cut show that the railroad actually rose around these rocks on a long-gone trestle. Below, the stream plunges over repeated ledges into deep pools.

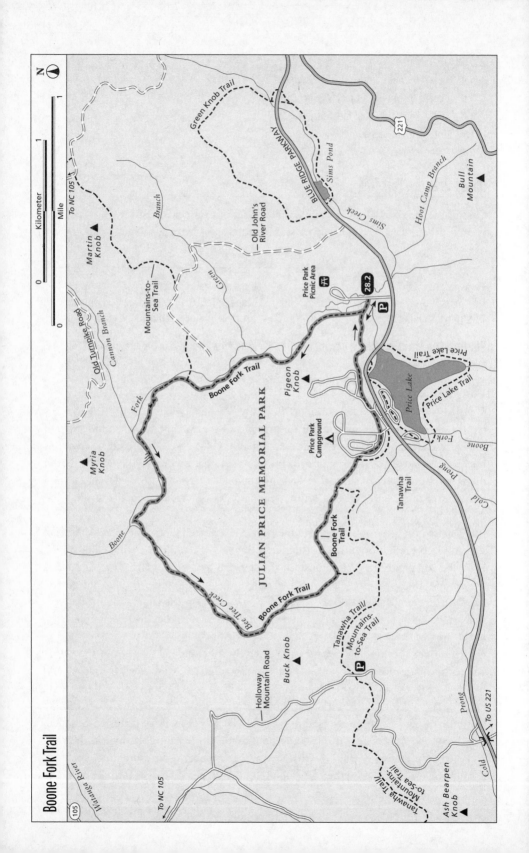

Boone Fork Trail

N

	Kilometer	
0		1
0	Mile	1

To NC 105

Watauga River

Old Turnpike Road

Cannon Branch

Martin Knob ▲

Mountains-to-Sea Trail

Green Branch

Green Knob Trail

To NC 105

BLUE RIDGE PARKWAY

Sims Pond

Old John's River Road

Sims Creek

Hoot Camp Branch

Bull Mountain ▲

221

Myria Knob ▲

Boone Fork

Boone Fork Trail

Price Park Picnic Area

28.2

P

Price Lake Trail

Price Lake

Pigeon Knob ▲

JULIAN PRICE MEMORIAL PARK

Price Park Campground ▲

Boone Fork

Price Lake Trail

Bee Tree Creek

Boone Fork Trail

Boone Fork Trail

Tanawha Trail

Cold Prong

Holloway Mountain Road

Buck Knob ▲

P

Tanawha Trail/Mountains-to-Sea Trail

To NC 105

Tanawha Trail/Mountains-to-Sea Trail

Ash Bearpen Knob ▲

Cold Prong

To US 221

The trail arcs across a forested hillside of birches and rhododendron. Just above what appears to be the remains of an old bridge crossing the stream, the trail bears left away from Boone Fork. It eventually returns to the stream. A bushwhack route follows Boone Fork but can be confusing.

The trail leaves the road grade and descends then climbs a ladder among crags (your cue to watch for the next turn) before veering sharply downhill to the right and dropping to the stream bank. (Here's where those who bushwhacked the stream-side would rejoin the trail.) Head left along the stream at 1.8 miles; the next few tenths of a mile pass truly impressive cascades. This is the biggest, steepest waterfall on the trail, with a wealth of places to sit and ponder the impressive plunges.

Get ready for more interesting evidence of railroading as you pass above deep pools amid hemlocks. The trail repeatedly rises and falls. It climbs stone or wood steps up to sections of railroad grade and then descends as the grade disappears. Then it climbs back to the next section of grade. You guessed it—long-gone bridges once carried trains across the space between these level grades. Don't expect this area to look like a construction site, but many hikers would miss the evidence that a railroad once ran here.

You cross a variety of side streams in this area then definitively switchback left out of the Boone Fork drainage (but the railroad grade keeps going) at about 2.5 miles. The trail climbs moderately, crossing Bee Tree Creek various times on logs, rocks, and then two bigger bridges. A wonderfully curving section of stream with a rock-lined trail and rhododendron tunnel follows. Then come more rocky crossings amid and among bubbling rivulets. This is scenic streamside hiking, especially in the light of late day.

A split-log bridge marks an upcoming section of steeper stone steps. The trail levels through an oak and hemlock forest carpeted with club moss then zigzags across various bridges, up stone steps, and into a wonderful grotto. Big hemlocks rise overhead, rhododendron cluster everywhere, and a paved portion of trail ducks beneath one of the rock outcrops that sprout above.

An eroded section of steep trail and a heart-thumping climb follow (with a bench halfway up). Then the scenery changes. Step through the fat-man squeeze to the edge of a meadow at 3.5 miles. The trail turns left and follows a rhododendron tunnel around the grassy bulge above. If you wish, go straight into the meadow following an obvious secondary path to the top for a great view of Grandfather Mountain to the southwest. Continue past the peak off the steeper side of the meadow and descend to the Boone Fork Trail, visible beyond as it arcs across the meadow.

The sandy trail leaves the meadow through white pines and reaches a junction at 3.9 miles where the Mountains-to-Sea Trail turns right and, along with the Tanawha Trail, heads south for Grandfather Mountain. (The short stretch of trail above, over the meadow to this junction, is part of a shorter Tanawha Trail loop hike.) Continue straight on the combined Boone Fork–Tanawha Trail through another fat-man squeeze and enter a true tunnel through the rhododendron. The trail splits at 4.1 miles. Tanawha descends right to its terminus trailhead near the Parkway just inside Price Park Campground. Stay left on the Boone Fork Trail and descend quickly to

Price Park Campground. Cross the road, go left of the restrooms, and veer sharp right, following a paved trail along the ridge bisecting the campground loop.

The trail again crosses the campground loop and becomes gravel as it passes above the Tanawha Trail parking area, visible off to the right. The trail passes between a ranger residence and the campground check-in kiosk at about 4.5 miles then crosses another road that rises left up to the RV campground loops. After a brief and gradual descent, the Boone Fork Trail reenters the meadow and reaches the sign where the loop started in the picnic area. Go straight across the bridge and back to your car.

Key Points

0.5 Extensive beaver activity across the stream.

1.0 Mountains-to-Sea Trail branches right to Moses Cone Park.

1.8 Rejoin Boone Fork near hike's biggest waterfalls.

2.5 Trail enters drainage of Bee Tree Creek.

3.9 Mountains-to-Sea and Tanawha Trail junction right from Grandfather Mountain.

4.1 Tanawha Trail branches right toward its Price Park Campground terminus.

4.5 Pass between a ranger residence and the campground check-in kiosk.

Option 3: Price Lake Trail

A great lakeside trail loops around the Parkway's largest body of water.

Parkway mile: 297.2
Distance: 2.5-mile loop
Difficulty: Easy to moderate

Elevation gain: Negligible
Maps: *USGS Boone;* Parkway handout map, available at Price Campground contact kiosk

Finding the trailhead: Either of two lakeshore overlooks is a potential starting point. The Boone Fork Overlook (oddly named because it overlooks Price Lake) is reached by a spur road at Milepost 297.2. Price Lake Overlook (which also overlooks the lake) is at Milepost 296.7.

The Hike

Price Lake is a memorable walk, in part through the lakeshore "A" loop of Price Lake Campground—easily one of the premier places on the Parkway to set up a tent.

Leave the southern end of the Boone Fork Overlook by the trail map sign and descend a wheelchair-accessible ramp past the top of the boat launch and behind the boat rental building. The first 0.7 mile of this trail has been nicely upgraded to permit wheelchair access to stream and lakeshore fishing spots. The trail scoots into the rhododendron immediately and crosses a bridge over Cold Prong. Most of this hike is right on the lakeshore, but now the path wanders a bit away and crosses a second bridge over the lake's main source, Boone Fork.

Staying away from the shoreline, the trail crosses a boggy area on a long boardwalk at about 0.5 mile. Here, opposite the boat launch, the trail returns to the shore at a lakeside fishing deck. This 1.0-mile or so out-and-back hike is one of the Parkway's

Price Lake may offer great views of surrounding mountains on a clear day, but there's something magical about a misty day by the lake.

best for the wheelchair-bound and beginning or very young cross-country skiers or hikers. From here to the Parkway, the trail is a woodsy and quiet walk—excepting the hollow *thunk* of paddle on canoe—around the longest arm of the lake.

The trail turns right and climbs its steepest grades (modest though they are) through a rhododendron grove before descending back to the lakeshore. The view is of the opposite bank as this prong of the lake constricts to a marshy area and the feeder stream of Laurel Creek. The trail turns left and crosses a bridge at about 1.0 mile then bears left again along the opposite bank, bound for the Parkway and the dam that impounds the lake. The entire trail has benches now and then, but just after a small bridge there's a bench tucked down by the lakeshore and surrounded by rhododendron at 1.2 miles. The views of Grandfather Mountain are particularly good along this eastern side of the lake. A variety of rocks reach into the water, enticing boaters to land and fishers to cast.

The trail exits the rhododendron near the bank to turn sharply right around a large rock at 1.4 miles. The path undulates its way to a flight of steps that lead out of the woods to the Parkway at 1.7 miles. Head left across the bridge over the dam, pass through Price Lake Overlook, and hug the roadside on a paved path. A lakeside deck creates another wheelchair-accessible place to fish or catch a view before leaving the open roadside and entering the tall hemlocks of the campground. The trail follows the lake then veers right to bisect Loop A. Just past a restroom at 2.2 miles, the trail crosses the road into the woods. At a junction go left; the trail to the right crosses the Parkway to the other campground loops and the Tanawha Trail Parking Area. The

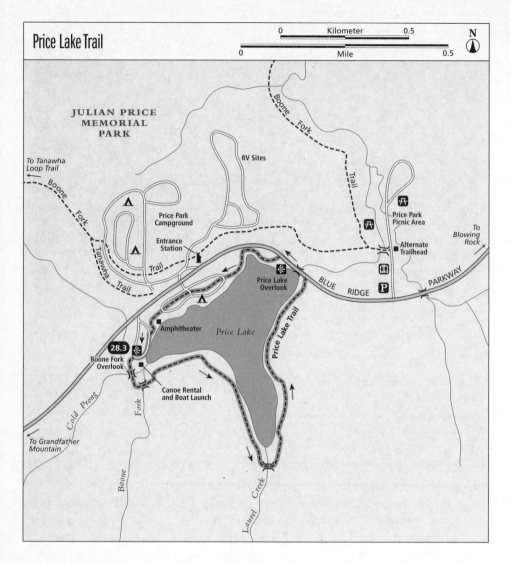

Price Lake Trail rises left to skirt the campground amphitheater. Emerging at the northern end of the Boone Fork Overlook, follow the edge of the parking lot along the lake and back to your car at 2.5 miles.

Key Points

0.5 Cross lengthy boardwalk

0.7 Fishing deck opposite boat ramp.

1.0 Bridge signals left turn along final side of the lake.

1.7 Turn left along Parkway to cross dam.

2.2 Pass restrooms.

2.5 Back to Boone Fork Overlook.

29 Tanawha Trail and the Parkway at Grandfather Mountain

Mileposts 298.6–304.4

The Tanawha Trail—the Cherokee word means "great hawk" or "eagle"—lies along the entire length of the Grandfather Mountain "missing link" portion of the Parkway. The trail reaches all the way to Julian Price Memorial Park and is the crowning achievement of the Blue Ridge Parkway trail network.

Hikers won't fail to notice the trail's intricate stone stairways, rock-paved treadways, and arching wood bridges (lowered here by helicopter), all designed to minimize hiker damage to this scenic environment. The federal government spent almost $750,000 in 1980s dollars on the 13.5 miles of trail between Beacon Heights, near Linville, and Price Park Campground, near Blowing Rock.

The Tanawha Trail's best views are from Rough Ridge, a high outcrop where boardwalks and handrails were required to keep the public from trampling the low, alpinelike vegetation, some of it rare and endangered. Please stay on the trails; dogs are prohibited, even on-leash. Happily, substantial effort has been devoted to preserving a truly unique area.

The Tanawha Trail, like many other sections of the Mountains-to-Sea Trail in North Carolina and the Appalachian Trail in Virginia, will rarely be hiked end to end by Parkway motorists. The most worthwhile sections of these roadside paths are the places that provide loop opportunities or attractive turnaround points. The hikes described below focus on those parts of what planners called the "Parkway parallel trail" before it was renamed.

Option 1: Tanawha Trail Hikes near Holloway Mountain Road

Two opportunities—a circuit hike and an out-and-back walk—allow you to sample the Tanawha and Mountains-to-Sea Trails in an area noted for outstanding meadow views.

Parkway mile: 298.6
Distance: 2.4-mile circuit to the north of the road; 1.6-mile out-and-back hike to the south (with greater distances and a higher-elevation hike possible)
Difficulty: Easy for the meadow hikes immediately north and south of Holloway Mountain Road; moderate for others
Elevation gain: 50 feet
Maps: USGS *Grandfather Mountain;* Tanawha Trail handout map, available at the Linn Cove Visitor Center (That map does not show the hike described first below; rely on the map provided here.)

Finding the trailhead: Leave the Parkway south of Blowing Rock at Milepost 298.6—the Holloway Mountain Road/US 221 exit. Turn immediately right onto the dirt road and park on the right in 1 mile at the Tanawha Trail crossing.

The Hikes

The circuit hike to the north patches together an easy sampling of the Tanawha, Boone Fork, and Mountains-to-Sea Trails without requiring that you completely retrace your steps. It also takes hikers along one of the premier unpaved roads near the Parkway. If you continue past the trailhead 1.2 miles and then turn right onto a paved road, you soon reach NC 105 between Boone and Banner Elk.

Head through the fat-man squeeze going north (to the right coming from the Parkway) on the combined Tanawha and Mountains-to-Sea Trail. Cross the first stretch of meadow, pass through another squeeze at 0.1 mile, then turn right onto an old gravel farm road. Follow the grade a short distance beneath a power line at 0.3 mile and then at 0.4 mile veer left up the log steps as the trail leaves the grade. At 0.5 mile cross the next fence and pass a Tanawha Trail signpost just beyond it onto another obvious gravel road grade.

Two hundred feet beyond the sign, at about 0.6 mile, near the edge of a meadow the trail goes right on the main grade. Leave the formal trail here, veering uphill where the road grade rises left. Emerge into the meadow and follow the obvious but faint, now grassy old roadway left through the grass for 100 feet parallel to rhododendron at the edge of the woods. The roadway wanders across the meadow, under the power line in the distance, and to the right of the rise beyond.

At about 0.9 mile the grade reaches a junction where the Boone Fork Trail comes in on the left. The junction is marked by a Mountains-to-Sea Trail signpost and signs in two directions reading BOONE FORK TRAIL, 4.9-MILE LOOP. Keep straight; the Boone Fork Trail turns left at the sign and onto your road grade.

Follow the rhododendron-arched Boone Fork Trail straight ahead, or turn right at the sign on an obvious secondary path and go up over the grassy bulge of the meadow for a great view of Grandfather Mountain to the southwest. Continuing over this meadow, head off the steeper side of the peak and down to the Boone Fork Trail, visible below as it leaves the rhododendron tunnel you avoided and arcs to the right across the field below.

Back on the main trail, descend from the meadow into white pines to a junction at 1.3 miles. This is the Mountains-to-Sea Trail/Tanawha Trail combination that you started on but left back at the meadow. Turn right off the Boone Fork Trail and head south along this section of trail you missed.

The first few hundred yards are beautiful—ferns, moss, and pine needles cover the ground under a grove of white pines. Notice the nearly decayed ruin of a tiny chestnut farm shed on the left as you start down from the turn. The path crosses a bridge, meets and follows a fenceline, crosses another small bridge, and gradually climbs right to reenter the meadow at an old apple orchard. Leveling off, the trail switchbacks left and passes a grove of white pines flanked by another apple orchard—a long-ago mountaineer homesite. The trail swings past the site and enters the woods at a trailside pit where an underground stream threatens to collapse the path.

Heading back into the woods at 1.8 miles, you immediately pass the uphill grade you earlier took to the left to exit the formal trail (now on your right). Now you're heading back the way you came. If you miss the last left turn from the road grade onto the Tanawha Trail to your car, don't sweat it. The gravel roadway empties onto Holloway Mountain Road 200 feet beyond where you parked (turn left), for a total hike of about 2.4 miles.

Just across the road from the hike above lies an even easier meadow walk to the south. The Tanawha Trail heads toward Grandfather Mountain, and views of the peak dominate the horizon in that direction.

The trail leaves the road through the fat-man squeeze, turns left at the roadside Tanawha Trail mileage sign, and arcs up the edge of the meadow. The path crosses another fence at 0.4 mile below an old cemetery that is just out of sight on the high right. It swings into the bowl of the next meadow then wanders through a grove of white pines with views down on the Holloway Mountain Road. When you reach a power line toward the end of the meadow at about 0.8 mile, a return from there creates an easy meadow stroll that's perfect for a picnic or ski tour of 1.6 miles.

The Tanawha Trail's elegantly arching spans, like this one at Rough Ridge, were lowered into place by helicopter.

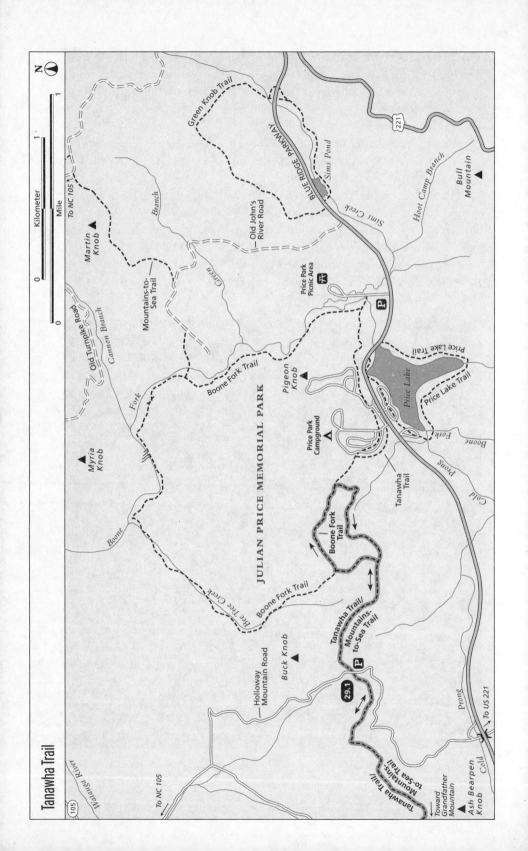

Tanawha Trail

Beyond the meadow turnaround point at 0.8 mile, the trail continues, descending into the woods and passing through a meadow at 1.1 miles and a nice clifftop view up to Grandfather Mountain's northernmost ridge at 1.6 miles. It crosses a small stream at 1.9 miles then rises to a junction at 2.0 miles. The Tanawha Trail continues right to the Boone Fork Parking Area. A side trail goes left 0.2 mile to Cold Prong Pond Parking Area (Milepost 299.0). With two cars you could hike beyond the turnaround meadow to Cold Prong Pond Parking Area, 1.4 miles farther, for a 2.2-mile one-way hike or, lacking a shuttle, a 4.4-mile out-and-back hike from Holloway Mountain Road.

Key Points for the Circuit to the North

0.4 Veer left off the grade and up log steps.

0.6 Turn left (north) onto the faint roadway to cross the meadow.

0.9 Join Boone Fork/Mountains-to-Sea Trail.

1.3 Turn right onto Mountains-to-Sea/Tanawha Trail.

1.8 Rejoin portion of trail you've already walked.

2.4 Holloway Mountain Road.

Option 2: Tanawha Trail from Cold Prong Pond Parking Area

An out-and-back hike or two-car shuttle heads uphill from Cold Prong Pond Overlook to Boone Fork Parking Area.

Parkway mile: 299
Distance: 3.8 miles out and back
Difficulty: Moderate
Elevation gain: 360 feet
Maps: USGS Grandfather Mountain; Tanawha Trail handout map, available at the Linn Cove Visitor Center. Parts of this hike are shown on Grandfather Mountain hiking map, free at Grandfather Mountain entrance (south from Cold Prong Pond Overlook 6.1 miles to US 221 exit; right 1 mile to entrance).

Finding the trailhead: Park at Cold Prong Pond Overlook. The trail leaves the north end of the parking lot and loops the now-drained site of Cold Prong Pond in 0.5 mile—but the formal start of the trail is so indirect that people have started an informal trail near the middle of the lot that dips left and down directly to the Tanawha Trail.

The Hike

Cold Prong Pond Overlook is the start of a noteworthy hike up to Boone Fork Parking Area. It's uphill, which means it's appropriately downhill on the way back, and has a logical destination—a scenic bridge over rushing Boone Fork, where a variety of hikes to the Grandfather summit region start. Another plus is that few people hike this scenic section of trail.

Take a left 0.2 mile below the parking area on the Tanawha Trail. The path crosses a wet slab of rock and turns right over a trail bridge to veer well away from the Parkway. At 0.5 mile cross another bridge to a right turn that deftly surmounts a crag to leave the drainage.

The trail rises past hemlocks, sharply switchbacks left, and enters an impressive cove hardwood forest with plentiful wildflowers at about 1.2 miles. The road can't be heard from here—this would be a great place for one of those (nearly) ubiquitous Parkway benches. The trail dips out of the cove and turns right around a ridge to enter an old road grade within earshot of the Parkway. The path climbs above the grade at 1.7 miles, where rock walls deflect the trail around a little stream. At about 1.9 miles bear right at the junction (the side trail goes left to Boone Fork Parking Area in 0.1 mile); the Boone Fork Trail bridge is a few hundred feet away. Nice pools lie below.

Key Points

0.2 Junction with Tanawha Trail; go left.

1.2 Nice cove hardwood forest.

1.9 Boone Fork Trail bridge.

Option 3: Tanawha Trail to Rough Ridge

Quite possibly the Parkway's easiest path to a spectacular view, here the Tanawha Trail traverses the alpine-appearing crest of a leading ridge to Grandfather Mountain.

Parkway mile: 302.8
Distance: Entire section is 1.5 miles, but the closest view is only a 0.6-mile round-trip. Out-and-back hikes of 1.2 and about 2.0 miles lead to the peak of Rough Ridge.
Difficulty: Moderate to strenuous
Elevation gain: 540 feet from Wilson Creek Overlook; 480 feet from Rough

Ridge Parking Area
Maps: *USGS Grandfather Mountain;* Tanawha Trail handout map, available at the Linn Cove Visitor Center. The Grandfather Mountain hiking map shows the trail best and is available free at the Grandfather Mountain entrance (south from Rough Ridge Overlook 2.3 miles to US 221 exit; right 1 mile to entrance).

Finding the trailhead: This hike is accessible from Wilson Creek Overlook (Milepost 303.6) and Rough Ridge Overlook (Milepost 302.8).

The Hike

The cliff-lined alpine crest of Rough Ridge offers startling vistas atop a stone face visible to Parkway motorists. From many places on this part of the Tanawha Trail, including boardwalks just 0.3 mile from the Rough Ridge Parking Area, the vista engulfs you.

As you're standing on the boardwalks, Rough Ridge rises to the three loftiest summits of Grandfather Mountain—a rocky, dramatic climax at nearly 6,000 feet. The Wilson Creek drainage drops like an expansive chute past the Linn Cove Viaduct and Parkway snaking to the south. Far below, across the rippling corduroy of Pisgah National Forest, the land descends to the edge of the Piedmont. This nearly vertical-mile relief is the greatest rise of the Blue Ridge escarpment. Mount Mitchell lies on the southern horizon; Grandfather Mountain's Pilot Knob is the rocky peak just to the north.

It's a dramatic view down to the North Carolina Piedmont from Rough Ridge—and when you turn the other way, there's an equally awesome rise up to the peaks of Grandfather Mountain.

Climbers call the faces below Rough Ridge "Ship Rock," and the crags are among the South's most popular rock-climbing sites. (The National Park Service requests that climbers reach the rock from the Wilson Creek Parking Area.)

The most direct route to the summit of Rough Ridge is from the parking area of the same name. Here the access trail ascends log steps to a junction. Take the Tanawha Trail left and immediately cross an arching wood bridge (near a NO PETS BEYOND THIS POINT sign) over a cascade that tumbles down beneath the parking area visible below. (To the right at the junction, the Tanawha Trail rises gently then descends in 4.0 miles through a luxuriant spruce forest around Pilot Knob to the Boone Fork Overlook.)

Across the bridge, the often-soggy trail ascends through evergreens, climbs a flight of stone steps, and then levels across a rocky shelf amid blueberry bushes and galax. It turns a corner, passes a distinctive stack rock formation on the right, and reaches 200 feet of ascending boardwalk designed to keep hikers from trampling the low vegetation that now surrounds you.

From this boardwalk—just 0.3 mile round-trip from the parking area—the view is remarkably similar to that found on the summit (another 0.3 mile ahead up rocky but nicely graded switchbacks). At the top, cable-defined pathways keep people on the paths amid fragile Allegheny sand myrtle and turkey beard. Unfortunately, dogs that are allowed off-leash don't stay within the barriers, so the Park Service prohibits all dogs from this trail.

Rough Ridge

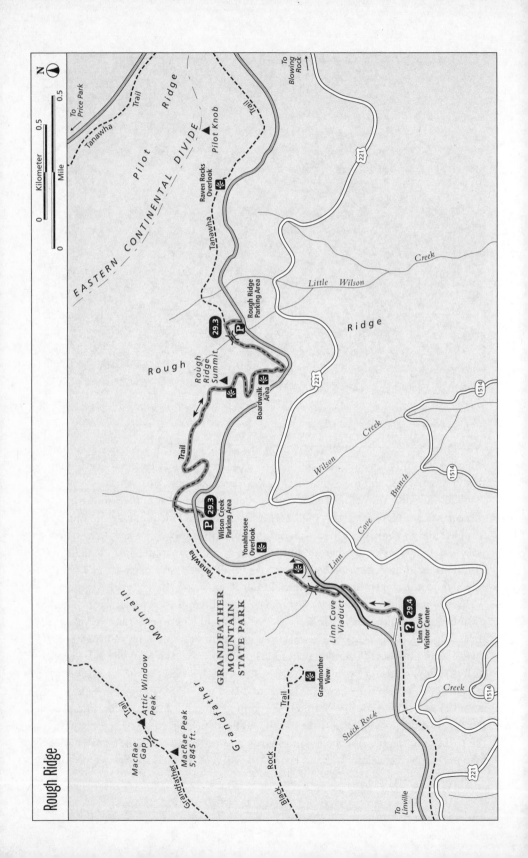

Either location is a nice spot to watch a sunset and get back to your car quickly. On a crystal-clear fall day, with electric foliage below, a summit dusting of snow, and racing clouds . . . you get the picture.

Wilson Creek Overlook is also a good start for an out-and-back hike to Rough Ridge. This approach is often less populated than the trail from Rough Ridge Parking Area.

Starting at Wilson Creek, take the side trail under the Parkway 0.1 mile to a junction with the Tanawha Trail and go right. Cross Wilson Creek (hence the name of the entire watershed above and below the mountain). The trail drops to within sight of the road then slips below the prow of an outcrop at 0.2 mile. Then comes a largely gradual and meandering climb across an ecosystem that recommends this Tanawha Trail hike—rock-garden boulder fields strewn with spring wildflowers and towering trees. After climbing through mixed evergreens to a saddle, stone steps artfully surmount the crag-capped summit of Rough Ridge, just under 1.0 mile from the Wilson Creek Parking Area (about 2.0 miles round-trip). From the summit to the Rough Ridge Parking Area, it's another 0.6 mile, for a 1.6-mile total hike.

An end-to-end hike would require leaving a car at both the Rough Ridge and Wilson Creek Parking Areas. If that's not possible, consider walking between the trailheads. The roadside walk is only 0.8 mile and is recommended by spectacular views of cliffs and climbers that motorists often only glimpse as they whiz by. That makes for a 2.4-mile hike.

Key Points from Rough Ridge Parking Area

0.3   Boardwalk views.

0.6   Views from the summit of Rough Ridge.

Option 4: Linn Cove Viaduct

A wheelchair-accessible paved path leads under this stunning span of the Parkway's Linn Cove Viaduct and then continues as a rougher trail through beautiful Linn Cove. The turnaround point is a classic postcard view of the viaduct.

Parkway mile: 304.4

Distance: 0.3 mile out and back for barrier-free trail; 1.0 mile out and back to classic views of the viaduct

Difficulty: Easy and barrier-free to moderate

Elevation gain: Virtually none for the paved trail; 50 feet for the moderate hike

Maps: USGS *Grandfather Mountain;* Tanawha Trail handout map, available at the Linn Cove Visitor Center. The Grandfather Mountain hiking map shows the trail best and is available free at the Grandfather Mountain entrance (south 0.7 mile to US 221 exit; right 1 mile to entrance).

Finding the trailhead: The trail starts at the end of the Linn Cove Parking Area opposite the small visitor center.

The Hike

The easiest walk to a view of the Linn Cove Viaduct begins at the Linn Cove Visitor Center, just north of Milepost 304.0. A paved and barrier-free trail winds 0.15 mile from the end of the parking lot opposite the vistor center to a viewpoint underneath the serpentine Linn Cove Viaduct.

The next-easiest walk lies just beyond. Stay on the trail past the pavement as it briefly climbs to the level of the bridge and zigzags through towering rhododendron, hemlocks, and birches. It undulates over impressive stone stairways among the jumble of huge boulders that tumble down from Grandfather Mountain's Black Rock Cliffs. This is the terrain that prompted the choice of span you see arcing around you. As you hike you'll hear the occasional whoosh and thump of a passing car. The trail crosses a bridge over Linn Cove Branch and ascends out of the stream drainage to a ridgeline above the road. At the 0.5-mile mark take a right on a side trail (a TANAWHA TRAIL sign with arrows that directs hikers back to the Linn Cove Parking Area marks the spot). This rock offers the picture-perfect perch for the oft-photographed view back to the bridge. Retrace your steps for a 1.0-mile out-and-back hike.

The trail continues 0.8 mile north to the Wilson Creek Overlook, the start of a recommended hike to Rough Ridge. Continuing from the viaduct view could lengthen that hike to Rough Ridge by 1.3 miles one-way. But this next section of Tanawha Trail is steep and very near the road. Lacking a strong desire for a longer hike, you'd do just as well to start at Wilson Creek.

Key Points

0.15 End of paved path.

0.5 Postcard view of viaduct.

THE "MISSING LINK"

Motorists are invariably attracted to this "newest" part of the Parkway in the Grandfather Mountain area. In addition to the scenic grandeur, they're wowed by the Linn Cove Viaduct, a multimillion-dollar space-age span made famous in nationally televised automobile advertisements.

The costly and curving Linn Cove Viaduct literally leaps away from the mountain. The segmented bridge was built with each ensuing section lowered out over thin air and affixed to the one before it. A small visitor center, the Parkway's Linn Cove Visitor Center, tells the inspiring technical story of the viaduct's construction. A portion of the Tanawha Trail takes you right beneath the viaduct.

The story of this long-awaited "missing link" in the Blue Ridge Parkway began after World War II, when young combat photographer Hugh Morton returned to his family's lands on Grandfather Mountain. The mountain had been part of a private tourist attraction and open to paying customers since the 1930s, and a "summit road" reached an overlook. Morton extended the road to "the top," actually one of the mountain's lower though spectacular summits. In 1951 he built the Mile-High Swinging Bridge, a suspension bridge between two rocky peaks. A summit visitor center later was built beside it. Habitat-style animal exhibits debuted in 1973, and a long list of annual events attracted thousands. Over the years, Morton's promotional genius and his gift for scenic photography made the mountain a high point of North Carolina tourism.

Not everything went smoothly. There is something about "owning a mountain," especially one being developed to attract tourists, that rubs people the wrong way. In retrospect, Morton's "ownership" is now widely seen as "stewardship." But in the early 1950s, public-spirited people lobbied hard to remove Grandfather Mountain from private ownership. An effort by the National Park Service was intended to wrest control of a portion of the mountain from Morton by completing the Blue Ridge Parkway on a "high route" that would have ridden well up on the mountain's flank, probably undermining the appeal of his Swinging Bridge. But Morton marshaled public opinion against a route that would have destroyed a significant swath of the mountain's wilderness. The irony of a private landowner defending wildlands against the nation's principal conservation agency was a potent marketing tool.

For thirty years the Department of the Interior wrangled with the private landowner over where the Blue Ridge Parkway would cross "his" mountain. Eventually, precluded from condemning land for a high route across this spectacular parcel of private land, the National

Park Service agreed on a lower route and the Parkway battle came to a close. Morton then donated the property for the route and expanded that acreage when the Tanawha Trail's designers wanted the new Parkway trail to climb higher on the mountainside.

After decades of controversy and acrimony, the National Park Service forged ahead to complete the project. The agency spared no expense to minimize the road's environmental impact. Fortuitously, the Parkway had been delayed long enough that it was now technologically feasible to build a computer-designed span that would lift the road above the fragile mountainside. The Park Service ultimately honored Morton for his role in what had become a reasonable solution for the public and a private landowner.

The two protagonists in the latter part of the controversy—Morton and longtime Parkway superintendent Gary Everhardt, who retired in 2001 after twenty-three years as head of the Parkway—ended up as friends who cooperated often for the benefit of the environment. The two worked closely to see that the USDA Forest Service acquired a parcel of private land under the viaduct.

The Linn Cove Viaduct and the Grandfather Mountain section of the Parkway debuted to wide acclaim on September 11, 1987—two years after the high road's fiftieth anniversary.

Exhibits at the Linn Cove Visitor Center explain the complex construction techniques that created the viaduct.

30 Grandfather Mountain

Mileposts 299.9–305.1

Hugh Morton's stewardship of his family's private lands on Grandfather Mountain has seen this spectacular North Carolina area evolve from a tourist attraction to an International Biosphere Reserve. His efforts set a national standard in preservation and public use of private land. Morton passed away in 2006.

Grandfather Mountain is a rocky, spectacular summit known to tourists for great views from its privately owned road and Mile-High Swinging Bridge. The peak is one of the region's premier natural areas, with a wonderful network of trails. Grandfather Mountain's 4,000 acres boast forty-three species of rare or endangered plants and animals, more than Great Smoky Mountains National Park.

As part of a private conservation park, the mountain's summit road has been open since the 1930s. After World War II, Morton extended the road upward, eventually connecting two lower summits with the Mile-High Swinging Bridge. Habitat-style animal exhibits debuted in 1973. The mountain became a high point of North Carolina tourism. Meanwhile, Grandfather Mountain's undeveloped backcountry—a nearly 5,000-acre parcel of jagged, evergreen-clothed cliffs and a nearly 6,000-foot summit—slumbered. An early book about the area described the wonderful hiking on the mountain, and at times during the development of the travel attraction, new trails were cut, signed, and occasionally "mowed" by park maintenance employees.

In 1978 Morton's Grandfather Mountain park successfully implemented a hiker fee system, establishing a pay-for-use trail preservation program that over the years became a significant example of wilderness management. The program attracted the country's leading backcountry researchers. The first peregrine falcons to be reintroduced into the wild Southern Appalachians were released here.

Spurred by the amicable resolution of Morton's "battle" with the Parkway (see sidebar) and the success of the trail management program, Grandfather Mountain's status as a natural area soared. More than 3,000 acres of its backcountry was eventually preserved through conservation easements granted to the North Carolina Nature Conservancy. In 1994 Grandfather Mountain became the nation's only privately owned Biosphere Reserve, one of 311 outstanding natural areas designated in eighty-one countries by UNESCO, the United Nations Educational, Cultural, and Scientific Organization.

In 2009 the bulk of the mountain's backcountry became a North Carolina state park. The acreage that includes the Mile-High Swinging Bridge is still privately owned, now as a nonprofit, and still offers the same attractions.

The mountain's new summit visitor center opened in early 2010, and for the first time the Mile-High Swinging Bridge is wheelchair accessible.

Halfway up the auto road—adjacent to habitats for deer, bears, cougars, and eagles—a first-class nature museum contains natural history exhibits. Daily nature films and educational events, such as a free June outdoor photography clinic, are often held in the museum theater.

Another new aspect of Grandfather Mountain: It has shrunk. No, the "Grand-fatherly" old summit isn't slumping, but it was remeasured in 2008. Calloway Peak became 5,946 feet (not 5,964—the elevation published by the state in 1917); Mac-Rae Peak is now 5,845 feet (not 5,939).

The mountain's innovative trail program has been based on a hiking permit system, which seems likely to continue—but at this point only camping requires a fee (registration is possible online). Permit outlets are plentiful, usually adjacent to trailheads, and the state park has installed trailhead registration posts. Please see trailhead signs for the latest information, or visit www.grandfather.com. Motor vehicle entrance fees to the mountain include hiking on trails from the attraction.

Hikers should be alert to weather conditions at Grandfather Mountain. People have died on the mountain from exposure, lightning strikes, falls, and heart attacks. The mountain is known for snowy winters and year-round high winds. A U.S. Weather Station caps the summit visitor center.

Option 1: Tanawha Trail and Daniel Boone Scout Trail to Calloway Peak

Tracking up the back side of Grandfather Mountain, the Daniel Boone Scout Trail climbs to Calloway Peak. Two other view-packed trails, one a nice beginning backpacking trip, also start on the Tanawha Trail from the Blue Ridge Parkway.

Parkway mile: 299.9
Distance: 5.8- or 4.9-mile out-and-back hike to Calloway Peak and a great view on the Boone Trail; 3.6-mile hike on the Crag Way Trail; 3.2 miles on the Nuwati Trail
Difficulty: Strenuous for the Boone Trail to Calloway Peak and for the Crag Way circuit; moderate for the Nuwati Trail

Elevation gain: 2,026 feet for the climb to Calloway Peak; 920 feet for the Crag Way circuit; 580 feet for the Nuwati Trail
Maps: USGS Grandfather Mountain; Tanawha Trail handout map, available at the Linn Cove Visitor Center. The best map for the hike is the trail map of Grandfather Mountain, available free at the Grandfather Mountain entrance (south 5.2 miles to US 221 exit; right 1 mile to entrance.)

Finding the trailhead: The best starting point for all these hikes is the Boone Fork Parking Area on the Blue Ridge Parkway. An alternative, especially in winter when snow closes the Parkway, is the Boone Trail's year-round trailhead on US 221, 8.5 miles north of the Grandfather Mountain entrance and 1.5 miles south of the US 221–Holloway Mountain Road junction south of Blowing Rock. Hiking permits are required on Grandfather Mountain's trails and are available at trailhead registration posts and online. (See trailhead signs for the latest information, or visit www.grand father.com.)

The author climbs the last few feet to the summit of MacRae Peak. PHOTO BY HELEN HOPPER

The Hikes

The Blue Ridge Parkway side of Grandfather Mountain was once the least-visited part of the peak. US 221 quietly snaked its way around the convoluted ridges, leading Parkway motorists past the portion of this national scenic road that wasn't completed until the late 1980s.

Looking west from Calloway Peak, the view is developed with everything from ski slopes lit for night skiing to condos. But the mountain bulks against the intrusion, and the Parkway side of the ridge gives campers on Grandfather a stunning vista of Piedmont cities sprawling like distant pinwheels of light over the dark isolation of Pisgah National Forest.

Since the early days of World War II, a primitive trail up this wilder side of the mountain has been in existence, built by a part-time Parkway ranger named Clyde Smith and a Blowing Rock troop of Boy Scouts. Smith moved back and forth between New England and North Carolina, pursuing his dedication to trails and handcrafting trail signs, many of which he installed on his favorite Southern summit: Grandfather Mountain. But the Boone Trail was only a memory a decade before the Parkway opened.

Grandfather Mountain's trail program reclaimed it in 1979. The route was pieced together from the remains of tin can–top trail markers, some bearing painted arrowheads. Also discovered was a decaying, half-century-old backpacking shelter felled by a wind-flattened grove of evergreens. By the early 1980s, the old backpacking shelter, Hi-Balsam, had been rebuilt. Then two new trails were added in the bowl-shaped valley beneath Calloway Peak that is spectacularly reminiscent of glacial bowls in New England.

In the 1970s two Appalachian State University professors hypothesized that the valley had been gouged by a glacier. Their conclusion was based on "glacial grooves" that were later discovered to have been left by logging cables.

Hike to Boone Fork Bowl

Starting at the Parkway's Boone Fork Parking Area, the connector to the Tanawha Trail leaves the lot and goes right at the first junction. (Left, a streamside trail connects a short distance north to the Calloway Peak Overlook—a good alternative if the Boone Fork lot is full.) The next junction is the Tanawha Trail. Go left and cross the laminated bridge spanning the creek. The connector to US 221 branches left just over the bridge (the 0.4-mile trail leads under a Blue Ridge Parkway bridge along an old road grade to the alternative trailhead). The Tanawha Trail wanders along, gaining elevation with moderate climbs to a junction on the right, at about 0.4 mile, with the Nuwati Trail.

The Nuwati Trail, formerly the Grandfather Trail Extension, was renamed in the early 1990s with a Cherokee word meaning "good medicine," a reference to the healing power of the wilderness experience, complementing the Tanawha Trail, which means "great hawk" or "eagle." Take a right on the blue-blazed trail, pass a trailhead signboard, and follow the level but rocky trail up an old logging railroad grade. A spring gushes under the trail at 0.7 mile. The trail winds along, gaining elevation until the bowl-like shape of the valley becomes noticeable. The sounds of the stream become audible far below on the right, and the old grade becomes a scenic rhododendron tunnel fringed by lacelike ferns. At 1.1 miles the Crag Way Trail goes left.

Within a few hundred feet is a designated campsite on the left beside a stream. From here to its end, the trail crosses numerous tributaries of Boone Fork, all of them easy hops. Another campsite appears on the left, where a large logging cable (like those that created the "ice-carved" grooves) is held firm in the V of a tree.

Cross Boone Fork at 1.4 miles and continue on the level path. The trail forks. A right dead-ends at a tent platform campsite. A left leads steeply to a prominent tooth of rock projecting above the valley floor at 4,500 feet (with a tent platform campsite at its base), 1.6 miles from the trailhead. The 360-degree panorama encompasses the entire high mountain valley—the upper bowl and headwall of the supposed "cirque," Calloway Peak above it, and the cliffs of White Rock Ridge above on the right. The rocky pinnacles on the Crag Way Trail lie on the opposite side of the valley. East, the view stretches along the Blue Ridge Parkway to Blowing Rock and Piedmont cities.

The Nuwati Trail gains only about 600 feet in 1.6 miles, making it a good beginning backpacking trip with moderate elevation gain, a number of trailside campsites, and spectacular scenery. The lowest crags on Crag Way and the bowl view at the end of the trail make nice evening viewpoints for campers.

Crag Way Loop

The best way to hike the steep Crag Way is down, and that involves hiking up the lower part of the Daniel Boone Scout Trail.

To do that, where the Nuwati Trail goes right from the Tanawha Trail, turn left and stay on Tanawha. The path ascends around a ridge; at 0.6 mile from the trailhead, the Daniel Boone Scout Trail goes right. Past the signboard and a flight of steps, the trail begins a gradual, switchbacking climb.

Emerging between two rock outcroppings 1.6 miles from the trailhead, the Boone Scout Trail continues left 0.1 mile to the "middle campsite," a group of tent platforms at about the center point on the trail. To the right, Crag Way starts its trip down to the Nuwati Trail. Go right, but first ascend Flat Rock View, the crag between the two—a table-flat vantage point on Boone Fork Bowl that makes a perfect lunch spot.

Going right on Crag Way, the trail skirts Flat Rock and winds along open crags, reenters the woods, and artfully broaches a line of small cliffs. Through dense rhododendron and occasional spruces, the path enters a heath bald of blueberry bushes and rhododendron before it abruptly encounters spectacular views at Top Crag. Keep to the trail here to avoid further impacting the Allegheny sand myrtle, a low-growing alpinelike plant that covers the open area. This expansive view is one of the best on the mountain.

The path steeply descends rocky crags with great views to a signed junction and a right on the Nuwati Trail (2.5 miles from the start). Going left on Tanawha, the round-trip back to the Boone Fork parking area is 3.6 miles. If you go left at the Crag Way–Nuwati Trail junction and hike to the view at the end of the Nuwati Trail and back, the hike is 4.6 miles.

Calloway Peak

To reach Calloway Peak, continue on the Boone Trail past the top of the Crag Way Trail—about 1.6 miles from the Boone Fork trailhead. The Daniel Boone Scout Trail enters a small flat where a left reaches the middle campsite. A side trail from there continues through a mixed deciduous and spruce forest about 100 yards to a small, reliable spring.

Heading up, the Boone Trail switchbacks in and out of a scenic red spruce forest. When the trail finally gains the crest of Pilot Ridge, a nice campsite with a view appears on the left. Continuing, the trail enters the spruce-fir forest zone—a dark, cool evergreen area carpeted with moss and wood sorrel. The trail climbs a rocky crag where a right turn at the top takes you out on the rock to good views. The trail reenters the woods and shortly reaches a signed trail on the left. Viaduct View is a rocky perch with a perspective on the Parkway's Linn Cove Viaduct.

The Daniel Boone Scout Trail crosses another crag; a second side trail on the left leads to Hi-Balsam Shelter, a tiny low-lying lean-to that sleeps five. The shelter, at about 2.6 miles, was built by Clyde Smith during World War II and later rebuilt to the same unique style and dimensions. No tent camping or fires are permitted at the shelter site.

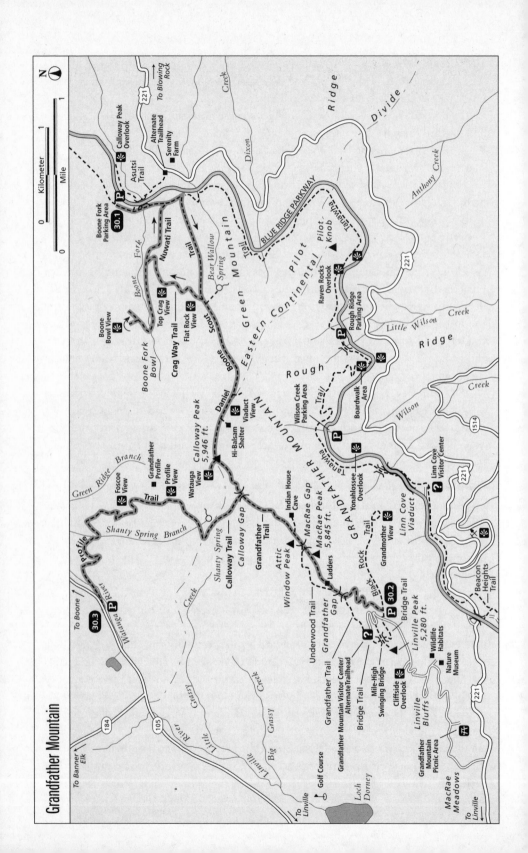

Grandfather Mountain

Just 100 yards from the shelter, the Daniel Boone Scout Trail continues past a tent platform campsite on the left (fires permitted). Opposite the campsite, across the trail and off in the woods, lie the remains of a single-engine plane that crashed in 1978. Past this point the trail suddenly stands on end, climbing steeply with the aid of one large ladder to Calloway Peak (5,946 feet; marked by a white X), 2.8 miles from the trailhead. The panoramic view takes in the dramatic drop to the Piedmont.

The Boone Trail terminates about 0.1 mile away at the Grandfather Trail and Watauga (*wa-TAW-ga*) View, the best vantage point to the west. Between the peak and the junction, the summit area is a rocky, evergreen-covered crest.

Retracing your steps, the entire hike is just under 6.0 miles with a visit to Watauga View. If you go left on the Crag Way Trail on the way down, the route is just under 5.0 miles, again assuming a Watauga View turnaround.

Key Points to Calloway Peak

0.4   Tanawha Trail junction with Nuwati Trail.

0.6   Right onto Daniel Boone Scout Trail.

1.6   Junction with Crag Way Trail.

2.6   Hi-Balsam Shelter.

2.8   Calloway Peak.

2.9   Watauga View turnaround.

Option 2: Grandfather Trail

One of the South's most rugged, spectacular, and storied trails traverses Grandfather Mountain's summit ridge. The route ascends peaks and scales ladders over cliffs to reach Calloway Peak, the highest summit in the Blue Ridge.

See map on page 208.
Parkway mile: 305.1
Distance: 2.0 miles out and back over the first major peak; 4.8 miles to Calloway Peak and back
Difficulty: Strenuous

Elevation gain: About 746 feet from the summit parking area for loop of MacRae Peak; 1,698 feet to Calloway Park and back returning on Underwood Trail
Maps: USGS *Grandfather Mountain.* The best map for the hike is the free trail map of Grandfather Mountain.

Finding the trailhead: Both trailheads lie at the top of the Grandfather Mountain motor road. A spur trail, the Grandfather Trail Extension, reaches the Grandfather Trail from the uppermost of the two Black Rock Trail parking lots just below the summit (next right after the 5,000 FEET ELEVATION sign). The trail itself starts at the highest parking lot opposite the new Linville Peak Visitor Center and the Mile-High Swinging Bridge.

Hikers may be asked to park at the lower of the two lots during busy times at the tourist attraction. If this is the case, and you do not wish to use the spur or would like to return to the visitor center (no walking is permitted on the road), take the Bridge Trail to the summit visitor center. That trail, which starts across the motor road from the Black Rock Cliffs Parking Area, is a moderate and meandering 0.4-mile climb through the cleft beneath the Swinging Bridge to the summit parking area.

The Hike

Starting at the Black Rock Trail Parking Area has its appeal. The Black Rock Trail itself is a 1.0-mile level path across the mountain's eastern flank. It passes a wonderful formation called Arch Rock on the way to an end loop with great views of the mountain—the summits above, the Parkway and Piedmont far below. The forest is a very New England–like mix of birches and spruce. And this is a nature trail; thirty-five stops interpret that inviting ecosystem.

The spur from the Black Rock Trail Parking Area to the Grandfather Trail is pleasant. The spur rises left out of the upper of the two parking areas (the Black Rock Trail goes right) and climbs first through a meadow then spruces and rhododendron to a junction with the Grandfather Trail.

Leaving the summit lot opposite the visitor center, the blue-blazed Grandfather Trail scrambles up a steep, rocky pitch and then turns right along a level path through open rhododendron areas and spruce forests and under an overhang called Head Bumpin' Rock. The cragtop view just beyond of the peaks is a nice turnaround for a family stroll. Left (west) is the resort development of Sugar Mountain (with the ten-story condominium now prohibited by state law) and Linville Ridge Country Club. Right (east), the land plummets to the Piedmont, a view that will get even better as you climb MacRae Peak (5,845 feet)—the cliff-faced, evergreen-covered summit straight ahead. If you peer closely at about ten o'clock on the peak, you might see hikers on a series of ladders that you'll climb.

Hikers climb ladders up the cliffs of MacRae Peak on Grandfather Mountain.

Descend along cables intended for use when the trail is a river of ice, and ascend over a crag. The spur trail from the Black Rock Trail Parking Area comes in on the right at 0.4 mile. You'll enter a large meadow with a junction just below the peak at 0.5 mile. The yellow-blazed Underwood Trail goes left to the gap beyond MacRae Peak, avoiding the climb over the summit. This is a nice return route that creates a great loop of the Grandfather Ridge. After crossing MacRae Peak, take a left on the Underwood Trail and return to this point and the visitor center for one of the truly spectacular short hikes in the region, 2.0 miles round-trip.

Turn right on the Grandfather Trail toward MacRae Peak and climb a steep section with the aid of cables. Ascending left, the trail then veers right into a fissure, where you'll encounter the first ladder. Not far above it, an opening on the left reveals a cliff that funnels a breeze in summer and a bitter wind in winter. Scramble up a few more rocks; the steepest ladders reach to the clifftops above. An experienced climber could scramble up the rocks around the ladders, but to the inexperienced, this is a truly adventurous section of trail. Consider pausing on the large ledge before the last ladder. The visitor center is now far below.

Ascend along the clifftop, climb another ladder, wander along a precipitous ridgeline, and emerge onto a knife-edge with a house-size boulder perched atop it. This is MacRae Peak (5,845 feet). An unnerving ladder leans against it. Climb and have lunch; the view is stupendous. To the east, the Blue Ridge escarpment plummets past the newest part of the Blue Ridge Parkway to the distant Carolina Piedmont. Farther along the ridge, the next summit, Attic Window Peak, rises with a deep cleft splitting its summit (the trail climbs through it). To the right of the peak, huge domes drop to the east. Continuing beyond the boulder, the trail reaches a steep chute where cables aid the descent to another ladder. In winter this is a frozen flow of ice.

At MacRae Gap, 1.0 mile from the visitor center, the Underwood Trail leads left 0.5 mile through crags, cliffs, mossy defiles, and a beautiful evergreen forest reminiscent of the far north. A return here nets a wonderfully adventurous day hike of 2.0 miles.

Keep on the Grandfather Trail, winding through a wood sorrel–covered gap of evergreens to more ladders, this time scaling their way through a boulder cave called THE SUBWAY on a mid-twentieth-century trail sign discovered here. Scramble higher through the massive split in the peak.

At the top of the couloir, a trail leads right to a tent platform campsite atop the domes. To the left, the trail emerges from between rocks to a stunning western view from Attic Window Peak at 1.2 miles.

Following the Grandfather Trail to the right, drop to the next gap. A side trail to the right at 1.3 miles leads to a massive overhanging rock called Indian House Cave. When discovered in the 1940s, the cave contained Native American artifacts, suggesting that it was a significant ritual site. This is a nice place to escape the rain.

Back at the gap, climb a small ladder; the trail follows an evergreen-, rhododendron-, and mountain laurel-covered knife-edge above a series of dramatic cliffs then descends into a high, alpinelike meadow with a fine campsite accessible to nearby evening views. Farther on, the trail crosses another clifftop and a tiny gap grown close with evergreens and wood sorrel.

Going over a whaleback of crags, the trail winds into Calloway Gap at 1.9 miles, a traditional ridgetop campground with a number of campsites. In the gap the red-blazed Calloway Trail descends steeply left 0.3 mile to a water source at Shanty Spring and the Profile Trail. (See Option 3.)

Right on the Grandfather Trail, the path climbs again, through a tiny meadow and past a campsite on the right with a spectacular view from a ledge. Farther up, the trail passes through dense evergreens. Almost immediately, the Grandfather Trail's last junction is reached at 2.3 miles. To the left, a short spur leads to Watauga View, a westerly ledge facing Banner Elk and overlooking the headwaters of the Watauga River. Just 0.1 mile to the right, on the white-blazed Daniel Boone Scout Trail, is Calloway Peak (5,946 feet).

The easiest way to gauge Grandfather Mountain's significance is to look east from Calloway, MacRae, or Attic Window Peaks and realize that Andre Michaux, the earliest and most important botanical explorer of the New World, clawed his way there in 1792 and completely lost all evidence of scientific objectivity. The result was perhaps the biggest error of Michaux's scientific career. In what biographer Henry Savage Jr. says was an unprecedented burst of emotion, the botanist told his diary that he'd "reached the summit of the highest mountain in all of North America." He was so inspired that he sang the "Marseillaise" and shouted "long live America and the Republic of France. Long live liberty, equality, and fraternity." Michaux's discovery of nearly 200 species of plants is a more fitting symbol of his achievements.

The Grandfather Trail gives hikers the best glimpse of the kind of scenery that prompted Michaux's famous flub. They'll also observe many of the plants he found so interesting. On the high, rocky clifftops, hikers encounter the fuzzy reddish-green leaves of Michaux's saxifrage, a delicate boreal plant that he might have first noticed here.

Key Points

0.4 Junction with Grandfather Trail Extension.

0.5 Junction with Underwood Trail.

1.0 Junction with Underwood Trail in MacRae Gap.

1.2 Attic Window Peak.

1.3 Right turn to Indian House Cave.

1.9 Calloway Gap.

2.3 Watauga View.

2.4 Calloway Peak.

Option 3: Profile Trail

This hike climbs the western flank of Grandfather Mountain to Calloway Peak.

See map on page 208.
Parkway mile: 305.1
Distance: 1.8 miles round-trip to Shanty Spring Branch; 7.0 miles round-trip to Calloway Peak
Difficulty: Easy to moderate to Shanty Spring Branch; strenuous to Calloway Peak

Elevation gain: 2,066 feet to Calloway Peak
Maps: USGS Grandfather Mountain. The best map for the hike is the free trail map of Grandfather Mountain, available at the Grandfather Mountain entrance, which you pass on the way to the trailhead (hiking permits also available).

Finding the trailhead: Leave the Parkway at Milepost 305.1 and turn right onto US 221. Continue past the Grandfather Mountain entrance (at 1 mile) and turn right onto NC 105 in Linville at about 3 miles. At about 7 miles pass the junction with NC 184, and in 0.7 mile turn sharply right into the trailhead parking area.

The Hike

The Profile Trail was built in the mid- to late 1980s to replace the ancient Shanty Spring Trail, a steep and eroding trail dating from the latter half of the nineteenth century.

Some of the earliest hikers who used the Shanty Spring Trail arrived at the trailhead on the old East Tennessee & Western North Carolina (ET&WNC) Railroad that paused in Linville Gap on its way from Johnson City, Tennessee, to Boone. The early romance of that time was eloquently told in the book *The Balsam Groves of the Grandfather Mountain* by Shepherd Dugger, published in 1907.

The Profile Trail has dramatic views of The Profile, the multifaceted namesake face of Grandfather Mountain that looks west. The face, or faces, is best seen north of the trailhead. (A few miles in that direction, the Grandview Restaurant is a nice place to appreciate the profile during a breakfast or lunch stop.)

The trail starts in an intimate spot beside the headwaters of the Watauga River where fringed phacelia blooms in April. The graded trail is largely level as it wanders for its first 0.9 mile along the beautiful stream through a mature, New England–like forest.

The trail leaves the river, climbs steeply for 0.2 mile or so, and passes a mileage sign at 0.5 mile, the first of such reminders along the trail. The trail winds into a scenic, dry drainage. Just beyond on the right, the large, waxy evergreen-leafed ground plant is Fraser's sedge, on the endangered list. At about 0.9 mile the trail dips across Shanty Spring Branch, the source of which is Shanty Spring, 1.8 miles ahead. Returning to the trailhead from here makes a nice out-and-back family hike of 1.8 miles.

Past the stream, the trail dips through a fissure in large rocks and then winds higher in and out of the drainages above on its way around Green Ridge.

As the trail crosses over Green Ridge and levels on its way into the next drainage, immediately below the Grandfather Profile, it reaches a nice view at about 1.7 miles. It looks north over the Watauga River Valley town of Foscoe and on to White Top (with its crescent-shaped bald) and Mount Rogers (just visible), the second-highest and highest summits in Virginia, respectively.

Now below the lowest, most facelike of the profiles, the trail repeatedly switchbacks to another crossing of Green Ridge at 2.0 miles, this time at a major campsite with numerous tent sites and a grandiose campfire pit. A small spring is on the left just beyond the spur trail to the campsite. From the campsite the trail ascends outstanding pathways of natural stone. A steep set of switchbacks reaches a huge boulder with a rock-paved shelter spot. A few hundred feet farther, the trail turns a corner to Profile View, a dramatic view of the face that early mountaineers said looked like a grandfather when hoarfrost blasted the mountain (the beard of the larger "face" that many people see from north of the mountain).

Rising more gradually, the trail passes a spring, parallels a small cliff, and then winds past the almost imperceptible junction with the old Shanty Spring Trail at 2.6 miles. At Shanty Spring, 2.7 miles from the start, water empties from below a cliff that is often spectacularly covered with ice in winter. In a typically Victorian claim, Dugger's *Balsam Groves* asserts that this is "the coldest water outside of perpetual snow in the United States."

Going right at the cliff, the red-blazed Calloway Trail rises on its historic, steep, and rocky route through increasing evergreens to Calloway Gap at 3.0 miles and a junction with the Grandfather Trail. (See Option 2.)

Left, hikers reach a side trail at 3.4 miles onto the often-windy western prow of the peak called Watauga View. Right, Calloway Peak is 0.1 mile away.

Key Points
- **0.9** Shanty Spring Branch.
- **1.7** Foscoe View.
- **2.3** Profile View.
- **2.7** Shanty Spring.
- **3.0** Calloway Gap.
- **3.4** Watauga View.
- **3.5** Calloway Peak.

The ground appears snow-covered at the start of the Profile Trail when Fringed Phacelia blooms profusely in early May.

31 Beacon Heights from the Parkway and via the Mountains-to-Sea Trail

Milepost 305.2

A short and popular leg-stretcher affords spectacular views of Grandfather Mountain and its nearly vertical-mile drop to the Piedmont. By adding either short or long stretches of the Mountains-to-Sea Trail, hikers can find solitude.

Parkway mile: 305.2
Distance: 0.7-mile out and back. Adding a short piece of the Mountains-to-Sea Trail creates a hike of about 1.1 miles. From Old House Gap the Mountains-to-Sea Trail hike is 4.8 miles out and back.
Difficulty: Mostly easy; strenuous from Old House Gap

Elevation gain: About 120 feet; 1,360 feet from Old House Gap
Maps: USGS *Grandfather Mountain;* Tanawha Trail handout map, available at the Linn Cove Visitor Center. The Grandfather Mountain hiking map shows the trail best and is available free at the Grandfather Mountain entrance (north 0.1 mile to US 221 exit; right 1 mile to entrance).

Finding the trailhead: The Parkway trailhead is located at Milepost 305.2, 0.1 mile south of the US 221 entrance to the Parkway, 3 miles east of Linville. To reach the lower Mountains-to-Sea Trail Parking Area, exit onto US 221 at Milepost 305.1. At the stop sign, turn left and drive under the Parkway, immediately passing NC 1513 on the right. About 0.4 mile from there, take the next right onto NC 1514 (at 0.5 mile there is a spectacular view of Grandfather Mountain). About 4.2 miles from US 221, turn right onto FSR 192. There's a nice roadside campsite at 0.8 mile, and Old House Gap is at 3.5 miles. The Mountains-to-Sea Trail enters the woods on the right.

The Hike

This is one of the Parkway's best leg-stretchers. The grades are gradual, the footing isn't very difficult, and the views are outstanding. It's a popular hike, but by adding a stretch of the Mountains-to-Sea Trail, hikers can easily outwit the crowds and picnic alone at scenic viewpoints.

From the trailhead (at 4,220 feet), hikers walk across a state road that parallels the Parkway (NC 1513) and enter the woods where the sign says TANAWHA TRAIL BEACON HEIGHTS 0.2. The path climbs gradually to a complex junction. The Tanawha Trail starts to the left. The Mountains-to-Sea Trail comes in from the right and goes left with the Tanawha Trail. Turn right on the Mountains-to-Sea Trail—that's also the Beacon Heights Trail to the top. You'll pass an overhanging rock on the left that makes an excellent rain shelter. There's a bench on the right before the steepest, rockiest part of the trail.

At a signed junction at 0.2 mile, the Mountains-to-Sea Trail goes right where the Beacon Heights Trail switchbacks left. At about 0.3 mile the Beacon Heights Trail reaches the crest, a bench, and a junction where a sign inspires you to get the most from the view: "The art of seeing nature is in essence the art of awareness. How much we see depends on what we bring to the encounter. —Unknown"

To the right the path emerges on the top of a south-facing exfoliated dome with great views to the Piedmont and the high peaks south along the Parkway, including Mount Mitchell and the Linville Gorge. To the left the path ascends stone steps to another dome with spectacular views of the eastern flank of Grandfather Mountain and the Parkway north toward Blowing Rock. To the east the mountain plummets into Pisgah National Forest's Wilson Creek drainage—a rippled, waterfall-filled area of scenic dirt roads.

Retrace your steps to the bottom (0.7 mile) or, to extend this walk, take the first left on the way down at the second junction with the Mountains-to-Sea Trail. This nice old logging grade, marked with round white blazes, is grown close with mountain laurel. The trail wanders down then bears sharply right to join NC 1513, the dirt road you crossed at the Parkway trailhead.

Just before reaching that road, turn left into the woods as the Mountains-to-Sea Trail descends to Old House Gap on the way to Linville Gorge. The trail slabs easily through an intimate forest of lichen-covered outcrops, galax, oak, pine, and rhododendron on a spongy, needle-covered trail. A nice ledge creates a quiet, private view of the valley that's perfect for a picnic.

The quickest route back to the Parkway trailhead retraces your steps on the Mountains-to-Sea Trail, then goes left on the grade to NC 1513. Turn right and walk on the gravel road back to the Parkway parking area on the left for a hike of 1.1 miles.

The longest Beacon Heights hike starts below, at Old House Gap, and rises through a different world—a secluded corner of the Pisgah National Forest that sees little foot traffic.

Leave the leafy parking area at Old House Gap (where there are roadside campsites) and go northwest on the white-blazed Mountains-to-Sea Trail across earth berms designed to deter four-wheel-drive traffic. Follow an eroded, then sandy and pleasant old logging grade bordered by mountain laurel, pine, oak, and rhododendron.

The path passes various orange boundary blazes. At about 0.3 mile from the gap, the more obvious road grade goes left and the Mountains-to-Sea Trail goes right. For a short distance the grassy path is bordered by ferns then wanders through tighter vegetation going northeast around the bulge of the ridge and into the upper drainage of Andrews Creek. The trail alternates between steeper and more gradual ascents before climbing through towering hemlocks and rhododendron beside the stream. In leafless seasons, Grandfather Mountain and Beacon Heights are visible above.

At the top end of the drainage, the trail turns right across the rhododendron-lined stream for the last time. It shifts back to the left side of the now-dry drainage a few tenths of a mile beyond and bears right up two final switchbacks bound for Beacon Heights. One major switchback breaks this general direction through sparser, drier vegetation.

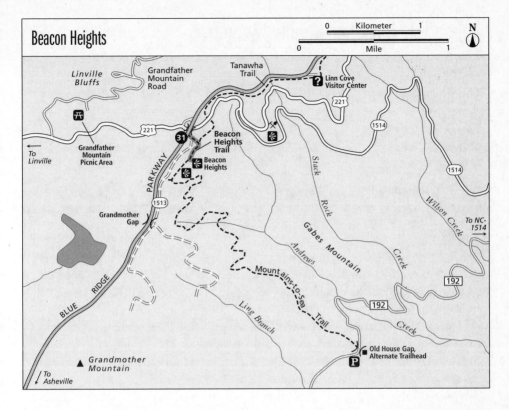

Beacon Heights

Linville Bluffs

Grandfather Mountain Road

Tanawha Trail

Linn Cove Visitor Center

221

221

1514

Grandfather Mountain Picnic Area

← To Linville

31

Beacon Heights Trail

Beacon Heights

1513

1514

Stack Rock Creek

Wilson Creek

To NC-1514

Grandmother Gap

Gabes Mountain

Andrews

Mountains-to-Sea Trail

192

192

Creek

BLUE RIDGE

Ling Branch

Creek

▲ Grandmother Mountain

↙ To Asheville

Old House Gap, Alternate Trailhead

A short, steep climb reaches the vista ledge described above—a private view for picnickers who'd rather not go any farther. Beyond, the trail slabs west through an intimate forest of lichen-covered outcrops, bisects two boulders, and crests the ridge at the old logging grade about 2.1 miles from Old House Gap.

To the left the grade reaches NC 1513 in 100 feet. (A right there takes you to the Parkway's Beacon Heights trailhead in 0.1 mile.) Hikers bound for the summit should go right and tie into the Beacon Heights Trail description above for a hike of about 2.4 miles from Old House Gap. The round-trip is just under 5.0 miles.

Key Points for Easy Hike

0.05 Go right; Tanawha Trail goes left.

0.2 Turn left; Mountains-to-Sea Trail goes right.

0.3 Reach crest with summit views.

0.7 Return to parking area; 1.1 miles with side trail.

32 Flat Rock Self-Guiding Loop Trail

Milepost 308.3

This educational trail offers natural history interpretive signs and good distant views.

Parkway mile: 308.3
Distance: 0.7-mile loop
Difficulty: Moderate

Elevation gain: About 100 feet
Maps: *USGS Grandfather Mountain;* no Parkway map available

Finding the trailhead: The trail begins at Milepost 308.3, 0.4 mile south of NC 1511—a local road that leads west to Linville and US 221 and east as a gravel road into Pisgah National Forest.

The Hike

Here's a rare hike—one not to miss for serious hikers and more casual Parkway motorists alike. This is a quick walk to a good view or a wonderful hour-plus stroll for a family that could include nature study or a picnic. Even the well-versed naturalist will find interesting insights in the twenty or so interpretive signs.

This well-maintained, popular trail ascends gradually then wanders northward along an outcrop with wonderful westward-facing views. Then it drops east back to the road. The trail passes through a Northern hardwood forest, with rhododendron and other more Southern species at an elevation of 4,000 feet.

Not far above the parking area, the trail loop splits. Head left at the first interpretive sign bearing David Brower's sage observation that humankind cannot make wilderness, it "can only spare it."

Beyond that junction, just as the trail jogs right, look off in the woods to the left. Parents might ask a child why that tree's standing on its tiptoes. The answer—the yellow birch perched above the forest floor on 3-foot-long, leglike roots sprouted long ago atop a huge fallen log—a nursery log—and took root around it. When the log rotted away, the birch was left standing on "stilts."

Interpretive signs point out a virgin remnant of a northern red oak on the right, then an American chestnut as you enter an area where the shiny heart-shaped leaves of galax cover the ground under the rhododendron. A short distance beyond, galax crops up at a sign, with a cucumber tree and a resting bench after that. Then comes withe rod (*Viburnum cassinoides*)—BREWED AS A TONIC FOR FEVER, the sign says, by mountaineers who called it "Shonny Haw." Nearby on Beech Mountain, the East's highest ski area, withe rod grows at nearly 5,500 feet, where it inspires the same name but a different spelling for ski runs Upper and Lower Shawneehaw.

Your next steps take you onto the outcrop of Flat Rock, a massive crop of quartzite with ribbons of white quartz. Slow down during the first 50 feet or so—at least notice the wonderful transition from rhododendron woods to a crag with gnarled pines, hemlocks, and a carpet of pine needles, luxuriant moss, and lichen. These pioneer plant communities struggle to turn the rock into soil and establish a foothold

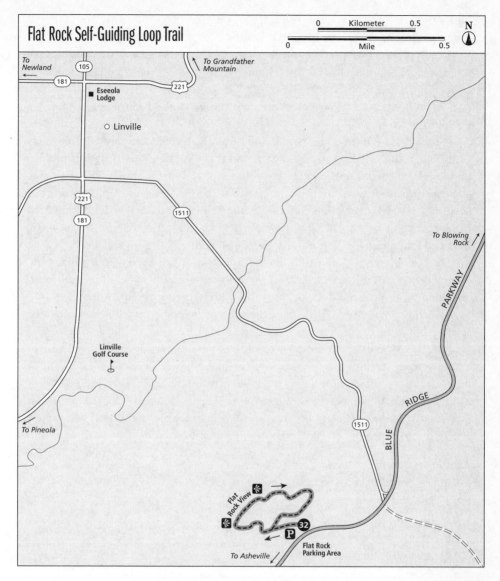

Flat Rock Self-Guiding Loop Trail

To Newland
To Grandfather Mountain
To Blowing Rock
Eseeola Lodge
Linville
Linville Golf Course
To Pineola
PARKWAY
BLUE RIDGE
Flat Rock View
32
Flat Rock Parking Area
To Asheville

for the forest. Part of that process is Flat Rock's "bathtubs," the interesting bowl-size basins just ahead that usually contain water—the key ingredient that permits wind-blown waves of water and freezing and thawing to break down this solid shelf of rock.

Turn right at the cement rectangle with a yellow painted arrow—three of these markers will guide you across a clifftop that could be an enigma in dense fog, not a rarity here. But on a clear day, the views are extensive.

From the breezy outcrop covered with wind-flagged hemlocks, there's a 180-degree view. You'll note the remains of two sighting devices in this area that once permitted hikers to align cones and point out the peaks beyond the golf course below at the summer resort of Linville, not far from its classic inn, the Eseeola Lodge.

The Appalachian Trail crosses the far western horizon dominated by the meadow-covered alpine-appearing peaks of Hump, Yellow, and Roan Mountains (right to left).

Follow the yellow arrows across the crest to one of the Parkway's best views of Grandfather Mountain.

Heading right, reenter the woods amid more galax. Surprisingly tall trees suddenly rise in the sheltered area below the rocks. The trail dips past a sign that points out both local species of rhododendron—the smaller-leafed Catawba (*Rhododendron catawbiense*) blooms reddish purple in early June; the longer-leafed rosebay, or great laurel (*Rhododendron maximum*), blooms white in July. Then comes hobblebush, red maple (the color king of the Southern Appalachians), and striped maple, one of many trees also found in New England that gives this forest a Northern feel.

The trail bears right and passes through a flat area of tall trees, then jogs left to an old log bench where a sign describes how entire forests of hemlocks like these were leveled for nothing more than the tannin-rich bark, used in tanning leather.

Turn right and start the descent to the end of the loop. A large bulge on the tree at the turn is a burl, a tree cancer the mountaineers used to make bowls. (The nearby Grandfather Mountain Nature Museum has a stunningly huge example.) The trail descends more steeply past a sign noting the high-altitude Fraser magnolia (named for botanist John Fraser by another famous early Appalachian explorer, John Bartram) and the white oak, "king of the mountain trees." The hard wood of this tree with light gray bark and round-lobed leaves was prized for tool handles and household items.

At the trail junction, head left back to the parking lot.

Key Points

0.0 Just after the start, the trail splits—head left.

0.2 Trail heads onto rocky outcrop.

0.3 Continue in same driection after leaving outcrop.

0.6 Trail intersects—turn left.

0.7 Return to parking area.

33 Linville Gorge Area

Milepost 312.2

Option 1: Hawksbill Mountain

Hawksbill Mountain is a crag-capped peak on the rim of the Linville Gorge Wilderness with panoramic summit views of Linville Gorge, a dozen major summits, and the Carolina Piedmont.

Parkway mile: 312.2
Distance: 1.4 miles out-and-back
Difficulty: Moderate
Elevation gain: 700 feet

Maps: USGS *Linville Falls* and *Ashford.* The best map is the USDA Forest Service map of the Linville Gorge Wilderness.

Finding the trailhead: Exit the Blue Ridge Parkway at the NC 181 junction near Pineola. Pass the NC 181/183 intersection and, measuring from there, turn right onto Gingercake Road (NC 1265) in 3 miles (where a sign reads PISGAH NATIONAL FOREST TABLE ROCK PICNIC AREA 8.7 MILES). Measuring from there, bear left in 0.3 mile onto NC 1261 (signed TABLE ROCK ROAD), which becomes gravel at 1.2 miles (and becomes FSR 210). Pass the trailhead for Sitting Bear and the Devils Hole Trail into the Gorge at 2.7 miles. At 3.7 miles the Hawksbill Trail leaves the road on the right, with a parking area on the left.

The Hike

Hawksbill is the easier to reach, less jagged summit of the prominent duo of peaks, Table Rock and Hawksbill, that dominate the skyline of Linville Gorge. It has a sloping, rocky crest and low vegetation that permits expansive views and offers relative privacy, at least compared with the more popular Table Rock (which is a stiffer climb and an additional 5-mile drive on steep, winding, and dusty roads). Views of Table Rock itself are especially good here, and the vista includes adjoining cliffs and crags that are nationally known among rock climbers.

The simple out-and-back walk to the peak begins at the Hawksbill Mountain Parking Area. The Hawksbill Trail enters the woods and climbs at a steady grade then steepens up the sunny side of Lettered Rock Ridge. The trail's big water bars are a step and a half high, and the steep trail is covered in loose rock, so the first 0.25 mile is not easy unless you take it slow.

The path flattens and then slips off the sunny side onto a fern-bordered grade through a shady forest of rhododendron, maple, mountain laurel, and chestnut oak. The trail descends gradually, and hikers should be alert: At about 0.5 mile you'll need to make a sharp left to the summit. After the turn, the trail gradually steepens. It's an undulating but decidedly uphill route through close vegetation and galax. After passing a rock shelter below the trail to the left, the path takes a hard right and reaches the sandy soils and pines of the peak at 0.7 mile.

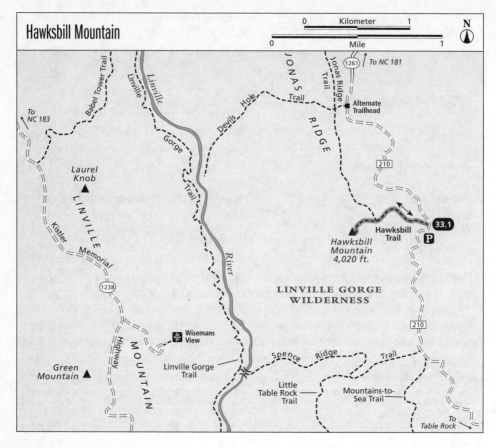

Here views and trails fan out like spokes of a wheel, and trees give way to low vegetation such as Allegheny sand myrtle and sedges. Bear left on an obvious trail; you'll wind down over prominent crags with fine views of Table Rock.

Key Points

0.5 Sharp left toward summit.

0.7 Summit.

Option 2: Table Rock Trail and Shortoff Mountain

The most distinctive summit flanking the Linville Gorge Wilderness, Table Rock Mountain is a craggy peak popular with rock climbers. Hikers have panoramic views from the summit, and views from nearby Shortoff Mountain are even better. There is no better vista of the rugged chasm of Linville Gorge.

Parkway mile: 312.2
Total distance: Table Rock, 2.2 miles out and back; Shortoff Mountain, 11.2 miles out and back
Difficulty: Moderately strenuous for Table Rock; strenuous for Shortoff Mountain

Elevation gain: 609 feet for Table Rock; 1,875 feet for Shortoff
Maps: USGS *Linville Falls* and *Ashford*. The best map is the Forest Service map of the Linville Gorge Wilderness.

Finding the trailhead: Exit the Blue Ridge Parkway at the NC 181 junction near Pineola. Pass the NC 181/183 intersection, and measuring from there, turn right onto Gingercake Road, NC 1265, in 3 miles (where a sign reads PISGAH NATIONAL FOREST TABLE ROCK PICNIC AREA 8.7 MILES). Measuring from there, bear left in 0.3 mile onto NC 1261 (signed TABLE ROCK ROAD), which turns to gravel at 1.2 miles and becomes FSR 210. Pass the Hawksbill parking at 3.7 miles, and at 4.7 miles pass parking for the Spence Ridge Trail. At 5.7 miles turn right onto FSR 210-B, following the sign to the Table Rock Picnic Area. At 6.3 miles pass the entrance to the North Carolina Outward Bound School. A paved, switchbacking ascent to the trailhead parking/picnic area starts at 7.25 miles. Reach the trailhead at 8.7 miles.

The Hikes

The hike to Table Rock is far simpler than the drive to the trailhead. The Table Rock Trail parking lot is a lightly developed recreation area with tables and grills for picnicking and modern pit toilets. There's no water, and no camping is allowed. There are, however, great views of Table Rock. Bring binoculars if you want to watch climbers scale the cliffs.

Table Rock

The Table Rock Trail, here combined with the Mountains-to-Sea Trail, leaves the north end of the parking area through profuse ferns and switchbacks left to the bottom of a long flight of gradual steps that get rockier and steeper.

Not far from the parking area, awesome views open up of Linville Gorge to the left; a climber's trail heads off to the right. The trail flattens, the footing gets easier, and at about 0.3 mile the trail switchbacks right as a side trail dips left into a little gap. This is the unmarked Little Table Rock Trail. Beyond, it joins Spence Ridge Trail.

Continuing on the Table Rock Trail, the white circle–blazed Mountains-to-Sea Trail goes left. The Table Rock Trail continues up and switchbacks left at the base of the first large crag. The trail squeezes between two boulders, then switchbacks twice before emerging into open, rocky terrain. There's a rock shelter on the right as you near the crest of the peak. (Side trails and switchback breaks are many up here; just keep to the widest rocky trail.)

A benchmark, its lettering illegible now from being struck with rocks, is on the left just as the views open up. This vista reaches the head of the gorge, toward Linville Falls. Gaining the crest, you're at the former site of a fire tower. A left through a gap in the wall of brush quickly takes you to a fine view of the upper gorge and Hawksbill Mountain, the rocky, gentle peak just north across the gap. Grandfather Mountain rises on the right. From out here, the gentle tinkling of rock-climbing hardware and

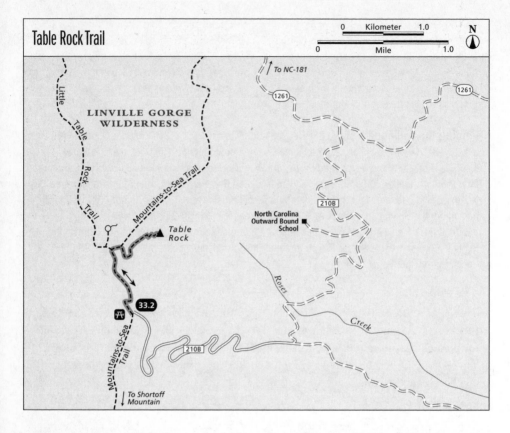

Kilometer 1.0
Mile 1.0
N

To NC-181

1261

1261

LINVILLE GORGE
WILDERNESS

Little Table Rock Trail

Mountains-to-Sea Trail

210B

North Carolina
Outward Bound
School

Table
Rock

33.2

Roses

Creek

Mountains-to-Sea Trail

210B

To Shortoff
Mountain

the conversation of climbers may drift up from Table Rock's North Ridge route. Summit vegetation is rooted in dry, almost sandy soil and includes various sedges, Allegheny sand myrtle, mountain laurel, blueberries, and pine, all waving in the gusts of wind so typical of a cliff-edge environment.

If you're surefooted, go south where the summit descends along a spectacular spine of rocks in a mix of rock scrambles and a wide dirt path. Many small trails disintegrate into climber's paths to the cliffs above stomach-churning drops. Grab a spectacular private crag and have lunch.

This part of the Linville Gorge is one of eastern America's premier rock-climbing areas. Looking south, just past the Table Rock Parking Area (visible below), you can see the convoluted ridge called the Chimneys, another famous climbing site. Farther away, Shortoff Mountain drops off to Lake James and the blue distance of the Carolina Piedmont. Across the gorge, the prominent cliff is Wisemans View, a developed vista reached by road. Off to the right, the long crest of the Black Mountains includes Mount Mitchell.

Key Points to Table Rock

0.3 Trail switchbacks right at a side trail to the left (spring).

0.4 Mountains-to-Sea Trail goes right.

1.1 Summit.

Shortoff Mountain

The Shortoff Mountain Trail leaves the same parking area but heads south. It follows a gradual ridgetop then slabs to the west of the Chimneys (3,557 feet) and their crags and cracks. The trail rejoins the ridge then swings southeast and begins a descent of 900 feet, much of it steeply, into Chimney Gap (2,509 feet). At about 2.0 miles the Cambric Branch Trail bears right along a ridgetop and then drops to a dead end at the Linville River.

Continuing along the Shortoff Mountain Trail (part of the Mountains-to-Sea Trail), a wet-weather spring is located 150 feet left of the trail at about 2.3 miles. The trail crosses a peak at about 3.0 miles and at 5.6 miles reaches the summit of Shortoff Mountain. Paths to the right reach clifftops with spectacular views directly up the deepest depths of the canyon, past all the highest summits along the rims. A spring is located beyond the summit in a small gap. Lake James sprawls below, a location for such memorable films as *The Last of the Mohicans* and the final scenes from *The Hunt for Red October,* which were supposed to be the coast of Maine.

Hikers atop Table Rock look out on Hawksbill and down into Linville Gorge.

34 Linville Falls Recreation Area

Milepost 316.4

Linville Falls Recreation Area is not to be missed. It's one of those periodic bulges in the narrow corridor of the Blue Ridge Parkway, so National Park Service property surrounds Linville Falls, the Parkway's biggest waterfall (by volume of water). There's almost always a thundering roar near this oft-photographed cataract that gushes 100 foaming feet into some serious scenery—Linville Gorge, the canyon and USDA Forest Service wilderness area that lies below the falls. The Parkway's National Recreation Trails offer a taste of this wild chasm.

Hikes on both sides of the Linville River offer views of the falls. The routes are grouped into two separate entries below, but they start at the same small visitor center (open seasonally; restrooms and a bookshop) that sits beside a placid stretch of the Linville River not far from the Linville Falls Campground and Picnic Area.

The remoteness of the gorge kept loggers out, and John D. Rockefeller donated the virgin-forested parcel to the National Park Service in 1952. Like the gorge itself, areas surrounding the falls have also never been logged and contain an inspiring forest. Near the river, towering hemlocks and white pines soar above an understory of rhododendron that blooms profusely in late May. This lofty forest gives way to gnarled scrub pines that cling to drier crags and rocky viewpoints that overlook Linville Falls. One trail reaches the wild base of the falls, but no swimming is permitted. Rock climbing is likewise off-limits.

In winter, cross-country skiers will find these trails inviting. Even when the Parkway is closed due to snow, a Forest Service spur trail provides access. (See "Finding the trailhead" under Options 1 and 2.) The bulk of the paths surrounding Linville Falls are gradual and make inspiring ski tours. Just ditch your skis for the short, steep detours to the viewpoints.

Option 1: Duggers Creek Loop, Linville Gorge Trail, and Plunge Basin Overlook Trail

Three trails on the visitor center side of the river make the most scenic, least visited hike to Linville Falls.

See map on page 229.
Parkway mile: 316.4
Distance: Duggers Creek, 0.25 mile one-way; Plunge Basin Overlook, 1.0-mile out and back; Linville Gorge, 1.4 miles out and back (about 1.8 miles for a combination of the Gorge and Plunge Basin Trails)
Difficulty: Easy for Duggers Creek Trail; moderate for Plunge Basin Overlook; moderate to strenuous for Linville Gorge
Elevation gain: 190 feet for the Linville Gorge Trail
Maps: *USGS Linville Falls;* Parkway handout map, available at the trailhead visitor center and campground

The perchlike overlooks of the Linville Falls trail system give hikers a bird's-eye view of the cataract.

Finding the trailhead: The trails to Linville Falls start at a visitor center and parking area 1.5 miles from the Parkway, past the Linville Falls Campground. The spur road to the trailhead leaves the Blue Ridge Parkway at Milepost 316.4, about 1 mile north of the US 221–Blue Ridge Parkway junction in the town of Linville Falls.

In winter, when the Parkway and the Linville Falls Spur Road to the falls can be closed due to snow, an alternative Forest Service trailhead can be used to reach these trails. From the US 221–Parkway junction near the town of Linville Falls (1 mile south of where the Linville Falls Spur Road joins the Parkway), go south on US 221 to the community of Linville Falls and turn left onto NC 183. In 0.7 mile from the US 221–NC 183 junction in Linville Falls, turn right onto Wiseman's View Road (NC 1238, also called the Kistler Memorial Highway), where prominent signs direct hikers to the Linville Gorge. Even if that unpaved road has not been plowed, the Linville Falls trailhead is just a few hundred yards from well-maintained NC 183. This road-width path is steep to start then levels to join the Linville Falls Trail. Turn left and cross the river to trails near the visitor center.

The Hikes

Two trails on the visitor center side of the river make a less-than-2.0-mile hike when combined, but a brief scenic stroll is also possible on the Duggers Creek Trail, which links the visitor center with the far end of the recreation area's long parking lot—a 0.2-mile walk you could enjoy heading back to your car after hitting the visitor center (or when finished with the two longer walks). Pass through the visitor center portico by the restrooms and ascend to take a left on Duggers Creek Trail at the junction where the Linville Gorge Trail goes right. The path wanders along beautiful Duggers Creek past plaques with inspiring sayings.

The Linville Gorge Trail heads right at that first junction and ascends gradually through hemlocks and rhododendron. At 0.3 mile from the visitor center, the Plunge Basin Overlook Trail heads right for the best view of the falls at about 0.5 mile. The path is level to a bench but then turns right and descends at times steeply but briefly down stone steps to a rock-walled perch above the falls. It's a truly inspiring sight. From here it's a 1.0-mile round-trip back to the visitor center.

Back at the junction, the Linville Gorge Trail bears right (a left if you avoid the Plunge Basin View) and reaches a fenced-off crag at a height of land before dipping over the edge and down. The gradual path has handrails as it skirts steep drops and then descends a steep flight of steps. Use care at the bottom of the steps—the trail turns hard right, but you could keep going left on the path created by countless others who have missed the turn. The trail continues a rocky though gradual descent to the bottom of a towering cliff. (Not far up the base of the cliff on the right is a sheltering overhang.) The trail descends with river noise off to the left. Avoid the first path left to the water, keeping right to emerge at the water's edge. Rock-hop to a vantage near the base of the thundering falls (ice may inhibit this in winter). This is a wonderful place to enjoy a lingering lunch at the lowest point of the trail system—about 3,040 feet—and soak up the wild atmosphere of the rock-hewn amphitheater below the falls. The craggy walls mark the start of Linville Gorge. On a warm summer day, the deep expanse of emerald water below the falls will surely tempt you—but swimming isn't allowed.

On a quiet day, amid the wildness and river noise, it's easy to imagine the hemmed-in feeling William Linville and his son must have felt near here in 1766 when confronted by Native Americans—who then scalped them.

A hike to the base of the falls and back is 1.4 miles. Include the side trip to the Plunge Basin Overlook and it's about 1.8 miles.

Key Points

0.3 Plunge Basin Overlook Trail branches from Linville Gorge Trail.

0.7 Gorge Trail reaches base of falls.

1.4 Return to parking area.

Option 2: Linville Falls Trail and Nearby Paths

Three hikes explore virgin forest and rugged scenery near Linville Falls, an impressive cataract that plunges into the Linville Gorge Wilderness. Two other walks—one on the access road from the Parkway, the other at Linville River Parking Area—also offer strolls.

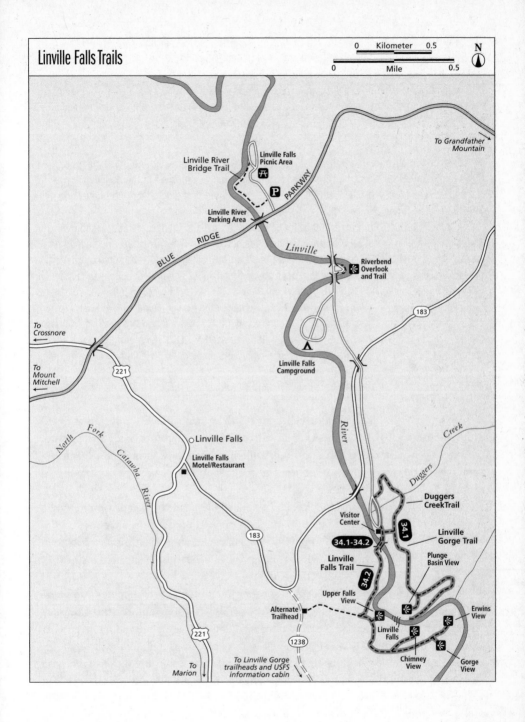

Linville Falls Trails

0 Kilometer 0.5
0 Mile 0.5

N

To Grandfather Mountain

Linville Falls Picnic Area

Linville River Bridge Trail

PARKWAY

Linville River Parking Area

BLUE   RIDGE

Linville

Riverbend Overlook and Trail

183

To Crossnore

221

To Mount Mitchell

Linville Falls Campground

North Fork Catawba River

Linville Falls

Linville Falls Motel/Restaurant

River

Duggers   Creek

Visitor Center

Duggers Creek Trail

34.1

Linville Gorge Trail

34.1-34.2

183

34.2

Linville Falls Trail

Plunge Basin View

Upper Falls View

Alternate Trailhead

221

1238

Linville Falls

Erwins View

Chimney View

Gorge View

To Marion

To Linville Gorge trailheads and USFS information cabin

Parkway mile: 316.4
Distance: Upper Falls View, 1.0 mile out and back; 2.0 miles out and back to Erwins View
Difficulty: Easy for Upper Falls View; moderate for trail to Chimney, Gorge, and Erwins Views

Elevation gain: Negligible for Upper Falls; about 200 feet to Chimney, Gorge, and Erwins Views.
Maps: USGS Linville Falls; Parkway handout map, available at the trailhead visitor center and campground

Finding the trailhead: The trails to Linville Falls start at a visitor center and parking area 1.5 miles from the Parkway, past the Linville Falls Campground. The spur road to the trailhead leaves the Blue Ridge Parkway at Milepost 316.4, about 1 mile north of the US 221–Blue Ridge Parkway junction in the town of Linville Falls.

In winter, when the Parkway and the Linville Falls Spur Road to the falls can be closed due to snow, an alternative Forest Service trailhead provides access for winter hikers and cross-country skiers. From the US 221–Parkway junction near the town of Linville Falls (1 mile south of where the Linville Falls Spur Road joins the Parkway), go south on US 221 to the community of Linville Falls and turn left onto NC 183. In 0.7 mile from the US 221/NC 183 junction in Linville Falls, turn right onto Wiseman's View Road (NC 1238, also called the Kistler Memorial Highway), where prominent signs direct hikers to the Linville Gorge. Even if that unpaved road has not been plowed, the trailhead is just a few hundred yards from well-maintained NC 183. The national forest contact station is 0.5 mile beyond on the right. This road-width path is steep to start then levels to join the Linville Falls Trail.

The Hike

Across the river from the visitor center, nice hikes reach higher, more distant, and more popular views of the falls. After crossing the Linville River on a footbridge from the visitor center, the level, road-width Linville Falls Trail leads through a scenic forest paralleling the river. A junction on the right at 0.4 mile is a Forest Service spur trail from NC 1238, a short distance away.

A side trail leads left to Upper Falls View, 0.5 mile from the visitor center, where the river funnels over its first big drop. Back on the main trail, the route rises through towering trees. White pine, oak, and birch trees complement this virgin hemlock forest. Here the trail starts a gradual rise to scrubbier vegetation associated with drier soils along the crags overlooking the gorge.

At 0.6 mile from the visitor center, another junction splits the trail at a rudimentary picnic/rain shelter. To the left the trail descends steep steps and reaches Chimney View at 0.7 mile, where hikers get an oft-photographed view of the entire falls. Back at the shelter, again head away from the visitor center as the trail climbs through dry, piney forest. Not far away on the right is Gorge View, a look down the gorge with an interpretive sign. The gorge appears again on the right, and on the left at about 1.0 mile is Erwins View, where the falls, gorge, and hikers on Chimney View are all in sight from the trail system's high point—about 3,360 feet. Retrace your steps from here for a 2.0-mile round-trip hike.

Key Points

0.4 Forest Service spur trail from NC 1238.

0.5 Side trail left to Upper Falls View.

0.6 Junction left to Chimney View.

1.0 Erwins View.

2.0 Return to parking area at visitor center.

The Riverbend Overlook Trail

On your way back on the Linville Falls Spur Road just past the campground—0.4 mile from the Parkway—pull into Riverbend Overlook. There's a bridge before and after this overlook, so here's the place to explore a big bend of the Linville River. Turning into the overlook and right on the one-way loop, trails dip into the woods at the first and last parking slips. Between them, paths wander the river rock–covered shore or just below the parking loop, on what looks almost like an old logging railroad grade.

Linville River Bridge Trail

Just 0.1 mile south of the Linville Falls Spur Road on the Parkway (Milepost 316.5), the Linville River Parking Area offers a leg-stretcher that arcs a gradual 0.1 mile down to the riverbank below the Parkway's largest stone structure (0.2 mile round-trip).

Just before you reach the river, a short, steep side trail drops off right to the first loop of the Linville Falls Picnic Area—the Parkway's biggest—and its first comfort station.

A trail does not follow the riverside through the picnic area as one might imagine, but you can wander nice paths through tall trees, short riverside sections of trail, even a flower-filled meadow between four parking areas. To the end of the picnic area and back can be a very rewarding, nearly flat walk of about 0.6 mile. At the end, the Parkway property line borders a big field of Christmas trees—a nice turnaround point for kids who wonder where their trees spend the summer.

35 Linville Gorge Wilderness

Milepost 317.5

The wild canyon of Linville Gorge, up to 2,000 feet deep in places, lies between Jonas Ridge to the east and Linville Mountain to the west. First protected as a primitive area by the Forest Service in 1951, it became an "instant wilderness" area with the passage of the 1964 Wilderness Act. A 1984 wilderness bill expanded the area to its current 12,002 acres.

Peaks on the rim of the gorge tower over Morganton and Lake James. The Blue Ridge Parkway skirts the head of the gorge on the northwest, where the Parkway's Linville Falls trails offer a nice glimpse into the chasm. If that peek intrigues you, these hikes will satisfy your curiosity.

This convoluted cleft is so rugged that no logging ever took place there. Towering virgin forest can be found in the gorge's isolated coves and rugged, wild tangles of primeval density in places where few people venture. For these reasons, Linville Gorge is the most popular of North Carolina's wilderness areas, and only a limited number of permits are available for weekend camping between May 31 and October 31. Campers can only remain in the area for three days and two nights.

The shape of the gorge funnels traffic into a narrow area, concentrating trail use on the river (almost the reverse of how trails at the Shining Rock Wilderness funnel hikers to the crest). Those who want solitude should pursue a rugged off-trail adventure or go in late fall, winter, or spring—also the best times for cross-country hikers because the gorge contains timber rattlesnakes and copperheads, active in warmer months.

If you must visit during peak season, go between Sunday and Thursday. The trail descriptions that follow include the Forest Service's assessment of how heavily each trail is used. The roughest, most strenuous, and primitive paths (generally, the southernmost gorge trails) will be the best bet for seeing the fewest people. Several of these trails access trackless areas where the terrain invites bushwhacking. Consult the map here and the Forest Service's Linville Gorge Wilderness map to locate those places. Some are obvious and just off popular trails, which makes it possible to find a secluded camp or lunch site. Others are large tracts just waiting for serious explorers. Whether or not you leave existing trails, be prepared for very primitive conditions. Though trailheads are signed, and the Forest Service feels that the gorge has more signing than "wilderness" might warrant, hikers get lost every year. Be aware that there is an active Internet-based network of bootleg trail builders in the Linville Gorge, and that could confuse even the savviest user of map and compass or GPS.

There is good news. Parts of the gorge have been damaged by recent forest fires and major summer storms—so funds have become available to improve trails. A bridge now spans the river at the Spence Ridge Trail, built in 2006. The burned over, obscure—and awesomely spectacular—Rock Jock Trail has been reopened. And in late 2009, Forest Service–funded crews reopened and stabilized the entire length of the Linville Gorge Trail along the river. On top of that, an active volunteer and adopt-a-trail effort is keeping trails into the gorge better maintained.

Nevertheless, gorge explorers should be savvy campers and follow precautions that include practicing zero-impact camping and wearing bright clothing during hunting season: late October to early January.

Parkway mile: Milepost 317.5

Distance: 0.2 mile out and back for the Wiseman's View Overlook Trail; 1.8 miles out and back for the Pine Gap Trail; 2.7 miles for the Bynum Bluff–Pine Gap circuit; 9.0-mile circuit at the southern end of the gorge using the Pinch-In, Conley Cove, and Rock Jock Trails

Difficulty: Easy for Wiseman's View and Pine Gap Trails; moderate for the Bynum Bluff–Pine Gap circuit; strenuous for the Linville Gorge Trail circuit

Elevation gain: 520 feet for the Bynum Bluff–Pine Gap circuit

Maps: *USGS Linville Falls and Ashford.* The best map is the USDA Forest Service map of the Linville Gorge Wilderness.

Finding the trailhead: Leave the Parkway at the US 221 exit and turn left to the town of Linville Falls (1 mile south of where the Linville Falls Spur Road joins the Parkway). In the community of Linville Falls, turn left onto NC 183. In 0.7 mile from that junction, turn right onto Wiseman's View Road

Linville Gorge plummets impressively from the craggy crest of Table Rock. The Shortoff Mountain Trail crosses the Chimneys in the middle ground on its way to the distant drop of Shortoff. The Rock Jock Trail runs the view-packed clifftops of the ridge at right.

(NC 1238, also called the Kistler Memorial Highway) where prominent signs direct hikers to the Linville Gorge. The Linville Falls trailhead parking is a short distance on the left. The national forest information cabin is 0.5 mile on the right (Apr through Oct, primarily Thur to Sat; 828-765-7550).

The trails descend from the left side of NC 1238 and are listed here by their distance south of the NC 183–NC 1238 junction: Pine Gap Trail, 0.9 mile; Bynum Bluff Trail, 1.5 miles; Cabin Trail, 1.9 miles; Babel Tower Trail, 2.7 miles; Sandy Flats Trail is closed (former trailhead at 3.7 miles); Wiseman's View Overlook Trail, 3.8 miles; Conley Cove-Rock Jock Trail, 5.3 miles; Pinch-In Trail, 8.2 miles.

Option 1: Wiseman's View, Pine Gap, and Bynum Bluff Trails

Trails here include a roadside view trail and a variety of other hikes into a wilderness chasm, varying from a down-and-back trip to the bottom of the gorge to a few circuit hikes. Even if you don't venture into the gorge, the 0.2-mile trail to Wiseman's View is a worthwhile side trip to get a feel for the gorge and its surrounding forest roads.

The Hikes

A nice prelude to a hike from the western side of the gorge is a warm-up on the Wiseman's View Trail. This easy 0.2-mile trail is not a long detour from the Parkway, and it will really give you the flavor of this primitive chasm in the Blue Ridge. The parking area is only 3.8 miles from the paved road. The view is spectacular, and you pass the Forest Service information cabin on the drive. (For two hikes that are rougher than Wiseman's View but generally not as strenuous as gorge hikes, check out entries for Table Rock and Hawksbill Mountain on the opposite rim of the gorge.)

Unless you just hike to the river and back—which many people do to swim, fish, picnic, or camp—you'll want to have cars at two trailheads to avoid a dusty walk along NC 1238. The trail descriptions below suggest ways to minimize that car-clouded trek. Most hikers intent on a longer jaunt into Linville Gorge enter and exit at two different western-side trails and follow the river on the Linville Gorge Trail between them. The easiest of these trails into and out of the gorge is the 0.7-mile Pine Gap Trail. It drops on a rare gradual grade and descends to a junction with the Bynum Bluff Trail. A left turn there leads out to a crag with spectacular views of a sharp bend in the river. (Avoid a right turn onto the Linville Gorge Trail on the way.) Retrace your steps for a 1.8-mile out-and-back day hike.

An easy circuit hike that requires just a 0.6-mile roadside walk pairs the Pine Gap Trail with the Bynum Bluff Trail. The Bynum Bluff Trail starts out gradually from the road and reaches a long promontory before plummeting down a sharp ridge to the Pine Gap Trail in 1.0 mile. Just beyond this junction, the Linville Gorge Trail goes right (downriver). Take in the views described above on the crag in a sharp bend in the river, or turn right for an out-and-back side trip along the river on the Linville Gorge Trail. Whichever you choose, make the easy climb out of the gorge on the Pine Gap Trail and walk the roadside for a 2.7-mile hike (if you don't go downstream).

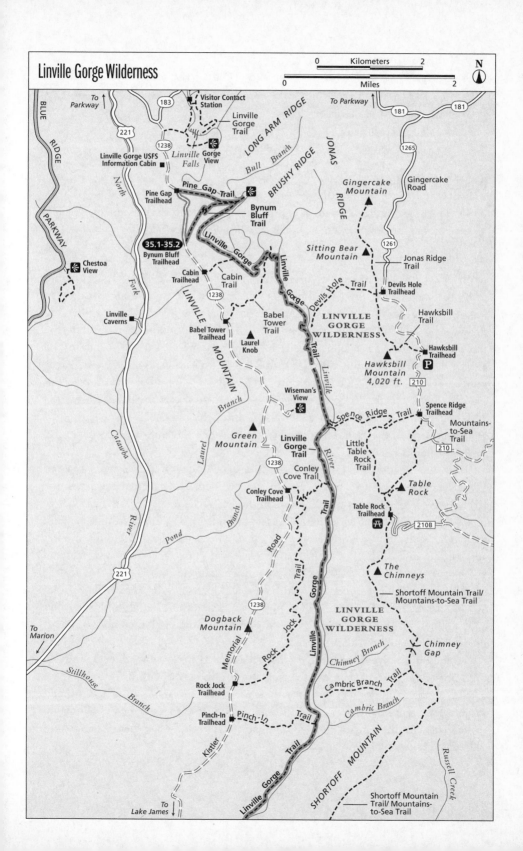

Linville Gorge Wilderness

Kilometers 0 — 2
Miles 0 — 2

N

To Parkway

183

Visitor Contact Station

Linville Gorge Trail

221

1238

Linville Gorge USFS Information Cabin

Linville Falls

Gorge View

LONG ARM RIDGE

Bull Branch

BRUSHY RIDGE

To Parkway

181

181

1265

JONAS RIDGE

Gingercake Mountain

Gingercake Road

Pine Gap Trail

Pine Gap Trailhead

BLUE RIDGE PARKWAY

North Fork

Chestoa View

Bynum Bluff Trail

35.1-35.2

Bynum Bluff Trailhead

Linville Gorge Trail

1261

Sitting Bear Mountain

Jonas Ridge Trail

Devils Hole Trail

Devils Hole Trailhead

Cabin Trailhead

Cabin Trail

Linville Caverns

1238

LINVILLE MOUNTAIN

Babel Tower Trailhead

Babel Tower Trail

Laurel Knob

LINVILLE GORGE WILDERNESS

Hawksbill Trail

Hawksbill Trailhead

Hawksbill Mountain 4,020 ft.

210

Laurel Branch

Linville Gorge Trail

Catawba River

Wiseman's View

Green Mountain

Linville Gorge Trail

1238

Conley Cove Trail

Conley Cove Trailhead

Pond Branch

Spence Ridge Trail

Spence Ridge Trailhead

Mountains-to-Sea Trail

210

Little Table Rock Trail

Table Rock

Table Rock Trailhead

210B

221

To Marion

Stillhouse Branch

Road

Rock Jock Trail

Dogback Mountain

1238

Memorial

Rock Jock Trailhead

Pinch-In Trailhead

Pinch-In Trail

Kistler

Linville Gorge Trail

The Chimneys

Shortoff Mountain Trail/ Mountains-to-Sea Trail

LINVILLE GORGE WILDERNESS

Chimney Gap

Chimney Branch

Cambric Branch

Cambric Branch Trail

SHORTOFF MOUNTAIN

Russell Creek

To Lake James

Linville Gorge Trail

Shortoff Mountain Trail/ Mountains-to-Sea Trail

1.0 Descend Bynum Bluff Trail to junction on left with Pine Gap Trail.

1.2 Viewpoint on river.

1.4 Right turn onto Pine Gap Trail.

2.1 NC 1238; turn left onto road.

2.7 Bynum Bluff trailhead.

Option 2: Linville Gorge Trail

It's hard to beat this classic route along the Linville River for wild scenery—even if recent Forest Service improvements make it a little easier to follow.

The Hike

From either the Pine Gap or Bynum Bluff Trail, the Linville Gorge Trail descends along the west side of the river for almost 11.5 miles. The other trails that drop to join it afford other in-and-out options. The trail starts south around a sharp bend in the river on side-hill terrain, close under NC 1238. At just more than 1.0 mile, the Linville Gorge Trail meets the Cabin Trail—a steep, strenuous 1.0-mile climb to NC 1238. On the left at the junction, a side trail juts out onto a bend in the river, reaching the peak of a 3,090-foot promontory. Continuing along the river another 0.8 mile, the trail switchbacks down then slabs to a junction with the Babel Tower Trail at 2.0 miles. A side trail goes left to another summit, this one 3,035 feet, encircled by an abrupt bend in the river. The popular Babel Tower Trail climbs a scenic ridge 1.2 miles to its trailhead on NC 1238.

From the junction, the Linville Gorge Trail switchbacks off a gap steeply down to the river. On the way to a bridgeless junction with the Devils Hole Trail across the river, there are great views of the gorge on the left at 3.4 miles as it rises east nearly 2,000 feet to Hawksbill Mountain. The Devils Hole Trail climbs 1.5 miles to FSR 210. At 3.9 miles on the Gorge Trail, the terrain flattens. There are plentiful campsites and a spring near the base of the old Sandy Flats Trail. (This super-steep 1.0-mile trail was permanently closed in 2005 after severe storm damage.)

The trail continues under Wiseman's View and intersects the Spence Ridge Trail at 4.5 miles. Spence Ridge is the most popular trail into the gorge from the east side. It leaves the Linville Gorge Trail, crosses the river on a bridge, and climbs somewhat gradually in 1.7 miles to FSR 210.

Lacking the convulsions at the head of the gorge, the river flows directly down— the Linville Gorge Trail with it—to a junction on the right with the Conley Cove Trail at about 5.5 miles. This is a heavily used route, due largely to its lesser grade. From the junction the Cove Trail rises on a graded tread to a spring and a junction on the left with the canyon rim–running view fest of the Rock Jock Trail at about 1.0 mile. It meets NC 1238 at 1.3 miles.

The Gorge Trail passes this junction and runs for its greatest uninterrupted length along the river, about 3.5 miles. There are plentiful places to swim and nice views across the river at popular rock-climbing areas. The bulk of this section of trail flattens out. (Along the way, on the opposite side of the gorge, the obscure Cambric Branch Trail descends from the Shortoff Mountain Trail to dead-end at the river.)

At just more than 9.0 miles, the junction on the right is Pinch-In Trail, a ruggedly steep, view-packed 1.4-mile route to NC 1238. Below this trail junction, the Linville Gorge Trail gradually runs the next 2.4 miles beside the river and then fords it, to terminate at private property.

An out-and-back hike on this portion of the lesser-used Lower Gorge Trail is nice, but a southern gorge circuit exists for the experienced hiker/backpacker. Parking at the Pinch-In Trail trailhead, descend into the gorge and hike up the canyon, exiting at the Conley Cove Trail. Go left on the Rock Jock Trail. When it exits onto NC 1238, it's only about 0.5 mile downhill south to the Pinch-In trailhead. This is a rugged 9.0-mile hike in either direction, exploring an area the Forest Service says is among the least used in the gorge.

The Museum of North Carolina Minerals, at Milepost 330.9, is a worthwhile stop between the Chestoa View Loop Trail and Crabtree Meadows Recreation Area.

36 Chestoa View Loop Trail

Milepost 320.8

From a popular roadside viewpoint, a quiet path leads to a nearby flat-topped knoll with a few good views.

Parkway mile: 320.8
Distance: 0.85-mile loop
Difficulty: Moderately easy

Elevation gain: Negligible
Maps: *USGS Linville Falls;* no Parkway map available

Finding the trailhead: The trail begins at the Chestoa View, just south of the US 221 entrance to the Parkway and the town of Linville Falls.

The Hike

Before hiking the longer trail, take the short, steep descent on stone steps to Chestoa View, a clifftop semicircular rock outlook with a dramatic drop to the North Cove Valley. The square-topped crag of Table Rock on the horizon marks the crest of the Linville Gorge (the chasm lies unseen below it). Directly below, US 221 can be seen heading down to Marion, North Carolina, and I-40.

The dramatic drop from that first overlook tells you what recommends this trail. Note that the first section of the short path to the formal viewpoint is bordered by an impenetrable wire-mesh fence—casual bushwhacking around here could very easily become a free fall from a vegetated clifftop. If the macabre thought suddenly surfaces that a villain might do away with someone here—well, it's happened.

The face of Chestoa is precipitously abrupt, and that relief makes the Chestoa ridge one Parkway landmark you'd do well to notice from a distance before taking this hike. If you've come from Marion and I-40 on US 221, you can't help but be awed on the way up by how Chestoa suddenly pinches the left side of North Cove Valley into towering cliffs. You'll notice the same thing on the side trip from Linville Falls to Linville Caverns (North Carolina's only commercial cavern—open year-round). It's just below, on the section of road you look down on from Chestoa View. Either way, you'll be on top of the cliffs you notice from below—at 4,090 feet.

From farther away—Grandfather Mountain's Mile-High Swinging Bridge, for instance—Chestoa is that saddlelike square-topped mountain to the south with the dramatic drop in front of it.

You'd be excused if you didn't even notice where the lengthiest Chestoa hike begins; the unpaved, unsigned trail scoots discreetly off to the right under an archway of rhododendron from the upper part of the paved viewpoint path. From that branch, the trail dips gradually down through a flat gap and then rises again—the steepest part of the entire trail is the last 0.1-mile climb before the trail splits into its end loop. Go left at the split and the grade moderates to a fence-lined view on the left of Grandfather Mountain and Table Rock, the dominating presence to the right.

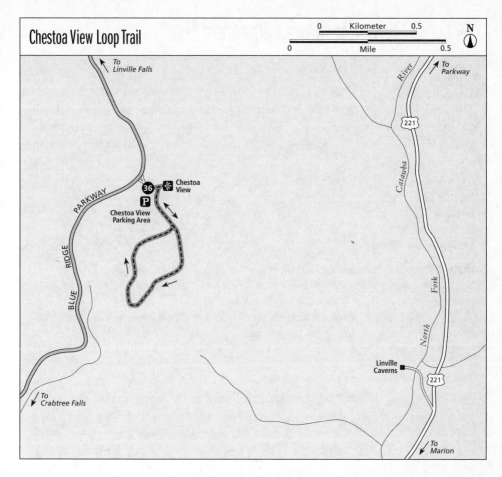

Chestoa View Loop Trail

0   Kilometer   0.5

0   Mile   0.5

N

To Linville Falls

To Parkway

River

221

Catawba

36

Chestoa View

P

Chestoa View
Parking Area

PARKWAY

BLUE RIDGE

North Fork

Linville Caverns

221

To Crabtree Falls

To Marion

The trail jogs back around toward the parking area. When there are no leaves on the trees, you get the full impact of how this side of the ridge drops through steep, gladed hillsides to sheer cliffs. Neighboring ridges rise grandly from the void beyond. The trail turns back toward the parking area, circling a marvelously flat-topped summit.

Parents might have a little fun with their kids near the turn back to the parking area. A tree just off the trail to the right is shaped remarkably like the number 4. You might wonder aloud, "Not every tree is tall and straight and looks like a number 1. Can you spot any other numbers out here?"

From there the path dips gradually again to the junction of the loop and return to the parking area.

Key Points

0.3   Trail splits; head left.

0.35   Nice view of Table Rock at Linville Gorge and Grandfather Mountain.

0.55   Return to loop split; head left.

0.85   Return to parking area.

37 Crabtree Meadows Recreation Area

Milepost 339.5

Though only 253 acres, Crabtree Meadows Recreation Area is a small but compelling scenic enclave on the Parkway. Crabtree Falls Loop Trail is one of western North Carolina's best waterfall hikes—especially on a sunny spring day after significant rain. You'll also find a campground, picnic area, snack bar, and gift shop with some camp supplies.

Parkway mile: 339.5
Distance: 2.5-mile loop
Difficulty: Strenuous
Elevation gain: 600 feet

Maps: *USGS Celo;* Parkway handout map, available at the snack bar and the campground kiosk

Finding the trailhead: Take the northernmost entrance to the Crabtree Meadows Recreation Area and bear right into the campground. Just past the contact station, turn right into the well-signed trailhead.

If the campground is closed, you can park in the snack bar lot and either walk the road to the campground or take the amphitheater trail to access the campground and trailhead (keep your eye on the map).

The Hike

This trail starts and descends on a wide gravel path to the loop junction and bench. Turn right and wind down into a hemlock-forested cove where steep stone steps mark two switchbacks. The trail between the switchbacks includes a bridge and is pretty wet when conditions for the falls are best. (On the way down, the falls are off to your left, plummeting down a steeper portion of this same descent.) You'll veer to the right, away from the second set of steps onto a sunnier slope. There's a bench in the last switchback where the trail turns left and heads back toward the waterfall.

A bridge with embedded benches spans Crabtree Creek near the base of the falls. Little paths on either side of the stream lead closer to the misty pool under the cataract. This is one of the most picturesque waterfalls in the Southern Appalachians—water dances down over ledges in a cascading fan of foam. Retrace your steps for a 1.8-mile out-and-back hike.

To continue, cross the stream and climb a sunny slope of switchbacks. On the way, stone steps afford another great view of the falls. The trail follows a rock retaining wall and then dips under a crag that marks the path's passage through the cliff line that forms the crest of the cataract. Just past stone steps and a metal railing, a bench marks the top of the climb.

The trail then becomes intimate and easy as you wander under a hemlock forest through a tunnel of rhododendron and mountain laurel. The stream appears off to your left. Sunny openings in the tall trees reveal mossy, grassy little bogs. It's A+ scen-

Crabtree Falls' dancing fan of foam is the perfect destination for a spring hike.

ery all along here as you cross a small side stream on a bridge and then a bigger span of Crabtree Creek at 1.3 miles. You may be tempted to aim your camera upstream, where the water cascades over ledge after ledge.

Past the stream, a stretch of rutted trail rises consistently then turns left past another big hemlock grove. The trail crosses a bridge and then parallels that stream as it ascends to its source in a bog beside a bench. Northern white hellebore grows here in late April. The trail then turns away to the right.

At about 2.1 miles a side trail branches right to campground Loop B. (You could turn left on the first paved road you reach and go straight through the next junction

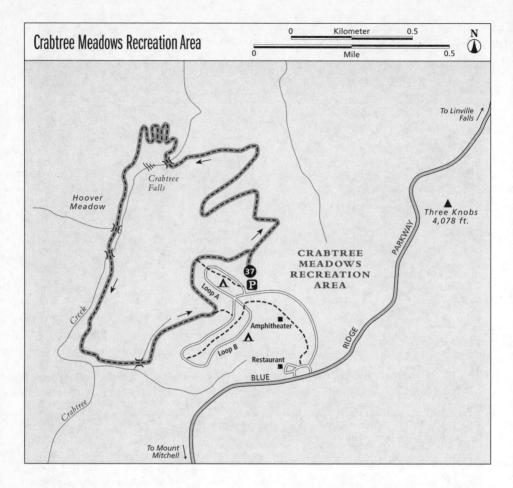

Crabtree Meadows Recreation Area

to the trailhead parking area.) Steer left and you have two ways back to your car, a few tenths of a mile away at the next junction. You can turn right, cross the road, and bisect campground Loop A on a path that leads directly to the trailhead past a restroom. Or you can keep straight, reach the loop trail junction beyond, and ascend the wide gravel path back to your car.

Key Points

0.15 Loop trail splits.

0.5 Descend long flight of stone steps.

0.9 Crabtree Falls.

1.3 Wooden bridge across Crabtree Creek.

2.1 Side trail to campground Loop B.

2.3 Side trail to campground Loop A; could go right.

2.4 Loop trail junction, go right.

38 Mount Mitchell

Mileposts 344.1–355.3

Mount Mitchell—the highest peak east of the Mississippi—is a crowning part of the Blue Ridge Parkway experience. The only motorized access to the mountain is from the Parkway, at Milepost 355.3, and the summit is only a 5-mile detour. Don't miss it—even on a dismal day.

The 1,700-acre Mount Mitchell State Park clings to the highest peak of the Black Mountains, a serrated string of summits that juts away from the Parkway and Blue Ridge to dominate the western skyline of North Carolina. Cut by landslides that appear as snow-and-ice-covered chutes in winter, the mighty Blacks are frequently seen from the Parkway as a dark ridgecrest rising above the clouds. Be sure to stop at the Black Mountains Overlook (Milepost 342.2) and the Mount Mitchell Overlook (Milepost 349.9). The range includes six of the ten highest peaks in eastern North America.

Unlike that contrastingly named New England range, the White Mountains, the Blacks would have to be nearly 8,000 feet in height to reach a climate cold enough to create the treeless alpine zone found in New Hampshire at just under 5,000 feet. But the Black Mountains reign supreme, and high winds and deep snow (104 inches

Mount Mitchell's new summit tower offers excellent views and signs that point out distant peaks.

annually) yield a surprisingly severe climate. Low vegetation, including a remarkable thornless blackberry, clings to the cliffs and crags. Vistas are everywhere among the mountains' evergreens.

The state park—North Carolina's first—was established in 1915 through the efforts of then Governor Locke Craig (1913–1917) and Theodore Roosevelt, among others. The park was created at a time when massive logging of the state's western mountains threatened to completely eradicate the last virgin forest. Much of the grandeur of that old-growth forest is gone, but this mountaintop preserve is a wonderful glimpse at a Canada-like forest in the American South.

Today the park is a microcosm of the environmental problems that are destroying high-elevation forests throughout eastern America and Europe. Early research had ascribed much of the defoliation and destruction of the mountain's evergreen zone to an infestation by the balsam woolly adelgid, a pest introduced into the United States around 1900. But the adelgid attacks only Fraser fir, which doesn't explain the decline of the red spruce forests. More recent studies suggest damage by acid rain—highly acidic precipitation that upsets the pH balance of the soil, freeing heavy metals that inhibit a tree's ability to ingest nutrients.

Robert Bruck, North Carolina State University, has discovered another significant factor: ozone. Bruck's measurements suggest that like the smog trapped in cities, airborne pollution from major upwind utilities and industries leads to startlingly high ozone levels on Southern summits. His research discovered that such pollution, often contained in cloud caps as acidic as vinegar, burns the needles of firs, dramatically inhibiting the growth and survival of evergreens already fighting a severe climate. The result is that stark tree skeletons stand tall and gray in ghostlike groves. The Balsam Nature Trail is an introduction to this ongoing ecological catastrophe.

The story of Mount Mitchell's crowning as the East's loftiest peak, and its naming, involve considerable controversy. Although Elisha Mitchell, a Connecticut native, is acknowledged as the first to measure the preeminent peak, that distinction was also claimed by Thomas Clingman, a North Carolinian and congressman, senator, and Confederate brigadier general. In 1835 Mitchell was intrigued by the claim of early botanist Andre Michaux that a peak in the Black Mountains was the highest in the United States. Mitchell began measuring summits in the Black Mountains barometrically and arrived at the conclusion that one of the summits, then called Black Dome, was 6,476 feet high. As a result, the mountain was listed in an 1839 atlas as the East's highest peak.

Clingman vaulted into what was apparently already a controversy in 1855, stating that Mitchell had not measured the loftiest peak and that he had; Clingman claimed 6,941 feet for the summit. Perhaps wishing to consolidate his advantage, the elderly Mitchell returned to the mountain in 1857. Stopping his work near the end of June, Mitchell left his party to visit the homes of former guides, including Thomas "Big Tom" Wilson. Five days later, Mitchell's son reached Wilson's cabin to learn that his father had never arrived. Wilson remembered an obscure route over the mountain that he'd shown Mitchell years before. Following that route to the base of a 40-foot waterfall, the party found Mitchell, who had apparently stumbled in the fading light and drowned in a large pool.

Needless to say, the public immediately flocked to Mitchell's side in the debate, and a year after his burial in Asheville, he was laid to vindicated rest on the mountaintop. The peak officially became Mount Mitchell in 1858. Ultimately, Mitchell's claim to the peak is enhanced by the fact that his final measurement of 6,672 feet is only 12 feet shy of the peak's true elevation—remarkable, since much later measurements were even further afield. Clingman's measurement was off by almost 300 feet. Nevertheless, I second Charlton Ogburn's lament that the East's highest peak might be more loftily named.

No one in this story could complain about his place in history. Mitchell may have the East's highest peak, but Clingman's name adorns Clingmans Dome (6,643 feet), the Great Smokies' highest summit, which he is also said to have measured. And Thomas "Big Tom" Wilson has his own summit—Big Tom (6,593 feet)—1.1 miles north of Mount Mitchell on the Deep Gap Trail.

Mitchell's gravesite on the summit sits below the primary tourist vista on the peak—a new stone tower and curving, wheelchair-accessible ramp that opened in 2009, the most recent of several memorials at this site.

In 1888 a 12-foot bronze monument was erected. By 1915 a pole-mounted view ladder was in place; and in 1916 when the park was created, a 15-foot wooden platform debuted. A medieval-looking stone tower appeared in 1926, and in 1959 the geometrical structure sprouted that was so recently replaced.

Mount Mitchell State Park has a variety of public facilities. The ranger office is on the right immediately after the park entrance, and a restaurant (open mid-May to late October) is next. The park's premier nine-site tent campground (open May through October) near the park maintenance area offers the coolest, highest camping in the South. Sites 5 and 6 are most sheltered from wind; Site 8 has its own little peak with a view of the tower. The summit facilities include a snack bar (open June 1 through Labor Day and weekends through October) and restrooms beside the parking lot; a highly recommended new nature museum was dedicated during summer 2001. The old museum on the wide paved path to the summit tower has been renovated as classroom space.

In winter the Blue Ridge Parkway closes during snowfall. Though the road to the summit, including the Parkway, is plowed for park personnel, the road often isn't safe for public use. When the road is plowed and stable weather permits, public access is allowed from the NC 80–Blue Ridge Parkway junction. Call ahead in winter, either to the state park or the Blue Ridge Parkway, before making the drive. Backpackers must register their vehicles on trailhead forms before camping.

Option 1: Mount Mitchell Trail to Mount Mitchell

This spectacular part of the Mountains-to-Sea Trail climbs through virgin forest to the summit of Mount Mitchell. Its vertical rise is one of the great elevation changes in the East. A lower circuit on the same trails is a shorter hike.

Parkway mile: Reached from Milepost 344.1
Distance: Approximately 11.4 miles out and back
Difficulty: Extremely strenuous to the summit; moderate for the lower virgin forest hike

Elevation gain: 3,700 feet
Maps: *USGS Old Fort and Mount Mitchell.* The best map is the Forest Service South Toe River Trail Map.

Finding the trailhead: Leave the Parkway at Milepost 344 going west on NC 80. In 2.2 miles turn left onto FSR 472. Black Mountain Campground is just more than 3 miles on the right. The trail begins in the upper campground loop.

The Hike

If only physically climbing a mountain makes you feel that you've earned the summit, this trail is your chance—all 4,000 vertical feet of it. The blue-blazed trail quickly skirts a small nature trail loop then crosses some small streams and climbs through impressive stands of virgin hardwoods and evergreens. Stay on the Mount Mitchell Trail past the junction with the Higgins Bald Trail on the left at 1.5 miles. The trail crosses Setrock Creek at 2.5 miles, passes another junction on the left with the Higgins Bald Trail at 2.7 miles, and climbs through more virgin forest, this time of red spruce and Fraser fir.

At about 3.9 miles join the Buncombe Horse Range Trail and at 4.0 miles pass the Camp Alice Shelter site. In another 0.1 mile the trail turns right and makes a rocky climb to a junction with the Balsam Nature Trail near the Mitchell summit. A left on the developed trail reaches the summit tower on Mount Mitchell at 5.7 miles. Consider taking a right on the white-blazed Higgins Bald Trail on the way down. It's only 0.3 mile farther than the Mount Mitchell Trail you've already hiked and includes a nice waterfall.

There is also a lower circuit with the Higgins Bald Trail. Follow it in the direction recommended above and then turn left onto the Higgins Bald Trail at 2.7 miles. At 3.4 miles you'll pass through an open area where a chimney still marks the former site of a Forest Service cabin and then pass a nice waterfall at Setrock Creek. At 4.2 miles turn back right onto the Mount Mitchell Trail and return to the campground for a 5.7-mile hike.

Keep in mind that Black Mountain Campground is one of the national forest campgrounds that's best-kept secret with easy Parkway access. (See the Mileage Log for access at Mileposts 344.1 and 351.9.)

Key Points

1.5 Higgins Bald Trail goes left.
2.7 Higgins Bald Trail returns left.
3.9 Left on Buncombe Horse Range Trail.
4.1 Right off horse trail to climb Commissary Ridge.

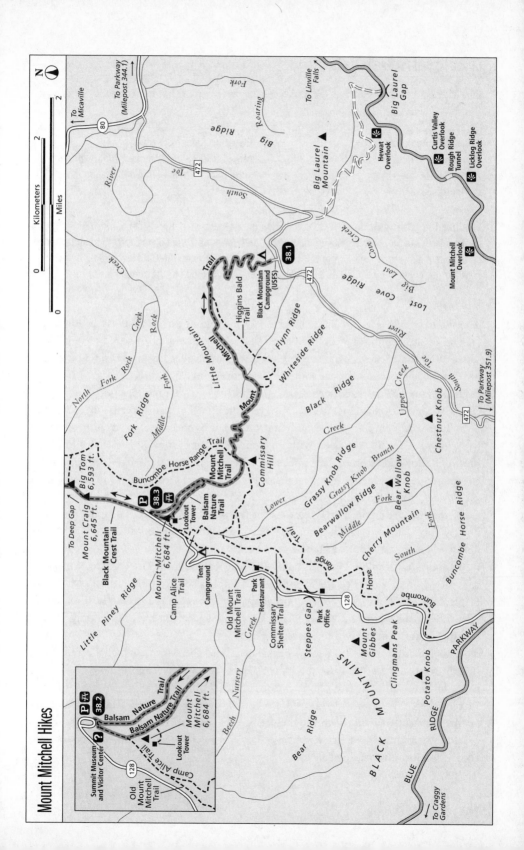

Mount Mitchell Hikes

N

0 1 2 Kilometers
0 1 2 Miles

To Micaville

To Parkway (Milepost 344.1)

80

River

Toe

472

South

Fork

Roaring

Ridge

Big

Creek

Cove

Big Laurel Mountain

To Linville Falls

Hewat Overlook

Big Laurel Gap

Curtis Valley Overlook

Rough Ridge Tunnel

Licklog Ridge Overlook

Mount Mitchell Overlook

Lost

Big

Cove

Ridge

472

Toe

River

South

472

To Parkway (Milepost 351.9)

Chestnut Knob

Creek

Creek

North Fork

Rock

Middle Fork

Rock

Fork Ridge

Higgins Bald Trail

Black Mountain Campground (USFS)

38.1

Flynn Ridge

Whiteside Ridge

Black Ridge

Grassy Knob Ridge

Grassy Knob Branch

Bearwallow Ridge

Bear Wallow Knob

Middle Fork

South Fork

Buncombe Horse Ridge

Mount Mitchell Trail

Little Mountain

Mount

Buncombe Horse Range Trail

Commissary Hill

Lower

Creek

Cherry Mountain

Mount Craig 6,645 ft.

Big Tom 6,593 ft.

To Deep Gap

Black Mountain Crest Trail

Mount Mitchell 6,684 ft.

P **38.3**

Lookout Tower

Balsam Nature Trail

Camp Alice Trail

Tent Campground

Old Mount Mitchell Trail

Park Restaurant

Commissary Shelter Trail

Little Piney Ridge

Mount Mitchell-

Nursery

Beech

Creek

Range Trail

Horse

Steppes Gap

Park Office

128

Buncombe

Mount Gibbes

Clingmans Peak

Potato Knob

Bear Ridge

BLACK MOUNTAINS

BLUE RIDGE

PARKWAY

To Craggy Gardens

Inset:

Summit Museum and Visitor Center

? **P** **38.2**

Balsam

128

Nature Trail

Balsam Nature Trail

Mount Mitchell 6,684 ft.

Lookout Tower

Camp Alice Trail

Old Mount Mitchell Trail

Option 2: Balsam Nature Trail

The Balsam Nature Trail is a self-guided interpretive trail that explains the spruce-fir forest and acid rain deforestation.

See map on page 247.
Parkway mile: Reached from Milepost 355.3
Distance: 0.8-mile loop
Difficulty: Easy

Elevation gain: Negligible
Maps: *USGS Mount Mitchell;* rudimentary state park map, available at the summit facilities

---

Finding the trailhead: Take NC 128, the state park access road, from Milepost 355.3 and go all the way to the Mount Mitchell summit parking area. Walk past the concession stand/museum on the ascending gravel trail toward the summit tower. Go left when the Old Mitchell Trail branches right and then take the next left at the trailhead sign. (A right leads to the summit tower.)

The Hike

The white triangle–blazed Balsam Nature Trail explores the highest, most Northern climate in the South. The recently improved interpretive path has trailside exhibits that feature the ecosystem, climate, plants, and animals that live in this rarefied evergreen zone, only found this far south at elevations above 5,500 feet.

In addition to the evergreen Fraser fir and red spruce, prevalent deciduous species at this elevation include mountain ash. Among other plants are many found in New England, including hobblebush and mountain wood sorrel, or oxalis, a cloverlike ground covering associated with boreal forests that blooms in late May and early June. The rhododendron blooms in late June. Yellow birch seen here also grows north to Minnesota and Quebec. The first leg of the trail passes Camp Rock, an east-facing shelter ledge used by explorers as early as 1850. The damp seeps at similar outcrops along the trail are favored growing sites for the purple turtlehead, a snapdragon-like flower. There's a view north along the Black Mountain range. Mount Craig is the dominant, nearer summit just beyond the parking lot.

In addition to yellow birch found on the trail, you might notice a grove of mountain paper birch, similar to the white-barked birches so often associated with New Hampshire and Vermont. The small heart-shaped leaves are the giveaway. If, as some scientists speculate, this grove is actually a separate species of birch, then only about 400 specimens exist, all within this state park.

The Balsam Nature Trail turns back left where the Mount Mitchell Trail goes straight to descend Commissary Ridge to Black Mountain Campground. This area is home to the most severe winter weather in North Carolina. In two days during March 1993, the mountain received a record 50 inches of snow. The trail passes a nearby stream that is likely the highest spring in eastern America. Its average temperature (when not frozen in winter) is 36°F. About 100 yards beyond, the nature trail ends at the summit parking lot.

Key Points

0.05 Old Mount Mitchell Trail goes right.

0.15 Tower trail goes right.

0.4 Balsam Nature Trail turns left from Mount Mitchell Trail.

Option 3: Black Mountain Crest Trail

An inspiring out-and-back summit-hopping hike/backpacking trip traverses a sparsely vegetated ridge well above 6,000 feet. Views plummet 4,000 feet into adjacent valleys.

See map on page 247.
Parkway mile: Reached from Milepost 355.3
Distance: 12.0 miles one-way; Mount Mitchell to Mount Craig, 2.0 miles round-trip; Mount Mitchell to Deep Gap, just under 8.0 miles round-trip; 6.6-mile summit loop
Difficulty: Moderate to Mount Craig; strenuous for longer hikes
Elevation gain: 535 feet to Mount Craig and back
Maps: USGS *Mount Mitchell* and *Celo* quads intersect, annoyingly, directly on the trail's ridgeline location. The best map is the Forest Service South Toe River Trail Map.

Finding the trailhead: Take NC 128, the state park access road, from Milepost 355.3 and go all the way to the Mount Mitchell summit parking area. When you round the last curve into the parking area, the Black Mountain Crest Trail (also called the Deep Gap Trail on the way to that landmark notch in the crest) begins on the left, between log cabin–style picnic shelters. The loop hike begins at the same trailhead as the Balsam Nature Trail. (See Option 2.)

The Hike

The first mile of the orange-blazed Black Mountain Crest Trail makes a great out-and-back 2.0-mile day hike to Mount Craig, with views in all directions. On the peak, a plaque memorializes Locke Craig, the governor who helped secure creation of this first North Carolina state park.

The trail leaves the north end of the parking lot, passes the picnic shelters, and descends through spruces. At the 0.5-mile mark, in the gap between the peaks (about 6,330 feet), the land drops away west to Mitchell Creek and Mitchell Falls (4,400 feet), where the body of Mount Mitchell's namesake, Elisha Mitchell, was found by his guide, Thomas "Big Tom" Wilson. The trail then rebounds to the open summit of Mount Craig (6,645 feet), the Blacks' second-highest and probably most spectacular peak. The view back to the tower on Mount Mitchell is what makes this short hike so memorable. From here the size of the summit development shrinks and the mountain you conquered by car gains in stature.

The next logical turnaround point for a day hike (and camping trip) is Deep Gap, the more than 700-foot cleft visible for miles in the ridge of the Blacks.

Continuing past Mount Craig, and after descending briefly to another gap, the trail ascends to the summit of Big Tom (6,593 feet) at 1.2 miles, an elevation virtually identical to Mount LeConte, a noteworthy peak in the Great Smokies. A plaque memorializes Wilson.

The Black Mountain Crest Trail then descends 0.4 mile to the Big Tom Trail, which drops east abruptly down the mountain. (This is the return leg of the loop hike described at the end of this entry.) The Crest Trail then climbs the west side of Balsam Cone and reaches the peak (6,611 feet) at about 2.0 miles. The trail crosses Cattail Peak at 6,583 feet, then leaves the state park for national forest land and drops 200 feet into a gap. It climbs again briefly to Potato Hill (6,440 feet—where a fixed rope aids a climb up a muddy section) before dramatically dipping into Deep Gap at just under 4.0 miles. Deep Gap's shelter was torn down in 1995, but there's a spring 300 yards down the mountain to the east in front of the shelter site.

Key Points

0.0 Start at north end of Mount Mitchell summit parking area.

1.0 Summit of Mount Craig.

1.6 Big Tom Trail intersects right.

3.9 Deep Gap, a good turnaround.

7.8 Return to the parking area.

End-to-End Trek

Few Parkway hikers get beyond Deep Gap—an end-to-end adventure on this trail requires two cars and substantial driving. But the Crest Trail does continue, climbing out of Deep Gap and over Deer Mountain (6,120 feet) at 4.5 miles. It jogs right to higher Winter Star Mountain (6,203 feet) and, just past there, gains the lower ridge of the northern Blacks with another fixed rope over a rock step that requires low-grade climbing. There are spectacular views on this section of the ridge.

The trail goes left of the crest at about 6.0 miles, passing Gibbs Mountain and Horse Rock. At just more than 7.0 miles, the trail pitches up and slabs west of the final and loftiest of the northern Black Mountain peaks, Celo Knob (6,327 feet), at 7.5 miles. The next 4.5 miles go downhill on a switchbacking descent to the Bolens Creek trailhead near Burnsville, North Carolina, at just under 11.0 miles. The trail follows cascades and pools to a timber road and reaches the dirt access road at just under 12.0 miles. Currently the Bolens Creek area is posted as a no trespassing zone, but local hikers are working with the owners to find a way that hikers can enjoy this beautiful creek. For more information, contact the Appalachian/Toecane Ranger Station, P.O. Box 128, Burnsville, NC 28714; (828) 682-6146.

Summit Circuit

If you'd prefer not to go out and back from the summit of Mount Mitchell, try this circuit that uses the Big Tom Trail to return on the Crest Trail: Leave the summit parking area on the tower trail, then veer off left onto the Balsam Nature Trail. (See that option for more detail.) When the nature trail bears left, continue straight on the Mount Mitchell Trail down Commissary Ridge to the scenic and easy Bun-combe Horse Range Trail, about 1.6 miles from the summit. This 15.0-mile, white-blazed horse trail parallels the ridgecrest north and south of the summit of Mount Mitchell.

Go left on the old logging road and in 0.1 mile pass the former site of the Camp Alice Shelter on the right. Follow the rocky but level trail north 3.0 miles to the Big Tom Trail. The horse trail goes right, to descend, but go left to make a steep 0.5-mile climb of about 560 vertical feet to the crest of the Black Mountains. Once on the ridge, turn left onto the Crest Trail at about 5.0 miles and prepare for a spectacular return to Mount Mitchell over Big Tom and Mount Craig for a 6.6-mile loop hike.

If you're inspired by the benchmark embedded in Mount Mitchell's new summit platform, you can buy a replica at the museum gift shop.

39 Douglas Falls Trail

Milepost 363.4

A rugged and steeply descending trail leads to a significant waterfall and a good campsite in an inspiring virgin forest.

Parkway mile: 363.4
Distance: 7.2 miles round-trip
Difficulty: Strenuous
Elevation gain: 1,326 feet

Maps: *USGS Craggy Pinnacle;* Parkway handout map, available at the Craggy Gardens Visitor Center

Finding the trailhead: Park north of the Craggy Gardens Visitor Center at the Graybeard Mountain Overlook (Milepost 363.4) trailhead for the Mountains-to-Sea Trail.

The Hike

Craggy Gardens may be high and almost alpine, but one of the area's best hikes plummets into the Pisgah National Forest's Craggy Mountain Scenic Area. A major waterfall and a prime example of western North Carolina's few remaining virgin hardwood forests make this a downhill walk worth considering. The hike starts on the Mountains-to-Sea Trail at the Graybeard Mountain Overlook. Take the white dot–blazed trail south then across the road. The trail follows a gated paved road downhill then reenters the woods.

About 1.3 miles from the parking area, the white-blazed Douglas Falls Trail heads right at a Forest Service trail sign. The trail descends switchbacks, and 1.0 mile from the Mountains-to-Sea Trail junction—at 2.3 miles—it passes Cascades Falls. Below that lies a truly impressive virgin evergreen and hardwood forest. There's a good campsite just before the 70-foot cataract of Douglas Falls at 3.6 miles (a 7.2-mile round-trip).

Many hikers start at a Forest Service trailhead 0.5 mile below the falls on FSR 74, but it's quite a drive from the Parkway.

Key Points

1.3 Go right on Douglas Falls Trail.
2.3 Cascades Falls.
3.6 Douglas Falls.

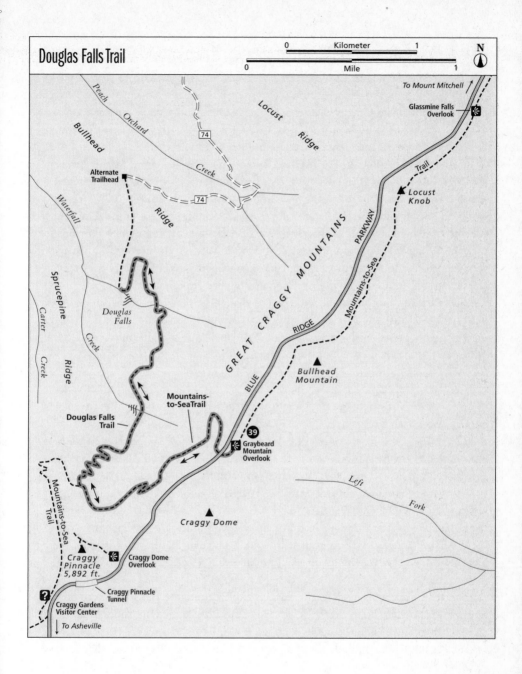

Douglas Falls Trail

40 Craggy Gardens

Mileposts 364.1–364.4

How can names like Craggy Gardens, Craggy Dome, and Craggy Pinnacle not be magnets for hikers? Visible from almost any corner of northwest North Carolina, these barren crests of the Craggy Mountains offer awesome views.

Coming from Asheville, the high road starts in sunny lowlands. As the Parkway climbs, eyes are drawn ahead, where the sun often disappears behind a microclimatic weather event caused by the Craggies. Summits and clouds coalesce. The dramatic elevation change often lends the area the feel of much higher mountains. The sunny warmth of Asheville yields to shade and chill breeze. During the coldest part of the year, the Craggy Gardens and the adjacent Mount Mitchell portions of the Parkway are often closed due to deep snow and severe weather. Some of that spills into even the warmest months—so be prepared for a truly peak experience.

Any Parkway motorist will likely agree that the Craggy–Mount Mitchell area possesses some of the high road's most dramatic scenery. You'd swear that the towering evergreen forests on the way by Mount Mitchell were straight out of the Pacific Northwest. And when you get to the Craggies, you'll swear the treeless peaks compare with Scotland.

That seemingly alpine, treeless environment is among the most unique ecosystems in the Southern Appalachians, and Craggy Gardens is one of the best places to experience the Southern balds.

The balds come in two varieties—grassy and heath. Grassy balds may be best exemplified by the meadow-covered crest of Roan Mountain, on the North Carolina–Tennessee state line west of the Parkway from Grandfather Mountain. Andrews Bald in the Great Smokies is another example. There are grassy balds atop the Craggies, but you'll also see heath balds—extensive crests covered in rhododendron, mountain laurel, blueberries, and other plants of the heath community. The mountaineers called them "slicks," and you will agree that they look just like that from a distance. They were also called "hells," which you would understand if you ever tried to bushwhack through one.

Native American legends offer various explanations for the formation of the Southern balds. One holds that the Catawba Indians challenged the tribes of Earth to a great battle. The ensuing struggle denuded the summits, and where every Catawba brave fell, a blood-red rhododendron sprang up as a memorial. Appropriately, the rhododendron found on these heights is the reddish-purple, or Catawba, rhododendron. The late-June bloom of rhododendron across these balds—perhaps most famous at Roan Mountain—is one of the Southern Appalachians' premier natural events, celebrated by festivals in North Carolina and Tennessee.

Theories about the balds speculate that fires claimed the trees and made the soil unsuitable for immediate reforestation. Natural or even man-made fires, perhaps created by Native Americans to foster better conditions for game, could explain the existence of the meadows. There is sentiment also that the balds have been in existence for thousands of years—perhaps starting with fire and then being maintained by the natural disturbance of continued grazing by buffalo and elk. The balds continued because Appalachian mountaineers also used them for grazing. A quarter century ago, revegetation of the balds may have gotten a helping hand when the Forest Service acquired the land and grazing was curtailed.

By the mid-1980s, a conference was called to weigh the future of the balds. "The alarms really went off," says Paul Bradley, a former Pisgah National Forest district ranger for the area that includes Roan Mountain and a section of the Appalachian Trail famous for balds. "Scientists, Forest Service officials, and the public realized that if we didn't start doing something immediately, we'd lose the balds," he says.

What a loss it would be. The Southern balds in the vicinity of Craggy Gardens provide key habitat for more than thirty endangered and threatened plant species. These plants, among them some with incredibly restricted ranges, constitute the greatest concentration of rare plants in the Southern Appalachians.

The statistics were ominous. Of 2,500 bald acres on Roan and adjoining summits, 1,641 acres had started growing in. The reforestation appeared to be a natural process; blackberry, hawthorn, and spruce were slowly taking over. The agency was directed to evaluate ways to preserve the balds. The long-term disturbance associated with activities like grazing had been helping the endangered and threatened species survive.

Efforts now under way could determine whether the scenic views of the Roan Mountain area will remain for future generations. The Forest Service now maintains 2,600 acres by mowing, controlled fires—even grazing.

Parkway travelers are some distance away from "the Roan," so Craggy Gardens is the best spot to savor the late-June extravaganza of blossoms and appreciate the beauty of the balds. Don't miss the trails of Craggy Gardens, and try to confine your steps to designated paths to preserve the grasses, sedges, shrubs, and wildflowers.

A visitor center (no phone) sits on the Parkway beside the start of the Craggy Gardens Trail; a nearby picnic area has restroom facilities and a trailhead.

Option 1: The Craggy Pinnacle Trail

This trail offers one of the Parkway's most inspiring 360-degree views.

Parkway mile: 364.1
Distance: 1.4 miles out and back
Difficulty: Moderate
Elevation gain: 252 feet

Maps: USGS Craggy Pinnacle; Parkway handout map, available at the Craggy Gardens Visitor Center

Finding the trailhead: The Craggy Pinnacle Trail begins in the Craggy Dome Parking Area at Milepost 364.1, north of the Craggy Gardens Visitor Center and the Craggy Pinnacle Tunnel. A spur road leads to the parking area from the Parkway.

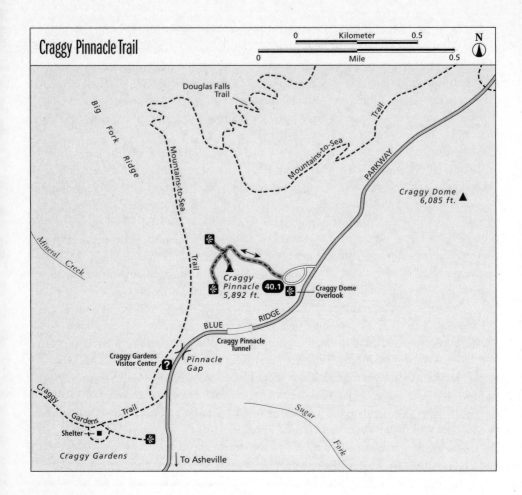

The Hike

Craggy Pinnacle is the Craggies' premier view. The path climbs to 360-degree vistas at 5,892 feet. The Mount Mitchell range dominates the northern horizon. On a clear day, a veritable who's who of Southern Appalachian summits stands out in all directions.

The path follows a level rhododendron tunnel then up stone steps on the way to a trail junction at 0.3 mile. A FRAGILE HABITAT RARE PLANTS sign exhorts hikers to stay on the main trails and within the designated viewing spots. The sign points right, to a lower overlook, and left, to the summit view. But first, take a hard right past a resting bench almost behind you and wander out a short ridge for other views.

Back at the sign, turn right and descend to a vista that looks down on the Craggy Gardens Visitor Center. Return again to the sign and go right to four stone-encircled viewpoints on top for stunning 360-degree views. Even on a wildly windy or overcast day, it's worth the short walk to soak up the otherworldly aura of the peak.

Key Points

0.3   View trail goes right.

0.7   Summit view.

Option 2: Craggy Gardens Trail via Mountains-to-Sea Trail

Great views from spectacular mountaintop balds recommend three Craggy Gardens hikes of varying lengths and difficulty.

Parkway mile: 364.5

Distance: 0.8 mile out and back from the visitor center; 1.2 miles out and back from the Craggy Gardens Picnic Area; 6.2 miles via a third and longer route on the Mountains-to-Sea Trail

Difficulty: Moderate to strenuous

Elevation gain: About 145 feet

Maps: USGS *Craggy Pinnacle;* Parkway handout map, available at the Craggy Gardens Visitor Center

Finding the trailhead: Craggy Gardens Visitor Center is located on the Blue Ridge Parkway at Milepost 364.5, about 20 miles north of Asheville. The Craggy Gardens Trail begins on the south side of the visitor center.

A second trailhead is located south of the visitor center in the Craggy Gardens Picnic Area. To reach it, turn from the Parkway onto the unpaved Stoney Fork Road at Milepost 367.6. Take the next right into the picnic area and go to the end of the parking area.

Many trails at Craggy Gardens are cozy rhododendron tunnels on the way to expansive views.

A third trailhead for the Mountains-to-Sea Trail circuit lies north of the visitor center at the Graybeard Mountain Overlook (Milepost 363.4).

The Hike

The Craggy Gardens Trail dips into the woods, and the Mountains-to-Sea Trail goes right at 0.1 mile. Beyond, the path climbs gradually through a marvelously cylindrical rhododendron tunnel. This first section of the hike is a self-guiding nature trail, with resting benches and signs identifying plants.

The trail leaves the woods and levels out at grassy Craggy Flats at a rustic, recently restored picnic shelter built by the Civilian Conservation Corps (CCC) in the 1930s. Side trails to the left just before and after the shelter lead across the wind-whipped grasses of the balds to a view from a stone observation platform at 5,640 feet. Retrace your steps and the round-trip from the Parkway to the summit viewpoint and back is about 0.8 mile. The main trail continues right through the shelter and descends to the Craggy Gardens Picnic Area.

For a longer walk of just more than 1.0 mile, start in the Craggy Gardens Picnic Area. The trail climbs gradually and at about 0.3 mile passes a short leftward trail that leads to a view from a gazebo shelter. From this direction, the rustic old picnic shelter at Craggy Flats is about 0.5 mile. The round-trip, including the summit, is about 1.2 miles.

Whichever route you choose, the grassy crest offers spectacular views. Vistas from the Craggy Flats picnic shelter look north to hikers atop Craggy Pinnacle (5,892 feet, left) and Craggy Dome (6,085 feet, right). The observation platform looks south over Craggy

Craggy Pinnacle rises beyond the restored Craggy Flats picnic shelter.

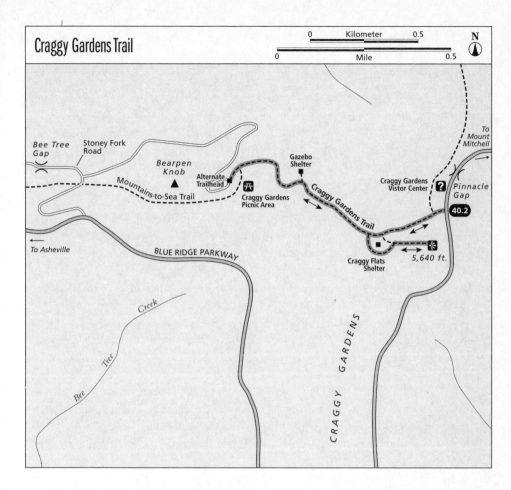

Knob (5,600 feet) and the Asheville Watershed's huge reservoir. Keep either of the two shelters in mind if the weather threatens, as it can quickly at this elevation.

Key Points to Viewpoint

0.3 Left turn at Craggy Flats picnic shelter.

Optional Longer Hike to Craggy Gardens

A longer walk to Craggy Gardens originates from the north on the Mountains-to-Sea Trail. From the Graybeard Mountain Overlook, take the white dot–blazed trail back south and across the road. The trail at first follows a gated paved road then enters the woods. About 1.3 miles from the parking area, a trail heads right to Douglas Falls.

Passing the waterfall cutoff, you'll swing out around a ridge of Craggy Pinnacle and approach the Parkway behind and below the Craggy Gardens Visitor Center. The trail joins the Craggy Gardens Trail and, about 3.0 miles from Graybeard Mountain Overlook, reaches the CCC shelter at Craggy Flats. Include the summit for a round-trip of 6.2 miles.

The Southern Appalachians

Mileposts 384.7 (US 74 at Asheville, North Carolina) to 469.1 (US 441 at Great Smoky Mountains National Park, North Carolina)

L iterally the loftiest part of the Parkway, the section from US 74 in Asheville (Milepost 384.7) to Great Smoky Mountains National Park (Milepost 469.1) has a feel all its own. It soars across the highest landmasses traversed by the high road. Add to that the sheer acreage of surrounding national forest lands, and you have a high and away-from-it-all experience that's second to none.

This is where the Blue Ridge meets the jumble of mountain ranges that make up the vast heart of the Southern Appalachians. On your way to Cherokee, North Carolina, and a memorable meeting with the massive wall of the Great Smokies, the mountaintop route surveys a mountain empire unmatched in eastern America. But off-Parkway options are nearby and noteworthy.

Asheville must lead that list. More Parkway visitors enter and exit the Parkway in Asheville than at any other place. Try the city's Urban Trail for an introduction to its vibrant downtown culture. (See Mileage Log 384.7.)

The biggest attraction is Biltmore House and Gardens, George W. Vanderbilt's 250-room summer place that is the United States' largest home. Its breathtaking gardens, interiors, and artwork are simply a must-see part of a Parkway experience. There's bike and horseback riding as well as kayaking, and the Inn on Biltmore Estate is a perfect platform for estate-raised foods and wines.

Festivals are an Asheville forte, with crafts and music as a focus. July's Belle Chere Festival is the state's largest street fest. And August boasts the Mountain Dance and Folk Festival, the nation's oldest event focused on mountain music.

The literary heritage of the Appalachians and the increasing popularity of modern fiction about the mountains are most apparent here. Visit Thomas Wolfe's boyhood home before you, yourself, go home again. Both Wolfe and O. Henry (William Sydney Porter) are buried in Asheville's Riverside Cemetery. You can make the short side trip to Carl Sandburg's home, Connemara, at nearby Hendersonville. Later, from the

Parkway, gaze at Cold Mountain, setting of the National Book Award–winning best seller of the same name.

Parkway travelers can literally check into local literary heritage at the Grove Park Inn, among the most quintessential of Appalachian hotels. The preserved historic heart of the inn, with its massive fireplace, has a room that was frequently occupied by F. Scott Fitzgerald. It's a favorite with readers. The hotel is renowned for top-notch facilities, including a nationally significant spa.

Once you're out of the city, this southernmost section of the Parkway has classic mountain towns that are at their liveliest during summer. Drop in (literally, from the Parkway) on Highlands, Cashiers, Rosman, Waynesville, and Brevard (with its internationally known summer music festival, June to August).

Indeed, this is one of the best places to hop off the Parkway and take side loops. After driving this National Park Service route, the Forest Heritage Scenic Byway is a perfect way to sample the best of the national forests flanking the road. One of the United States' most popular scenic byways, this 79-mile national forest circuit crosses the Parkway on both sides of Shining Rock Wilderness and follows US 276, NC 215, and US 64 in the vicinity of Brevard. The trip includes the Cradle of Forestry facility, the nation's earliest forestry school.

This is the "Land of Waterfalls." Looking Glass Falls is one of the roadside attractions of the Forest Heritage Byway, as is the national forest's natural water slide, Sliding Rock. Many national forest campgrounds and picnic areas line the route.

Other tours from town include Handmade in America's seven craft heritage routes. From Asheville's eateries, with a focus on locally grown seasonal produce, to the Grove Arcade Market downtown and on to out-of-the-way craft shops and galleries, these mountains are a hotbed of tradition. This is the city where the Southern Highland Handicraft Guild was born, and one of the Parkway's major facilities, the Folk Art Center, just north of the city, is a showcase for the work of its members. There are many, many other galleries all over town, some in unique shopping settings like Biltmore Village, a multiblock neighborhood of historic homes converted to distinctive shops.

Here also is the Parkway Visitor Center (Milepost 384). The brand-new, primary visitor center for the high road is just in time for the seventy-fifth anniversary. The environmentally green building has a meadow-covered roof and exhibits on the Parkway's vistas, history, geology, and culture. An interactive wall map covers the entire journey. And there's a large bookstore, theater, and restrooms.

Save time for Cherokee, the largest Indian reservation in eastern America. The tribe's stirring culture and history come alive at *Unto These Hills,* an outdoor drama that tells the Trail of Tears saga (early June to late August). The Museum of the Cherokee Indian has top-notch interactive exhibits. Oconaluftee Indian Village re-creates a Cherokee town. Craft and fine artworks by members of the oldest Native American art organization are available at the Qualla Arts and Crafts Mutual, Inc. And Harrah's Cherokee is the high road's only casino hotel, and the only place in Cherokee permitted to serve alcohol (after a recent referendum).

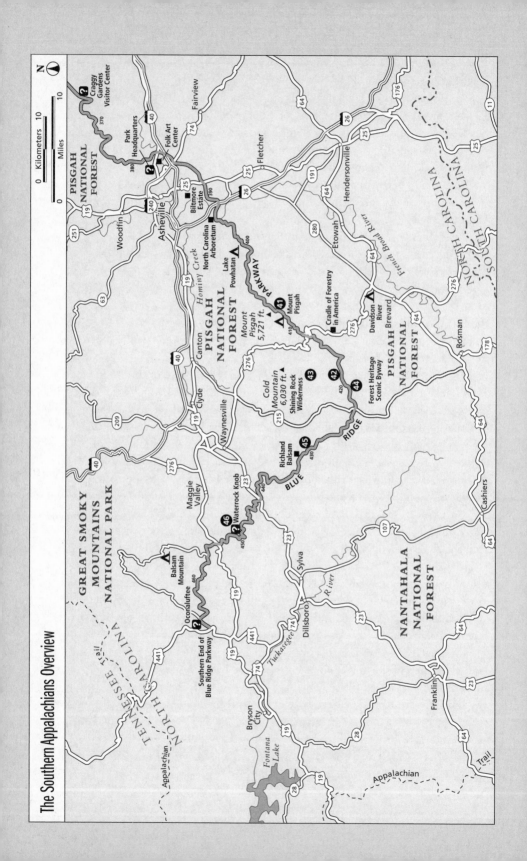

The Southern Appalachians Overview

Between the French Broad and Nantahala Rivers and many other watercourses, this is the best part of the Parkway for canoeing, kayaking, or whitewater rafting. The Asheville area also is full of film locations. Not far east of town is scenic Lake Lure (*Dirty Dancing*) and Chimney Rock, the latter a trail-laced natural area where the most memorable scenes from *The Last of the Mohicans* were filmed. Anywhere you go in Asheville—and especially as you take the Parkway in and out—you'll marvel at the city's cinematic setting.

Check Appendix B for relevant Web sites and contact information.

Asheville's recommended Urban Trail goes right by the Grove Arcade, a historic neo-Gothic city market.

41　Mount Pisgah Area Trails

Mileposts 407.6–411.9

Driving the Parkway from Asheville to Mount Pisgah is a humbling experience—especially if you stopped by Biltmore House and Gardens on the way through town. George W. Vanderbilt's fascinating palatial home—and the surrounding landscaped forest preserve that was Frederick Law Olmsted's last major project—is tiny compared with what surrounds you now as you rise out of the city. This, too, was once Vanderbilt's.

His Asheville empire illustrates the positive role played by the wealthy in the Parkway's achievement of preservation. Of course the Biltmore estate is still privately owned and, though not inexpensive, delivers a not-to-be missed travel experience on many levels. The tastefully managed private preserve still sets the stage for Vanderbilt's public land legacy.

A huge chunk of his 125,000-acre estate became the Pisgah National Forest. Indeed, Vanderbilt named this acreage Pisgah Forest after the mountain that dominates the area. (Scotch-Irish minister James Hall had named the peak in 1776 for the biblical mountain from which Moses saw the Promised Land.)

Vanderbilt hired two of the United States' earliest foresters to restore and manage his lands responsibly. Following that effort at forest stewardship, America's first school

This chair's for you—after the hike. Pisgah Inn offers hearty meals and rooms with a great view.

of forestry was located not far from Mount Pisgah. The aptly named Cradle of Forestry, a must-see stop for Parkway visitors, is located just off the Parkway on US 276 at Milepost 411.8, a turnoff 0.8 mile south of the Cradle of Forestry Overlook. US 276 is part of the Forest Heritage Scenic Byway, a highly recommended 79-mile loop in the Mount Pisgah area.

Vanderbilt built a 17.0-mile trail from his estate to a hunting lodge on the heights of what is now the Parkway's multifaceted Mount Pisgah Recreation Area (the lodge site is on the Buck Spring Trail). From 5,000 feet the views over Pisgah National Forest are as astounding now as they were in the late 1800s—and that includes the vistas from the rooms, front porches, and restaurant at Pisgah Inn. The campground is the Parkway's highest, so expect cool nights. It is the only Parkway campground with showers (at publication time). A picnic area, camp store, and gift/craft shop round out the resources.

The trail to the site of Vanderbilt's hunting lodge is still in use; the Shut-In Trail was reclaimed and is now part of the Mountains-to-Sea Trail. Between that trail, other easy paths, and the notoriously steep ascent of Mount Pisgah itself, Vanderbilt's former forest domain endures as a place where hikers would do well to get out of the car.

Option 1: Mount Pisgah Trail and Picnic Area Connector

A heart-pumping climb leads to great views atop the conical summit of one of western North Carolina's landmark mountains.

Parkway mile: 407.6
Distance: 2.6 or 3.6 miles (from picnic area) out and back
Difficulty: Strenuous

Elevation gain: 726 feet
Maps: *USGS Dunsmore Mountain and Cruso;* Parkway handout map, available at the lodge, campground, and other facilities

Finding the trailhead: Don't become befuddled trying to find this trailhead. Its location reflects an oddity of the Parkway's mileage system. Just south of the Buck Spring Tunnel, turn east into the Buck Spring Gap Overlook at Milepost 407.7, but stay left of the parking area and follow the road extension. This brings you back north to the Mount Pisgah Parking Area, which actually sits atop the Buck Spring Tunnel. Thus the parking area is back at Milepost 407.6, but you have to get there from Milepost 407.7. The trail mentioned from the picnic area (Milepost 407.8) leaves from the northeast end of the lot.

The Hike

Pass the STRENUOUS TRAIL WARNING sign at the end of the lot; the trail connector to the picnic area goes off to the left. (You can start there; see below.) The trail is pretty gradual at first as it slabs around the ridges on the northwest side of Little Pisgah Mountain, a mile-high summit in its own right that forces the Parkway through two nearby tunnels. (The picnic area connector goes by one of them.)

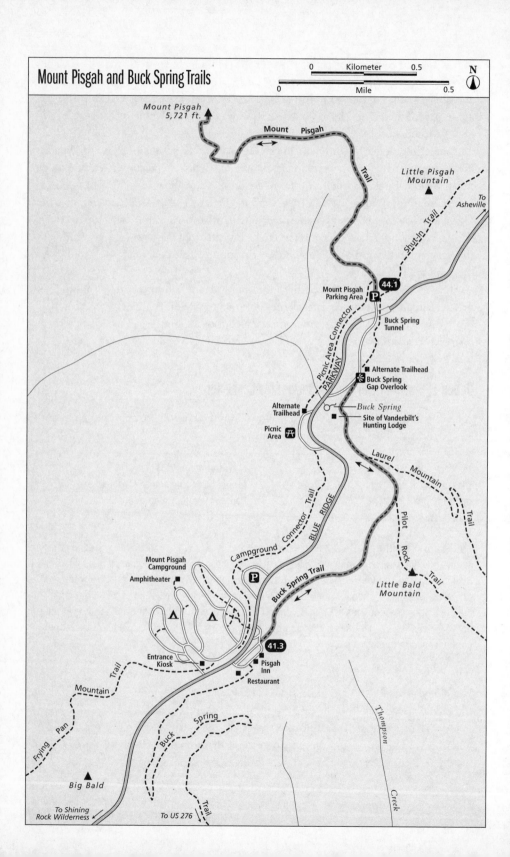

Mount Pisgah and Buck Spring Trails

0 Kilometer 0.5

0 Mile 0.5

N

Mount Pisgah
5,721 ft.

Mount Pisgah Trail

Little Pisgah
Mountain

Shut-In Trail

To Asheville

Mount Pisgah
Parking Area

P

44.1

Buck Spring
Tunnel

Picnic Area Connector

PARKWAY

Alternate Trailhead

Buck Spring
Gap Overlook

Alternate
Trailhead

Buck Spring

Site of Vanderbilt's
Hunting Lodge

Picnic
Area

Laurel

Mountain

Trail

Campground Connector Trail

BLUE RIDGE

Pilot Rock Trail

Little Bald
Mountain

Mount Pisgah
Campground

Amphitheater

P

Buck Spring Trail

Entrance
Kiosk

41.3

Pisgah
Inn

Restaurant

Mountain

Trail

Buck

Spring

Thompson

Frying Pan

Big Bald

To Shining
Rock Wilderness

To US 276

Trail

Creek

Pass a spring at 0.4 mile and rise along the ridgecrest at 0.6 mile. The trail swings left of the ridge, and a few benches appear as the trail steepens to the 1.0-mile mark. As you ascend the summit cone, the trail switchbacks and climbs back to the right to emerge at the observation tower (5,721 feet). The astounding vista stretches from the chasm of the Asheville Valley and the Black Mountains to the north, back across the crest of the Shining Rock Wilderness (including Cold Mountain) to the Smokies and beyond. Pisgah is perfectly situated to provide one of the Parkway's best views.

You can add 1.0 mile (0.5 mile in each direction) to the Mount Pisgah hike by starting at the picnic area parking lot and going right on the connector.

This trail is another of the "transportation" paths you'll find in developed Parkway recreation areas. These trails usually serve as routes for picnickers or campers to stroll between their tents or RVs and other facilities (including restaurants and camp stores).

Most campground and picnic area loop trails fall into this category and are usually of little interest to hikers. But some are destination trails in themselves—the Rocky Knob Picnic Loop in Virginia is a good example. Others can be used to extend walks, and that's the case with the connector paths that link the picnic area to the Mount Pisgah Trail as well as to the Mount Pisgah Campground and the trailhead for Frying Pan Mountain Trail.

The northernmost end of the connector leaves the picnic area toward Mount Pisgah and descends through an open area into the woods. It dips below and along the road and then rises into rhododendron and past the Buck Spring Tunnel—a rare view from the roadside rather than through the windshield. The trail climbs left and intersects the Mount Pisgah Trail at 0.5 mile.

Starting at the picnic area makes a lot of sense if you're planning to climb Mount Pisgah after lunch.

Another connector trail leaves the picnic area bound for the campground. (See the Frying Pan Mountain option for more on that hike.)

Key Points
0.4 Spring.
0.6 Ascend sharp ridge.
0.9 Trail steepens.
1.3 Summit tower.

Option 2: Frying Pan Mountain Trail

A short, long, and longer way allow you to sample views of the Pisgah area from the base of a fire tower at about 5,260 feet.

Parkway mile: 408.8
Distance: 2.0, 4.0, and 6.4 miles out and back
Difficulty: Moderate to strenuous

Elevation gain: 410 feet
Maps: USGS Dunsmore Mountain and Cruso; Parkway handout map, available at the lodge, campground, and other facilities

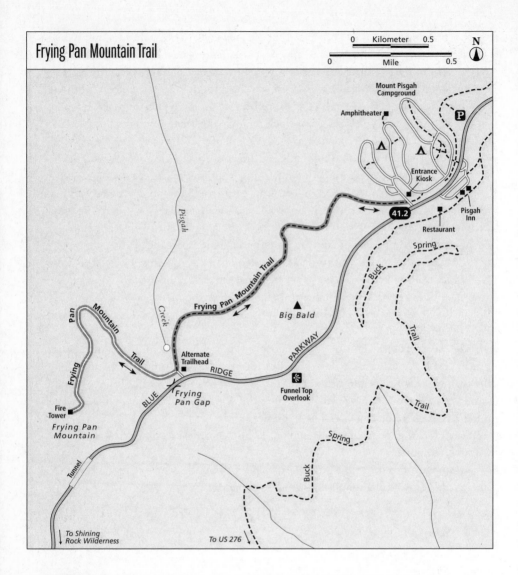

Frying Pan Mountain Trail

0 — Kilometer — 0.5
0 — Mile — 0.5

N

Mount Pisgah Campground

Amphitheater

P

Entrance Kiosk

41.2

Pisgah Inn

Restaurant

Spring

Pisgah

Creek

Frying Pan Mountain Trail

Big Bald

Buck

Trail

Mountain

Frying Pan

Trail

Alternate Trailhead

RIDGE

PARKWAY

BLUE

Frying Pan Gap

Funnel Top Overlook

Fire Tower

Frying Pan Mountain

Trail

Spring

Tunnel

Buck

To Shining Rock Wilderness

To US 276

Finding the trailhead: Start near the campground entrance station (Milepost 408.8) or at the picnic area via the campground connector trail (Milepost 407.8) and head south.

The Hike

Any version of this hike reaches another great vista on a lofty section of the Parkway. But unlike the Mount Pisgah view, one of the focal points from Frying Pan Mountain is Mount Pisgah itself. There is no access to the fire tower atop the mountain.

The trail leaves the roadside near the campground check-in kiosk and rises over the northwest ridge of Big Bald Mountain before swinging left to slab the mountainside. The Parkway is on the opposite side of the mountain, so this is a quiet stretch of trail through a scrubby forest that offers good winter views. At about the 0.5-mile mark, the trail begins a general descent into Frying Pan Gap (Milepost 409.6). This roadside pull-off, at 1.0 mile, marks the start of the portion of trail that follows a dirt road to the fire tower. Indeed, the last mile of the hike takes a big hairpin turn to the left and reaches the tower for commanding views. From Frying Pan Gap it's only a 2.0-mile round-trip hike—still a climb, but shorter. From the campground it's a 4.0-mile round-trip.

You could also make this a 6.4-mile hike by starting at the picnic area on the trail from the south side of the lot. The path dips quickly into a damp green corridor below the road through dense rhododendron and spruce forest. The first side trail to the left, at 0.8 mile, goes a few hundred feet to an unnamed parking area at Milepost 408.3. As the campsites appear off to the right at 1.0 mile, a trail goes right to the campground and left 0.1 mile to the Parkway across from the camp store. At 1.1 miles the trail joins and follows the campground loop road for 100 feet before heading back into the woods and arriving at the campground entrance kiosk at the 1.2-mile mark. Cross the road to the Frying Pan Mountain Trail. The round-trip from picnic area to the peak makes for a 6.4-mile hike that's strenuous mostly due to distance.

Key Points

0.5 Trail begins descent to Frying Pan Gap.

1.0 Frying Pan Gap.

2.0 Summit tower.

Option 3: Buck Spring Trail

A mostly graded trail makes for a pleasant walk from the Pisgah Inn to the site of George Vanderbilt's Buck Spring Hunting Lodge. A much longer but very easy section of the trail on Forest Service property is also inviting.

See map on page 266.
Parkway miles: 407.7, 408.6, and 411.8
Distance: 1.6 miles, 2.0 miles, or as much as 12.0 miles out and back
Difficulty: Easy to moderate

Elevation gain: About 480 feet from Pisgah Inn to hunting lodge site and back
Maps: *USGS Dunsmore Mountain and Cruso;* Parkway handout map, available at the lodge, campground, and other facilities

---

Finding the trailhead: On the north end of the trail, park at Buck Spring Gap Overlook (Milepost 407.7). On the south end (Milepost 408.6), park in the lot at the Pisgah Inn and start beside the trail map sign at the parking area's north end. You can also walk between the lodge office and the restaurant, descend the stone steps, and follow the grassy path right to US 276. To start at the bottom of the trail, most of which is on USDA Forest Service property, drive to Milepost 411.8. Go south 2 miles on US 276 and park on the left.

The Hike

This pleasant path is a perfect place for an aimless amble, particularly for lodge or campground guests.

The Buck Spring Trail sees most use as an untaxing walk to the site of Vanderbilt's hunting lodge for people starting from the Pisgah Inn, on the Parkway's section of the trail. The trail leaves the inn area at the map sign, passes a junction on the right with the Thompson Creek Trail and then lodge employee housing on the left, gains a ridge at 0.3 mile, and at 0.6 mile passes the Pilot Rock Trail. That trail goes a bit more than 2.0 miles to Yellow Gap Road. (In that direction, the path reaches the summit of Little Bald Mountain 0.2 mile from the Buck Spring Trail—a nice side trip or turnaround point for a round-trip walk of 1.6 miles.)

Just 0.1 mile beyond that junction, the Laurel Mountain Trail also goes right, this time to Yellow Gap Road in 7.0 miles. Keeping to the Buck Spring Gap Trail, you reach the lodge site at 1.0 mile (just 0.1 mile beyond is Buck Spring Gap Overlook). Interpretive signs describe the history of buildings that were removed in 1963. That's a 1.0-mile walk for a 2.0 mile round-trip (2.4 miles if you take in Little Bald Moun-tain's summit). Much of both these routes is part of the Mountains-to-Sea Trail.

Another option is to return to your car at the lodge via the Mount Pisgah Trail and campground connector. Go to the other end of Buck Spring Gap Overlook, the upper trailhead for the Shut-In Trail, and head into the woods there. Hike to the next parking lot, the start of the Mount Pisgah Trail, at about 1.3 miles. Switch to the Mount Pisgah Trail and immediately turn left onto the campground connector. Cross the parking lot at the picnic area at about 1.9 miles and continue toward the campground. Pass the side trail to a no-name parking area, and as the campsites appear off to the right, go left on the trail to the Parkway at about 3.0 miles. Cross the road past the camp store to the parking area at the map sign for a 3.1-mile circuit.

The easiest route to the old lodge site is to start at the north end of the trail at the Buck Spring Gap Overlook. From there the lodge site is 0.1 mile. Along the way, informal paths lead left to the edge of the ridge—surely viewpoints in Vanderbilt's time.

You'll need more ambition to tackle the lengthy Forest Service portion of the Buck Spring Trail. It leaves US 276, passes junctions left and right, respectively, with the Mountains-to-Sea Trail and the MST alternate at 1.0 mile and 1.2 miles, and climbs gradually through very scenic vegetation with many small stream crossings. The path switchbacks more steeply to an old road grade and then becomes grassy as it reaches the front of the Pisgah Inn at about 6.0 miles. From that lowest trailhead, the inn could be a great hike to lunch at the restaurant, for a long but doable 12.0 miles round-trip.

Key Points

0.6 Pass Pilot Rock Trail.

0.7 Laurel Mountain Trail goes right.

1.0 Arrive at site of Buck Spring Hunting Lodge.

42 Graveyard Fields Loop

Milepost 418.8

This loop reaches three waterfalls and explores a high, alpinelike valley. A second circuit involves a portion of the Mountains-to-Sea Trail.

Parkway mile: 418.8

Distance: Loops of 2.0 and 3.0 miles; 4.5-mile Mountains-to-Sea Trail circuit

Difficulty: Easy to moderately strenuous; easy backpacking for beginners

Elevation gain: About 300 feet for the 2.0-mile loop; about 700 feet with the side trip to Upper Falls and the Mountains-to-Sea Trail circuit

Maps: *USGS Shining Rock.* Pisgah National Forest's Shining Rock–Middle Prong Wilderness map covers the area best.

Finding the trailhead: The trail begins at Graveyard Fields Overlook at Milepost 418.8 on the Blue Ridge Parkway, 30 miles south of US 25 in Asheville. The trail is about 7 miles south of the US 276 junction and about 4.5 miles north of the NC 215 junction.

Loop Trail

The Hike

Hikes on the well-maintained but heavily traveled Graveyard Fields Loop can range from a short out-and-back hike to a full-length streamside loop, with or without scenic waterfalls. Though this lofty area—the trailhead is at 5,100 feet and the high point at 5,400 feet—never gets very warm, the pool below the lower falls is a great summer spot to cool off.

The easy return leg of the Graveyard Fields Loop rises back to the Parkway through grassy woods.

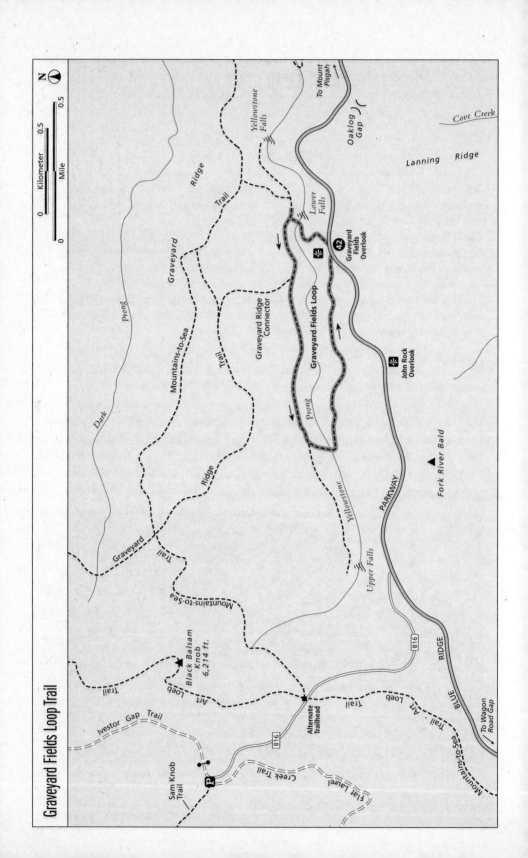

Graveyard Fields Loop Trail

N

0   Kilometer   0.5

0   Mile   0.5

To Mount Pisgah

Cove Creek

Oaklog Gap

Lanning   Ridge

Yellowstone Falls

Ridge

Trail

Graveyard

Prong

Dark

Lower Falls

Graveyard Ridge Connector

Graveyard Fields Loop

Graveyard Fields Overlook

42

Mountains-to-Sea

Trail

Ridge

Prong

John Rock Overlook

Graveyard

Trail

Yellowstone

Fork River Bald

Mountains-to-Sea

Upper Falls

PARKWAY

816

BLUE   RIDGE

Black Balsam Knob 6,214 ft.

Art Loeb   Trail

Ivestor Gap Trail

Sam Knob Trail

P

Creek Trail

816

Alternate Trailhead

Trail - Art Loeb

Flat Laurel

To Wagon Road Gap

Mountains-to-Sea

One caution: Probably the most daunting part of the entire hike is the steep descent from the Blue Ridge Parkway to the stream valley. It's short, only a few tenths of a mile, but it is steep on the way back up if you return the same way. (The return described here climbs much more gradually.) Otherwise, the Graveyard Fields Loop is a relatively easy way to explore a lofty area near the Shining Rock Wilderness, one of North Carolina's most scenic areas.

The logged open fields here were named following a devastating fire in 1925. The thousands of stumps remaining reminded some people of grave markers. The entire watershed was consumed by wildfires in the 1920s and again in the 1940s; the little valley burned again in the late 1990s. The earliest massive fires gave the Shining Rock area its above–tree line appearance; the results of the 25,000- and 50,000-acre conflagrations can still be seen in the largely treeless landscape. Few places in North Carolina afford better views.

This gentle stream valley makes the perfect place for a day hike, picnic, or back-packing trip, especially for beginners or those who want scenic camping without arduous walking. The area is very popular in summer and fall, though, so campers in this fragile area should observe scrupulous camping practices. Although accessible campsites may be filled during the busy seasons, it is easy to find out-of-the-way sites for zero-impact camping. Best advice for campers—go during the week.

Leaving the right side of the Parkway overlook, the trail descends the steep paved path to wood steps and a boardwalk bridge across Yellowstone Prong. Go right at the junction beyond, signed TO LOWER FALLS, and cross a small bridge. Descend another elaborate wooden boardwalk with some steps to the base of a cataract with a deep pool beneath it (called Second Falls on the topo map).

Retrace your steps to the junction, at about 0.5 mile, and continue past the split-rail fence with the GRAVEYARD FIELDS UPPER FALLS sign. This is a place of plentiful side trails, so watch closely as you emerge into the open meadows on a worn path along more fence. Views reach up to the balds above, along the skyline of the Art Loeb Trail and Shining Rock Wilderness. All around, evergreens mingle with deciduous trees and blueberry bushes. Beyond a boardwalk, bear right. (A side trail left leads to a dead-end campsite by the stream where you could mistake fishing trails for the path upriver.) Soon meet the Graveyard Ridge Trail branching right at an unsigned junction. Stay left and cross a short boardwalk over a drainage that confirms your choice. Good campsites become visible as you arrive at the loop's final signed junction at the 1.0-mile mark. The return part of the loop heads left over the bridge.

The right-hand trail goes 0.7 mile to Upper Falls, a much less visited, more pre-cipitous cascade with impressive views down the valley. This section of trail, about 1.4 miles round-trip, is steeper and rockier than the rest of the route and would up the elevation gain of the hike to a not-insignificant 700 feet. From Upper Falls, retrace your steps downstream and take a right turn across Yellowstone Prong at about 2.7 miles.

The return route gradually ascends through boggy areas with a high-altitude feel. You'll cross bog logs and a sloping boardwalk on the way and in about 0.5 mile be back at the parking lot (this time climbing a short flight of wood steps to the left side of the overlook). The entire hike is slightly more than 3.0 miles and moderately strenuous. Without the side trip to Upper Falls, the loop is about 2.0 miles and rated moderately easy.

Key Points

0.5 Return to bridge after side trip to Second Falls.
1.0 Return leg of loop goes left; side trail to Upper Falls goes right.
2.0 Return to parking area for hike without Upper Falls.
3.0 Return to parking lot with side trail to Upper Falls.

COLD MOUNTAIN

Charles Frazier's 1999 National Book Award–winning best seller *Cold Mountain* sparked increasing national interest in the rich literature of the Appalachians. Robert Morgan's *Gap Creek* rose on the best-seller list soon after. A wealth of other writers offer a deeper sense of the culture and setting of these mountains. Indeed, you won't go wrong reading *Cold Mountain* before a visit to Shining Rock (or the entire southern part of the Parkway, for that matter). That goes double if you're hiking into Shining Rock Wilderness.

The book, which became a motion picture in 2003, tells the story of a wounded Civil War veteran who escapes from the hospital and heads for home. He walks the length of North Carolina, then the route of the Blue Ridge Parkway from Grandfather Mountain to a farm on the flank of this evocatively named summit. Indeed, if you stand on Shining Rock and look north to Cold Mountain, you can see a tiny farm perched on the right flank of the peak far below the summit. It doesn't take much to imagine that this view could have inspired Frazier's plans for his protagonist.

You'll see far fewer people on this western side of Shining Rock, but if Cold Mountain is your destination, its newfound notoriety as a literary landmark has no doubt increased visitation, even though it's a dead end—at least for everyone except author Charles Frazier.

43 Shining Rock Wilderness

Mileposts 411.8–423.2

Shining Rock—like the Craggy Mountains and Mount Mitchell just north of Asheville—is where the Parkway delivers some of the Southern Appalachians' most stunning scenery.

As you drive south out of Asheville and climb past Mount Pisgah, the Shining Rock Wilderness can't help but catch your attention. The horizon peels back on an almost Western scale, and meadow-covered mountaintops march off to meet summits cloaked in evergreens and accented by milk-white crags of quartz—the area's namesake "shining rocks."

Unlike the "natural" balds of the Craggy Mountains and Roan Mountain, the meadows of the Shining Rock area were created by periodic wildfires. Few places in the South offer better views than the grasslands of the Art Loeb Trail that border the Blue Ridge Parkway. The area north and beyond the balds, the 19,000-acre evergreen-forested tract now designated as the Shining Rock Wilderness, was not as impacted by fire. In the middle of the wilderness, Shining Rock Mountain (5,940 feet) thrusts its crystal-covered crest above the trees. A more distant and appropriately named peak, Cold Mountain, rises to 6,030 feet near the northern boundary of the wilderness area. This is the isolated summit made famous in Charles Frazier's National Book Award–winning best seller *Cold Mountain*.

The Shining Rock Wilderness is popular, but many hikers plan to visit during the week or gladly accept the presence of other people to savor the scenery on the balds of the Loeb Trail.

Backpackers, regardless of where they're headed, should try to avoid Shining Rock Gap. Just a glance at the trail map suggests why this is one of the most overused campsites in the wilderness. Regulations prohibit groups of more than ten persons, and all campfires are banned. Any backpacking plans for this area should include time to find a more secluded site farther into the wilderness or east or west of the ridge on the side trails that access the area. Take this suggestion as an opportunity to have a true wilderness experience. Find what looks like flatter ground on the Forest Service trail map and go check it out!

Aside from the scenery, part of Shining Rock's appeal is the number of circuit hikes available from surrounding valleys. Luckily these access points are very easy to reach from the Parkway. This entry offers an overview of the trail network and then recommends a variety of multitrail loops from the south, east, and west. (Please check the map as you read this description.)

Basically the Shining Rock Trail network centers on the ridgetop Art Loeb Trail, which runs from the Parkway north across various balds and Shining Rock Mountain before turning left off the ridge just before another trail leads to Cold Mountain. This ridgetop route can be divided into roughly three sections.

The most southerly section crosses the balds of Black Balsam Knob and Tennent Mountain to Ivestor Gap. This part of the trail is flanked on both sides by gradual routes—the Ivestor Gap Trail on the west and, on the east, the Graveyard Ridge Trail and a Mountains-to-Sea Trail section. Together the side trails form a big loop around the Loeb Trail. You'll notice, though, that this southernmost section of the Ivestor Gap Trail isn't included in the recommended hikes—it is very popular with hikers and horseback riders and open to vehicles to Ivestor Gap (the wilderness boundary) during the fall hunting season.

The middle section of the Loeb Trail, from Ivestor Gap to Shining Rock Gap, is also flanked on the west by part of the Ivestor Gap Trail; this section is less crowded. Beyond Shining Rock Gap, the northernmost part of the Loeb Trail wanders alone to the valley, while the Cold Mountain Trail continues out the ridge to its summit dead end.

The drawback of the trail system is that everybody ends up on the crest. The beauty of the layout is that the Loeb Trail and its flanking paths form wonderful summit circuits reachable by no fewer than seven access trails from nearby valleys. You'd need a calculator to count the possibilities—a situation unmatched by other Parkway-adjacent wilderness parcels, such as Virginia's James River Face.

Option 1: Shining Rock Wilderness Circuits from the East Side

A variety of streamside hikes start on the east side and rise to the crest of Shining Rock Wilderness.

Parkway mile: 411.8
Distance: Major circuits ranging from 8.4 to 12.9 miles
Difficulty: Strenuous

Elevation gain: About 3,000 feet for all
Maps: USGS *Shining Rock*. Pisgah National Forest's Shining Rock–Middle Prong Wilderness map covers the area best.

Finding the trailhead: Trailheads for the Old Butt Knob, Shining Creek, and Greasy Cove–Big East Fork Trails are all located at the Big East Fork Parking Area on US 276, on the left just under 3 miles north of the Parkway.

The Hikes

A trio of trails ascends the east side of the wilderness, and they all start at virtually the same trailhead. The more northerly two, the Old Butt Knob Trail (3.6 miles) and the Shining Creek Trail (4.1 miles), terminate in Shining Rock Gap to form the shortest circuit to the heights (8.4 miles). This hike crosses Shining Rock.

The most southerly trail, a combination of the Big East Fork Trail (3.6 miles) and Greasy Cove Trail (3.0 miles), makes a 6.8-mile climb to the ridge at Ivestor Gap (which includes a 0.2-mile stretch on the Graveyard Ridge Trail). Heading north from there 1.8 miles on the ridgetop Art Loeb Trail to Shining Rock Gap creates much larger loops—12.7 miles with a descent of the Shining Creek Trail and 12.9 miles going down

White quartz caps the evergreen-fringed peak of Shining Rock Mountain.

the Old Butt Knob Trail. The level Ivestor Gap Trail also links these access trails. The winding route it takes to slab west of the Art Loeb Trail adds 0.3 mile to each hike.

To take the shortest circuit, leave the parking area on the Shining Creek Trail as it climbs away from the East Fork of the Pigeon River. At 0.7 mile keep left in Shining Creek Gap where the Old Butt Knob Trail, your return route, goes right. The trail drops out of the gap to join Shining Creek above its confluence with the Pigeon. From here most of the way up, the trail is within sight of the tumbling stream. You'll cross Daniel's Cove Creek at 2.0 miles and a stream rising right at 3.0 miles. High above, this branch starts as a trailside spring you might be stopping at when you pass through Beech Spring Gap on the Old Butt Knob Trail. The trail starts its steepest climb up out of the drainage and switchbacks across the headwaters of the North Prong of Shining Creek to Shining Rock Gap at 4.1 miles.

The gap is a popular campsite, and with tents and tall summer grasses, the Old Butt Trail can be a challenge to find (not an issue if you climb it; see below). Turn right at Shining Rock Gap to the Old Butt Knob Trail and reach Shining Rock Mountain's crystal cap in 0.2 mile. Descend beyond to Beech Spring Gap at 4.7 miles (that spring is on the right). This next section of ridge—across Dog Loser Knob at 4.9 miles, to Spanish Oak Gap at 5.5 miles, back up to Old Butt Knob at 5.7, and even beyond, to the 6.0-mile mark where the trail plummets—has gradual sections. Notice on the way down the

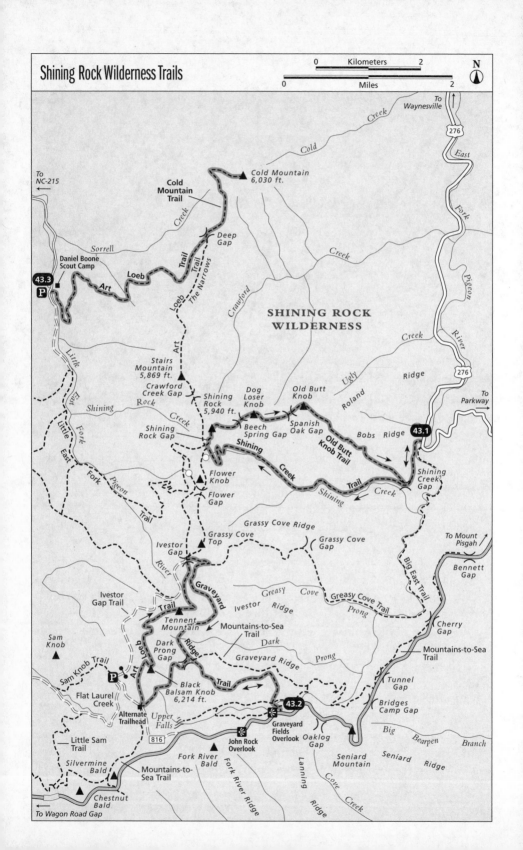

Shining Rock Wilderness Trails

SHINING ROCK WILDERNESS

Kilometers 0 — 2
Miles 0 — 2

N

To Waynesville

276

East Fork

To NC-215

Cold Mountain
6,030 ft.

Cold Mountain Trail

Cold Creek

Cold Creek

Crawford Creek

Pigeon River

276

To Parkway

Sorrell Creek

Daniel Boone Scout Camp

43.3 P

Art Loeb Trail

Deep Gap

Loeb Trail

The Narrows

Stairs Mountain
5,869 ft.

Crawford Creek Gap

Shining Rock Creek

Little East Fork

Shining Rock Gap

Shining Rock
5,940 ft.

Dog Loser Knob

Old Butt Knob

Beech Spring Gap

Spanish Oak Gap

Old Butt Knob Trail

Bobs Ridge

Ugly Roland

43.1

Little East Fork Pigeon River

Flower Knob

Flower Gap

Shining Creek

Shining Creek Trail

Shining Creek

Shining Creek Gap

Grassy Cove Ridge

Ivestor Gap

Grassy Cove Top

Grassy Cove Gap

To Mount Pisgah

Big East Trail

Bennett Gap

Ivestor Gap Trail

Graveyard Trail

Greasy Cove

Ivestor Ridge

Greasy Cove Trail

Greasy Cove Prong

Sam Knob

Tennent Mountain

Mountains-to-Sea Trail

Dark Prong

Cherry Gap

Mountains-to-Sea Trail

Sam Knob Trail

P

Art Loeb Trail

Dark Prong Gap

Graveyard Ridge

Tunnel Gap

Flat Laurel Creek

Black Balsam Knob
6,214 ft.

Ridge Trail

43.2

Bridges Camp Gap

Alternate Trailhead

Upper Falls

816

John Rock Overlook

Graveyard Fields Overlook

Oaklog Gap

Seniard Mountain

Big Bearpen Branch

Little Sam Trail

Silvermine Bald

Mountains-to-Sea Trail

Fork River Bald

Fork River Ridge

Lanning Ridge

Cove Creek

Seniard Ridge

Chestnut Bald

To Wagon Road Gap

steepest section—aptly named Chestnut Ridge—how the young American chestnuts still struggle up to respectable height before falling victim to chestnut blight. There are plentiful campsites for the finding and fine views from outcrops on both sides of the trail. The trail then drops very steeply for 1.5 miles to the Shining Creek junction at 7.7 miles. Take a left to the trailhead for an 8.4-mile circuit.

If your muscles are better on the uphill than your knees or ankles are on the way down—the case with many baby-boomers—you could do this trip in reverse. (The Old Butt Knob Trail is the least used on this side of the wilderness, but it's a punishing climb.)

Going down Shining Creek Trail is a nice way to form the largest loop from this side. That requires a start on the Big East Fork–Greasy Cove Trail combo to the south. Start from the next pull-off above the Big East Fork trailhead parking and heading right. This old railroad grade continues for miles up the drainage amid lush streamside scenery and plentiful campsites. Cross Bennett Branch at 1.3 miles; at 3.6 miles the old railroad grade goes left up the river.

Cross and continue up Greasy Cove Trail for the steepest part of the climb. The trail veers away from the stream at 4.5 miles and climbs steeply until 5.3 miles, when the grade slackens substantially at the crest of Grassy Cove Ridge. The trail is only steep in spots from here much of the way to the Graveyard Ridge Trail at 6.6 miles; there are possible campsites where the ridge is broadest.

Go right on the Graveyard Ridge Trail; at 6.8 miles turn right in Ivestor Gap onto the Art Loeb Trail. The path switchbacks past the peak of Grassy Cove Top, dips across a gentle gap, and heads over the next rise to a sharp drop into Flower Gap at 8.0 miles. The path joins an old railroad grade there and slabs east of Flower Knob past a spring on the right at 8.4 miles. Shining Rock Gap is at 8.6 miles.

The descent of the Shining Creek Trail makes a 12.7-mile route (the first streamlet you encounter on the way down is from the Loeb Trail spring you just passed); a descent of the Old Butt Knob Trail is 12.9 miles.

Key Points on the Shortest Circuit

0.7 Keep left in Shining Creek Gap where Old Butt Knob Trail goes right.
4.1 Shining Rock Gap.
4.3 Shining Rock summit.
4.7 Beech Spring Gap.
5.7 Old Butt Knob.
7.7 Left on Shining Rock Creek Trail.

Option 2: Bald Summit Circuits on the Art Loeb Trail from the South Side

The Shining Rock area's most southerly summits are among the most spectacular balds in the South. The recommended circuits avoid the popular high-elevation trailheads and can be extended to include the namesake Shining Rock in the heart of the wilderness area.

See map on page 278.
Parkway mile: 418.8
Distance: Day or overnight circuit hikes across the area's southerly bald summits of 5.2 and 8.8 miles; longer circuits that include Shining Rock of 9.1 or 12.7 miles; a recommended

out-and-back hike of 0.8 mile
Difficulty: Moderate to strenuous
Elevation gain: 1,674 feet
Maps: USGS *Shining Rock.* Pisgah National Forest's Shining Rock–Middle Prong Wilderness map covers the area best.

Finding the trailhead: Park at Graveyard Fields Overlook. To reach the parking on FSR 816 below Black Balsam Knob, turn right at Parkway Milepost 420.2. The trailhead is 0.8 mile on the right. The Black Balsam Parking Area for Ivestor Gap Trail is another 0.5 mile beyond. The Ivestor Gap trailhead is the Shining Rock area's busiest, and that section of the trail isn't recommended, but modern privies are available at the parking area.

The Hikes

Descend from the right side of Graveyard Fields Overlook on the steep paved path and cross Yellowstone Prong on a boardwalk bridge. Turn left and continue past the split-rail fence with the GRAVEYARD FIELDS UPPER FALLS sign. This is a place of plentiful side trails, so watch closely as you emerge into the open meadows on a worn path along more fence. Beyond a boardwalk, bear right. (A side trail left leads to a dead-end campsite by the stream where you could mistake fishing trails for the path upriver.) At about 0.3 mile take a right onto the Graveyard Ridge Trail. Follow this gradual logging railroad grade to a crossing of the Mountains-to-Sea Trail in a gap between Black Balsam Knob to the left and an unnamed peak. This is Dark Prong Gap, informally named by Forest Service personnel and trail volunteers who built the route that crosses the Graveyard Ridge Trail here. This first 1.8-mile section of the hike is rich with campsites.

Turn left onto the Mountains-to-Sea Trail as it swings north out of the gap at about 5,400 feet, rises abruptly to the 5,600-foot level, then climbs gradually past the upper edge of a large flat visible just above the 5,600-foot contour line on the Forest Service wilderness map. There are good campsites in this area and the remains of an old railroad camp used during logging days. From there the trail crosses a bridge over the headwaters of Yellowstone Prong and follows an old railroad grade into evergreens and grasses to a junction a few feet from FSR 816 and a parking spot for the Art Loeb Trail (about 1.0 mile from the last junction, just under 3.0 miles from the start).

Take an immediate right onto the Loeb Trail and quickly ascend in 0.4 mile (3.2 miles from your starting point) to the open vistas and waving grasses of Black Balsam Knob (6,214 feet). This view is among the best along the Parkway. North, the Mount Mitchell range bulks beyond Asheville, with the High Country resort area and Grandfather Mountain beyond that. The Smokies rise dramatically to the west. This is a 360-degree panorama worthy of bringing your binoculars and a camera.

Retracing your steps from here creates an out-and-back hike of about 6.5 miles from the Parkway trailhead. If you don't have much time, this can be a quick 0.8-mile hike from the parking area you just passed on FSR 816.

Follow the Art Loeb Trail north along the open ridgetop into a shrubby gap at about 5,880 feet and then back up to eye-popping views atop Tennent Mountain (6,046 feet), about 1.2 miles from Black Balsam Knob (4.4 miles from the Parkway). The descent from Tennent Mountain brings you in 0.7 mile to the Ivestor Gap Trail and a right turn onto the Graveyard Ridge Trail at 5.1 miles. Continue out of the gap; the Greasy Cove–Big East Fork Trail combination heads left to US 276 at 5.3 miles. Continue right; after crossing the Mountains-to-Sea Trail, you'll reach the Graveyard Fields Loop at 8.5 miles. Go left then right back to the trailhead at about 8.8 miles.

Keeping in mind that much of this hike is pretty gradual, backpackers or well-conditioned walkers could extend the above circuit to include the ridgetop stretch of the Loeb Trail that continues north to Shining Rock Gap. From Ivestor Gap, that section of the Loeb Trail forms another loop with the nearly level Ivestor Gap Trail. The combination creates a big figure eight that adds another 3.9 miles to the hike, for a 12.7-mile walk from the Graveyard Fields Overlook.

If you have less time, start at the recommended spot on FSR 816. From the parking area the first loop of the above circuit is about 5.2 miles (instead of 8.8 miles from the Parkway). Extend that to include Shining Rock Gap and the hike is 9.1 miles (instead of 12.7). Either of these hikes will be 0.4 mile farther if you go to Shining Rock itself—a 0.2-mile hike each way out of Shining Rock Gap on the Old Butt Knob Trail.

Key Points on the Art Loeb Circuit

0.3 Turn right from Graveyard Fields Loop onto Graveyard Ridge Trail.

1.8 Turn left onto Mountains-to-Sea Trail.

2.8 Turn right from FSR 816 onto Art Loeb Trail.

3.2 Black Balsam Knob.

4.4 Tennent Mountain.

5.1 Turn right in Ivestor Gap onto Graveyard Ridge Trail.

8.5 Rejoin Graveyard Fields Loop.

Option 3: West Side Circuit and Cold Mountain

This hike includes a less-frequented circuit and an out-and-back option to Cold Mountain—the most isolated, least-visited part of the Shining Rock Wilderness.

See map on page 278.
Parkway mile: 423.2
Distance: 10.6 miles out and back to Cold Mountain
Difficulty: Strenuous

Elevation gain: About 2,790 feet to Cold Mountain from the trailhead
Maps: USGS *Shining Rock*. Pisgah National Forest's Shining Rock–Middle Prong Wilderness map covers the area best.

Finding the trailhead: The Daniel Boone Scout Camp trailhead for the Art Loeb and Little East Fork Trails is reached via NC 215. Leave the Parkway at Milepost 423.2 and go north 13 miles. Turn right onto Little East Fork Road (NC 1129) and drive 3.8 miles to parking at the Scout camp.

The Art Loeb Trail goes to the left from the parking area just after the Boy Scout camp's main lodge. To start the Little East Fork Trail, cross the bridge and walk on the road as it becomes the trail along an old railroad grade.

The Hikes

There's really only one circuit from the west side of Shining Rock—a 12.0-mile combination of the Little East Fork and Art Loeb Trails that starts at the same trailhead. One of the area's best out-and-back hikes also starts there—the 10.6-mile hike to Cold Mountain. This is the least-popular side of the wilderness.

The choice of which direction to hike this circuit will be arbitrary for most, as both trails gain the ridge at similar grades. Backpackers will surely decide based on where they want to camp. Starting on the Art Loeb Trail is the fastest route to the least-populated part of the wilderness—the Cold Mountain hike. It also approaches the highest terrain by climbing up the leading ridge. Taking the Little East Fork Trail descends that ridge and gets you to Shining Rock Gap sooner.

Leaving the roadside, the Art Loeb Trail switchbacks north to round a ridgeline at 1.1 miles. At 2.0 miles the trail crosses tumbling Sorrell Creek at the first good campsites. The trail continues to rise across the richly forested flank of the Shining Rock Ledge, weaving in and out of green drainages (the deepest of which is at 3.1 miles). Deep Gap's grassy expanse arrives at 3.8 miles.

Those intent on solitude should consider Cold Mountain. From the Art Loeb Trail at Deep Gap, take a left. The area's least-visited peak is just 1.5 miles north for a 5.3-mile hike from the valley. For backpackers, that plan puts Shining Rock within striking distance for day hikes.

To continue the circuit, go right from this breezy gap across a rocky, knife-edge ridge called The Narrows. The ridge broadens then narrows again to Stairs Mountain (5,869 feet) at 5.9 miles. The trail enters an old railroad grade at 6.1 miles in Crawford Creek Gap and reaches Shining Rock Gap at 6.7 miles. Turn right here onto the old railroad grade of the Ivestor Gap Trail. The Little East Fork Trail turns off right 0.4 mile ahead, at 7.1 miles. This old railroad grade switchbacks just below the Ivestor Gap Trail as it leaves the spruces and birches of the crest. It crosses the Little East Fork of the Pigeon River at 9.3 miles and follows the stream to emerge at the Scout Camp at 12.1 miles.

There is one other trail of interest on the west side of Shining Rock. The little-used Fork Mountain Trail also climbs to the crest, but its trailhead is miles from the Boy Scout camp starting point of the other two paths. Without two cars, an exciting option for the adventurous would be to go up the Little East Fork Trail from Daniel Boone Camp and descend the Fork Mountain Trail. On the way down, a right turn almost anywhere would create a bushwhack route back to the Little East Fork Trail and your car.

Key Points to Cold Mountain

2.0 Sorrell Creek campsites.

3.8 Deep Gap.

5.3 Cold Mountain summit.

44 Devil's Courthouse Trail

Milepost 422.4

A short, steep climb leads to a spectacular viewpoint with devices for sighting distant peaks. This is a popular peregrine falcon viewing area.

Parkway mile: 422.4
Distance: 1.0 mile out and back
Difficulty: Strenuous

Elevation gain: 258 feet
Maps: USGS *Sams Knob*

Finding the trailhead: Park at Devil's Courthouse Overlook.

The Hike

Before you hit the trail, look across the drop-off east of the parking area and up to the crag of Devil's Courthouse at 5,720 feet. Chances are you can see a few tiny hikers enjoying the view.

Though steep, this largely paved path is rewarding. The rock wall–encircled overlook atop the Courthouse offers great views. East is the plummet down into the Carolina Piedmont. West is the crest of the Shining Rock Wilderness, one of the loftiest, most alpine-appearing areas to abut the Parkway. Close in, you're likely to see the high-speed "stoops," or dives, of peregrine falcons.

Leave the parking lot and wander along the side of the Parkway toward the 665-foot-long Devil's Courthouse Tunnel. Enter the woods and breathe in the rich smells of a high-elevation Canadian-zone forest of spruce, fir, and birch. The paved trail climbs steeply, with ribbed water breaks to divert the deluges. The pavement ends where a spur to the Mountains-to-Sea Trail veers left to cross the top of the tunnel on its way in 0.1 mile to the Sam Knob area. (See the map and below for more.)

The unpaved trail wanders to the right, ascending stone steps to a wall-enclosed viewing area that was refurbished and expanded in 2000. Rock gnome lichen grows on the crag; nearby you'll see Gray's lily and spreading avens.

The name Devil's Courthouse reflects the many folk tales about the peak. Some say there's a cave in the mountain where the devil holds court. Cherokee legend calls it a dancing chamber and dwelling of a slant-eyed giant named Judaculla. If you're ever on the peak when a thunderstorm rumbles nearby, you may understand the origin of such folklore.

Peregrines have been known to nest just under the overlook. The birds were reintroduced in the nearby Sam Knob area in the late 1980s using the process of "hacking." The chicks were placed in a cage, surreptitiously fed, and released when ready to fly. The birds have since returned to many places in the Southern Appalachians.

Look west to see the area where the peregrines were reintroduced, and use the sighting device to locate the rocky summit of Sam Knob, 2.0 miles away.

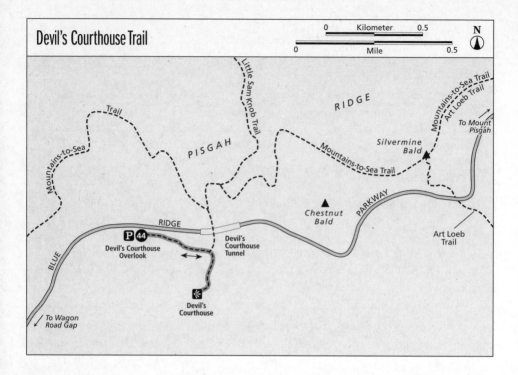

Devil's Courthouse Trail

Another option is to take the Mountain-to-Sea Trail over the tunnel; there are great views not far away. Take the spur across the tunnel to the MST and turn right (0.2 mile from the overlook). The Little Sam Knob Trail goes left at 0.4 mile, and there's a rocky crag at 0.5 mile that offers a vista of the alpinelike area that lies just south of Shining Rock Wilderness. The round-trip to the crag is 1.0 mile, for a 2.0-mile total hike including Devil's Courthouse.

Key Points

0.2 Mountains-to-Sea Trail spur goes left.

0.5 Summit viewpoint.

45 Richland Balsam Self-Guiding Trail

Milepost 431.0

Numbered posts keyed to an interpretive brochure describe the changing composition of a lofty spruce-fir forest at 6,410 feet—the highest elevation reached by a Parkway trail.

Parkway mile: 431
Distance: 1.4-mile loop
Difficulty: Moderate

Elevation gain: 390 feet
Maps*: USGS Sam Knob;* no Parkway map available

Finding the trailhead: The trail starts at the Haywood-Jackson Overlook (named for the boundary of the two counties), 9.2 miles south of NC 215.

The Hike

Here's an oddity—a kind of rough, rooty trail a lot like the backcountry tracks that wind everywhere in western North Carolina's national forests. The Richland Balsam Trail is the perfect counterpoint to the Parkway's generally groomed paths. It's a reminder that nature's "beauty" can be untidy and unkempt—and more real in its roughness. It's also the Parkway's best path to experience the aromatic lushness of the dripping, cloud-dampened spruce-fir forest.

The recently landscaped sign at Richland Balsam provides a perfect parking pedestal for Parkway souvenir photos.

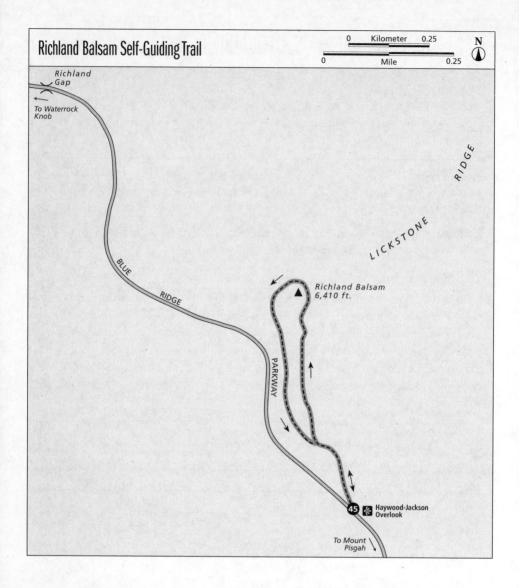

Richland
Gap

To Waterrock
Knob

BLUE

RIDGE

PARKWAY

LICKSTONE

RIDGE

Richland Balsam
6,410 ft.

45 Haywood-Jackson
Overlook

To Mount
Pisgah

0   Kilometer   0.25

0   Mile   0.25

N

Before you start your hike, enjoy the fine view of the Shining Rock Wilderness on the overlook's skyline. Prominent peaks run from Cold Mountain on the left, to the gentle pyramid of Mount Pisgah, the white-quartz summit of Shining Rock, and on to Devil's Courthouse on the far right.

Just up the paved first 100 yards of the trail is a brochure box with laminated trail brochures to borrow for your hike. The theme here, as it is at Mount Mitchell State Park's Balsam Nature Trail, is a Fraser fir forest in decline. The brochure's twenty-plus interpretive stops explore the topic.

Go right after the pavement ends at the first two of many benches, these in a tiny clearing where the loop splits. The trail passes an odd mileage sign (3,100 feet to the summit) then winds around through dense summer growths of sedge grasses and briers.

The trail passes rich Canadian-zone vegetation and a sign reading 1,600 FEET TO SUMMIT. It rises over a series of small peaks to a bench at 0.6 mile where the summit sign reads 6,410 feet. The path drops off the back of the peak, descending flights of stone steps amid evergreens and grasses.

The evergreen needle–carpeted trail levels off and glides through a very scenic fir forest full of ferns. A faint side trail goes right to the top of the road-cut with views of the Richland Balsam Overlook, the next view south on the Parkway (highest point on the motor road). You'll pass another few benches at about 1.2 miles, the second with the trail's best view—a look along the Parkway to the next overlook heading north, the Cowee Mountain Overlook. The trail passes through more spruce forest and ferns to the loop junction and a right back to the parking area at about 1.4 miles.

Even on a warm, dry day, the summit shade is cool, which explains the seemingly drunken bumblebees fighting to do their summer duty amid the gusty chill. It's that evergreen forest feeling that recommends this trail. If that feeling and not the summit is your goal, just go left when the loop starts for a short, easy, and atmospheric out-and-back walk to the last few benches. (Oh … don't forget to return your brochure to the box.)

Key Points

0.15 Loop branches; go right.

0.6 Summit bench.

1.2 Bench with good view.

1.3 Loop returns.

1.4 Return to parking lot.

The damp evergreen zone of high Parkway peaks such as Richland Balsam is home to more species of salamanders than any other place on the planet. PHOTO BY HUGH MORTON

46 Waterrock Knob Trail

Milepost 451.2

This steep-paved path climbs from one of the Parkway's small visitor centers to a designated must-see viewpoint. A rougher path continues on to the wilder summit of Waterrock Knob (6,292 feet).

Parkway mile: 451.2
Distance: 1.2 miles out and back
Difficulty: Moderate to strenuous

Elevation gain: 472 feet
Maps: *USGS Sylva North;* no Parkway map available

Finding the trailhead: Park in the Waterrock Knob Visitor Center parking lot and ascend the paved path.

The Hike

Waterrock Knob is one of the key viewpoints that recommend the high-altitude southernmost section of the Blue Ridge Parkway. Luckily there are two sides to this steep and strenuous trail that make it a suitable walk for less-than-serious hikers.

The trail soars out of the parking area as a steep and paved path. Take your time; a bench appears just where the grade slackens to nearly level. Not far beyond on the left, notice the huge fan-shaped root system of a wind-downed spruce. The solid rock barely below the soil surface explains the shape of the root system and illustrates the challenge faced by these high-altitude evergreens.

The trail ascends past another bench before switchbacking up two flights of stone steps to a rock wall–encircled observation point. The mountains ripple away; below, the Parkway arcs across a mountainside. This is the place to head back if you're tired or unsure of foot.

Above the viewpoint, the trail rises over steps, becomes rocky then gravel covered, and levels out as it leaves the evergreens and enters an open meadow of filamentous ferns where northern

The view of the Parkway from Waterrock Knob's observation platform is expansive.

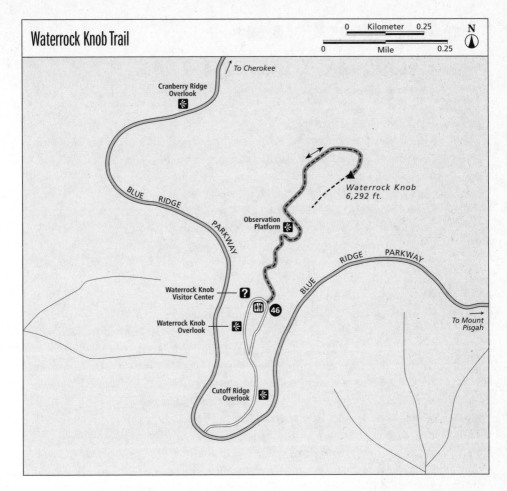

Waterrock Knob Trail

0   Kilometer   0.25

0   Mile   0.25

N

To Cherokee

Cranberry Ridge
Overlook

BLUE   RIDGE

PARKWAY

Waterrock Knob
6,292 ft.

Observation
Platform

RIDGE   PARKWAY

Waterrock Knob
Visitor Center

BLUE

46

To Mount
Pisgah

Waterrock Knob
Overlook

Cutoff Ridge
Overlook

white hellebore still grows in July. There's a bench in this clearing. Farther on, the trail gets rougher, eroded in some spots, and ascends steeply, at times over crags and up one flight of steep stone steps. The trail winds around the back of the peak on switchbacks with stone steps to a nice view into Maggie Valley. The trail climbs again and, after a last flight of steps, reaches an evergreen-bordered bench on the largely open top of Waterrock Knob at 6,292 feet.

More than 80 percent of mature firs on this part of the Parkway have died from the balsam woolly adelgid, and the destruction is evident here and in many places on the way up. If you walk the informal path over the crest, you can descend through the lush meadow greenery (annual rainfall exceeds 60 inches on the summit) and actually peer down on the parking lot.

Key Points

0.2   Developed viewpoint.

0.6   Summit bench.

Blue Ridge Parkway Mileage Log

This mileage log is your guide to the Parkway, its trails and facilities, and the resources just off the road. Consult it frequently on your trip, especially for access points to the Appalachian and Mountains-to-Sea Trails. The mileage points highlighted in **boldface** refer you to all hikes near the Parkway.

0.0   Rockfish Gap • Elevation: 1,909 ft. (582m) • Signboard: history of Rockfish Gap • Facilities: Tourist Information Center (9:00 a.m. to 5:00 p.m. daily).

0.0   US 250/I-64 underpass • Access to US 250 and I-64 West; 4 miles to Waynesboro, VA (west); 16 miles to Charlottesville, VA (east).

0.2   Afton Overlook, east • Elevation: 2,054 ft. (626m).

1.5   Rockfish Valley Overlook, east • Elevation: 2,148 ft. (655m).

2.2   VA 610 access, west • Trail: Appalachian Trail crossing.

2.9   Shenandoah Valley Overlook, west • Elevation: 2,354 ft. (718m) • Wayside panel: Virginia's profile.

4.4   VA 609 crossing • Access VA 610, west.

5.8   Humpback Rocks Visitor Center and Pioneer Farm Exhibit, west (Hike 1, Option 1) • Elevation: 2,353 ft. (717m) • Facilities: restrooms, water, self-guiding trail • Trail: **Mountain Farm Self-Guiding Trail,** 0.5 mile (Easy).

6.0   Humpback Gap Parking Area, east (Hike 1, Option 2) • Elevation: 2,360 ft. (719m) • Cars: 20 • Facilities: picnic table • Wayside panel: pioneer methods of clearing fields • Trail: Appalachian Trail access.

8.5   Humpback Rocks Picnic Area, east (Hike 1, Option 2) • Facilities: 91 sites, water, restrooms • Trails: **Catoctin Trail.** This short path reaches a lofty perch over the Shenandoah Valley. Go to the end of the Humpback Rocks Picnic Area and take the trail to the right. (The path to the left reaches the Appalachian Trail.) Appalachian Trail access.

8.8   Greenstone Overlook, west (Hike 2) • Elevation: 3,007 ft. (916m) • Cars: 8 • Signboard: old stone fences • Trail: Greenstone Self-Guiding Trail, 0.2 mile (Easy).

9.2   Laurel Springs Gap, east • Trail: 300 yards to Appalachian Trail on east.

9.6   Dripping Rocks Parking, east • Trail: Appalachian Trail access.

10.4   Rock Point Overlook, west • Elevation: 3,113 ft. (949m) • Cars: 5 • Lift-top easel: Catoctin greenstone (geologic formation).

10.7   Raven's Roost Overlook, west • Elevation: 3,200 ft. (975m) • Facilities: picnic table • Interpretive device: orientation • Recreation: hang gliding, rock climbing.

11.7   Hickory Spring Parking, east • Facilities: picnic table • Hunter access west during hunting season only.

13.1   Three Ridges Overlook, east • Elevation: 2,697 ft. (822m) • Facilities: picnic table • Trail: Appalachian Trail access.

Roadside azaleas bloom in May on the northern part of the Parkway.

13.7   Reeds Gap • Elevation: 2,637 ft. (804m) • Trail: Appalachian Trail access.

13.7   VA 664 crossing (Hikes 3 and 4; Hike 5, Option 2) • West to VA 814; east to US 29.

15.4   Love Gap • Elevation: 2,597 ft. (792m) • Trails: Appalachian Trail access—fire road to Maupin Field Shelter on Three Ridges Wilderness circuit.

16.0   VA 814 staggered crossing • Right to Love Maintenance Area; left to Massies Mill, VA.

16.0   Love Maintenance Area • Elevation: 1,700 ft. (518m).

17.6   The Priest Overlook, east • Elevation: 2,695 ft. (821m) • Cars: 10 • Wayside panel: hickory trees • Facilities: picnic table • Trail: The Priest Trail, 0.2 mile (Easy). This easy walk terminates 100 yards from the parking area at a roadside hilltop and a bench. You can wander into the woods on an informal path that dips around and below the overlook.

The prominent summit and leading ridges of The Priest, 4,026 feet, rise in the distance. Other peaks of the adjacent Religious Range include The Cardinal and The Friar. The Appalachian Trail crosses The Priest's summit and makes a nice hike from the area of **Crabtree Falls (Hike 7).**

Note the Parkway interpretive easel about hickory trees at this overlook. You will see many hickories on your hikes—mockernut, pignut, bitternut, and shagbark. Just a minute with this exhibit and you'll be able to recognize the long, gray bark strands of the shagbark—at 100 feet, one of the tallest hickories. Fifteen of the twenty known species of hickory are found in the United States.

18.5 **White Rock Gap (Hike 5)** • Elevation: 2,549 ft. (777m) • Trails: White Rock Gap Trail to Slacks Trail circuit and USDA Forest Service (USFS) Sherando Lake, west; White Rock Falls Trail, east (Moderate).

19.0 20 Minute Cliff Overlook, east • Elevation: 2,715 ft. (827m) • Signboard: story of 20 Minute Cliff • Facilities: picnic table.

19.9 **The Slacks Overlook, west (Hike 5)** • Elevation: 2,800 ft. (853m) • Trails: White Rock Falls Trail, east, to falls, 1.3 miles (Moderate) and on to Slacks circuit • Slacks Trail circuit access, west, past picnic table.

22.1 **Bald Mountain Parking Area, west (Hike 6)** • Elevation: 3,250 ft. (991m) • Facilities: picnic table.

22.1 USFS road access, west (gated).

23.0 **Fork Mountain Overlook, east (Hike 6)** • Elevation: 3,294 ft. (1,004m).

24.3 Federal Aviation Administration (FAA) road access (to radar site), east.

25.6 Spy Run Gap • Elevation: 3,033 ft. (924m).

25.6 VA 686 access, east.

26.4 **Big Spy Overlook, west** • Elevation: 3,185 ft. (971m) • Trail: **Big Spy Mountain Overlook Trail**, 0.1 mile (Easy). Many of the Parkway's best views are from roadside meadows. This grassy trail reaches a wonderfully breezy hilltop with a bench and views west to the Shenandoah Valley across the ridgetops of the Saint Mary's Wilderness Area (Hike 6). The prominent more-pointed peak with the boulder-covered scree slopes is Big Spy—so named because it served as a lookout for troop movements in the Shenandoah Valley during the Civil War. To the east, the grassy, high fields of adjacent farms lend a pastoral feel to the scene.

27.2 Tye River Gap • Elevation: 2,969 ft. (905m).

27.2 **VA 56 crossing, underpass (access east, north of crossing) (Hike 7)** • Right to Vesuvius, 4 miles; Steele's Tavern, VA, 6.5 miles; left to Montebello, VA, 0.75 mile • Trails: access left to Crabtree Falls Trail, AT trailhead for Three Ridges Wilderness circuit • AT hikes to The Priest and Spy Rock.

29.0 Whetstone Ridge • Elevation: 2,990 ft. (911m) • Facilities: restrooms and picnic tables, west.

29.0 VA 603 access, east.

29.5 VA 603 crossing, underpass (no access).

31.4 Stillhouse Hollow parking, east • Elevation: 3,000 ft. (914m) • Facilities: picnic table.

31.9 VA 886 crossing.

33.0 Fence exhibit, west.

34.4 **Yankee Horse Ridge Parking Area, east (Hike 8)** • Elevation: 3,140 ft. (957m) • Facilities: picnic table • Trails: **Yankee Horse Trail,** 0.2 mile (Easy); Appalachian Trail access. • Signboard: old logging railroad • Exhibit: 200 feet of railroad track, trestle • View: Wigwam Falls.

34.8   Yankee Horse Ridge.

37.4   Irish Gap • Elevation: 2,200 ft. (671m).

37.5   US 60 access, east.

37.5   VA 605 crossing, underpass (access east, north of crossing) • Right to Irish Creek and Buena Vista, VA; left to US 60 and Amherst, VA (maintained dirt road).

38.8   **Boston Knob Parking Area, west** • Elevation: 2,508 ft. (764m) • Trail: **Boston Knob Trail,** 0.1 mile (Easy; 5-minute leg-stretcher). Leave the overlook to the right; the trail rises on a grassy tread and circles left around a small tree-topped hummock. It's an often-breezy wander, with limited views down into a grove of white pines before the trail dips back to the center of the overlook.

40.0   Clarks Gap • Elevation: 2,177 ft. (663m).

40.1   USFS road access, east.

40.9   USFS road access, east (gated).

42.2   Irish Creek Valley Parking, west • Elevation: 2,665 ft. (812m).

44.2   USFS road crossing • (Old Jordan Road).

44.4   Whites Gap Overlook, east • Elevation: 2,567 ft. (782m) • Facilities: picnic table.

44.9   Chimney Rock parking, west • Elevation: 2,485 ft. (757m).

45.6   Humphries Gap, east • Elevation: 2,312 ft. (705m).

45.6   US 60 crossing, underpass (access east, north of crossing) • Right to Buena Vista, VA, 4 miles; Lexington, VA, 11 miles; left to Amherst, VA, 22 miles.

45.7   Buena Vista Overlook, west.

47.5   **Indian Gap Parking Area, east (Hike 9)** • Elevation: 2,098 ft. (639m) • Trail: **Indian Gap Trail,** 0.3 mile (Easy; 10-minute trail to Indian Rocks).

48.9   Licklog Spring Gap • Elevation: 2,481 ft. (756m).

49.3   House Mountain Overlook, west • Elevation: 2,498 ft. (761m).

50.5   Robinson Gap • Elevation: 2,412 ft. (735m).

51.1   USFS road access, west (gated) • To Bluff Mountain/Punch Bowl area.

51.5   Appalachian Trail crossing and parking area.

52.8   Bluff Mountain Overlook, east • Elevation: 1,850 ft. (564m) • Signboard: George Washington National Forest's multiple resources.

53.1   Bluff Mountain Tunnel • Length: 630 feet • Max height: 19 feet, 1 inch • Min height: 13 feet, 7 inches.

53.6   Rice Mountain Overlook, east • Elevation: 1,755 ft. (535m).

53.8   USFS road access, east (gated).

55.1   **White Oak Flats Overlook, west** • Elevation: 1,460 ft. (445m) • Facilities: picnic table • Trail: **White Oak Flats Trail,** 0.1 mile (Easy). From White Oak Flats, at 1,460 feet, south to the James River, at 650 feet, the Parkway descends for nearly 9 miles through a rich streamside environment of beautiful evergreen and deciduous forests. There are streamside "flats" all along the way. White Oak Flats is the loftiest, and it leans to its namesake white oak trees, with a scrubby understory of mountain laurel and young white pines. A formal trail is difficult to discern. You can wander past the picnic table to the right and reach the stream. Or go left at the table and stroll the greater distance to the creek, where rocks invite you to hop across and head up the side drainage.

Driving south, you'll want to stop and savor a few other flats, especially along Otter Creek, with its extensive trail system. Otter Creek Flats Overlook (Milepost 58.2) is a nice place to pause; on the way, be sure to notice the chimney standing off the right side of the road at Milepost 58.

55.9   Dancing Creek Overlook, west • Elevation: 1,300 ft. (396m) • Facilities: picnic table.

56.1   USFS road crossing (gated).

57.0   USFS road crossing (gated).

57.6   Upper Otter Creek Overlook, east • Elevation: 1,085 ft. (331m).

58.2   Otter Creek Flats Overlook, east • Elevation: 1,005 ft. (306m) • Facilities: picnic table.

59.7   Otter Creek Overlook, west • Elevation: 885 ft. (270m).

60.4   The Riffles Overlook, east • Elevation: 822 ft. (251m).

60.8   Otter Creek Recreation Area, east (Hike 10, Option 1) • Elevation: 777 ft. (237m) • Campground: 42 tents, 26 trailer sites • Facilities: water, restrooms, campfire circle, restaurant, gift shop. • Trails: Otter Creek Trail trailhead, 3.4 miles (Moderate).

61.0   Otter Creek Bridge #6.

61.4   Terrapin Hill Overlook, west • Elevation: 760 ft. (232m) • Facilities: picnic table • Trails: Otter Creek Trail access.

61.4   VA 130 access • Right (west) to US 501, 2 miles; Glasgow, VA, 8 miles; Natural Bridge, VA, 15 miles; left (east) to US 29, 15 miles; Lynchburg, VA, 20 miles.

61.6   VA 130 crossing, underpass (no access) • Right to US 501, 2 miles; Glasgow, VA, 8 miles; left to Elon, VA, 12 miles; Lynchburg, VA, 20 miles.

62.5   Lower Otter Creek Overlook, east • Elevation: 685 ft. (209m) • Facilities: picnic tables across trail bridge to left • Trail: Otter Creek Trail access.

63.1   Otter Lake Overlook, east (Hike 10, Option 2) • Elevation: 655 ft. (200m) • Parking: additional parking on west side • Trail: Otter Lake Trail, 1.0 mile (Moderate; lake loop).

63.2   Lowest elevation on Blue Ridge Parkway, 646.4 ft. (197m).

63.6   James River Overlook, east (Hike 10, Option 1; Hike 11) • Elevation: 668 ft. (204m) • Facilities: visitor center, restrooms, water • Trails: James River Trail, 0.4 mile (Easy; trail to Kanawha Canal lock exhibit); Trail of Trees, 0.5 mile (Moderate; self-guiding nature trail) • Exhibits: Kanawha Canal locks • Signboard: James River Visitor Center and trails; Trail of Trees. Also Otter Creek Trail.

63.7   James River Bridge.

63.7   C&O Railroad crossing, underpass.

63.9 **US 501 crossing, underpass (access east; south of crossing) (Hike 12, Option 1)** • Right (south) to Big Island, VA, 2 miles; Lynchburg, VA, 11 miles; left (north) to Glasgow, VA, 9 miles; Natural Bridge, VA, 15 miles.

69.1 James River Valley Overlook, east • Elevation: 1,874 ft. (571m) • Facilities: picnic table.

69.1 FSR 951 access, east (Battery Creek Road).

71.0 **Petites Gap (Hike 12, Options 2 and 3)** • Elevation: 2,361 ft. (720m).

71.0 FSR 35, west • Trails: Appalachian Trail access parking (50 yards west); Sulphur Spring, Belfast, and Gunter Ridge Trails • Cave Mountain Lake Recreation Area, 8 miles.

72.6 Terrapin Mountain parking, east • Elevation: 2,885 ft. (879m).

74.6 National Park Service road, west (gated).

74.7 **Thunder Ridge Parking Area, west (Hike 13)** • Elevation: 3,485 ft. (1,062m) • Facilities: picnic table • Trails: Thunder Ridge Trail, 0.2 mile (Easy; 10-minute loop trail to pedestrian overlook; view of Glasgow and Natural Bridge); Appalachian Trail access.

74.8 Thunder Hill • Elevation: 3,510 ft. (1,070m).

74.9 Appalachian Trail crossing • Right: to Thunder Ridge Parking Area • Left: to Thunder Hill Shelter (USFS). • Trails: Hunting Creek Trail (USFS); AT access 150 feet east to FSR 45.

75.2 Arnold Valley Parking (north), west • Elevation: 3,510 ft. (1,070m) • Cars: 5 • Hunter access east and west during hunting season.

75.3 Arnold Valley Parking (south), west • Elevation: 3,700 ft. (1,128m) • View: Devil's Hopper and Snake Den Ridge, west.

76.2 U.S. Air Force access road, east (gated).

76.3 Appalachian Trail crossing • Right: to Apple Orchard Mountain • Left: to Thunder Hill Shelter, 0.3 mile north.

76.5 Apple Orchard parking, east • Elevation: 3,933 ft. (1,199m) • Signboard: Apple Orchard Mountain.

76.7 Highest point on the Blue Ridge Parkway in Virginia • Elevation: 3,950 ft. (1,204m).

76.7 U.S. Air Force access road to Apple Orchard Mountain, west (gated).

78.4 **Sunset Field Overlook, west (Hike 14)** • Elevation: 3,472 ft. (1,058m) • Trails: **Apple Orchard Falls Trail;** Appalachian Trail access as it crosses Apple Orchard Falls Trail (NPS–USFS), west • Gated entrance to former Camp Kewanzee, east.

78.4 FSR 812 access, west • Parkers Gap Road to Apple Orchard Falls; North Creek Campground (USFS).

79.7 **Onion Mountain Overlook, east** • Elevation: 3,145 ft. (959m) • Facilities: picnic table • View: Suck Mountain, east • Trails: **Onion Mountain Loop Trail,** 0.2 mile (Easy; 6-minute loop). The Onion Mountain Loop circles the little summit that sits just south of the parking area. A few stone steps lead to a

Near Milepost 76, the Parkway reaches its highest point in Virginia—3,950 feet.

split in the trail. Take the right fork, then bear left at a second, heavily trodden trail. (An informal path that leads to the top of the Parkway road-cut provides an interesting photo spot from above the road.)

The trail weaves around and down among rocks, dipping significantly off the back of the crag. Heading left on a flat section, there are views down into the surrounding forest. Then the trail rises over stone steps, sloping rocks, between crags, and over a final few flights of steps to the top. A right turn steps down to the parking lot. Though easy, the climb back to the parking area and rocky footing make this leg-stretcher a bit more challenging. For some it could take longer than the 6 minutes noted on the sign.

79.9 Black Rock Hill Parking, west • Elevation: 3,195 ft. (974m).

80.5 FSR190 crossing • Right: gated • Left: open to public; to VA 640 • Trails: Appalachian Trail access to Cornelius Creek Shelter (USFS), west • Appalachian Trail leaves Parkway, heading down into Middle Creek (USFS).

81.9 Head-first parking, east • Elevation: 2,860 ft. (872m) • Lift-top easel: tulip poplar tree.

83.1 Falling Cascades Parking Area, west (Hike 15, Option 1) • Elevation: 2,557 ft. (779m) • Trail: **Fallingwater Cascades Trail,** 1.6-mile loop (Moderate; to cascades).

83.1 USFS road access, west (gated).

83.4 Wilkerson Gap • Elevation: 2,511 ft. (765m).

83.5 Flat Top Parking Area, east (Hike 15, Option 2) • Elevation: 2,610 ft. (795m) • Trail: **Flat Top Trail,** 4.4 miles (across Flat Top Mountain, elevation 4,001 ft., to Peaks of Otter Picnic Area).

85.2   Peaks of Otter Maintenance Area, west • Trail: Road to Johnson Farm (4 historic buildings—house restored to 1930s).

85.6   Peaks of Otter Lodge, east (Hike 15, Option 3) • Elevation: 2,525 ft. (770m) • Facilities: lodge—58 rooms/3 suites; restaurant with lounge, coffee shop, gift shop, parking areas • Abbott Lake: 24-acre lake, east; managed for smallmouth bass • Trail: **Abbott Lake Trail,** 1.0 mile (Easy) • Feature: Polly Woods Ordinary.

85.9   Peaks of Otter developed area, east (Hike 15, Option 4) • Elevation: 2,875 ft. (876m) • Facilities: Camp store, restrooms, bus station for concession bus up Sharp Top Mountain (bus goes to within 1,500 feet of summit) • Campground: 90 tents, 53 trailer sites • Picnic Area: 62 sites • Signboards: Big Springs, weather at work; boulders of Sharp Top, Sharp Top summit, Elk Run Trail • Wayside: Sharp Top Mountain, Polly Woods Ordinary, Johnson Farmhouse • Trails: **Sharp Top Trail,** 1.5 miles (Strenuous); Sharp Top Summit Trails (Strenuous), with spur trail to Buzzards Roost.

85.9   Peaks of Otter Visitor Center, west (Hike 15, Option 5) • Elevation: 2,550 ft. (777m) • Facilities: visitor center, district ranger office, restrooms, water, amphitheater • Trails: **Johnson Farm Loop Trail,** 2.1 miles (Easy); **Harkening Hill Trail,** 3.3 miles (Moderate); **Elk Run Self-Guiding Trail,** 0.8 mile (Easy).

85.9   VA 43 access, east • Straight to Bedford, VA, 15 miles; left to public road (VA 614) by bus station to Sheep Creek; private road right off public road (VA 614) and R.A. Church Camp.

89.1   Powell Gap, west • Elevation: 1,916 ft. (584m).

An alert deer has one eye on a hiker below and the other on Sharp Top rearing overhead.

89.1   VA 618 access, west • To Arcadia • North Creek Campground (USFS)

89.4   Upper Goose Creek Overlook, east • Elevation: 1,925 ft. (587m).

90.0   Porter's Mountain Overlook, east • Elevation: 2,100 ft. (640m) • Lift-top easel: different types of oak.

91.0   Bearwallow Gap • Elevation: 2,258 ft. (688m) • Trails: Appalachian Trail crosses under Parkway bridge and parallels and traverses the Parkway for the next 7 miles.

91.0   VA 695 crossing, underpass (access east and west) • West to VA 43; Buchanan, VA, 5 miles; east to US 460 at Montvale, VA, 10 miles.

91.8   Mills Gap parking, west • Elevation: 2,435 ft. (742m) • Facilities: picnic table.

91.9   Mills Gap • Elevation: 2,425 ft. (739m).

92.1   Purgatory Mountain parking, west • Elevation: 2,400 ft. (731m) • Wayside panel: hawk migration.

92.5   Sharp Top Parking, east • Elevation: 2,415 ft. (736m) • Trail: Appalachian Trail crossing • Wayside panel: Appalachian Trail.

93.1   Bobblet's Gap Overlook, west • Elevation: 2,150 ft. (655m) • Facilities: picnic table • Trail: Appalachian Trail access to Bobblet's Gap Shelter, west.

93.2   Bobblet's Gap • Elevation: 2,148 ft. (655m) • Trail: Appalachian Trail near Parkway.

93.2   VA 617 crossing, underpass (no access) • Right to I-81; left to US 460.

94.9   USFS Hammond Fire Trail access, west • On Appalachian Trail north for 250 paces then Fire Trail down mountain to VA 645.

95.2   Pine Tree Overlook, east • Elevation: 2,490 ft. (759m).

95.3   Harvey's Knob Overlook, west • Elevation: 2,524 ft. (769m) • Trail: Appalachian Trail crossing. Excellent scenery in fall and winter.

95.9   Montvale Overlook, east • Elevation: 2,441 ft. (744m) • Trail: Appalachian Trail accesses overlook, east • Facilities: picnic table.

96.0   USFS Spec Mine Fire Trail access, west • To VA 645, 2.8 miles; 5.6 miles round-trip.

96.2   Iron Mine Hollow parking (north), west • Elevation: 2,364 ft. (720m).

96.4   Iron Mine Hollow parking (south), west • Elevation: 2,372 ft. (723m) • History: Pre–Civil War iron mining (low-grade ore).

97.0   Taylor Mountain Overlook, east • Elevation: 2,340 ft. (713m) • Trail: Appalachian Trail crossing.

97.7   Black Horse Gap • Elevation: 2,402 ft. (732m).

97.7   FSR 186 access, west (gated) • Goes down to Wilson Creek (USFS) to Camp Bethel and VA 640.

97.7   Abandoned Virginia Forestry Service road, east (gated) • 0.3 mile to old Black Horse Tavern site.

99.6   The Great Valley Overlook, west • Elevation: 2,493 ft. (760m) • Facilities: picnic table • Interpretive sign: the Great Valley.

100.9   The Quarry Overlook, east • Elevation: 2,170 ft. (661m).

101.5   Curry Gap • Elevation: 1,985 ft. (605m).

101.5   FSR 191 crossing • Right to Fullhardt Knob, Shay Hollow at access 1 mile; left to US 460.

105.0   Interpretive board.

105.8   US 460 crossing, overpass (access west and east) • Right (west) to Roanoke, VA, 9 miles; left (east) to Bedford, VA, 21 miles.

106.9   N&W Railroad Overlook, east • Elevation: 1,161 ft. (354m).

107.0   Coyner Mountain Overlook, west • Elevation: 1,150 ft. (350m).

109.8   Read Mountain Overlook, west • Elevation: 1,163 ft. (354m).

110.6   Stewarts Knob Overlook, east (Hike 16, Option 1) • Elevation: 1,365 ft. (416m) • Trail: **Stewarts Knob Trail,** 0.1 mile (Easy).

112.2   VA 24 crossing, underpass (access west and east) • Right (west) to Roanoke, VA, 5 miles; Vinton, VA, 2 miles; left (east) to Booker T. Washington National Monument, 33 miles; Stewartsville, VA, 4 miles.

112.9   Roanoke Basin Overlook, east • Elevation: 1,250 ft. (381m).

114.7   Roanoke River Bridge • Elevation: 825 ft. at river (251m) • Other: N&W Railroad bridge, 0.25 mile long.

114.9   Roanoke River Parking Area, west (Hike 16, Option 2) • Elevation: 985 ft. (300m) • View: Appalachian Power Dam • Trails: **Roanoke River Trail,** 0.4 mile (Easy; 20-minute trail to river level and patio; angler trail to river edge; loop trail).

115.0   Former access to Explore Park (now closed), east. Parkway visitor center open on a seasonal basis.

115.1   Pine Mountain Parking Area, east • Elevation: 1,002 ft. (305m).

118.0   Horse trail crossing.

119.8   Roanoke Mountain Loop exit, east.

120.3   Roanoke Mountain Loop entrance, east (Hike 16, Option 3) • Length: 4-mile loop road • Restrictions: no recreational vehicles over 20 feet • Overlooks: 5 • Trail: **Roanoke Mountain Summit Trail** (10-minute trail) • View: Excellent views of City of Roanoke, Roanoke Valley, Mill Mountain, and surrounding areas.

120.4   Mill Mountain Spur Road, west (Hike 16, Options 4 and 5).
0.1   Gum Spring Overlook • Elevation: 1,445 ft. (440m) • Trail: Horse trail crossing.
0.4   Welcome Valley Road/(VA 672) crossing (no access).
1.1   Chestnut Ridge Overlook • Elevation: 1,465 ft. (446m) • Interpretive: map and access to 5.4-mile **Chestnut Ridge Trail.**
1.3   Roanoke Mountain Campground • Facilities: 74 tent sites, 31 trailer sites, 3 designed for barrier-free accessibility; 200-person capacity campfire circle • Trail: access to Chestnut Ridge Trail (barrier free).
1.4   View of back side of Mill Mountain Star.
2.5   **End Blue Ridge Parkway jurisdiction • Left to Mill Mountain**

Stonework enhances the overlook on the Roanoke Mountain Loop Road (Milepost 120.3).

Park, Playhouse, and Zoo • Begin J. B. Fishburn Parkway down Mill Mountain to Roanoke, VA (2 miles).

120.6 Horse trail crossing • Trail: Roanoke Valley Horse Trail, 18.5 miles (Moderate).

121.4 US 220 crossing, underpass (access west and east) • Right to Roanoke, VA, 5 miles; left to Rocky Mount, VA, 21 miles.

123.2 Buck Mountain Overlook, east (Hike 17) • Elevation: 1,465 ft. (446m) • Cars: 15 • Trail: **Buck Mountain Trail.**

126.2 Masons Knob Overlook, east • Elevation: 1,430 ft. (436m).

128.7 Metz Run Overlook, west • Elevation: 1,875 ft. (571m) • View: Cascade Falls, east (no access).

128.8 Circular bridge crossing Metz Run (creek).

129.3 Poages Mill Overlook, west • Elevation: 2,035 ft. (620m) • View: Roanoke Valley.

129.6 Roanoke Valley Overlook, west • Elevation: 2,100 ft. (640m) • View: Roanoke Valley • Wayside panel: Roanoke.

129.9 Lost Mountain Overlook, west • Elevation: 2,200 ft. (671m).

132.0 Dividing Springs • Elevation: 2,800 ft. (853m).

132.9 Slings Gap Overlook, east • Elevation: 2,817 ft. (859m).

133.0 Slings Gap • Elevation: 2,825 ft. (861m) • VA 612 crossing: (no access).

133.6 Bull Run Knob Overlook, east • Elevation: 2,890 ft. (881m).

134.3 Lancaster Gap • Elevation: 2,786 ft. (849m).

134.9 Poor Mountain Overlook, west • Elevation: 2,975 ft. (907m).

135.9 US 221 access, west • Right: to Roanoke, VA, 19 miles.

136.0 Adney Gap • Elevation: 2,690 ft. (820m).

138.5 Sweet Annie Hollow • Elevation: 2,889 ft. (881m) • Trail: to Smith Tract.

139.0 Cahas Knob Overlook, east • Elevation: 3,013 ft. (918m).

143.5 Cemetery, east (Confederate soldier buried here).

143.9 Devils Backbone Overlook, east • Elevation: 2,687 ft. (819m) • Cars: 22 • View: Western Piedmont of Virginia.

144.3 Pine Spur Gap.

144.8 Pine Spur Overlook, east • Elevation: 2,703 ft. (824m) • Cars: 10.

145.3 VA 610 access, west.

145.7 VA 791 crossing.

146.4 VA 642 staggered crossing.

148.1 VA 641 crossing.

148.2 Honeytree Development.

148.4 VA 663 crossing.

149.1 VA 640 crossing.

149.5 Cannady Woods.

150.5 VA 639 crossing • Right to VA 221 to Roanoke, VA; Payne Creek Church.

150.8 Kelley Springhouse, east (no sign).

150.9 Public road crossing • Right to VA 681 (Floyd–Franklin Turnpike); left to VA 640 (Five Mile Mountain Road) and Ferrum, VA.

152.0 VA 888 staggered crossing.

153.6 VA 993 crossing.

154.1 Smart View Overlook, east • Elevation: 2,560 ft. (780m).

154.5 Smart View Parking Area, east (Hike 18) • Map: **Smart View Loop Trail** • Signboard: describing Trails Cabin; brief history of log cabins • Facilities: picnic area (42 sites), 2 comfort stations, picnic shelter, 8 tables, fireplace; first-come, first-served basis.

155.3 VA 793 crossing • Left to Endicott, VA, 4 miles; right to VA 680.

156.3 VA 635 crossing.

157.6 Shortts Knob Overlook, east • Elevation: 2,806 ft. (855m).

158.9 VA 637 crossing • Right to Floyd, VA, 6 miles; left to Endicott and Ferrum, VA (Shooting Creek Road).

159.3 VA 860 crossing • Right to Floyd, VA, 6 miles; left to Endicott and Ferrum, VA (Shooting Creek Road).

161.3 VA 615 crossing.

162.1 VA 711 crossing.

162.4 Rakes Mill Pond Overlook, west • Elevation: 2,477 ft. (755m) • Signboard: history of Rakes Mill Pond.

162.6 Staggered road crossing.

162.9 VA 710 crossing.

163.2   VA 797 crossing • Thomas Grove Baptist Church, east.

163.5   VA 709 crossing.

165.3   Tuggle Gap • Elevation: 2,752 ft. (839m).

165.3   VA 8 crossing, underpass (access west, north of crossing) (Hike 19, Option 1) • Right to Floyd, VA, 6 miles; I-81, 28 miles; left to Stuart, VA, 21 miles; Fairy Stone State Park, 30 miles.

167.1   Rocky Knob developed area, west • Facilities: campground (81 tent sites, 28 trailer sites, 150-person capacity campfire circle), restrooms, trailer dumping station • Trails: **Rock Castle Gorge Trail,** 10.6 miles (Strenuous); 3 miles to Rock Castle Gorge and Rock Castle Creek • CCC camp for backcountry camping (backcountry permit required).

This chimney along the Rock Castle Gorge Trail (Milepost 165.3) is all that remains of a former homestead.

168.0   Saddle Overlook, east (Hike 19, Option 2) • Trails: access to Rock Castle Gorge Trail; old AT shelter; 1.0 mile to Rocky Knob Picnic Area; 0.7 mile to Rocky Knob Campground, east.

168.2   Rocky Knob, east (no sign) • Elevation: 3,572 ft. (1,089m).

168.8   Rock Castle Gorge Overlook, east • Elevation: 3,195 ft. (974m) • Trails: access to Rock Castle Gorge Trail • Views: Brammer Spur, Rock Castle Gorge, Western Piedmont • Wayside panel: Rock Castle Gorge.

169.0   Rocky Knob Picnic Area, west (Hike 19, Options 3 and 4) • Sites: 72 • Facilities: Rocky Knob Contact Station, comfort stations, phone, picnic shelter • Trails: **Black Ridge Trail,** 3.1 miles (Moderate); **Rocky Knob Picnic Loop Trail,** 1.3 miles (Easy).

169.1   Twelve O'Clock Knob Overlook, east.

169.2   Pump House Road access, west.

170.4   VA 720 crossing.

171.3   VA 720 crossing.

171.7   VA 726 crossing • Elevation: 3,471 ft. (1,058m) • Highest motor road elevation between Apple Orchard and Doughton Park.

172.7   Belcher Curve (no sign).

174.0   Rock Castle Gap • Elevation: 2,970 ft. (905m).

174.0   VA 799 access, west • Right to Willis, VA; Hubbards Mill.

174.1   VA 758 access, east (Woodberry Road) • Left to Meadows of Dan and Rocky Knob Cabins (8 housekeeping cabins).

175.9   VA 603 crossing • Entrance to Mabry Mill overflow parking area.

176.2   Mabry Mill, east (Hike 20) • Elevation: 2,855 ft. (870m) • Facilities: Coffee shop, gift shop, restrooms, and phone; water-powered sawmill, carpenter shop, and working gristmill • Trail: **Mountain Industry Trail,** 0.5 mile (Easy; self-guiding Pioneer Industry Trail, including blacksmith and wheelwright shop exhibit and whiskey still) • Signboard: rural life in Appalachia • Wayside panel: whiskey still, mill challenges/mill operation.

176.3   Entrance to Mabry Mill overflow parking area.

177.7   Meadows of Dan • Elevation: 2,964 ft. (903m).

177.7   US 58 crossing, underpass (access west, north of crossing) • Right to Hillsville, VA, 21 miles; left to Stuart, VA, 16 miles; Cochran's Mill, 3 miles.

178.8   VA 744 crossing.

179.2   Round Meadow Overlook, west (Hike 21) • Elevation: 2,800 ft. (853m) • Views: excellent mountain cove with large hemlocks.

179.4   Round Meadow Viaduct • Elevation: 2,800 ft. (853m) • Creek elevation: 2,690 ft. (Round Meadow Creek).

180.1   VA 600 crossing • Mayberry Presbyterian Church and Cemetery.

180.5   VA 634 crossing • Mayberry Crossing; 0.1 mile to Mayberry Trading Post, gas, apple butter making.

180.6   Mayberry Gap.

180.7   Mayberry Creek • Elevation: 2,775 ft. (846m).

183.4   Pinnacles of Dan Gap • Elevation: 2,875 ft. (876m).

183.9   VA 614 access, east • To Mount Airy, NC.

187.7   VA 639 crossing.

188.8   Groundhog Mountain Picnic Area, east • Elevation: 3,025 ft. (922m) • Facilities: picnic area (26 sites), one comfort station, trail from parking area to observation tower (leg-stretcher) • Views: excellent 360-degree view from tower • Cemetery in parking area island • Wayside panel: different types of rail fences • Exhibits: 4 types of rail fences • Trail: **Groundhog Mountain Observation Tower,** 300 feet (Easy). Parkway motorists can see this hilltop observation tower long before they reach it. And the easy 100-yard stroll that leads to the amazing log structure means that even if you don't climb the tower, no one should miss exploring the hilltop. Like other key exhibits along the Parkway, this one truly informs—this time about fences. The variety and elegance of the ways mountaineers used logs to fence animals in and out is nothing short of amazing. The exhibit explores many of the fence types you'll see being maintained by the Park Service along the road—or rotting on the forest floor in remote trail locations.

188.9   VA 608 crossing, underpass (no access).

189.1   Pilot Mountain Overlook, east • Elevation: 2,950 ft. (899m) • Views: excellent view of distinctive summit in North Carolina Piedmont.

189.2 VA 608 crossing, underpass.

189.2 Doe Run Lodge.

189.9 Puckett Cabin Parking Area, west • Elevation: 2,848 ft. (868m) • Wayside panel: history of Puckett Cabin • Trail: Puckett Cabin, 150 feet (Easy). Pause at this roadside cabin where Orelena Hawks Puckett spent the second half of a 102-year life. The rude cabin and outbuilding sit beside a fenced garden space. Puckett was married at sixteen and lived her entire life near Groundhog Mountain. She turned to midwifery in midlife and helped deliver more than 1,000 babies—the last in 1939, the year she died. None of "Aunt" Orelena's own twenty-four children lived beyond infancy. A photo of the woman during the last year of her life appears on the roadside interpretive easel.

190.0 Crossing to Puckett Primitive Baptist Church.

190.6 VA 910 crossing.

191.4 VA 608 crossing.

192.2 VA 648 crossing (no sign) • Left to Willis Gap (VA 771); Mount Airy, NC.

193.2 Volunteer Gap crossing • Elevation: 2,672 ft. (814m) • Access: Old Volunteer Road.

193.7 Orchard Gap • Elevation: 2,675 ft. (815m).

193.7 VA 691 crossing • Right to Hillsville, VA; left to Mount Airy, NC.

194.7 VA 608 crossing.

195.5 Wards Gap • Elevation: 2,750 ft. (838m).

196.4 VA 682 crossing, underpass (Guynn Town Bridge).

197.7 Cascade Mountain Development, east • Access from VA 608 only.

198.4 VA 685 crossing • Left to VA 608.

198.9 VA 608 access, east, start of staggered crossing.

199.1 Fancy Gap Maintenance Area, west.

199.1 VA 608 access, west, end of staggered crossing.

199.4 Fancy Gap • Elevation: 2,925 ft. (891m) • Diverse services.

199.4 US 52 crossing, underpass • Right to Hillsville, VA, 8 miles; left to Mount Airy, NC, 14 miles.

199.9 VA 778 crossing.

202.2 VA 608 crossing.

202.8 Granite Quarry Overlook, east • Elevation: 3,015 ft. (919m) • Signboard: Mount Airy granite, with a sample of granite. • Views: excellent view of North Carolina Piedmont, including Hanging Rock and Pilot Mountain State Parks.

203.9 Piedmont Overlook, east • Elevation: 2,900 ft. (884m) • Views: excellent view of North Carolina Piedmont.

204.8 VA 700 crossing.

206.1 Pipers Gap • Elevation: 2,759 ft. (841m).

206.3 VA 608 crossing • Right to VA 620, 97, and 775; Galax, VA, 10 miles; Lambsburg, VA, 4 miles; I-77, 5 miles.

206.9 Mount Carroll Methodist Church (inactive) and Cemetery, east.

207.7 VA 608 crossing.

208.1 Blue Ridge Chapel, church and cemetery, west • Access to VA 608.

209.3 Parsons Gap • Access to VA 715 and Galax, VA.

209.8 VA 716 crossing.

211.1 VA 612 crossing • Right to Galax, VA.

213.0 Blue Ridge Music Center, east (Hike 22) • Elevation: 2,620 ft. (799m) • Facilities: visitor center, restrooms, water, music performance amphitheater • Trails: **High Meadow Trail,** 1.3 miles; **Fisher Peak Loop,** 3.0 miles.

213.3 VA 612 crossing.

215.3 VA 799, start of staggered crossing, west.

215.6 VA 799, end of staggered crossing, east.

215.8 VA 89 crossing, overpass (access west, north of crossing) • Right to Galax, VA, 7 miles; left to Mount Airy, NC, 22 miles.

216.9 Virginia–North Carolina state line.

217.1 North Carolina history plaque noting beginning of Parkway.

217.3 NC 18 crossing, underpass (access west, north of crossing) • Right to Sparta, NC, 15 miles; left to Mount Airy, NC, 22 miles.

217.5 Cumberland Knob (Hike 23, Options 1 and 2) • Facilities: visitor center, parking, picnic area with 33 sites, comfort stations, trail shelter, cemetery.

217.8 Leaving Cumberland Knob.

218.6 Fox Hunter's Paradise Overlook, east (Hike 23, Option 3) • Elevation: 2,805 ft. (855m) • Signboard: fox hunting at this site • Short spur road to view trail at High Piney Spur.

220.4 NC 1460 access, west.

220.5 NC 1461 access, east.

221.8 Saddle Mountain Church • Elevation: 2,755 ft. (840m).

221.8 NC 1461 crossing.

223.1 Staggered NC 1486 crossing, west • NC 1479, east.

225.3 Hare Mill Pond • Elevation: 2,590 ft. (789m).

225.3 NC 1463 crossing.

226.3 NC 1433 staggered crossing, west • NC 1472, east.

227.6 NC 1433 access, west (Rich Hill Road).

227.6 NC 1472 access, east (Mountain View Church Road).

229.2 NC 1468 access, east.

229.7 US 21, underpass (access west and east) • West to Sparta, NC, 7 miles; east to Stone Mountain State Park (about 13 miles; turn right from US 21 onto NC 1100 in 4.6 miles) and Elkin, NC, 25 miles.

230.1 Little Glade Mill Pond Overlook, east • Elevation: 2,709 ft. (826m) • Facilities: 5 picnic tables • Trail: **Little Glade Mill Pond Trail,** 0.3 mile (Easy). Circling this old millpond from the overlook past picnic tables is a flat and pleasant stroll. The place takes on added appeal early or late in the day.

230.9   NC 1108 access, east.

230.9   NC 1111 access, west.

231.5   NC 1109 crossing.

231.8   NC 1110 access, west.

232.5   Stone Mountain Overlook, east • Elevation: 3,200 ft. (975m) • Facilities: picnic table • Wayside panel: Stone Mountain.

233.7   Bullhead Mountain Overlook, east • Elevation: 3,200 ft. (975m).

234.0   Deep Gap • Elevation: 3,193 ft. (973m).

234.0   NC 1115 access, west (Cable Car Road).

235.0   Mahogany Rock Overlook, west (Hike 24) • Elevation: 3,420 ft. (1,042m) • Facilities: picnic table.

235.7   Devil's Garden Overlook, east • Elevation: 3,428 ft. (1,045m). • Trail: access to Mountains-to-Sea Trail (MST)

236.9   Air Bellows Gap Overlook, west • Elevation: 3,729 ft. (1,137m).

237.1   Air Bellows Gap • Elevation: 3,729 ft. (1,137m).

237.1   NC 1130 crossing, underpass (Air Bellows Road).

238.5   Brinegar Cabin Overlook, east • Elevation: 3,508 ft. (1,069m) • Trails: Cedar Ridge Trail, 4.2 miles (Moderate); **Bluff Mountain Trail/Mountains-to-Sea Trail,** 7.5 miles (Moderate) • Signboard: Brinegar Cabin and loom • Wayside panel: Appalachian garden.

238.5   Enter Doughton Park.

239.2   Doughton Park Campground, east • Facilities: west, 110 campsites, 3 comfort stations, 250-person capacity campfire circle; east, 25 trailer sites, 1 comfort station.

240.1   Low Notch • Elevation: 3,482 ft. (1,045m).

241.1   Wildcat Rocks Overlook, east • Wayside panel: homestead (Martin Caudill) • Historic plaque: Robert L. Doughton • View: Basin Creek watershed and homestead of Martin Caudill • Trail: Fodder Stack Trail, 1.0 mile (Moderate).

241.1   Doughton Park concession area (Hike 24, Option 1) • Facilities: west, coffee shop, gift shop, service station, and information center; east, 24-room lodge, picnic area • Trails: **Bluff Ridge Trail,** 2.8 miles (Strenuous); **Bluff Mountain Trail/**Mountains-to-Sea Trail, 7.5 miles (Moderate).

242.0   Ice Rock (no access)

242.4   Alligator Back Overlook, east (Hike 24, Option 2) • Elevation: 3,388 ft. (1,033m) • Signboard: predator birds and mammals • Trail: access to Bluff Mountain Trail/Mountains-to-Sea Trail, 7.5 miles (Moderate).

243.4   Bluff Mountain Overlook, east • Elevation: 3,421 ft. (1,043m) • Trail: access to Bluff Mountain Trail/Mountains-to-Sea Trail, 7.5 miles (Moderate).

243.7   Grassy Gap, east • Elevation: 3,218 ft. (981m) • Trails: Grassy Gap Fire Road Trail, 6.5 miles (Moderate); access to Bluff Mountain Trail / Mountains-to-Sea Trail, 7.5 miles (Moderate).

244.7   Basin Cove Overlook, east (Hike 24, Option 3) • Elevation: 3,312 ft. (1,009m) • Trails: **Flat Rock Ridge Trail,** 5.0 miles (Moderate); access to

Bluff Mountain Trail/Mountains-to-Sea Trail, 7.5 miles (Moderate) • Sign: Doughton Park Trail System.

245.5   Bluffs Maintenance Area/Ranger Offices, west • Residences: 34 and 35.

246.1   NC 1143 access, west (Elk Knob Road).

246.9   NC 1144 access, west.

247.2   NC 1175 access, west (Miller's Campground Road).

248.1 NC 18 crossing, underpass (access west and east) (Hike 24, Option 4) • West to Laurel Springs, NC, 2 miles; east to North Wilkesboro, NC, 24 miles.

248.9   Laurel Fork Viaduct.

249.3   NC SR 1613 crossing.

250.0   NC SR 1615 access, west.

250.8   NC 1616 crossing, west, to Upper Mountain Experiment Station.

250.8   NC 1620, east.

251.5   Alder Gap • Elevation: 3,047 ft. (914m).

252.3   Sheets Cabin, west.

252.4   NC 1619 access, west (Ashe Court).

252.8   Sheets Gap parking, east • Elevation: 3,342 ft. (1,019m) • Facilities: 2 picnic tables.

258.7   NC 1648 access, east.

258.7   Northwest Trading Post, west • Facilities: comfort station, craft store, limited snacks, picnic table.

259.2   NC 1632 access, west.

259.8   NC 1634 access, west (Doyle Bare Road).

260.3 Jumpinoff Rocks Parking Area, east (Hike 25) • Elevation: 3,165 ft. (965m) • Facilities: 2 picnic tables.

261.2   Horse Gap • Elevation: 3,108 ft. (958m).

261.2   NC 16 crossing, underpass (access west and east) • East to Jefferson, NC, 12 miles; west to North Wilkesboro, NC, 22 miles.

262.2   Daniel Gap • Elevation: 3,167 ft. (965m).

263.7   Gilliam Gap • Elevation: 3,238 ft. (990m).

264.4 The Lump Overlook, east • Elevation: 3,465 ft. (1,056m) • Facilities: picnic table • Signboard: Tom Dula (Tom Dooley of folk song fame) • Trail: **The Lump Trail,** 0.2 to 0.4 mile (Easy). The Lump is a rounded meadow with an expansive view in all directions. Step through the fence at the fat-man squeeze and take the informal path to the top—or circle the meadow for a longer, more level side-hill walk that will make you feel far away from the Parkway. There are plenty of picnic spots across the top and around the edges of the fields. It's not unusual to see kites—even the stray radio-controlled model airplane—in the air above the breezy hilltop.

The interpretive sign at the overlook is interesting. Tom Dula—the subject of the song made popular by the Kingston Trio during the 1960s folk music resurgence—lived just below this hill in Wilkes County, North Carolina. A handsome Civil War hero, Dula was hanged for a murder that resulted from a lover's triangle. Although defended by Governor Zebulon B. Vance, Dula was convicted and hanged in Statesville, North Carolina, in 1868. The story became one of the nation's first highly publicized crimes of passion.

265.1 Calloway Gap • Elevation: 3,439 ft. (1,032m).

265.1 NC 1360 access, east.

265.1 NC 1165 access, west.

266.3 Radio relay tower (Watson's Dome), west.

266.8 Mount Jefferson Overlook, west • Elevation: 3,699 ft. (1,127m) • Signboard: Mount Jefferson.

267.6 NC 1167 crossing.

267.8 Betsey's Rock Falls Overlook, east • Elevation: 3,400 ft. (1,036m) • Facilities: picnic table.

268.0 Benge Gap • Elevation: 3,296 ft. (1,005m).

268.0 NC 1166 crossing (Park Vista Road).

269.7 NC 1365 access, east.

269.8 Phillips Gap • Elevation: 3,221 ft. (982m).

269.8 NC 1168 crossing.

270.2 Lewis Fork Overlook, east • Elevation: 3,290 ft. (1,003m).

271.9 Cascades Overlook, east (Hike 26, Option 1) • Elevation: 3,570 ft. (1,088m) • Facilities: picnic tables (30), cinder pits (4), comfort station, water fountain • Trails: **Cascades Self-Guiding Trail,** 1.0 mile (Moderate; to Cascades pedestrian overlook); trail to Cool Spring Baptist Church and Jesse Brown Cabin (Easy) • Signboard: E. B. Jeffress Park.

272.4 Cool Spring Baptist Church/Jesse Brown Cabin, east • Signboard: the church.

272.5 Tompkins Knob Parking Area, east (Hike 26, Option 2) • Elevation: 3,657 ft. • Trails: trail to Jesse Brown Cabin and Cool Spring Baptist Church, 500 feet (Easy); **Tompkins Knob Trail,** 0.6 mile (Easy).

273.6 Tompkins Knob.

274.2 Leaving Jeffress Park.

274.3 Elk Mountain Overlook, east • Elevation: 3,795 ft. (1,157m).

276.4 Deep Gap • Elevation: 3,142 ft. (958m).

276.4 US 421 crossing, underpass (access west, south of crossing) • left to Boone, NC, 12 miles; right to North Wilkesboro, NC, 26 miles • Newest Parkway bridge—rockwork and span completed 2002.

277.3 Stoney Fork Valley Overlook, east • Elevation: 3,405 ft. (1,038m).

277.9 Osborne Mountain View Overlook, east • Elevation: 3,500 ft. (1,067m).

278.3 Carroll Gap Overlook, west • Elevation: 3,430 ft. (1,045m).

280.9 US 421 and US 221 access, west • Right to Deep Gap, NC, 4 miles; left to Boone, NC, 7 miles.

The newest of the Parkway's handcrafted stone bridges soars across the now four-lane expanse of US 421 in Deep Gap, east of Boone, North Carolina.

281.4 Grandview Overlook, east • Elevation: 3,240 ft. (988m).

285.1 Boone's Trace Overlook, east • Feature: historical marker about Daniel Boone • Facilities: picnic table.

285.5 Bamboo Gap • Elevation: 3,262 ft. (994m).

285.5 Public road access, west, underpass (Bamboo Road) • Left: to Boone, NC.

286.3 Public road crossing, underpass (George Hayes Road; no access).

286.3 Goshen Creek Bridge.

288.0 Aho Gap • To US 321 between Boone and Blowing Rock, NC.

288.1 Staggered public road crossing (Aho Road).

289.5 Raven Rocks Overlook, west • Elevation: 3,810 ft. (1,161m) • Spectacular view of Grandfather Mountain.

289.8 Yadkin Valley Overlook, east • Elevation: 3,830 ft. (1,167m).

290.4 Thunder Hill Overlook, east • Elevation: 3,795 ft. (1,157m).

290.7 Public road access, east (Green Hill Road).

291.8 US 321 and US 221 crossing, underpass (access west, north of crossing, and east, south of crossing) (Hike 27, Option 6) • West to Boone, NC, 8 miles; east to Blowing Rock, NC, 2 miles.

292.7 Enter Moses H. Cone Memorial Park.

293.5 Moses Cone Overlook, east • Elevation: 3,888 ft. (1,185m).

November is a special season on the Parkway. Before snow falls, hoarfrost often turns Cone Park and its trails into a fairyland.

294.0 Moses Cone Manor House, east (Hike 27, Options 1 and 2) • Facilities: visitor information center, craft center, comfort station, Cone family cemetery, Bass Lake, carriage barn, apple barn, public telephone • Trails: **Moses Cone Carriage Trails** (Easy to moderate); access to Mountains-to-Sea Trail • Wayside panel: Moses H. Cone Memorial Park.

294.6 US 221 access road, east (Hike 27, Options 3–5, 7, and 8) • Trail: **Trout Lake Trail,** 1.0 mile (Easy) • Left to Blowing Rock, NC, 2 miles; left to Bass Lake, 1 mile.

294.6   Trout Lake Parking Area (access via Shull's Mill Road).

294.7   NC crossing, underpass (Flannery Fork and Shull's Mill Roads).

295.3 Sims Creek Overlook, west • Elevation: 3,608 ft. (1,100m) • Trail: access to Green Knob Trail.

295.4   Sims Creek Bridge.

295.8   Leave Moses Cone and enter Julian Price Memorial Park.

295.9 Sims Pond Overlook, east (Hike 28, Option 1) • Elevation: 3,447 ft. (1,051m) • Trail: **Green Knob Trail,** 2.1 miles (Moderate) • Signs: fishing regulations.

296.1   National Park Service road staggered crossing (Old John's River Road).

296.4 Price Park Picnic Area, west (Hike 28, Option 2) • Facilities: 100 picnic sites; 2 comfort stations (one with barrier-free facilities) • Trail: Boone Fork Trail (loop), 4.9 miles (Strenuous) • Signboard: old lakebed.

296.7   Price Lake Overlook, east • Elevation: 3,380 ft. (1,030m) • Trail: Price Lake Loop Trail, 2.3 miles (Moderate) • Signboard: Julian Price Memorial Park • Sign: lake-use regulations.

296.9   Price Park Campground, west and east • west: 62 trailer sites, 100 tent sites, 5 comfort stations, kiosk, bulletin board, public telephones, PRICE PARK TRAILS sign • East: 29 tent sites (2 barrier-free sites), 6 trailer sites, 1 comfort station (barrier free) • Trails: Tanawha Trail, 13.5 miles (easy to strenuous); access to Boone Fork, Price Lake, and Mountains-to-Sea Trails.

297.2   Boone Fork Overlook, east (Hike 28, Option 3) • Elevation: 3,410 ft. (1,039m) • Facilities: boat dock, canoe/rowboat rentals, 68 trailer sites, 129 tent sites, limited snacks, amphitheater (seating capacity 300) • Trails: **Price Lake Trail,** 2.5 miles (Moderately easy); access to Tanawha, Mountains-to-Sea, and Boone Fork Trails • Wayside panel: beavers—aquatic engineers; beavers—friend or foe? • Signs: Price Park Trails.

298.6   Public road crossing, underpass (access west, north of crossing) • Right 1 mile on gravel Holloway Mountain Road to Tanawha Trail **(Hike 29, Option 1)** and beyond to NC 105 between Banner Elk/Boone; left on pavement to Rufus Lenoir Gwyn Trail and 1 mile to US 221 • Trail: **Gwyn Memorial Trail,** 0.1 mile (Easy) • Sign: memorial to Rufus Lenoir Gwyn.

This is a rare Parkway beauty spot—it isn't even visible from the road. Tucked below the Parkway within the curving exit to Holloway Mountain Road and US 221, this tiny loop trail crosses a tiny stream while it circles a glade. There's a bench and plentiful places to spread a picnic blanket. The enclave honors Rufus Lenoir Gwyn, a member of the first committee organized to secure the Parkway route for North Carolina.

299.0   Cold Prong Pond Overlook, west (Hike 29, Option 2) • Elevation: 3,580 ft. (1,091m) • Trails: No-name loop trail, 0.3 mile (Easy), unmarked beyond trailhead; access to Tanawha Trail.

299.7   View of Calloway Peak Overlook, east • Elevation: 3,798 ft. (1,158m) • Trails: leg-stretcher (0.5 mile) along Boone Fork to Boone Fork Parking Area; access to Tanawha Trail.

299.9   Boone Fork Parking Area, west (Hike 30, Option 1) • Elevation: 3,905 ft. (1,190m) • Trails: access to **Tanawha Trail, Nuwati** and **Daniel Boone Scout Trails** on Grandfather Mountain.

300.6   Green Mountain Overlook, east • Elevation: 4,134 ft. (1,260m).

301.8   Pilot Ridge Overlook, east • Elevation: 4,400 ft. (1,341m).

302.1   View Wilson Creek Valley Overlook, east • Elevation: 4,356 ft. (1,328m).

302.4   Boulder Field Overlook, west • Elevation: 4,335 ft. (1,321m) • Trail: access to Tanawha Trail.

302.8   Rough Ridge Parking Area, west (Hike 29, Option 3) • Elevation: 4,293 ft. (1,308m) • Trails: access to Tanawha Trail (10-minute hike to Rough Ridge Boardwalk).

303.0 "Great Wall of China" Bridge.

303.6 Wilson Creek Overlook, east • Elevation: 4,357 ft. (1,328m) • Trail: access to Tanawha Trail.

303.9 Yonahlossee Overlook, east • Elevation: 4,412 ft. (1,345m).

304.0 Linn Cove Viaduct.

304.4 Linn Cove Parking Area, east (Hike 29, Option 4) • Elevation: 4,315 ft. (1,315m) • Facilities: visitor contact station, comfort station • Trails: connects to Tanawha trail; barrier-free trail to view of Linn Cove Viaduct • Wayside panel: Linn Cove Viaduct construction.

304.8 Stack Rock Parking Area, east • Elevation: 4,286 ft. (1,306m) • Trail: access to Tanawha Trail.

305.1 US 221 crossing, underpass (access west, north of crossing). US 221 is NC Scenic Byway in both directions **(Hike 30, Options 2 and 3)** • Right: Grandfather Mountain entrance, 1 mile; Linville, NC, 3 miles; left: Blowing Rock, NC, 13 miles.

305.2 Beacon Heights Parking Area, east (Hike 31) • Elevation: 4,220 ft. (1,286m) • Facilities: interpretive display • Trails: **Beacon Heights Trail,** 0.7 mile (Easy); access to Tanawha (begin/end Tanawha Trail) and Mountains-to-Sea Trails.

306.2 Grandmother Mountain Gap • Elevation: 4,051 ft. (1,235m).

306.6 Grandfather Mountain Overlook, west • Elevation: 4,154 ft. (1,266m).

307.4 Grandmother Parking Area, east • Elevation: 4,063 ft. (1,238m).

307.6 No-name parking, west • Elevation: 4,015 ft. (1,224m).

Beacon Heights (Milepost 305.2) showcases the dramatic drop to the Piedmont from the Grand-father Mountain area.

Yellow arrows lead hikers across the crest of the Flat Rock Trail toward distant Grandfather Mountain.

307.9　NC 1511 crossing (Roseboro Road) • Right to Linville, NC, 2 miles; left to Roseboro and Mortimer, NC, and USFS recreation areas in Wilson Creek area.

308.3　Flat Rock Parking Area, west (Hike 32) • Elevation: 3,987 ft. (1,215m) • Trail: **Flat Rock Trail,** 0.7 mile (Moderate)—interpretive signs of flora and fauna and directional dials on summit • Signboard: Flat Rock Trail.

310.0　Lost Cove Cliffs Overlook, east • Elevation: 3,812 ft. (1,162m) • Facilities: picnic table • Wayside panel: Brown Mountain lights.

311.2　NC 1518 crossing • West to Pineola, NC, 3 miles; east to Old Jonas Ridge Road to Edgemont and Mortimer, NC.

312.2　NC 181 crossing, overpass (access west, north of crossing) (Hike 33, Options 1 and 2) • Right to Pineola, NC, 2 miles; left to Morganton, NC, 32 miles • Trails: access to **Hawksbill** and **Table Rock Trails.**

315.6　Camp Creek Overlook, west • Elevation: 3,443 ft. (1,049m) • Trail: **Camp Creek Trail,** 0.4 mile (Easy). Not much more than a glorified parking area side trail, Camp Creek is a quick descent from the overlook to the edge of a rushing, rhododendron-choked trout stream alive with the sounds of the Southern Appalachians. White pines soar overhead. This is a fisher's access trail—a sign proclaims FISHING WITH SINGLE HOOK ARTIFICIAL LURES ONLY. CREEL LIMIT 4, SIZE

LIMIT 7 INCHES. POSSESSION OF NATURAL BAIT ILLEGAL. In fifteen minutes on this old trail—blowdowns have been in place so long that sidestepping hikers have almost rerouted the trail—you can feel miles from the road.

316.4 Linville Falls Spur Road, east (Hike 34, Options 1 and 2):

0.1 Linville Falls Maintenance Area.

0.4 Riverbend Overlook, east • Trail: Riverbend Overlook Trail, 0.1 mile (Easy).

0.5 Linville Falls Campground, west • Facilities: campground (55 tent and small RV sites, 15 large RV sites), 150-person capacity campfire circle.

1.5 Linville Falls Visitor Contact Station • Facilities: contact station, restrooms, water fountain • Trails: **Linville Falls Trail,** 0.9 mile (Moderate); **Linville Gorge Trail,** 0.8 mile (Strenuous); **Duggers Creek Trail,** 0.3 mile (Easy); Riverbend Overlook Trail, 0.1 mile (Easy); Linville River Bridge Trail, 0.2 mile (Easy) • Falls: Lower Linville Falls, total drop 60 feet; upper falls, total drop 12 feet.

316.5 Linville River Parking Area, west (Hike 34, Option 2) • Elevation: 3,250 ft. (991m)

316.5 Linville Falls Picnic Area, west • Facilities: 100 sites, 3 comfort stations.

316.6 Linville River Bridge • Elevation: 3,257 ft. (993m) • Largest stone structure on Parkway.

317.5 US 221 crossing, underpass (access west, north of bridge) (Hike 35) • Right: to Newland, NC, 11 miles; left to Linville Falls, NC, 1 mile and turn left again for Linville Gorge trails; to Marion, NC, 24 miles.

318.4 North Toe Valley Overlook, west • Elevation: 3,540 ft. (1,079m).

319.8 Humpback Mountain Viaduct.

320.8 Chestoa View Parking Area, east (Hike 36) • Elevation: 4,090 ft. (1,247m) • Facilities: 3 picnic tables. • Trail: **Chestoa View Trail,** 0.8 mile (Moderately easy).

323.0 Bear Den Overlook, east • Elevation: 3,359 ft. (1,024m).

325.9 Heffner Gap Overlook, east • Elevation: 3,067 ft. (935m) • Signboard: apple trees.

326.0 NC SR crossing, west and east.

327.3 North Cove Overlook, east • Elevation: 2,815 ft. (858m) • Wayside panel: crest of the Blue Ridge Highway.

327.5 McKinney Gap • Elevation: 2,790 ft. (850m).

327.5 Public road crossing, underpass (access west, south of crossing; Altapass Road) • Right to Spruce Pine, NC, 5 miles; left to US 221, 10 miles.

328.6 The Loops Overlook, east • Elevation: 2,980 ft. (908m) • Wayside panel: Carolina, Clinchfield, and Ohio Railway (at Loops).

329.5 Swafford Gap • Elevation: 2,852 ft. (869m).

329.5 NC 1113 crossing.

329.8 Table Rock Overlook, east • Elevation: 2,870 ft. (875m).

330.9 Gillespie Gap • Elevation: 2,819 ft. (859m).

330.9   NC 226 crossing, underpass (access west, north of crossing) • Right to Spruce Pine, NC, 4 miles; left to NC 226A; to Little Switzerland, NC, 4 miles; to Marion, NC, 14 miles.

330.9   Minerals Museum • Facilities: three-sided interpretive/informational display • Open year-round; Mitchell County Chamber of Commerce.

330.9   Gillespie Gap Maintenance Area • Facilities: ranger and maintenance offices.

332.6   Lynn Gap (Dale Road) • Elevation: 3,109 ft. (948m).

333.4   Little Switzerland Tunnel • Length: 542 feet • Min height: 14 feet, 4 inches.

333.9   Public road crossing, underpass (access east, north of crossing) • Elevation: 3,490 ft. (1,064m) • Left to NC 226A; Little Switzerland, NC.

335.4   Bearwallow Gap • Elevation: 3,490 ft. (1,064m).

336.3   Gooch Gap • Elevation: 3,360 ft. (1,024m).

336.3   Public road crossing (access east; Wild Acres Road).

336.8   Wildacres Tunnel • Length: 330 feet • Min height: 13 feet, 1 inch.

337.2   Deer Lick Gap Overlook, west • Elevation: 3,452 ft. (1,052m) • Facilities: 2 picnic tables • Wayside panel: groundhogs.

338.8   Three Knobs Overlook, west • Elevation: 3,875 ft. (1,181m).

339.5   Crabtree Meadows Recreation Area (Hike 37) • Facilities: restaurant, gift shop/camp store • Campground: 71 tent and small RV sites, 22 large RV sites, 3 comfort stations, 300-person capacity amphitheater • Trails: **Crabtree Falls Loop Trail,** 2.5 miles (Strenuous) • Crabtree Falls, total drop 90 feet.

340.2   Picnic area, east • Facilities: 82 sites, 1 comfort station.

342.1   Public road crossing (Victor Road access).

342.2   Black Mountains Overlook, west • Elevation: 3,892 ft. (1186m) • Wayside panel: Black Mountain Range.

344.1   Buck Creek Gap Overlook, east • Elevation: 3,355 ft. (1023m) • Trail: Woods Mountain Trail, 2.0 miles.

344.1   NC 80 crossing, underpass (access east, south of crossing) (Hike 38, Option 1) • Right to Marion, NC, 16 miles; left to Burnsville, NC, 17 miles.

344.5   Twin Tunnel (north) • Length: 300 feet • Min height: 16 feet.

344.7   Twin Tunnel (south) • Length: 401 feet • Min height: 14 feet, 7 inches.

345.3   Singecat Ridge Overlook, east • Elevation: 3,406 ft. (1,038m).) • Trail: access to Mountains-to-Sea Trail.

347.6   Big Laurel Gap • Elevation: 4,048 ft. (1,234m).

347.6   USFS road crossing • Right to Black Mountain Campground and Mount Mitchell Trail; left to Curtis Creek Road.

347.9   Hewat Overlook, west • Elevation: 4,175 ft. (1,272m).

348.8   Curtis Valley Overlook, east • Elevation: 4,460 (1,359m).

349.0   Rough Ridge Tunnel • Length: 150 feet • Min height: 13 feet, 9 inches.

349.2   Licklog Ridge Overlook, east • Elevation: 4,602 ft. (1,403m).

349.9   Mount Mitchell Overlook, west • Elevation: 4,825 ft. (1,471m) • View: Mount Mitchell (elevation 6,684 ft.).

350.4 **Green Knob Overlook, east** • Elevation: 4,761 ft. (1,451m) • **Green Knob Trail/Lost Cove Ridge Trail,** 1.0 mile to tower from Parkway; 5.2 miles from Black Mountain Campground (Moderate). On the way toward Mount Mitchell from the north, you'll notice the fire tower atop Green Knob, at 4,950 feet. If you want to savor the view of the East's highest summit from there, leave the Green Knob Overlook heading south on the trail then cross the Parkway. Following white blazes, the trail rises to a left that brings you to the tower at 0.5 mile (1.0-mile round-trip). The route continues past the tower another 2.6 miles to Black Mountain Campground—a best-kept secret camping spot with easy Parkway access. To reach the campground, or start from the lower trailhead, go south and turn right at Milepost 351.9 onto FSR 472. The campground is 5 miles from the turn.

351.9 Deep Gap • Elevation: 4,284 ft. (1,306m) • Trail: Deep Gap Trail, 0.2 mile.

351.9 FSR 472 access, west • USFS Black Mountain Campground (54 sites, showers, flush toilets; 828-675-5616) and Mount Mitchell Trail, 5 miles; NC 80, 8 miles.

352.4 No-name parking, west • Elevation: 4,500 ft. (1,372m).

354.8 Toe River Gap • Elevation: 5,158 ft. (1,572m).

355.3 Black Mountain Gap • Elevation: 5,160 ft. (1,573m).

355.3 Ridge Junction Overlook, west • Elevation: 5,160 ft. (1,573m).

355.3 **NC 128 access, west (Hike 38, Options 2 and 3)** • To Mount Mitchell, 4.8 miles.

355.3 Enter Asheville Watershed.

358.5 Highest point on Parkway north of Asheville • Elevation: 5,676.5 ft. (1,730m).

359.8 **Balsam Gap Parking Area,** west • Elevation: 5,317 ft. (1,621m) • Trails: Big Butt Trail—leads north (left side of parking). Good day hikes to superb views. Mountains-to-Sea Trail leaves right—views of Craggy Mountains and Mount Mitchell (Strenuous). For rare close-in views of the Mitchell Range, take the Big Butt Trail left out of the parking area and follow the prominent ridge northwest. The trail eventually plummets down to NC 197, but the first 2.4 miles lead to campsites and especially great views at 1.6 miles, and to Little Butt at 2.4 miles. Between Balsam Gap and NC 128 (trailhead is 0.6 mile from the Parkway at Milepost 355.3), the Mountains-to-Sea Trail traverses a 5.0-mile stretch along the Parkway through the spectacular evergreen forests that clothe the intersection where the Black and Craggy Mountains collide. For a highly recommended and scenic day hike, climb 3.6 miles across the flank of Blackstock Knob to great views at Promontory Rock and return for a hike of about 7.0 miles. In Balsam Gap, the Big Butt Trail goes left and a forest road leaves straight ahead. Follow the white circles out of the parking area uphill and to the right.

361.1 Cotton Tree Gap • Elevation: 5,141 ft. (1,567m).

361.2 Glassmine Falls Overlook, east • Elevation: 5,200 ft. (1,585m) • View: Glassmine Falls (800 feet high) • Trails: **Glassmine Falls Trail,** 0.1 mile (Easy); Mountains-to-Sea Trail access. This 300-foot leg-stretcher offers a nice view across the headwaters of the Asheville Watershed to where Glassmine Falls feeds the North Fork of the Swannanoa River. The "waterfall" requires a good rain to be very visible on its drop to the vicinity of an old mica mine. The surrounding area, especially west of the Parkway near Spruce Pine, has historically been a major mining region. Mica, a prominent area mineral, was once called isinglass—hence the name of the falls. The Blackstock Knob area above the falls is explored by two trails from nearby Balsam Gap.

363.4 Bullhead Gap • Elevation: 5,592 ft. (1,704m).

363.4 Graybeard Mountain Overlook, east (Hike 39) • Elevation: 5,592 ft. (1,704m) • Trails: **Douglas Fall Trail;** Mountains-to-Sea Trail crossing • View: Mountains (elevation 5,365 ft.) • Signboard: Asheville Watershed (20,000 acres).

364.1 Craggy Dome Overlook, west (Hike 40, Option 1) • Elevation: 5,640 ft. (1,719m) • Trail: **Craggy Pinnacle Trail,** 0.7 mile (Moderate) • Wayside panel: Catawba rhododendron, rare plants, heath balds.

364.4 Craggy Pinnacle Tunnel • Length: 245 feet • Min height: 14 feet, 1 inch.

364.5 Craggy Gardens Visitor Center and Parking Area, west (Hike 40, Option 2) • Elevation: 5,497 ft. (1,675m) • Trail: **Craggy Gardens Self-Guiding Trail,** 0.8 mile (Moderate) • Signboard: Craggy Gardens Trail.

From Craggy Pinnacle Trail, the Parkway snakes across the Craggy Mountains with Mount Mitchell's spruce-fir forests rising dark in the distance.

365.5 Craggy Flats Tunnel • Length: 400 feet • Min height: 14 feet, 4 inches.

367.6 Bee Tree Gap • Elevation: 4,900 ft. (1,493m).

367.6 Craggy Gardens Picnic Area (Bear Pen Gap) • Elevation: 5,220 ft. (1,591m) • Facilities: 86 sites, 2 comfort stations, 3 water fountains, 2 barrier-free picnic sites, 1 comfort station semi–wheelchair accessible • Trail: Mountains-to-Sea Trail access.

368.2 Potato Field Gap • Elevation: 4,600 ft. (1,402m).

370.3 Leave Asheville Watershed.

372.1 Lane Pinnacle Overlook, east • Elevation: 3,890 ft. (1,186m).

373.8 Bull Creek Valley Overlook, east • Elevation: 3,483 ft. (1,062m) • Sign: the last buffalo seen in this area.

374.4 Tanbark Ridge Tunnel • Length: 780 feet • Min height: 14 feet, 1 inch • Trail: Mountains-to-Sea Trail access.

375.2 Bull Gap • Elevation: 3,107 ft. (947m).

375.6 NC 694 access, west (Ox Creek Road/Scenic Elk Mountain Highway) • Trail: Mountains-to-Sea Trail access; right to Weaverville, NC, 8 miles.

376.7 Tanbark Ridge Overlook, east • Elevation: 3,175 ft. (968m).

377.4 Craven Gap • Elevation: 3,132 ft. (955m) • Trail: Mountains-to-Sea Trail crossing.

377.4 NC 694 access, west (Town Mountain Road/Webb Cove Road) • Right to Asheville, NC, 7 miles.

380.0 Haw Creek Valley Overlook, west • Elevation: 2,720 ft. (829m).

381.0 Mountains-to-Sea Trail access.

382.0 Folk Art Center • Facilities: visitor information center, craft center, craft demonstrations, restrooms, public telephone • Trail: Mountains-to-Sea Trail access at both ends of parking lot.

382.3 Asheville District Maintenance Area, east • Facilities: communications center, Asheville district offices.

382.5 US 70 crossing, underpass (access west and east) • Right to Asheville, NC; left to Black Mountain, NC, 9 miles.

383.6 Swannanoa River • Elevation: 2,040 ft. (622m).

383.6 I-40 crossing, underpass (no access).

384.4 Parkway Visitor Center • Facilities: the Parkway's newest, most complete visitor information center, extensive exhibits, travel counseling, book/gift shop, restrooms, public telephone • Trail: Mountains-to-Sea Trail access from parking lot.

384.7 US 74 crossing, underpass (access west and east) • West to Asheville, NC, 5 miles; I-40, 0.25 mile; east to Chimney Rock, NC, 20 miles • Trails: Mountains-to-Sea Trail access at crossing; **Asheville Urban Trail,** downtown.

  The Asheville Urban Trail is a nice amble through Asheville's vibrant downtown and the perfect way to enjoy a surprising mountain city that is second only to Miami Beach as the South's greatest concentration of art deco architecture. With thirty sculptures and exhibits, this "museum without walls" is packed with rich historical insight. Highlights include the Grove Arcade, a classic neo-Gothic city market. The Saint Lawrence Basilica illustrates how artisans from all over the world were lured to Asheville in the late nineteenth century by the building of Vanderbilt's Biltmore Estate, still the United States' largest private home. Italian-born engineer Rafael Guastavino was struck by the mountain setting and stayed. The basilica he created has North America's largest freestanding elliptical dome. Dancers and musicians at another stop commemorate the 1927 launch of the nation's oldest mountain music event, the Mountain Dance and Folk Festival.

The Urban Trail's markers change by district; angels represent the neighborhood of *Look Homeward, Angel* author Thomas Wolfe. The book's setting— his mother's real-life boardinghouse—is here, and the Thomas Wolfe Memorial Visitor Center wonderfully interprets the man who literally couldn't go home again after parodying his hometown's provinciality. Another exhibit treats O. Henry, and an arbor-sculpted bench honors Elizabeth Blackwell, the country's first female physician, who started her medical training while an Asheville schoolteacher. Urban Trail guide brochures are available all over town. Factor in the great restaurants and diversity of craft and fine art shops along the way, and an afternoon (or longer) on Asheville's Urban Trail is a highlight of any Parkway trip.

388.8   US 25 crossing, underpass (access east and west) • Right to Asheville, NC, 5 miles; left to Hendersonville, NC, 17 miles • Trail: Mountains-to-Sea Trail access.

392.1   Mountains-to-Sea Trail crossing.

393.5   French Broad River • Elevation: 2,000 ft. (610m).

393.6   NC 191 crossing, underpass • Ramp on south side of bridge to NC 191; left on NC 191 to Asheville, NC, 9 miles; right to Hendersonville, NC, 18 miles.

393.6   North Carolina Arboretum; take first left on ramp before NC 191. Mountains-to-Sea Trail leaves left from ramp before arboretum.

This is a must-see facility for gardeners or anyone seriously interested in the flora of the Southern Appalachians. The 426-acre arboretum includes 36 acres of impressively landscaped gardens. From the Visitor Education Center and its impressive entrance plaza gardens, the Grand Garden Promenade leads to a satellite garden area. Extensive exhibits in the Visitor Education Center include an internationally renowned bonsai collection. Recent improvements have been fast and furious and more are expected.

There are miles of hiking and biking trails, a few of which continue into the adjoining Bent Creek Experimental Forest, one of the nation's earliest forest research areas. Those trails and the arboretum are increasingly popular with locals as Asheville's premier place for walking, running, and mountain biking.

North Carolina Arboretum (Milepost 393.6) is a worthwhile side trip.

The 0.7-mile Natural Garden Trail makes a nice walk if you're interested primarily in the Visitor Education Center and gardens. Start from trailheads in the arboretum's major parking area, at the end of the Grand Garden Promenade, or adjacent to the Visitor Education Center in a garden called Plants of Promise. This foot travel–only trail overlooks Bent Creek and the National Native Azalea Repository. The Carolina Mountain Trail, 1.6 miles, explores three types of forest between the Visitor Education Center, the greenhouse, and Bent Creek Road.

A "recreation area" trailhead is located just inside the park on the left. Hikers and mountain bikers can take the 3.4-mile gravel and natural-surface road-grade loop of the Hard Times Road, Owl Ridge Trail, Rocky Cove Road, Bent Creek Road, and a connector trail back to the parking area. A short side trail explores the National Native Azalea Repository. Near the repository, Running Cedar Road connects Bent Creek Road and this longer loop with the core area. Closer to the recreation area trailhead, the Wesley Branch Trail also links the longer loop with the Natural Garden Trail and the core area. Just outside the arboretum entrance, the combined Mountains-to-Sea Trail and Shut-In Trail leaves the roadside bound for the Mount Pisgah area of the Parkway.

The latest trail map should be available at the recreation area trailhead or when you pay the parking fee. Consider supporting the arboretum. Visitation is soaring, and the world-class facility is coming into its own. Members

of the arboretum have unlimited access. For more information visit www
.ncarboretum.org.

393.8 French Broad Overlook, east • Elevation: 2,100 ft. (640m) • Trail: **Start of Shut-In Trail,** 16.3 miles (Strenuous, to Mount Pisgah) • Wayside panel: the French Broad River.

395.1 Glenn Gap • Elevation: 2,495 ft. (760m).

396.4 Walnut Cove Overlook, east • Elevation: 2,920 ft. (890m) • Trail: access to Shut-In Trail (Mountains-to-Sea Trail to Milepost 407.6).

396.8 Reynolds Gap • Elevation: 2,865 ft. (873m).

397.1 Grassy Knob Tunnel • Length: 770 feet • Min height: 13 feet, 7 inches.

397.3 Sleepy Gap • Elevation: 2,930 ft. (893m).

397.3 Sleepy Gap Overlook, west • Elevation: 2,930 ft. (893m) • Facilities: 2 picnic tables • Trails: Grassy Knob Trail, 0.9-mile connector to USFS trails in Bent Creek Experimental Forest; access to Shut-In Trail, .09 mile to Milepost 398.3.

398.3 Chestnut Cove Overlook, east • Elevation: 3,035 ft. (925m) • Facilities: 2 picnic tables • Trail: access to Shut-In Trail, 2.8 miles to Milepost 400.3.

399.1 Pine Mountain Tunnel • Length: 1,434 feet (longest tunnel on Parkway) • Min height: 14 feet, 2 inches.

399.7 Bad Fork Valley Overlook, east • Elevation: 3,350 ft. (1,021m).

400.3 Bent Creek Gap • Elevation: 3,270 ft. (997m) • Trail: access to Shut-In Trail, 1.9 miles to Milepost 401.7.

400.3 USFS road crossing, underpass (access east; gated).

400.9 Ferrin Knob Tunnel No. 1 • Length: 561 feet • Min height: 14 feet, 2 inches.

401.1 Wash Creek Valley Overlook, east • Elevation: 3,435 ft. (1,047m).

401.3 Ferrin Knob Tunnel No. 2 • Length: 421 feet • Min height: 14 feet.

401.5 Ferrin Knob Tunnel No. 3 • Length: 375 feet • Min height: 13 feet, 9 inches.

401.7 Beaver Dam Gap • Elevation: 3,270 ft. (1,088m).

401.7 Beaver Dam Gap Overlook, east • Elevation: 3,570 ft. (1,088m) • Facilities: picnic table • Trail: access to Shut-In Trail, 0.9 mile to Milepost 402.6.

402.6 Stony Bald Overlook, east • Elevation: 3,750 ft. (1,143m) • Trail: access to Shut-In Trail, 1.2 miles to Milepost 403.6.

403.0 Young Pisgah Ridge Tunnel • Length: 412 feet • Min height: 14 feet, 6 inches.

403.6 Big Ridge Overlook, east • Elevation: 3,820 ft. (1,164m) • Trail: access to Shut-In Trail, 1.1 miles to Milepost 404.5.

404.0 Fork Mountain Tunnel • Length: 389 feet • Min height: 14 feet.

404.2 Hominy Valley Overlook, west • Elevation: 3,980 ft. (1,213m).

404.5 Mills River Valley Overlook, east • Elevation: 4,085 ft. (1,245m) • Trail: access to Shut-In Trail, 1.2 miles to Milepost 405.5.

405.5 Elk Pasture Gap • Elevation: 4,235 ft. (1,291m) • Trail: access to Shut-In Trail, 1.9 miles to Milepost 407.6.

405.5 NC 151 access, west • To Candler, NC, 15 miles.

406.9 Little Pisgah Tunnel • Length: 576 feet • Min height: 13 feet, 10 inches.

407.3 Buck Spring Tunnel • Length: 462 feet • Min height: 13 feet, 8 inches.

407.6 **Mount Pisgah Parking Area, east (Hike 41, Option 1)** • Elevation: 4,995 ft. (1,522m) • Trails: **Mount Pisgah Trail,** 1.3 miles (Strenuous); access to Shut-In Trail and Mountains-to-Sea Trail • Signboard: Mount Pisgah.

407.7 **Buck Spring Gap Overlook, east (Hike 41, Option 3)** • Elevation: 4,980 ft. (1,518m) • Trails: access to Mountains-to-Sea Trail; **Buck Spring Trail,** 1.1 miles (Moderate).

407.8 Mount Pisgah Picnic Area, west • Facilities: 50 sites, bear-proof trash cans, restrooms • Trail: access to Mount Pisgah Trail.

408.3 No-name parking, west.

408.4 Flat Laurel Gap • Elevation: 4,980 ft. (1,518m).

408.6 **Pisgah Inn, east (Hike 41, Option 3)** • Facilities: lodging (50 rooms/1 suite), restaurant and gift shop, camp store, public telephones • Trails: access to Buck Spring and Mountains-to-Sea Trails.

408.8 **Mount Pisgah Campground, west (Hike 41, Option 2)** • Facilities: 70 tent sites, 70 trailer sites, 100-seat amphitheater, public telephone, comfort stations, dump station • Trails: access to **Frying Pan Mountain Trail** (Strenuous); access to Mountains-to-Sea Trail.

409.3 Funnel Top Overlook, east • Elevation: 4,925 ft. (1,501m).

409.6 Frying Pan Gap • Elevation: 4,931 ft. (1,503m) • Trail: access to Frying Pan Mountain Trail, west.

409.6 USFS road access, west (to fire tower).

410.1 Frying Pan Tunnel • Length: 577 feet • Min height: 13 feet, 8 inches.

410.3 The Pink Beds Overlook, east • Elevation: 4,822 ft. (1,470m).

411.0 The Cradle of Forestry Overlook, east • Elevation: 4,710 ft. (1,436m) • Facilities: trash can • Wayside panel: Cradle of Forestry.

411.8 Wagon Road Gap • Elevation: 4,535 ft. (1,382m).

411.8 **US 276 crossing, underpass (access east, north of bridge) (Hike 41, Option 3; Hike 43, Option 1)** • USFS Forest Heritage Scenic Byway • Right to Waynesville, NC, 22 miles; left to Cradle of Forestry, 4 miles; Brevard, NC, 18 miles.

Cradle of Forestry (Milepost 411.8) • Total distance: 2.3 miles (Easy).

The 6,500-acre Cradle of Forestry is a must-see stop for Parkway visitors. The nation's first school of forestry grew out of George Vanderbilt's efforts to manage his massive holdings in western North Carolina in the late 1800s.

To manage his lands, in 1889 Vanderbilt hired Gifford Pinchot, a forester and conservationist. In 1895 he was succeeded by Dr. Carl Schenck, a German forester. Schenck's expertise drew budding foresters to the estate, and in 1898 he started the United States' first forestry school. A decade later, North Carolinians were among the first to see the need to protect the nation's forests from over-logging, forest fires, and erosion. The state supported the adoption of the Weeks

Act in 1911, the legislation that created the national forests. The first chief of the Forest Service was Pinchot, Vanderbilt's first forester. After Vanderbilt's death, his lands were among the earliest parcels of the new national forests.

Encountering the history of the forests that surround the Parkway is fun at "the Plymouth Rock of Forestry." State-of-the-art exhibits in the Forest Discovery Center include a jostling simulator that replicates a ride on a firefighting helicopter. The entire facility is a cooperative effort between the Forest Service and the Cradle of Forestry Interpretive Association.

The easy, 1.0-mile **Biltmore Campus Trail** explores the early facility. Students lived and learned in the rustic assortment of mountain cabins and early buildings preserved here. The school closed in 1913, victim to a proliferation of university forestry programs. The 1.3-mile Forest Festival Trail is a masterpiece of interpretation on how and why the science of forestry is practiced.

Looking Glass Rock (Milepost 411.8) • Total distance: 6.2 miles (Strenuous). Go east from the Parkway on US 276. Pass Sliding Rock and Looking Glass Falls to take a right onto FSR 475, the Davidson River Road. The trailhead is on the right 0.4 mile from the turn.

The hike to 3,960 feet atop this spectacular dome of rock is probably the most popular in the entire Pisgah Ranger District. The yellow-blazed trail has been significantly hardened to withstand all the use, and it's important to stay on the trail to avoid damage to the mountain as well as to limit impact on the peregrine falcons that are partial to its cliffs and crags. (Rock climbing is restricted on certain routes during the January to August breeding season.) The trail is steep and rugged, with switchback after switchback, but the view from the top is awesome.

411.9 Cold Mountain Overlook, west • Elevation: 4,542 ft. (1,384m).

412.2 Wagon Road Gap Parking Area, east • Elevation: 4,550 ft. (1,387m) • Facilities: picnic table.

412.5 Pigeon Gap • Elevation: 4,520 ft. (1,378m) • Trail: access to Mountains-to-Sea Trail.

413.2 Pounding Mill Overlook, east • Elevation: 4,700 ft. (1,433m).

414.5 Bennett Gap • Elevation: 4,404 ft. (1,342m) • Trail: access to Mountains-to-Sea Trail.

414.9 Bennett Cove • Elevation: 4,525 ft. (1,379m).

415.6 Tunnel Gap • Elevation: 4,325 ft. (1,318m) • Trail: access to Mountains-to-Sea Trail.

415.7 Cherry Cove Overlook, east • Elevation: 4,327 ft. (1,319m) • Wayside panel: monarch butterfly migration.

416.3 Log Hollow Overlook, east • Elevation: 4,445 ft. (1,355m) • Facilities: picnic table.

416.6 Log Hollow Gap • Elevation: 4,488 ft. (1,368m).

416.8 Bridges Camp Gap • Elevation: 4,450 ft. (1,356m) • Trail: East Fork Trail access, west.

417.0 Looking Glass Rock Overlook, east • Elevation: 4,492 ft. (1,369m) • Trail: access spur to Mountains-to-Sea Trail • Wayside panel: Looking Glass Rock.

417.8 Seniard Gap • Elevation: 4,775 ft. (1,455m).

418.3 East Fork Overlook, west • Elevation: 4,995 ft. (1,522m).

418.8 Graveyard Fields Overlook, west (Hike 42 and Hike 43, Option 2) • Elevation: 5,120 ft. (1,561m) • Trail: **Graveyard Fields Loop Trail,** 2.0 miles (Moderate); access to Mountains-to-Sea Trail. • Wayside panel: history of the name "Graveyard Fields."

Art Loeb Trail on Black Balsam Knob is one of many hikes near Shining Rock Wilderness (Milepost 420.2).

419.4 John Rock Overlook, east • Elevation: 5,330 ft. (1,625m) • Facilities: 2 picnic tables • Trail: **John Rock Trail,** 0.1 mile (Easy). John Rock Overlook is a peephole view from a ledge on the edge of Pisgah Ridge and its drop of more than 2,000 vertical feet. A longer bootleg trail heads left past the view made by people assuming there must be a better view farther on. There isn't. Looking Glass Rock can be seen; to its right and behind is John Rock.

420.2 Balsam Spring Gap • Elevation: 5,550 ft. (1,692m).

420.2 FSR 816 access, west • Entrance to Shining Rock Wilderness, 1.3 miles to parking area • Facilities: modern privies only • Trails: access to Art Loeb Trail and Shining Rock Wilderness Trail System.

421.2 Art Loeb Trail crossing.

421.7 Fetterbush Overlook, east • Elevation: 5,494 ft. (1,675m) • Facilities: picnic table.

422.1 Devil's Courthouse Tunnel • Length: 665 feet • Min height: 14 feet, 2 inches.

422.4 Devil's Courthouse Overlook, east (Hike 44) • Elevation: 5,462 ft. (1,665m) • Facilities: picnic table • Trail: **Devil's Courthouse Trail,** 1.0 mile (Strenuous); access to Mountains-to-Sea Trail • D.A.R. Memorial Plaque • Wayside panel: superstitions of Devil's Courthouse.

422.8 Mount Hardy Overlook, west • Elevation: 5,415 ft. (1,650m) • Facilities: picnic table.

423.2 Beech Gap • Elevation: 5,340 ft. (1,628m).

423.2 NC 215 crossing, underpass (access west, south of bridge) **(Hike 43, Option 3)** • USFS Forest Heritage Scenic Byway • Right to Rosman, NC, 18 miles; left to Canton, NC, 24 miles.

423.5 Courthouse Valley Overlook, east • Elevation: 5,362 ft. (1,634m) • Facilities: 2 picnic tables.

424.2 Mount Hardy Gap • Elevation: 5,490 ft. (1,673m).

424.4 Herrin Knob Parking, east • Elevation: 5,510 ft. (1,679m).

424.8 Wolf Mountain Overlook, east • Elevation: 5,500 ft. (1,676m).

425.3 Wolf Bald.

425.4 Rough Butt Bald Overlook, east • Elevation: 5,300 ft. (1,615m) • Trail: access to Mountains-to-Sea Trail.

425.5 Buckeye Gap • Elevation: 5,377 ft. (1,639m).

426.5 Haywood Gap • Elevation: 5,225 ft. (1,593m) • Trail: Mountains-to-Sea Trail crossing.

427.1 Rough Butt Bald.

427.6 Bear Pen Gap Parking Area, east • Elevation: 5,560 ft. (1,695m) • Trail: access Mountains-to-Sea Trail.

427.8 Spot Knob Overlook, west • Elevation: 5,652 ft. (1,723m) • Facilities: picnic table.

428.0 Caney Fork Overlook, east • Elevation: 5,650 ft. (1,722m).

428.3 Little Bear Pen Gap • Elevation: 5,600 ft. (1,707m).

A bench and this atmospheric old sign mark the Richland Balsam summit.

428.5 Beartrap Gap Overlook, west • Elevation: 5,580 ft. (1,701m) • Facilities: picnic table • Wayside panel: Parkway bears.

429.1 Reinhart Gap • Elevation: 5,455 ft. (1,663m).

430.0 Reinhart Knob.

430.4 Beartrail Ridge Parking Area, east • Elevation: 5,872 ft. (1,790m) • Facilities: picnic table.

430.7 Cowee Mountain Overlook, east • Elevation: 5,950 ft. (1,817m).

431.0 Haywood Jackson Overlook, west (Hike 45) • Elevation: 6,020 ft. (1,835m) • Trail: **Richland Balsam Self-Guiding Trail,** 1.4 miles (Moderate) • Facilities: picnic table.

431.4 Richland Balsam Overlook, east • Elevation: 6,047 ft. (1,843m)—highest point on motor road • Wayside panel: forest decline.

432.7 Lone Bald Overlook, east • Elevation: 5,635 ft. (1,718m).

433.3 Roy Taylor Forest Overlook, east • Elevation: 5,580 ft. (1,701m) • Facilities: pedestrian overlook and exhibit 100 feet down the trail.

433.4 Locust Gap • Elevation: 5,575 ft. (1,699m).

434.8 Racking Horse Gap • Elevation: 5,400 ft. (1,646m).

435.3 Doubletop Mountain Overlook, east • Elevation: 5,365 ft. (1,635m) • Facilities: picnic table • Trail: access to Mountains-to-Sea Trail.

435.5 Licklog Gap • Elevation: 5,135 (1,565m).

435.7 Licklog Gap Overlook, west • Elevation: 5,135 ft. (1,403m) • Facilities: picnic table.

436.8 Grassy Ridge Mine Overlook, east • Elevation: 5,250 ft. (1,600m) • Facilities: picnic table • Trail: access to Mountains-to-Sea Trail.

437.0 Deep Gap • Elevation: 5,260 ft. (1,603m).

438.9 Steestachee Bald Overlook, west • Elevation: 4,780 ft. (1,457m).

439.4 Cove Field Ridge Overlook, west • Elevation: 4,620 ft. (1,408m).

439.7 Pinnacle Ridge Tunnel • Elevation: 813 feet • Min height: 13 feet, 10 inches.

440.0 Saunook Overlook, west • Elevation: 4,375 ft. (1,333m).

440.9 Waynesville Overlook, west • Elevation: 4,110 ft. (1,253m) • Facilities: picnic table.

441.4 Standing Rock Overlook, west • Elevation: 3,915 ft. (1,193m) • Facilities: picnic table.

441.9 Rabb Knob Overlook, west • Elevation: 3,725 ft. (1,135m) • Facilities: picnic table • Wayside panel: Rutherford's expedition.

442.2 Balsam Gap Overlook, west • Elevation: 3,630 ft. (1,106m)

443.1 Balsam Gap • Elevation: 3,370 ft. (1,027m).

443.1 US 74/23 crossing, underpass (access west, south of crossing) • West to Sylva, NC, 12 miles; east to Waynesville, NC, 8 miles.

444.6 The Orchards Overlook, west • Elevation: 3,810 ft. (1,161m) • Facilities: 2 picnic tables.

445.2 Mount Lynn Lowry Overlook, east • Elevation: 4,000 ft. (1,219m) • Facilities: picnic table.

446.0 Woodfin Valley Overlook, east • Elevation: 4,120 ft. (1,382m).

446.7 Woodfin Cascades Overlook, east • Elevation: 4,535 ft. (1,382m).

448.1 Wesner Bald Overlook, east • Elevation: 4,912 ft. (1,497m).

448.5 Scott Creek Overlook, east • Elevation: 5,050 ft. (1,539m).

449.0 Fork Ridge Overlook, east • Elevation: 5,280 ft. (1,609m).

450.2 Yellow Face Overlook, east • Elevation: 5,610 ft. (1,710m).

451.2 Browning Knob Overlook, west • Plaque: honoring R. Getty Browning (engineer).

451.2 Waterrock Knob Overlook, west (Hike 46) • Elevation: 5,718 ft. (1,723m) • Facilities: comfort station, visitor information and sales center (May through October) • Trail: **Waterrock Knob Trail,** 1.2 miles (moderate to strenuous) • Wayside panels: North Carolina horizons.

452.1 Cranberry Ridge Overlook, east • Elevation: 5,475 ft. (1,669m).

452.3 Woolyback Overlook, east • Elevation: 5,425 ft. (1,652m).

453.4 Hornbuckle Valley Overlook, east • Elevation: 5,105 ft. (1,556m).

454.4 Thunder Struck Ridge Overlook, east • Elevation: 4,780 ft. (1,457m).

455.1 Fed Cove Overlook, east • Elevation: 4,550 ft. (1,387m).

455.5 Soco Gap Overlook, east • Elevation: 4,570 ft. (1,393m) • Facilities: water fountain; toilets during winter.

455.7 Soco Gap • Elevation: 4,340 ft. (1,323m).

455.7 US 19 crossing, underpass (access west and east) • East to Maggie Valley, NC, 4 miles; west to Cherokee, NC, 12 miles.

456.2 Jonathan Creek Overlook, west • Elevation: 4,460 ft. (1,359m) • Facilities: 2 picnic tables.

457.6 Docks Gap • Elevation: 4,930 ft. (1,503m).

457.7 Entering Cherokee Indian Reservation.

457.9 Plott Balsam Overlook, east • Elevation: 5,020 ft. (1,530m) • Signboard: Plott Balsam Mountains.

458.2 Wolf Laurel Gap • Elevation: 5,100 ft. (1,554m).

458.2 Heintooga Spur Road

0.1 Indian Service Road • Left to Big Witch Gap, Hyatt Cove; right to US 19.

0.5 Plott Ridge.

0.9 Mollie Gap • Elevation: 5,352 ft. (1,631m). • Public road access, east (Indian Road) • To Soco Bald.

1.3 Mile High Overlook, east • Elevation: 5,250 ft. (1,600m) • Signboard: Great Smoky Mountains National Park.

1.4 Maggie Valley Overlook, west • Elevation: 5,220 ft. (1,591m).

2.3 Lake Junaluska Overlook, west • Elevation: 5,034 ft. (1,534m).

3.3 Horsetrough Ridge parking, east • Elevation: 4,540 ft. (1384m).

3.4 Horsetrough Ridge parking, west • Elevation: 4,540 ft. (1384m).

3.6 Black Camp Gap Parking Area, west • Elevation: 4,496 ft. (1370m) • Trail: Paved walkway (100 yards) to historic Masonic marker • Facilities: picnic table. • Boundary, Great Smoky Mountains National Park.

3.9 Overlook, east.

4.8 Overlook, east.

6.0 Polls Gap.

6.2 Overlook, east.

8.4 Balsam Mountain Campground, east • Elevation: 5,340 ft. (1628m) • Facilities: 40 campsites, 100-person capacity campground circle.

8.9 Heintooga Ridge Picnic Area • Facilities: 37 sites.

9.0 Parking area—end of paved road • One-way motor nature road, open May 15 to October 15. For autos and light trucks; *no trailers)*.

458.8 Lickstone Ridge Tunnel • Length: 402 feet • Min height: 11 feet, 1 inch.

458.9 Lickstone Overlook, east • Elevation: 5,150 ft. (1,570m) • Signboard: Qualla Indian Reservation.

459.3 Bunches Bald Tunnel • Length: 255 feet • Min height: 10 feet, 6 inches.

459.5 Bunches Bald Overlook, east • Elevation: 4,925 ft. (1,501m).

459.7 Bunches Gap • Elevation: 4,850 ft. (1,478m).

460.8 Jenkins Ridge Overlook, east • Elevation: 4,445 ft. (1,355m).

461.2 Big Witch Tunnel • Length: 348 feet • Min height: 11 feet, 3 inches.

461.6 Big Witch Gap • Elevation: 4,160 ft. (1,268m).

461.9 Big Witch Overlook, west • Elevation: 4,150 ft. (1,265m) • Facilities: 2 picnic tables.

462.3 Barnett Fire Tower Road access, east.

463.9 Thomas Divide Overlook, west • Elevation: 3,735 ft. (1,138m) • Facilities: picnic table.

465.6 Rattlesnake Mountain Tunnel • Length: 395 feet • Min height: 14 feet, 5 inches.

466.2 Sherrill Cove Tunnel • Length: 550 feet • Min height: 14 feet, 4 inches.

467.4 Ballhoot Scar Overlook, west • Elevation: 2,550 ft. (777m).

467.9 Raven Fork Overlook, west • Elevation: 2,400 ft. (631m).

468.4 Oconaluftee Overlook, west • Elevation: 2,200 ft. (671m).

468.9 Parkway interpretive display.

469.1 US 441 T-junction • Left to Cherokee, NC, 2 miles; right to Great Smoky Mountains National Park Oconaluftee Visitor Center, 0.3 mile; Gatlinburg, TN, 29 miles.

The first of the worthwhile hikes you'll encounter in Great Smoky Mountains National Park lies just past the Parkway's last Milepost, number 469. The Oconaluftee River Trail follows the riverbank under the bridge and links Cherokee, North Carolina, and the Smokies' Oconaluftee Visitor Center. See Best Easy Day Hikes Great Smoky Mountains National Park *(FalconGuides) by Randy Johnson, for more on that and other Smokies hikes*

Appendix A: Wildflowers Are Blooming!

The Blue Ridge Parkway is a wildflower lover's paradise, offering a huge variety of native species during spring, summer, and fall. Depending on your elevation and north–south orientation, some species can be found blooming over a considerably long period. The following list is a highlight of some of the most popular wildflowers, their months in bloom, and places along the Parkway where you can find them. Photograph them, sketch them, or simply enjoy the view, but remember that all park resources are protected—leave them for others to enjoy. Download the Parkway's complete bloom calendar at www.nps.gov/blri/planyourvisit/brochures.htm.

Species	Months in Bloom	Suggested Mileposts
Skunk Cabbage	Feb–Mar	176.1, 185.8, 217.0
Dwarf Iris	Mar–Apr	260.5
Spring Beauty	Mar–Apr	Craggy Picnic Area (PA)
Mayapple	Mar–Apr	76.2–76.4, 296–297, 320.8, 339.5
Serviceberry (Sarvis)	Mar–May	241–242, 294–297, 368–370
Silver-bell Tree	Mar–May	344.1–355.3
Buttercups	Mar–June	Common along roadsides
Crested Dwarf Iris	Apr–May	195, 198, 210, 217, 379
Tulip Poplar	Apr–May	Common in low woods and coves
Indian Paintbrush	Apr–May	369–371
Solomon's Seal	Apr–May	Common on moist wooded slopes and in coves
Bloodroot	Apr–May	85.6, 191–193, 198.7, 294
Pinxter Flower	Apr–May	4, 92–97, 145.5, 211.6, 350–351, 412–423
Trillium	Apr–May	68–69, 175, 200–216, 339–340
Redbud	Late Apr–May	54–68
Dutchman's Breeches	Apr–June	367.6 PA, 458.2
Carolina Rhododendron	Late Apr–June	308–310, 404–411
Dogwood	May	6, 85.8 PA, 230–232, 378–382
Fraser Magnolia	May	173–174, 252–253
Bluets	May–June	200.2, 355–368 PA
Wild Geranium	May–June	84–86, 170–172, 211.6, 375
Small's Groundsel	May–June	29.1, 85.8 PA, 330–340
Pinkshell Azalea	May–June	305.2, 342–343, 419–424
Flame Azalea	May–June	138.6, 144–145, 164–166, 308–310, 412–423
Fire Pink	May–June	1–2, 154.5 PA, 367–375

Species	Months in Bloom	Suggested Mileposts
Bowman's Root	May–June	24–45, 260, 368–369
Columbine	May–June	74–75, 339.3 PA, 370–378
Queen Anne's Lace	May–Sept	Common along open fields and roadsides
Mountain Laurel	Late May–June	130.5, 162.9, 347.9, 380, 400
Catawba Rhododendron	June	44.9, 77–83, 280.5, 348–350
Goat's Beard	June	10–11, 24, 240, 337.6
Spiraea	June–July	368–378
Sourwood	June–July	102–106, 231–232, 321–327
Butterfly Weed	June–Aug	63–65, 238–346
Coreopsis	June–Aug	29.6, 77, 157, 190, 306
Butter and Eggs	June–Aug	Common along roadsides and waste places
Turk's-cap Lily	June–Aug	187.6, 364–368, 406–411
Mullein	June–Sept	Common along roadsides
Bull Thistle	Late June–frost	Common along roadsides
Tall Meadow-Rue	July	85.8 PA, 155.2, 248
Fleabane	July	Common along roadsides
Ox-Eye Daisy	July	Common in fields
Black-Eyed Susan	July	Common in fields
Common Milkweed	July–Aug	85–86, 167–176
Bergamot/Bee Balm	July–Aug	38.8, 368–374
Tall Coneflower	July–Aug	36, 161.2, 228.1, 314
Oswego Tea	July–Aug	Common in wet areas
Bellflower	July–Sept	370–375
Jewel Weed	Aug	Common in wet areas
Ironweed	Aug	245, 248
Joe-Pye Weed	Aug	6, 85.8 PA, 146, 248, 339.3 PA, 357–359
Pokeberry	Aug	6, 74.7, 151, 376.9
Cardinal Flower	Aug	Infrequently in wet areas
Blazing Star	Aug–Sept	305.1, 369–370
Goldenrod	Sept	Common in fields along roadsides
Aster	Sept	Common in fields along roadsides
Yellow Ironweed	Sept–Oct	6, 88, 154.5, 271.9

Appendix B: Contact Information

The Blue Ridge Parkway
199 Hemphill Knob Road
Asheville, NC 28803-8686
(828) 271-4779
(828) 298-0398 (recorded information, such as road closures, and mailing requests)
In case of emergency, call (800) PARK-WATCH (800-727-5928).
www.nps.gov/blri.
The Blue Ridge Parkway Web site provides extensive up-to-date information about facilities on the Parkway, including PDFs of visitor trail maps and brochures. Reserve a campsite in advance at Julian Price Park, Linville Falls, and Mount Pisgah Campgrounds by using the www .recreation.gov Web site or calling (toll-free) (877) 444-6777.

Otter Creek Campground
(434) 299-5125 (year-round)
Restaurant, gift shop, and visitor center.

Peaks of Otter Lodge (year-round)
(540) 586-1081 or (800) 542-5927
Campground (seasonal): (540) 586-7321
Lodge, restaurant, gift shop, and picnic area; visitor center (seasonal).

Roanoke Mountain Campground
(540) 982-9242

Rocky Knob Campground
(540) 745-9664)
Visitor center with picnic area and cabins: (540) 593-3503

Doughton Park Campground
(336) 372-8877
Bluffs Lodge: (336) 372-4499

Price Park Campground
(828) 963-5911

Parkway Craft Center
Moses Cone Manor House
(828) 295-7938 (seasonal)
Southern Highland Craft Guild shop; visitor center

Linville Falls Campground (year-round)
(828) 765-7818
Picnic area, visitor center

Crabtree Meadows Campground
(828) 675-5444
Restaurant, gift shop, and picnic area

Pisgah Inn
(828) 235-8228
Campground: (828) 648-2644
Restaurant, gift shop, camp store

Travel Information Sources

Asheville Area Convention and Visitors Bureau
(800) 280-0005
www.exploreasheville.com

Blue Ridge Parkway Association
P.O. Box 2136
Asheville, NC 28802-2136
www.blueridgeparkway.org (highly recommended site)
Organization publishes invaluable free Parkway road guide to adjacent services and sights.

Blue Ridge Travel Association of Virginia
P.O. Box 1395
Wytheville, VA 24382
(800) 446-9670

Cherokee Visitor Center
P.O. Box 460
Cherokee, NC 28719
(800) 438-1601
www.cherokee-nc.com

North Carolina Division of Tourism Film and Sports Development
301 North Wilmington St.
Raleigh, NC 27601
(800) VISITNC (800-847-4862)
www.visitnc.com

NC High Country Host
1700 Blowing Rock Rd.
Boone, NC 28607
(828) 264-1299 or (800) 438-7500

Roanoke Valley Convention and Visitors Bureau
101 Shenandoah Ave.
Roanoke, VA 24016
(800) 635-5535
www.visitroanokeva.com

Shenandoah Valley Travel Association
277 West Old Cross Rd.
New Market, VA 22844
(540) 740-3132
www.visitshenandoah.org

"The Crooked Road, Virginia Music Heritage Trail"
www.thecrookedroad.org

Virginia Tourism Commission
901 East Byrd St.
Richmond, VA 23219
(800) 321-3244
www.virginia.org

Parkway Preservation Organizations

Blue Ridge Parkway Foundation
717 South Marshall St., Suite 105B
Winston-Salem, NC 27101
(336) 721-0260
www.brpfoundation.org

Friends of the Blue Ridge Parkway
P.O. Box 341
Arden, NC 28704
In Virginia:
P.O. Box 20986
Roanoke, VA 24018
(800) 228-7275
www.blueridgefriends.org

National Forests

The national forest Web sites below provide extensive up-to-date information about campgrounds adjacent to the Parkway, including information on how to reserve campsites. The ranger districts below abut or include the Parkway.

Virginia

Supervisor's Office
5162 Valleypointe Parkway
Roanoke, VA 24019-3050
(540) 265-5100 or (888) 265-0019
www.fs.fed.us/r8/gwj

Glenwood and Pedlar Ranger Districts

27 Ranger Lane
Natural Bridge Station, VA 24579
(540) 291-2188

North Carolina

Supervisor's Office
National Forests in North Carolina
160A Zillicoa St., Suite A
Asheville, NC 28801
(828) 257-4200
www.cs.unca.edu/nfsnc

Nantahala National Forest
Highlands Ranger District

2010 Flat Mountain Rd.
Highlands, NC 28741
(828) 526-3765
Visitor Information Center:
(828) 526-3462

Nantahala Ranger District

90 Sloan Rd.
Franklin, NC 28734
(828) 524-6441

Pisgah National Forest
Grandfather Ranger District

109 East Lawling Dr.
Nebo, NC 28761-9707
(828) 652-2144

Pisgah Ranger District

1001 Pisgah Highway
Pisgah Forest, NC 28768
(828) 877-3350

Appalachian/Toecane Ranger District

P.O. Box 128
Burnsville, NC 28714
(828) 682-6146

The Cradle of Forestry

US 276/Pisgah Highway
Pisgah Forest, NC 28768
(828) 877-3130
www.cradleofforestry.com

State Parks

The Parkway passes close to various state parks, especially North Carolina's Mount Mitchell State Park. Other state parks are visible from Parkway overlooks and are not too far away.

North Carolina Department of Environment, Health, and Natural Resources

Division of Parks and Recreation
512 North Salisbury St.
Archdale Building, 7th Floor, Room 742
1615 MSC
Raleigh, NC 27699
(919) 733-4181
parkinfo@ncmail.net

Mount Jefferson State Park

P.O. Box 48
Jefferson, NC 28640
(336) 246-9653
E-mail: mount.jefferson@ncmail

Mount Mitchell State Park
2388 State Highway 128
Burnsville, NC 28714
(828) 675-4611
E-mail: mount.mitchell@ncmail.net

Stone Mountain State Park
3042 Frank Parkway
Roaring Gap, NC 28668
(336) 957-8185
E-mail: stonemtn@ncmail.net

Other Sources and Trail Organizations

Great Smoky Mountains National Park
107 Park Headquarters Rd.
Gatlinburg, TN 37738
(865) 436-1200 (recorded information)
(865) 436-1231 (backcountry reservations)

Appalachian Trail Conservancy
P.O. Box 807
Harpers Ferry, WV 25425-0807
(304) 535-6331
www.appalachiantrail.org

Friends of the Mountains-to-Sea Trail
P.O. Box 10431
Raleigh, NC 27605
(919) 698-9024
www.ncmst.org

Chimney Rock Park
P.O. Box 39
Chimney Rock, NC 28720
(800) 277-9611
www.chimneyrockpark.com

Grandfather Mountain
P.O. Box 129
Linville, NC 28646
(828) 733-2013 or (800) 4MT-PEAK
(800-468-7325)
www.grandfather.com

Wintergreen Resort
Wintergreen, VA 22958
(434) 325-2200
www.wintergreenresort.com

Hike Index

About the Author

Randy Johnson has lived near the Parkway most of his life and has repeatedly hiked the high road's trails and driven its entire length.

He was an early member of the Virginia Wilderness Committee, and his first published magazine article supported designation of Virginia's first legislated wilderness.

He proposed and implemented the trail management program at Grandfather Mountain that helped keep the peak open to public use and laid the groundwork for the mountain's designation as a United Nations Biosphere Reserve and, more recently, a state park. He was a trail design consultant for the Parkway's Tanawha Trail and worked to mesh the private and Park Service trails into the system in place today. Randy was instrumental in making the Tanawha Trail part of the Mountains-to-Sea Trail, and as co-chairman of the Central Blue Ridge Task Force, he helped design and construct a portion of the Mountains-to-Sea Trail.

Until 2009, Randy was the longtime editor of *Hemispheres,* the magazine of United Airlines and, under his stewardship, the United States' most award-winning in-flight magazine. He has written widely for national newspapers and ski and travel magazines and is the author of *Southern Snow: The Winter Guide to Dixie* and *Hiking North Carolina* and the editorial director and contributing author of *The Age of Flight: The History of America's Pioneering Airline.*

He is a member of the Society of American Travel Writers and the North American Snowsports Journalists Association.

He invites you to visit his Web site (www.randyjohnsonbooks.com) for special features about his books or to send him an e-mail.